A Travelling Man

DONALD DAVIE was born in Barnsley in 1922 and educated at Barnsley Holgate Grammar School and St Catharine's College, Cambridge. During the Second World War he served in the Navy and travelled widely. He was a Fellow of Trinity College, Dublin, lecturer at Dublin University and Fellow of Gonville and Caius College, Cambridge before becoming Professor of English and Pro-Vice-Chancellor at the University of Essex. In 1968 he left England for America to take up a chair at Stanford, and later at Vanderbilt. Donald Davie returned to England in 1988; he died in 1995. Carcanet publish a number of his works, including *Under Briggflatts* (1989), *Slavic Excursions* (1990), *Studies in Ezra Pound* (1991), *With the Grain: Thomas Hardy and Modern British Poetry* (1998), *Two Ways Out of Whitman: American Essays* (2000) and *Collected Poems* (2001).

T0294085

Donald Davie

A Travelling Man

eighteenth-century bearings

edited with an introduction

by Doreen Davie

A TRAVELLING MAN
For Augustine Martin

Travelling by train
  − For I am a travelling man −
Across fields that I laid
  Under this private ban,

I thought: a travelling man
  Will come and go, here now
And gone tomorrow, and
  He cannot keep a vow…

          . . .

Easy pronouncements from
  The stranger, as he leaves!
The truth is, he was home
  − Or so he half-believes.

First published in Great Britain in 2003 by
Carcanet Press Limited
Alliance House
30 Cross Street
Manchester M2 7AQ

A CIP catalogue record for this book
is available from the British Library.

ISBN 1 85754 634 2

The publisher acknowledges financial assistance
from the Arts Council of England.

Set in Bembo by XL Publishing Services, Tiverton
Printed and bound in England by SRP Ltd, Exeter

THE FOUNTAIN

Feathers up fast, and steeples; then in clods
Thuds into its first basin; thence as surf
Smokes up and hangs; irregularly slops
Into its second, tattered like a shawl;
There, chill as rain, stipples a danker green,
Where urgent tritons lob their heavy jets.

For Berkeley this was human thought, that mounts
From bland assumptions to inquiring skies,
There glints with wit, fumes into fancies, plays
As by a law of nature, to its bowl
Of thus enlightened but still common sense.

We who have no such confidence must gaze
With all the more affection on these forms,
These spires, these plumes, these calm reflections, these
Similitudes of surf and turf and shawl,
Graceful returns upon acceptances.
We ask of fountains only that they play,

Though that was not what Berkeley meant at all.

Contents

Introduction

It was a happy chance that led Donald Davie to Dublin to take up his first academic appointment at Trinity College in 1950. At that time, Dublin was a spacious, elegant city, planned and laid out in the eighteenth-century by the Dublin Wide Street Commissioners. There, in its centre, 'Trinity College united strength and elegance, passion and rationality, in ways that I had learned to venerate in eighteenth-century writers.'[1] Davie's first book, *Purity of Diction in English Verse,* to be published in 1952, was already with the publisher. In it he sought to define the principles of purity of diction through the study of poetry written in the later eighteenth century.

Goldsmith Burke, Swift, Berkeley – all eighteenth-century men, all Trinity men, in whose shadow Davie walked through the halls and squares of Trinity College, and it was to George Berkeley, Bishop of Cloyne, that he turned when writing his next book, *Articulate Energy* (1955): 'When I found myself in *Articulate Energy* pushed reluctantly into poetic theory, and so into a sort of philosophy, Berkeley had to serve me, since he was the only philosopher I had read and thought I understood. (He has got into my poems, too.) It was the winning personality of the man, and the tough clarity of his style, that appealed to me as much as the rigour of his arguments.' Living in a time of energetic scientific enquiry and achievement, a contemporary of Isaac Newton, Berkeley explored the problems of language, how scientific language could serve poetry's purposes. Davie's fascination with his work is evident in all that he wrote at that time, and the early essays in this collection of eighteenth-century essays are explorations of Berkeley's style and philosophy. There is some overlapping, inevitably, but it is useful to have in a group these close studies of Berkeley's writings.

Dublin in the 1950s was a thriving city, and a peaceful one. It very quickly became home to us, as we settled into the house we'd bought in Raheny, a suburb on the northern side of the city. Friendly rivalry between the two universities – Trinity College and University College – stimulated lively discussions between colleagues, Denis Donoghue among them, and Dublin's young poets widened their circle to welcome the

1   *Contemporary Authors,* Autobiography Series, Vol.3 (Detroit, 1986), p. 37.

newcomer. As I remember, Liam Miller, the publisher and owner of the Dolmen Press, was at the centre of that circle, which included Thomas Kinsella and Sean White and, on occasion, Philip Larkin from Belfast, where he was the University Librarian. They were fruitful years for the young Davie, but among the poems he wrote at that time there was one that sounded a darker note:

> *Belfast on a Sunday Afternoon*
>
> Visiting Belfast at the end of June,
> We found the Orange Lodge behind a band:
> Sashes and bearskins in the afternoon,
> White cotton gloves upon a crippled hand.
>
> Pastmasters pale, elaborately grim
> Marched each alone, beneath a bowler hat;
> And, catapulted on a crumpled limb,
> A lame man leapt the tram-line like a bat.
>
> And first of all we tried to laugh it off,
> Acting bemusement in the grimy sun;
> But stayed to worry where we came to scoff,
> As loud contingents followed, one by one.
>
> Pipe bands, flute bands, brass bands and silver bands,
> Presbyter's pibroch and the deacon's serge,
> Came stamping where the iron Maenad stands,
> Victoria, glum upon a grassy verge.
>
> Some brawny striplings sprawled upon the lawn;
> No man is really crippled by his hates.
> Yet I remembered with a sudden scorn
> Those 'passionate intensities' of Yeats.

There were other rumblings. In 1956, I think it was, a 'mixed marriage' took place in Fethard-on-sea, a small town in County Wexford. That is to say, a young Roman Catholic married a young Protestant, in disobedience to his church's ruling. The marriage was denounced from the pulpit by the priest, who ordered his congregation to boycott the local Protestant-owned grocery shop, whose takings fell sharply in consequence. In sympathy with that persecuted minority, co-religionists in Dublin, some ninety miles distant, began buying their groceries by mail from Fethard-on-sea. At the time, it was difficult for us to comprehend those old religious rifts that had come down through the years, unhealed. In this case, the young couple eventually emigrated to Canada to get on with their lives, and ours resumed their regular routine. However, when a letter arrived from Cambridge a while later, advising Donald of a vacant post there, it seemed time to move on, though not without regret.

His return to Cambridge in 1958 marked the beginning of a busy, not to say hectic, period. Higher education was expanding rapidly in England in the early 1960s, new universities opening to students as fast as they were being built in East Anglia, Warwick, Kent, York, Essex. The academic world was abuzz: new staff to be appointed, new syllabuses to be set up, new professors to be promoted, new faculties to be created. From the English Faculty at Cambridge, Matthew Hodgart and David Daiches had already been appointed to Chairs in the University of Sussex, one of the earliest of the new campuses. Ian Watt had come from Berkeley in California to set up the Department of English in East Anglia (though he did not stay long on this side of the Atlantic) and it is well known that Donald Davie was lured to the University of Essex. For a year or more he drove several times a month to meetings in Colchester, where the new university was to be, in addition to his full-time commitments in Cambridge. The following excerpt from his journal, reflecting on the course of English Studies he planned with his newly appointed colleagues, is not irrelevant to this collection:

The vision that I had, of how literary studies could be re-directed at Essex, was shared I think by George Dekker and Gordon Brotherston, and even, with a certain detached but amiable amusement by that one of my Social Science colleagues with whom I had most to do and felt most at home – the expansive Frenchman Jean Blondel, Professor of Government. By decisions taken before we were appointed, Blondel and I, and later some half-hearted sociologists and economists and art-historians, were committed to paying particular attention, along with British experience through the centuries, to the historic experience of three regions of the earth's surface: North America, European and Asiatic Russia, and Latin America. The reasons why these areas had been picked on, were nothing to do with us; we had to make such sense as we could of the arrangement. And of course there were those who from the first declared that the arrangement was senseless, as well as others who really thought so but pretended otherwise, who joined the Essex team with the private determination to subvert it from within. For my part, as soon as I pondered these three regions and cradles of human culture I recognized that they had much in common. The first common feature I detected was disconcerting and unwelcome: for all practical purposes (since we were thinking about undergraduates) the history of Russia, of North America and of Latin America began in the second half of the eighteenth century, and it seemed to follow that our studies of English literature, if they were to keep meaningfully in step with study of a foreign literature (and it was clear to us that they should), would have to be disproportionately weighted towards literature of the last two hundred years. This meant that a very painful sacrifice – of our earlier literature – was exacted from us at the very beginning: and it let us in for some awkward fudging, as when, having recognised that no course in English literature could exclude Shakespeare, we made provision for study of him on the precarious grounds that debate about him and his achievement was very lively around 1800, in Russia and the Americas as well as in Britain and Western Europe. On the other hand, I thought, could we not turn this very disadvantage to good account by giving particular attention (as we could hardly avoid doing anyway) to the category or phase of cultural history that goes by the name – even in English, though significantly less than in other languages – of 'the Enlightenment' (*die Aufklarung, le siècle des lumières*)? Was it not indeed just here that Blondel and I could begin to meet another of the obligations that had been wished upon us – of breaking down the fences normally erected between the Social Sciences and the Arts? For those social or behavioural sciences – Economics, Political Science, Sociology, along with others that in truth attracted me more, like Anthropology and Cultural Geography – by common consent emerged, in anything like their modern form, out of the climate of ideas that we call 'the Enlightenment'. And so our students from the first should at one and the same time be given a grounding in eighteenth-century history and forced into a critical scrutiny of one or another scholarly discipline, obliged indeed to address themselves to the philosophical problem of just what 'discipline' in this sense means…

[…] However it might be with my associates and allies, I at any rate made a new connection here with 'the Enlightenment'. For if I asked myself what poems in English … had last gone for imaginative substance to geography on an oceanic and continental and millennial scale, I found myself naming those classics (surely) of the English Enlightenment: Goldsmith's 'The Traveller', Gray's 'Education and Government', Thomson's 'The Seasons'. It was later, after I had left Essex for California, that I came to see how this aspect of the Enlightenment, not its rationalistic arrogance but on the contrary its humbled awe before the revealed plenitude of human terrains and human cultures, was inscribed – as on language by Gray and Montesquieu, Thomson and Goldsmith – so on the maps and charts of the world by Cook and George Vancouver, La Perouse and La Verendrye, Abel Tasman and Vitus Behring. It was the discovery of Melanesian and Polynesian cultures by the great Enlightenment navigators like Cook and Bligh, Bougainville and the American John Ledyard, which finally exploded, for thoughtful and responsible people in Western Europe, the assumption that cultural and moral and civic standards had been established once and for all, at the start of the

Christian era, by three Mediterranean cultures: Greek, and Roman, and Hebrew. So at least it seemed to me; and I have held to it ever since as a more humane and plausible explanation than any that the literary histories supply me with, more appropriate in its global scale to the psychologically global change it has to account for, of how at the end of the eighteenth-century a 'classical' culture gave way to a culture that we have to call, however uneasily, 'romantic'. Thinking and feeling and imagining along these lines I was diverging widely and rapidly from whatever consensus I had established or appealed to between myself and the readers of my earlier poems. Just how widely I had diverged was brought home to me, as late as 1980, when a critic who was by and large sympathetic rapped me over the knuckles for supposing that any British reader of poetry today knew, or was prepared to learn about, such a figure from the British past as George Vancouver. It might be said that my Essex plans, aborted by political make-believe, were designed to produce a sort of reader for whom the choice of Vancouver as subject of a poem would seem eminently natural. The plans miscarried; and for the reader I hoped to interest with poems about Vancouver and Ledyard and Cook I can now look only in that very dubious unsatisfactory dimension of time called 'posterity'. My poem about Vancouver, and another poem about the Cornishman James Trevenen who like Vancouver sailed as a midshipman on Cook's last voyage, are in no sense apologies for imperialism; but they are celebrating that global scope for the imagination, those continental and inter-continental vistas, which were natural for the English during the centuries of British imperialism, which have shrunk away to nothing in the years since the Empire was dismantled.[1]

It would take too long, and this is not the place to discuss in detail the events of 1968 which erupted across university campuses in France, America, England and elsewhere. To turn briefly once more to the journal:

It was contended at the time, and has been ever since, that the 'difficulties' at Essex and Warwick, as also at Kent and LSE and Berkeley and the Sorbonne and elsewhere, saw an amorphous entity called 'democracy' ranged against an equally nebulous 'authoritarianism'. Among my colleagues at Essex who deceived others and perhaps themselves with this fraudulent simplification were some who left the Communist party only in 1956, as well as others who could not break with the party even then. But of course we were not the victims of 'a communist plot'; for the ring-leaders, who were not all of them even nominally students, were as incapable of obeying the party's directives

1   Donald Davie, Journal, 12 July 1980.

as of abiding any other sort of discipline. Their revolution was, as some
of them would admit, 'open-ended'; that's to say, they were mischief-
makers on principle. The principle was solidarity with their allegedly
suffering brothers and sisters in Paris and Berkeley; and in support of
that principle they would, as some of them admitted to me in private,
pretend that they suffered on the Essex campus from injustices that did
not exist. Some who lost patience with this situation felt it as an affront
to themselves personally, or to the dignity of the university offices that
they held; others were those like me who had invested much time and
trouble in an ambitious and difficult re-structuring of the curriculum
of studies, who foresaw accurately that the politicising of the university would have the effect of pouring studies back into the accredited
and orthodox moulds we had tried to break. A modest but genuine
attempt at an intellectual revolution was thus aborted for the sake of a
political revolution that was only frivolous play-acting in any case.

This comment, part of a much longer account of those 1968 protests,
could be regarded as Davie's first experience of political involvement.
Elsewhere in that account, he noted that 'far from the university being
"structured according to the principle of absolute loyalty and responsibility to its chief executive, the Vice-Chancellor", my frustration as Pro-
Vice-Chancellor at Essex was that I could seldom or never be sure of
securing for my Vice-Chancellor a majority on his own Senate.' He
resigned, not only as Pro-Vice-Chancellor, but also from the University.
As I recall, he wrote a private letter to the Vice-Chancellor warning him
of this before doing so officially, and indeed before the worst of the
student riots had taken place at Essex. Meanwhile, Stanford University
wrote, repeating an earlier invitation to accept the Professorship left
vacant by the death of Yvor Winters. 'Head-hunting', it would be called
today. It seemed the answer to the problem of his immediate future, and
thus it was that the family emigrated to California in 1968. It has been
remarked, with some amusement, that moving from Essex to California
in 1968 was hardly a retreat from student confrontations, but Davie never
again took an active part in politics, university or otherwise (though I do
recall in 1971 joining a protest march in San Francisco against the invasion of Cambodia). On the other hand, he was never again apolitical, as
he had been in the 1950s.

It is possible to follow Davie's academic progress as he moved on, not
only through his poems but also through his essays. Just as throughout his
years in Ireland he had adopted the culture of those among whom he was
living, so, following his move to California, his commitment to the
country and its people is reflected in this collection of his essays on the
eighteenth century. He was, by 1976, so wholly accepted into the
American academic community that Yale University invited him to inau-

gurate its series of essays to commemorate America's Bicentenary. That essay, 'Edward Taylor and Isaac Watts' is included in this volume, followed by others exploring the nature of American, as distinct from English, Dissent.

Donald Davie grew up in a family with a Dissenting background. He attended the local Baptist church with his parents, and his grandfather was a Baptist deacon and lay preacher. The history of the non-conformist churches, as they came to be known, had always interested him and when asked, also in 1976, to deliver the Clark Lectures in Cambridge he chose as his title *A Gathered Church,* subtitled 'The Literature of the English Dissenting Interest, 1700–1930'. Again, I have chosen to include in this volume the two lectures relating to the eighteenth century. *A Gathered Church* was published by Routledge and Kegan Paul in 1978. He loved and knew by heart the well-known hymns of Isaac Watts, the Wesleys, and others, which he discusses in these pages. He would sing them as he moved about the house, though frequently off-key. In retirement he went on to write *The Eighteenth-Century Hymn in England,* which was published by Cambridge University Press in 1993.

As I have remarked, the scope and range of these essays follow the geographical range of Davie's travels within the academic community, through which he moved with such ease. Throughout, however, the eighteenth century remained a central point of reference, from which he took bearings both as academic and as poet.

DOREEN DAVIE
Silverton, 2002

I Berkeley's Style in Siris

Berkeley in *Siris* seeks a cure for all ills; not only physical, but psychological, and in the last analysis spiritual ills. The most startling feature of his book is implicit in its curious form. It is a 'chain' of reflections. And the reflections begin in the world of physic, and end in metaphysic. The form implies that the distinction between the physical and the metaphysical is artificial. This realization may be compared with the conviction, in modern medicine, that mind and body are intimate, so that a psychological malady may produce physical symptoms. And thus Berkeley's panacea on the medical level, tar-water, is not really distinguishable from the root-element on the chemical level (where Berkeley feels towards the notion of oxygen), nor from the invariable ground of existence on the metaphysical level (the aethereal fire). The aethereal fire is, as it were, the root-element in its field; and faith in the fire, as such, is a sort of panacea for spiritual unrest, as tar-water for physical unease.

Berkeley, like Dr Johnson, deals often in the no-man's-land between mind and body, where wander the nervous languors of *angst* and hypochondria. And while Johnson resolutely denied the possibility of any panacea (his Christian faith was far too troubled to qualify as that, and throughout *Rasselas*, for instance, he insists that every seeming panacea is illusion), yet Johnson and Berkeley see the human predicament (the ills for which the panacea is needed), in strikingly similar terms. For both of them were a prey to the form of hypochondriac melancholia which attacked so many of the best minds of the eighteenth century. It may be that one source of this melancholia was the impossibility, for the sensitive mind, of finding satisfaction in Shaftesbury's and Hume's world of good-sense and good-nature, to which ideal they clung nevertheless, in their conscious minds, as the only cement of stability and order. But the unrest could be seen with equal justice as a physical or, better, a nervous disorder. It is thus seen by Berkeley:

> The soul of man was supposed by many ancient sages to be thrust into the human body as into a prison, for punishment of past offences. But the worst prison is the body of an indolent epicure, whose blood is inflamed by fermented liquors and high sauces, or rendered putrid, sharp, and corrosive, by a stagnation of the animal juices through sloth and indolence; whose membranes are irritated by pungent salts; whose

mind is agitated by painful oscillations of the nervous system, and whose nerves are mutually affected by the irregular passions of his mind. This ferment in the animal economy darkens and confounds the intellect. It produceth vain terrors and vain conceits, and stimulates the soul with mad desires, which, not being natural, nothing in nature can satisfy. No wonder, therefore, there are so many fine persons of both sexes, shining themselves, and shone on by fortune, who are inwardly miserable and sick of life.

The hardness of stubbed vulgar constitutions renders them insensible of a thousand things that fret and gall those delicate people, who, as if their skin was peeled off, feel to the quick everything that touches them. The remedy for this exquisite and painful sensibility is commonly sought from fermented, perhaps from distilled, liquors, which render many lives wretched that would otherwise have been only ridiculous. The tender nerves and low spirits of such poor creatures would be much relieved by the use of tar-water, which might prolong and cheer their lives. I do, therefore, recommend to them the use of a cordial, not only safe and innocent, but giving health and spirits as surely as other cordials destroy them. (§§ 104, 105.)

From one point of view, the clue to this passage is 'mutually'. The effect of physical constitution upon moral behaviour had been the basis of the medicine of the humours; Berkeley sees a two-way traffic, and a moral characteristic, such as 'sloth', can operate through the nerves to effect 'a stagnation of the animal juices'. This may not have been new in Berkeley's day and is certainly not new today. But the importance of this notion in Berkeley is to be seen from the way it impregnates his style; that is, his thinking.

For Berkeley's diction, in *Siris*, is based upon a choice of terms which are nicely ambiguous in reference. We speak of a 'mild' purgative as we speak of a 'mild' disposition; and 'mild' therefore can be used so that the reader feels, in the word, the identity of the spiritual and the physical worlds. This is the sort of ambiguity which Berkeley exploits throughout *Siris*. Some such usage was commoner to his age than to ours. We, for instance, should not normally describe a 'cordial' as 'innocent'; for 'innocent' is a word we reserve to describe a spiritual state. In Berkeley's age, however, it carried the meaning we now express by 'innocuous'. Compare Donne:

The trepidation of the spheres,
Though greater far, is innocent

– where the word has for us the force of a Latinate pun, though it would not have had that force for Donne's contemporaries. On the other hand, 'cordial' retains, for us, both its connotations, and, as a noun, describes a medicine having certain properties, while, as an adjective, it describes human temperament and human behaviour. The word, therefore, implies, if we scrutinize it closely, an identity between the world of physical medicine and the world of the human spirit. But of course we do *not* scrutinize it closely. The metaphor, for us, is dead. In practice, the world of spirit can only be described by analogy from the world of appearance, of physical nature; and therefore all the words we use to describe the spiritual world are metaphorical in origin. But those metaphors are dead, for us. And it was part of Berkeley's achievement to revivify such metaphors, already dead in his time as in ours. In this way, he insisted, in each turn of phrase, on the identity which his whole train of argument was to expound. He took metaphors which had ossified into meanings, and by a slight change of focus clothed them with flesh to rise as metaphors once again.

I should not like to say that, in the passage quoted, his use of 'innocent' restored metaphorical force to 'cordial'. It does so for us, I think. But for the reader of 1744 'innocent' in this sense would have been more 'dead', more of a literal meaning, more usual and accepted than it is for us. But there can be no doubt about the first sentence of that paragraph. 'I fretted ...', 'It galled me ...', 'It cut me to the quick ...': these usages would be dead metaphors in 1744, hardly less than they are today.[1] And the surprising felicity of 'stubbed' would enliven them in 1744 as it does now. The image is sustained and developed, almost like a conceit, from 'stubbed' to 'the quick'. And, paradoxically, as the 'fretting', the 'galling', and the 'feeling to the quick' take on a metaphorical life long lost, so the word 'stubbed' loses some of its life. At first it shocked the reader as a violent catachresis; now it subsides, and is seen to be no more metaphorical than the usage, 'feeling to the quick', which we have used time and again with no metaphorical force whatever. In the end, therefore, Berkeley's diction moves in an ambiguous field, neither plain metaphor nor literal meaning. And this equivalent territory is just what Berkeley requires for his chain which begins in physic and ends in metaphysic. The chain does not lead from one territory into another. Rather it is coiled and piled, physical or metaphysical according as we look on this coil or on that. There is really no question of going 'beyond'.

To say that the activities and the changes of the human sensibility are here *compared* with the activities and the changes of the skin of the hand, would be to miss the point. The two halves in the comparison are lost in a new compound which is neither one nor the other. It has been argued that this 'fusion' is peculiar to metaphor, and that all true metaphors act in this way. The drawing of a comparison, on the other hand, is the func-

---

1   The *Shorter Oxford English Dictionary* finds this figure in North in the sixteenth century: 'Tigranes ... was galled to the quick, and hit at the heart.'

tion of the simile, which is not to be distinguished from metaphor mechanically, according as the word 'like' appears or is omitted. And it would probably be true to say that 'stubbed' is subdued, by the resurrected metaphors which follow, not from metaphor to something less, but simply from catachresis to metaphor. In that case we have only proved that Berkeley's style is metaphorical in an exact sense.

But this is not all. The whole of *Siris*, we may say, is one great metaphor. At any rate, the metaphors throughout are drawn from one restricted field, a field which is proper to the medical speculation from which the first links of 'the small chain' were forged. Again, the metaphor is not, we have shown, a comparison. It cannot, therefore, 'work one way'. From the cuticle of the finger we work (with imperceptible rapidity), towards the human sensibility, as the cuticle of the personality. But equally we work from the sensibility to the finger. Thus when we learn (§ 92) that 'the animal salts of a sound body are of a neutral, bland, and benign nature', it cannot be said that the physical properties of the salts are expressed by analogy from the moral properties of a virtuous human temperament. 'Bland' and 'benign' are suspended between the physical order and the moral order, partaking equally of both, and implying that the two orders are not to be ultimately distinguished.

Of course this ambiguous vocabulary was not Berkeley's creation. It was largely the creation of the scientists of the seventeenth century. 'Cordial', as a medicine, is Chaucerian; and of course this ambiguity was the range of the alchemists, for whom a metal, for instance, could be noble or ignoble. Again, the vocabulary of the humours depended upon such ambiguities as 'melancholy'. And perhaps the most pregnant and momentous of the ambiguities was coined extempore by Bacon, when he chanced upon the word 'lex', with its moral connotations, to express his conception of what we now, following him, call 'scientific law'.[1] But the ambiguous vocabulary proliferated most richly in the hands of the natural philosophers of the Royal Society. The *Shorter Oxford English Dictionary* finds 'bland' first applied to inanimate 'things' in 1667. To call them 'inanimate' begs the question which such words as 'bland' successfully evade. So, too, the dictionary finds 'innocent' first used as opposed to 'malignant' by a pathologist of 1662; and 'benign' used of medicines in 1735.

These usages have had an interesting history. Some – 'bland', 'benign' and 'innocent', as applied to medicines – have merely disappeared. Others have been pruned of their ambiguity by dividing into two, as the seven-

---

1 Bacon, *Novum Organum*, II, 2, cf. Owen Barfield 'Poetic Diction and Legal Fiction' in *Essays presented to Charles Williams*, pp. 124 and 125. Mr Barfield points out that Bacon proposed for his novel conception the Platonic word 'forma', but in the course of this proposal he threw out the metaphor of 'lex'. The casual metaphor was adopted; the consciously proposed equivalent was dropped.

teenth century 'melancholy' is now divided between 'melancholy' and 'melancholia', having caused many confusions in the process.[1] Others again retain their metaphorical power; what layman, hearing of a person afflicted with a 'malignant' cancer, does not feel a tug in the word, towards the idea of possession by evil spirits? And others again, like scientific 'law', sham dead, awaking again to dangerous metaphorical life, when least expected.

One would only claim for Berkeley that in *Siris*, whether by accident or design, he exploited this field of ambiguity with exceptional thoroughness and consistency:

The balsam or essential oil of vegetables contains a spirit, wherein consist the specific qualities, the smell and taste of the plant. Boerhaave holds the native presiding spirit to be neither oil, salt, earth, or water; but somewhat too fine and subtle to be caught alone and rendered visible to the eye. This, when suffered to fly off, for instance, from the oil of rosemary, leaves it destitute of all flavour. This spark of life, this spirit or soul, if we may so say, of the vegetable departs without any sensible diminution of the oil or water wherein it was lodged.

It should seem that the forms, souls, or principles of vegetable life subsist in the light or solar emanation; which in respect of the macrocosm is what the animal spirit is to the microcosm – the interior tegument, the subtle instrument and vehicle of power. No wonder, then, that the *ens primum* or *scintilla spirituosa*, as it is called, of plants should be a thing so fine and fugacious as to escape our nicest search. It is evident that nature at the sun's approach vegetates, and languishes at his recess: this terrestrial globe seeming only a matrix disposed and prepared to receive life from his light; whence Homer in his Hymns styleth earth the wife of heaven, ἄλοχ' οὐρανοῦ ἀοτερόεντος.

The luminous spirit which is the form or life of a plant, from whence its differences and properties flow, is somewhat extremely volatile. It is not the oil, but a thing more subtle, whereof oil is the vehicle, which retains it from flying off, and is lodged in several parts of the plant, particularly in the cells of the bark and in the seeds. This oil, purified and exalted by the organical powers of the plant, and agitated by warmth, becomes a proper receptacle of the spirit: part of which spirit exhales through the leaves and flowers, and part is arrested by this unctuous humour that detains it in the plant. It is to be noted this essential oil, animated, one may say, with the flavour of the plant, is very different from any spirit that can be procured from the same plant by fermentation. (§§ 42, 43, 44.)

---

1   Cf. Amy Reed, *The Background of Gray's Elegy.*

Here the ambiguity is patent. It centres upon 'spirit'. The 'spirit' of the last sentence quoted I take to be a spirit as wood-alcohol is a spirit. This, too, presumably is the 'spirit' which appears in the first paragraph. But this is immediately qualified as 'too fine and subtle to be caught alone and rendered visible to the eye'. Yet this is not the immaterial spirit which equals 'soul'; for Berkeley guards against this conclusion by explaining, against his normal practice, that this identification is 'only metaphorical' – 'This spark of life, this spirit or soul, *if we may so say* ...' But this is an old trick. The writer takes the precaution of 'if I may say so', but he knows very well that that disclaimer weakens little the metaphorical force; so he has it both ways. And so he is able to move at once to 'forms, souls, or principles' (with no disclaimer this time) to *ens primum* or *scintilla spiri-tuosa*. By this time, the spirit of vegetables is for the reader a spirit as an angel is a spirit; and this is cunningly reinforced by the 'luminous spirit' who soars into the last paragraph. Berkeley is safe. He 'means', logically, the spirit derived from light; but all the force of the locution derives from the disreputable, illogical part of the meaning, by which the 'spirit' is bright and shining as angels are. Finally, in a casual parenthesis, Berkeley returns to the 'spirit', as of wood-alcohol. And so, in the end, the reader has been inveigled into accepting an ambiguity as a meaning.

It may be argued of course that this is rank dishonesty, mere word-spinning. And perhaps, if *Siris* were a philosophical treatise, this would be all one could say. But the work is a chain of reflections. And one could argue that it has its own logic, the logic not of philosophy but poetry. For after all one is unable to say: 'This is the true meaning of spirit, in the terms of the argument. And this other is the fanciful meaning, which Berkeley, by vicious sleight of hand, passes off as the true.' For there is no argument, there is only the 'chain'. And there is not one level of rational discourse, another of metaphor. For all is metaphorical. What is to be made, for instance, of that nature, which 'at the sun's approach vegetates, and languishes at his recess'? Does it 'really' languish? Or is the expression 'figurative'? Truly, we cannot say. For in this world where 'spirit' is something comparable with wood-alcohol, yet also a soul, subsisting in the light, we cannot be sure about the languor in nature. Most readers will feel at any rate that when Berkeley speaks of nature languishing, he means something less metaphorical, more nearly literal, than the modern speaker who says of a person that he 'vegetates'. And languour, too, it will be noted, belongs in this ambiguous territory where a moral and spiritual condition seems open to diagnosis by physicians.

Again and again, tar-water is described in terms which strike the modern reader as proper only to descriptions of moral or spiritual condi-tion. It is 'unctuous', 'subtle', 'active'. It is (§49) 'gentle, bland and temperate'. And (§ 72) 'it is of so just a temperament as to be an enemy of all extremes' – phrasing which one could think to find in Hume, describing a moral man. So too, 'There is a lentor or smoothness in the blood of healthy strong people; there is often an acrimony and solution in that of weakly morbid persons'; and we cannot, perhaps we should not, dismiss the human and moral connotations of 'acrimony' from a passage which purports to be scientific accounting. The truth seems to be that for Berkeley here, if not for his age in general, the discrimination which we make between the scientific and the moral was unnecessary and positively unwanted. And that, we recall with a start, is what *Siris* is about. The means which Berkeley employed and the end which he proposed are one and the same. It is the definition of poetry. And perhaps this is part of what Yeats meant when he said that Berkeley the philosopher was 'a mask'.

Cambridge Journal, no. 4 (April 1951), pp. 427–33.

II Berkeley and 'Philosophic Words'

When I speak of 'philosophic words' here I mean by it what W.K. Wimsatt means, in his book of this title on the style of Dr Johnson.[1] This is to use 'philosophic' as Johnson used it, to mean whatever pertains to 'natural philosophy' or, as we should say, to the natural sciences. Such words as 'acrimony' or 'volatile' are, in this sense, eminently philosophic words, being adopted into the language at large from the special terminology of chemistry.

Mr Wimsatt has shown, in his admirable and momentous study, that Johnson the lexicographer set out quite deliberately to assist the adoption of these words into the language, and to attract them out of the laboratory into the drawing-room. At the same time, in *The Rambler*, Johnson the essayist was doing the same thing by other means, exemplifying in practice what, in the Dictionary, he urged as theory. For, as Mr Wimsatt shows, the prevailingly abstract, Latinate, and sesquipedalian character of Johnson's style, especially in *The Rambler,* is brought about very largely by his consistent use of these words which he called 'philosophic'.

But the essays in *The Rambler* are moral disquisitions, and have nothing to do with the natural sciences, except occasionally for purposes of illustration. How, then, could Johnson use so many scientific words in a non-scientific context? He does so by extending their significations, and giving them a metaphorical, as well as a literal bearing. So, when 'acrimony' is used, it still means literally, what it meant in the laboratory, 'corrosiveness'; but it means metaphorically, in the context of moral disquisition, 'severity, bitterness of thought or language'. One tends to think that an abstract style is a style devoid of images, hence unmetaphorical; but, as Mr Wimsatt shows, what makes Johnson's style abstract is also what makes it highly metaphorical.

What is more, every metaphor thus used derives from, and helps to maintain, one philosophical system, that of Locke. For to bring over into morals and psychology the terminology of natural philosophy is to imply that the workings of the mind are precisely analogous to the workings of matter, so that the one set of terms is equally applicable in both fields; and this was one of the implications of Locke's philosophy. The point is taken

---

1 W.K. Wimsatt, Jr. *Philosophic Words. A Study of Style and Meaning in the* Rambler *and* Dictionary *of Samuel Johnson* (New Haven, 1948).

beautifully by Blake in his notes to Reynolds's Discourses. Reynolds writes 'My notion of nature comprehends not only the forms which nature produces, but also the nature and internal fabrick and organization … of the human mind and imagination.' This is precisely the assumption that underlies Johnson's metaphorical use of terms from natural science; and Blake sees all the implications: 'Here is a Plain Confession that he thinks Mind and Imagination not to be above the Mortal and Perishing Nature. Such is the End of Epicurean or Newtonian Philosophy; it is Atheism.'[1] Hence, it is not surprising to find, in Mr Wimsatt's words, that 'Locke was evidently the British philosopher chosen to represent his kind in the Dictionary.' Berkeley had challenged the Lockean system; but Johnson, it seems, chose to ignore the challenge. This goes along with Johnson's known dislike of Berkeleyan thought as he understood it; and again it is not surprising to find that Berkeley is quoted in the Dictionary only eight times – a marked contrast to the strongly Berkeleyan cast of Ephraim Chambers's *Cyclopaedia*, a work that in other respects was one of Johnson's main sources.[2]

It follows that 'philosophic' words could have no such attraction for Berkeley, who did not accept the Lockean system, as for Johnson, who did. To be consistent Berkeley ought to refuse to use such words except in their literal meaning; for to extend them metaphorically to refer to the workings of the mind was to assume a philosophical postulate which he rejected. And this is just what we find, for instance, in the sixth dialogue of *Alciphron*, where Lysicles, the free-thinker, has been deducing the nature of the human soul from the behaviour of vegetables, and using, in the process, such 'philosophic' words as 'unctuous' and 'volatile'. Crito, Berkeley's spokesman, objects:

> But what relation hath the soul of man to Chymic Art? The same reason that bids me trust a skilful Artist in his Art, inclines me to suspect him out of his Art. Men are too apt to reduce unknown Things to the Standard of what they know, and bring a Prejudice or Tincture from Things they have been conversant in, to judge thereby of Things in which they have not been conversant.[3]

Crito's question brings the whole matter to a head. 'What relation …?' Why, the relation established by Locke, which Berkeley rejected, which Johnson accepted so whole-heartedly that it informed the whole of his diction and his style. Berkeley's opposition to Locke's system, like Johnson's adherence to it, is as apparent in the turn of a phrase as in the tenor of a whole argument. And yet Crito, even as he refuses to accept

---

1   William Blake, *Poetry and Prose* (Nonesuch edn) p. 807.
2   Wimsatt, op. cit. p. 96.
3   Dialogue VI.

the metaphoric extension of philosophic words, falls into just such a metaphor himself – 'a Prejudice or *Tincture*'.[1] 'Tincture' is a 'philosophic' word, and used metaphorically to refer to the working of the mind. It is, in fact, included by Mr Wimsatt in his glossary of such words from *The Rambler*. Berkeley betrays his principles even as he announces them.

Elsewhere, I believe, he can be seen taking pains to exclude these ambiguous terms even where the context almost aches for them. In the nature of things this is something that cannot be demonstrated, except perhaps by a statistical word-count. Otherwise, what is excluded is excluded; and if a word strikes one reader as conspicuous by its absence he has no way of proving this to another. But I will give one example of a passage, from which I think the philosophical word has been deliberately excluded to striking and beautiful effect:

> Whatever may be the Effect of pure Theory upon certain Spirits, of a peculiar Make, or in some other Parts of the World; I do verily think that in this Country of ours, Reason, Religion, Law, are all together little enough to subdue the Outward to the Inner Man; and that it must argue a wrong Head and weak Judgment to suppose, that without them Men will be enamoured of the golden Mean. To which my Countrymen perhaps are less inclined than others, there being in the Make of an *English* Mind a certain Gloom and Eagerness, which carries to the sad Extreme; Religion to Fanaticism; Free-thinking to Atheism; Liberty to Rebellion ...[2]

The collocation 'Gloom and Eagerness' is delightful, I suggest, in a poetic way; the marriage of such dissimilars is surprising yet just. The pleasure it gives is different only in degree from the pleasure we get from Congreve's choice of epithets:

> Sententious Mirabell! Prithee don't look with that violent and inflexible wise Face, like Solomon at the dividing of the Child in an old Tapestry Hanging ...[3]

– where the coming together of 'violent', 'inflexible' and 'wise', like Berkeley's marriage of 'gloom' and 'eagerness', is at once unlikely and inevitable. Now Nathan Bailey's *Dictionarium* of 1730 gives the following under 'Acrimony':

> Acrimony. Sharpness, Eagerness, Tartness.

1   cf. *Dialogue, VI* '...Prospects viewed but in part, and by the broken tinged Light of our Intellects, though to us they seem disproportionate and monstrous, may nevertheless appear quite otherwise to another Eye, and in a different Situation ...'
2   *Dialogue III*.
3   Quoted by L.J. Potts, *Comedy* (London, 1949, p. 66), who comments 'the image as well as the two adjectives ("violent" and "inflexible") are beyond the range of any but the highest poetic imagination: unexcelled by Chaucer and Shakespeare' (ibid., p. 102).

And Johnson's Dictionary gives an example of the metaphorical sense of 'acrimony', from Robert South's Sermons of 1692. There can be little doubt that in Berkeley's context 'gloom and acrimony' would be a combination less surprising to the modern reader than the combination 'gloom and eagerness'. The evidence from Bailey and South goes to suggest that even in Berkeley's day 'acrimony' rather than 'eagerness' would be the first word to spring to mind for the idea wanted in the context given. There is at least a possibility, therefore, that Berkeley hit upon the felicitous 'eagerness' in his efforts to avoid metaphorical use of the philosophic 'acrimony'.

But this, as I am aware, is not evidence. What evidence there is can only be circumstantial. Mr Wimsatt, for instance, supports his case that Johnson deliberately used metaphors from natural science in single 'philosophic' words, by pointing out how often extended similes from natural philosophy are used by him to introduce or illustrate moral arguments. These more elaborate figures obviously derive from the same sort of interest as would find metaphors in single philosophic words; therefore to find these similes so frequently in *The Rambler* ('it is,' says Mr Wimsatt, 'one of the favourite opening patterns of a *Rambler* essay')[1] helps to explain the high frequency of philosophic words in the essays, and to establish that this high frequency is no accident. In Berkeley's writing, on the other hand, such similes are very rare. The only example that comes to mind as even remotely resembling the scientific similes to be found in *The Rambler* (Mr Wimsatt calls the device 'a philosopher's version, as it were, of epic simile') is at the end of *Three Dialogues between Hylas and Philonous*:

> *Hyl.* ... You set out upon the same principles that Academics, Cartesians, and the like sects usually do; and for a long time it looked as if you were advancing their philosophical Scepticism; but, in the end, your conclusions are directly opposite to theirs.
> *Phil.* You see, Hylas, the water of yonder fountain, how it is forced upwards, in a round column, to a certain height; at which it breaks, and falls back into the basin from whence it rose; its ascent, as well as descent, proceeding from the same law or principle of gravitation. Just so, the same Principles which, at first view, lead to Scepticism, pursued to a certain point, bring men back to Common Sense.[2]

The difference between this and any *Rambler* example is more striking than the formal similarity. The tone indicates that it is graceful and fanciful, no more; we are not led by it to think, even for a moment, that there is any law of correspondence between the processes of the mind and

---

1 Wimsatt, op. cit. p. 58. See the whole passage pp. 54–66, for examples.
2 Berkeley's *Works*, annotated by A.C. Fraser (Oxford, 1901), I, p.485.

the processes of the external world. One such correspondence is noted for our amusement, but there is no implication that this is anything but fortuitous. And it is no accident that this comes at the end of an argument where analogous similes in *The Rambler* come at the start; Johnson establishes the correspondence in order to develop it, Berkeley implies that to develop it would be to prove its absurdity.

In the *Alciphron* at any rate, when Berkeley resorts to simile or to metaphor (deliberately, that is, not trapped into one unknowing, as with 'tincture'), his range is more like Dryden's. Both he and Dryden most often find their correspondences between mental operations on the one hand, and, on the other, not the behaviour of gases in a retort or toads in a stone, but the behaviour of man in society:

> O Alciphon! these Minute Philosophers (since that is their true Name) are a sort of Pirates who plunder all that come in their way. I consider my self as a Man left stript and desolate on a bleak Beach.[1]

> But allowing what Beauty you please to Virtue in an Irreligious System, it cannot be less in a Religious, unless you will suppose that her Charms diminish as her Dowry increaseth ...

> To me it seems, those heroic Infidel Inamorato's of abstracted Beauty are much to be pitied, and much to be admired.[2]

> I would observe, that in this Charge of *Lysicles* there is something right and something wrong. It seems right to assert as he doth, that the real Belief of Natural Religion will lead a Man to approve of Revealed: But it is as wrong to assert, that Inquisitions, Tyranny, and Ruin must follow from thence. Your Free-thinkers, without Offence be it said, seem to mistake their Talent. They imagine strongly, but reason weakly; mighty at Exaggeration, and jejune in Argument! Can no method be found, to relieve them from the Terror of that fierce and bloody Animal, an *English* Parson? Will it not suffice to pare his Talons without chopping off his fingers?[3]

> Your Men of Fashion, in whom animal Life abounds, are a sort of Bullies in Morality, who disdain to have it thought they are afraid of Conscience; these descant much upon honour, and affect to be called Men of Honour, rather than conscientious or honest Men. But, by all that I could ever observe, this specious Character, where there is nothing of Conscience or Religion underneath, to give it Life and Substance, is no better than a Meteor or painted Cloud.[2]

In the last of these examples, where Berkeley has slipped, with 'Meteor',

1   *Dialogue I.*
2   *Dialogue III.*
3   *Dialogue V.*

into an image from science, he hastens to mute the metaphor and restrict its application, by tying it up with an image from theatrical decor, the 'painted Cloud'. His happiest and most common imagery is all from human life – minute philosophers as pirates, virtue as a bride, men of fashion as moral bullies. All in all, it seems true to say that Berkeley deliberately avoided finding metaphors for the operations of the mind in the operations of external nature as embodied in the vocabulary of natural scientists. In this his practice was the direct opposite of Dr Johnson's practice; and this is only what we should expect, since Berkeley rejected, as Johnson endorsed, the Lockean postulate on which such metaphorical usage depended.

To this, however, there is one glaring exception – the case of *Siris*. Here 'philosophic' words could not be excluded, for in a treatise on the medicinal virtues of tar-water it was inevitable that Berkeley should draw upon the 'philosophic' words in the special vocabularies of physicians, chemists and botanists. This in itself constitutes no exception and calls for no comment; for like Mr Wimsatt, we are not interested in 'philosophic' words as such, but only when they are used by metaphoric extension to describe operations of the mind. So long as Berkeley uses 'salt', 'sulphur' or 'corrosion' only as the chemist uses them, he is not departing from his avowed principles. But, as I have argued elsewhere,[1] Berkeley in fact uses these terms metaphorically:

> There is a lentor or smoothness in the blood of healthy strong people; these is often an acrimony and solution in that of weakly morbid persons.

Plainly here there is a drift from acrimony in diet ('fermented liquors and high sauces'), through acrimony in the blood ('rendered putrid, sharp, and corrosive'), to acrimonious disposition or temperament; the whole argument of *Siris* (though 'argument' is hardly the word for it) depends upon just such a drift. The ambiguity that we noted elsewhere in an isolated instance (the 'tincture' of *Alciphron*) is the very staple of Berkeley's diction in *Siris*.

And yet this style in *Siris* brings Berkeley nearer not to Johnson but to Lewis Carroll:

> 'When *I'm* a Duchess,' she said to herself (not in a very hopeful tone though), 'I won't have any pepper in my kitchen *at all*. Soup does very well without – Maybe it's always pepper that makes people hot-tempered', she went on, very much pleased at having found out a new kind of rule, 'and vinegar that makes them sour – and camomile that makes them bitter – and – and barley-sugar and such things that make

---

1   See above, 'Berkeley's Style in *Siris*'.

children sweet-tempered. I only wish people knew *that:* then they wouldn't be so stingy about it, you know.'[1]

Alice's 'new kind of rule' is not new at all. Berkeley had found it before her. And it was not new, even then. It is as old, no doubt, as Galen. For Berkeley is not implying an exact correspondence between the outward and the inward world. As we see from the drift of the whole work he is implying an *identity;* which is a very different matter. Metaphor after all, does not enter into it. The acrimony of salts is not, according to Berkeley, *analogous* to the acrimony of human temperaments. It *is* that acrimony. He is being quite literal about it. Hence Berkeley in *Siris* is no longer a Berkeleyan, but still less is he a Lockean, as Johnson is.

Studies. An Irish Quarterly, no. 44 (Winter 1955), pp. 319–24.

1   *Alice's Adventures in Wonderland.* Chapter IX. cf. Charles Lever, *Charles O'Malley* (Dublin, 1841) I. 163. Captain Power recommends the punch – 'eh, doctor? you advise it yourself, to be taken before bed-time; nothing inflammatory in it; nothing pugnacious; a mere circulation of the better juices and more genial spirits of the marly clay, without arousing any of the baser passions; whiskey is the devil for that.'

III Irony and Conciseness in Berkeley and in Swift

Officially, as it were, the model of English prose-writing is Addison. But it is notable that this claim for Addison is never made with enthusiasm. 'If one must have a model,' writes James Sutherland,[1] 'Addison could hardly be bettered'; but Matthew Arnold is quite explicit that when he plumps for Addison, he does so *faute de mieux*.[2] There is general agreement that what is lacking in Addison's style is force or 'punch'. He 'thought justly, but he thought faintly' – his writing is not trenchant. The only question is: whether any other writer in English has all the Addisonian virtues, and trenchancy into the bargain. It has been sometimes asserted that Swift is such a writer.

In the first place, however, it may be maintained that there is no such thing as a model writer; and that any attempt to find one is only a literary parlour-game which soon palls because it has no rules. Probably no writer ever put himself to school to 'the best models'; or, at anyrate, no one ever learnt in that way to write well. In this sense it may well be true that there is no model writer. But the idea of 'the model' can still be fruitful, if it is taken, as Arnold took it, to mean centrality, a sort of norm or standard, academic in the best and rarest sense, by which, as other writers depart from it, their departures can somehow be charted. Arnold would claim further that the writers who embody this norm, who occupy this centre, are by virtue of that the most civilised writers in any given language; that others may have deeper insight or more persuasive force or more compelling beauty, but that the model writer is the most civil writer (again in the best sense of the word). The rules of the game are likewise those implicit or expressed in Arnold's classic essay, and they can be reduced to one assumption or convention. If there is to be any point to the game of 'find the model', we have to assume with Arnold, what is by no means proven (it was challenged in Arnold's day by Gerard Manley Hopkins), that the writing of prose and the writing of poetry are two distinct disciplines. It follows that prose is not better (rather, it is likely to

1   James Sutherland, 'Some Aspects of Eighteenth-Century Prose' in *Essays on the Eighteenth Century Presented to David Nichol Smith* (Oxford, 1945), p. 95.
2   Matthew Arnold, 'The Literary Influence of Academies' (1864).

be worse) according as it approaches the condition of poetry. It is on this assumption that Arnold excludes the masters of poetic or poetical English prose, from Jeremy Taylor through Burke to Ruskin or Kinglake; and, for the game to be played properly, we have to do the same.

From the still enormous range of possible candidates, we select Swift and Berkeley; in the first place, because both candidates have been put forward before, and secondly because, game or no game, it is Berkeley we are concerned with, and the virtues of his prose appear most clearly by comparison with Swift.

Now, Swift is often taken to possess pre-eminently just that trenchancy the lack of which is Addison's limitation. Louis Bredvold writes, for instance:

> The satire of Swift, even at its bitterest, never depends for its intensity on any sense of frustration; it has the force of intellectual statement – often mock-scientific in tone – and has the effect of arousing in the reader, by means of the *vis comica* and indignation, a will to action which is sympathetic with Swift's own character.[1]

Herbert Davis[2] agrees, and argues that this was what was meant by Orrery when he wrote of Swift: 'If we consider his prose works, we shall find a certain masterly conciseness in their style that has never been equalled by any other writer.' To use 'conciseness' in this way is open to misunderstanding, and Herbert Davis appeals to authority:

> I use the term 'conciseness' not quite as Ben Jonson used it to describe the style 'which expresseth not enough, but leaves somewhat to be understood', though that is perhaps the reason why we feel in Swift a strength and force lacking in other plain writers. He leaves somewhat to be understood. But I use the term rather as Dryden used it, when he spoke of ' the conciseness of Demosthenes', quoting the remark of Speroni, the Italian wit, that Tully wished to achieve the copiousness of Homer, and Virgil the conciseness of Demosthenes. It will be remembered that Swift compares the art of Demosthenes and Cicero in his *Letter to a Young Clergyman*, recommending the former, with whom most divines were less conversant, as the more excellent orator. And he draws attention to the chief purpose of their oratory, 'to drive some one particular Point, according as the Oratory on either Side prevailed.'

Davis goes on to claim, and to demonstrate, that conciseness in this sense is such a constant feature of Swift's prose that by its presence or

1   Louis Bredvold, 'The Gloom of the Tory Satirists' in *Pope and His Contemporaries. Essays Presented to George Sherburn* (Oxford, 1949), p. 6.
2   Davis, 'The Conciseness of Swift' in *Essays on the Eighteenth Century Presented to David Nichol Smith*.

absence the editor of Swift can decide whether to accept or reject pieces of writing doubtfully attributed to him.

There is, however, another sort of comment frequently made on the style of Swift, which tends to qualify or (implicitly) to dispute his conciseness, in this special sense of his trenchancy. I mean the comments made by critics on Swift's use of irony as a satirical weapon. This is a point that has to be made at length, so I must apologize for another page or so of quotation and citation.

Maynard Mack remarks, of irony in the Augustan writers:

> At its most refined, in fact, as in Swift's *Modest Proposal* or Pope's praise of George II in the *Epistle to Augustus*, it asks us to lay together not two, but three, different perspectives on reality. First, the surface, and, second, the intended meanings, these two corresponding roughly to vehicle and tenor in a metaphor; and then, third – to use again the Pope and Swift examples – the kind of propositions that English projectors were *usually* making about Ireland, or the poets about George II.[1]

The meaning that struggles to expression through Mr Mack's not very happy phrasing is that of Professor Quintana when he speaks of '*situational* satire' in Swift. And undoubtedly irony so complex as this can be called satirical, but only by refining and extending the normal meaning of 'satire':

> If one had to justify this irony according to the conventional notion of satire, then its satiric efficacy would be to make comfortable non-recognition, the unconsciousness of habit, impossible.[2]

This may be that 'universal satire' that plays so elusive a role in the older appreciations of Swift. But what it is *not* is that satire of Mr Bredvold which arouses 'a will to: action', or that conciseness of Mr Davis which has as its purpose 'to drive some one particular Point'. As Dr Leavis says: 'Its function is to defeat habit, to intimidate and to demoralise.' We seem to draw near to that 'sense of frustration' on which, according to Mr Bredvold, Swift's satire never depends.

I hasten to correct the impression that the Swiftian irony of which Dr Leavis writes is solely that defined by Maynard Mack. It comprehends that; but, in Dr Leavis' treatment, Swift's irony is 'demoralising' (frustrating), whether or not the 'situational' element is present. The essay in *Determinations* seems to me much the best account available, or known to me, of this feature of Swift's style, and indeed of that style in general. Since so much of it is analysis of an extended passage from *The Tale of a*

---

1   Maynard Mack, 'Wit and Poetry and Pope' in *Pope and his Contemporaries*, p. 33.
2   F.R. Leavis, 'The Irony of Swift' in *Determinations* (London, 1934), p. 85.

Tub, I can only direct the reader to it. But the upshot of it is that the reader is first persuaded to eschew curiosity, because 'Last week I saw a woman flayed, and you will hardly believe how much it altered her person for the worse'; but then, having been taken by Swift from curiosity to its opposite, credulity, the reader finds the trap sprung upon him when credulity turns out to be 'the serene peaceful state of being a fool among knaves'. And this, as Dr Leavis implies, is the very opposite of a call to action or a driving of 'some one particular point'. On the contrary, it painfully suspends action, offers two 'particular points', and, having led the reader to each in turn, destroys both.

Mr Davis seems uneasily aware of this when he writes

> After *A Tale of a Tub* was put behind him, he rarely permitted himself to indulge his humour or his literary skill in parody or raillery or any of the tricks of the trade for his amusement only. His irresponsible play was almost entirely limited to verse and the various bagatelles in which the little group of Dublin friends engaged for sport.

James L. Clifford will hardly appreciate 'irresponsible play' put in such close conjunction with *A Tale of a Tub*, the volume which includes *The Mechanical Operation of the Spirit*.[1] And C.S. Lewis has Dr Johnson's authority for not limiting Swift's enjoyment of the bagatelle to his writings for his group of Dublin friends.[2] In any case, it will not do; as Dr Leavis shows, this same frustrating irony is at the heart of Book IV of *Gulliver's Travels*, where we are left suspended, as before, between curiosity and credulity, so there between Houyhnhnms and Yahoos. It is rather disingenuous of Mr Davis to declare: 'Nothing is quite so concise as the conciseness of irony; the meaning is tight-closed, until the reader stays to pick it up and open it.' Quite. But this is suddenly the conciseness of Ben Jonson, not that of Dryden and Swift, not the sort that goes with trenchancy.

This suggests to me that 'irony', as a term of criticism, is being overworked. For the three-tiered or 'situational' irony is not confined to Pope and Swift, though in Swift it may be more constant and more elaborate than anywhere else. It is worth considering whether in fact this is not the only sort of irony that deserves the name; and whether all other apparently simpler types of irony are not in fact varieties of sarcasm. If this terminology were adopted, it would appear, I believe, that irony is not strictly satirical at all, though sarcasm is. Obviously irony is potentially present in almost any satirical writing, but where it appears, one might argue, the satirical edge is blunted and the satire becomes for the moment something else.

These, perhaps, are quibbles. The point to be made is this: that if irony is a fairly constant feature of Swift's writing, and if it works as Dr Leavis says it does, then Swift's style is less trenchant, and in this sense less concise, than is commonly supposed. How, then, we may ask, does Berkeley's style compare with Swift's in this point of trenchancy?

The grounds for such a comparison are obvious and inevitable. It was probably Percival, in the anonymous introduction to the first London edition of *The Querist*,[1] who invited comparison of Swift's writings on Irish economics, with Berkeley's. In any case, no one who reads *The Querist* but must be reminded time and again of Swift's *Drapier's Letters* and his *Modest Proposal*; and there can be little doubt that Berkeley had Swift in mind, as he wrote his own book. When readers have compared the procedures of the two men, they have made the point that Swift's treatment is the more trenchant:

> Berkeley had an interest in economics for their own sake, or as a problem: *The Querist* has a place in the general history of the science, universal as well as local significance. Swift's *Drapier's Letters* are simply *ex parte* statements arising out of the particular controversy of Wood's half-pence, a fascinating revelation of polemical skill, but without any suggestion of deep doctrine. Berkeley is not less characterised in *The Querist* than in his more famous metaphysical writings by the taste for speculative thought, and by that affection for problems which was notably absent from Swift's composition. For Swift, the 'whole doctrine' is always 'short and plain' – there are no new truths, for a Plato or for a ploughman, and there is nothing that cannot be demonstrated by immediate efficacious arguments.[2]

There is no disputing the justice of this, and yet it is a comparison of Swift with Berkeley as men, rather than as writers. It will give the wrong impression, for instance, if we do not remember that Berkeley's 'more famous metaphysical writings', however speculative, are also, without exception, polemical. And on the other hand, as we have seen, the *Modest Proposal* has not the effect of a 'whole doctrine', 'short and plain', but rather of a painful indecision.

In another place, Mr Hone has written:

> The oddity of Ireland is Berkeley's favourite theme in *The Querist*, and he gives his sense of satire full rein. He himself, with a string of innocent-seeming questions, figures as the bewildered observer of the

1   Cf. J.M. Hone and M.M. Rossi, *Bishop Berkeley* (London, 1931), p. 263
2   Berkeley, *The Querist*, ed. J.M. Hone (Dublin & Cork, 1935), pp. 16, 17.

paradoxes of the Irish political, social and economic life. It was in the same interrogative way that he had recently rebuked the extravagances of the mathematicians. The form as a method of argument gives full play to the satirical and controversial vein of Berkeley – even better than does the dialogue – and it is a sort of dialogue in which Berkeley speaks and fixes the term of controversy, and the supposed interlocutor can only answer Yes or No … as Berkeley will have him reply.[1]

This does not quite correspond with my impression of *The Querist*. I do not find that Berkeley 'figures as the bewildered observer'; he does not pose his questions in any assumed character, and when his tongue goes into his cheek ('Whether the subject of free-thinking in religion be not exhausted? …'), it is only for a moment. The form is such as to encourage irony, and irony of the Swiftian kind; but nothing is so remarkable, I find, as the absence of irony from *The Querist*. Mr Hone admits as much, and makes the really important point, when he points out how little room for manoeuvre Berkeley leaves to his 'supposed interlocutor'. The questions are all rhetorical; each contains in itself the only possible answer to it. It is this that makes the writing polemical. The mind behind the writing is a speculative mind, yet *The Querist* is not speculation, but argument.

This comes out very clearly if we compare *The Querist* with the earlier *Essay towards preventing the Ruine of Great Britain*. The two works have much in common. The reforms that Berkeley demanded of the English in 1721 are in some cases not very different from those he recommended to the Irish in 1735. He even uses the same examples.[2] But in form and expression the two pieces are poles apart. The Essay is pathetically ineffectual; it has every mark of conviction except its force. Berkeley's prose here has as little edge to it as Addison's, without any of the more insidious plausibilities that are Addison's substitute. There can be little doubt that the rhetorical questions of *The Querist* are the result of Berkeley's endeavour to give to his writing the polemical force and cut that at first it had wanted. Such self-consciousness in the act of writing is only to be expected from the writer who first detected and mocked the iambic rhythms of Shaftesbury's rhapsodic prose. *The Querist*, then, is far more satirical, and so more cutting, than the Essay.

But this increase in satirical effect has nothing to do with irony, which is hard to find in either piece of writing. Where irony appears in

---

1   Hone and Rossi, op. cit., p. 200.
2   For example, the *Essay:* 'If it be considered that more fine Linnen is worn in *Great Britain* than in any other Country of Europe, it will be difficult to assign a Reason why Paper may not be made here as good, and in the same quantity, as in *Holland* or *France*, or *Genoa*.' cf. *Querist*, 89; 'How it comes to pass that the Venetians and Genoese, who wear so much less linen, and so much worse than we do, should yet make very good paper, and in great quantity while we make very little?'

Berkeley, it is of the complex Swiftian kind; and of enormous interest, from this point of view, is the MS discovered by Hone and Rossi and printed as Appendix IV to their biography. This is *The Irish Patriot or Queries upon Queries*, Berkeley's retort to those who had attacked the views he promoted in *The Querist*. The thirty-six queries in this document are wholly different from those in *The Querist*. They do not require of the reader that he answer Yes, or No, according as Berkeley directs. Instead, they frustrate and embarrass him, and trap him into assenting to absurdities:

> (12) Whether a man who is versed in the doctrine of opposition and influence, can conceive it possible for the Government and people to unite in any one view for the public interest?

> (13) Whether a true Irishman should not by all means contrive and project that neither England nor the Government be better for the Kingdom?

> (14) Whether it be not a sure axiom that, *where nothing is, thence nothing can come out?*

The irony here is the three-fold irony discerned by Maynard Mack in the *Epistle to Augustus* and the *Modest Proposal*. In addition to the two levels of sarcasm (what is said, first; second, what is meant), there is also the ironical echo of the kind of question that Irish patriots were *usually* making about Ireland. These queries, in fact, are made *in character*, as is Swift's Modest Proposal. And there is some point in saying, that as the *Modest Proposal* and *Queries Upon Queries* are more ironical than *The Drapier's Letters* and *The Querist*, respectively, so they are less satirical; irony may barb the satiric thrust, but it also blunts it. It is notable, for instance, that Bishop Percy of Dromore, who was no fool, seems to have missed the whole point of *Queries upon Queries*, when the MS was in his possession.[1] He took the queries at their face-value, and never realised that Berkeley's tongue was in his cheek. That he should have done so is a tribute to Berkeley's skill as an ironist; but when irony is so accomplished as this, whether in Berkeley or in Swift, it is a weapon too delicate for satire, which drives to action. If Berkeley inspired (as he probably did) the view put forward in the anonymous introduction to the English edition of *The Querist*, if he thought with Percival (if it was Percival) that Swift's Irish tracts had only 'exasperated', then it may explain why his *Queries upon Queries* were never published. For that exasperated too; in fact, as Dr Leavis has established, exasperation is the special effect of all irony of this Swiftian kind. Berkeley, it seems probable, thought exasperation could

---

1 Hone and Rossi, op. cit., p. 264.

only do harm in Ireland in 1735, and so he suppressed his own work:

> (23) Whether it be not our great comfort and security that we can cry
> out upon all occasions: poor Ireland, beggarly Ireland? But if
> Ireland once became rich, what cry could we cry?

There can be little doubt that this arose out of exasperation in the writer. But it is hardly less plain that its effect, mounted as it is, so aptly, upon plaintive rhythms, would be to exasperate the reader. In suppressing it, Berkeley acted as a moralist. And Swift, too, was a moralist – that, we are often told, is the key to his character and his career. But Berkeley the moralist is as straightforward as Dr Johnson himself; in fact, as one sees from the *Essay towards preventing the Ruine of Great Britain*, he was, to begin with, altogether too straightforward to be effective. By comparison with Johnson and Berkeley, Swift seems sheerly irresponsible; and this is particularly true of Swift the ironist.

Dublin Magazine, n.s. 27 (October–December 1952), pp. 20–9.

IV Scientist; Philosopher; Poet

The English poet of the eighteenth century thought he had much to be thankful for, in taking the language from the hands of Denham and Waller and Dryden, who 'first gave it regular harmony, and discovered its latent powers'. But we tell one another that they were living in a fool's paradise:

> The whole movement of philosophy which started with Descartes and which was accompanied by the vast expansion of scientific inquiry and achievement, has been seen, and no doubt rightly, as producing an atmosphere inimical to poetry. The view of the universe its influence had made the generally accepted one, was that of a mechanism run on mathematical principles and devoid of colour, scent, taste, and sound. Science had enlarged the size of the universe, but had turned it into a lifeless machine, which worked by forces that could be expressed in mathematical formulae, but not in poetry. What was real was what could be measured, weighed and expressed in numbers, not what could be made the subject of poetry. Such writers as A. N. Whitehead, Basil Willey and Douglas Bush have all made the point that the mechanical view of the world is one that does not commend itself to the poet. Its declaration that what is 'really real', is a world of atoms in motion, devoid of all secondary sense qualities such as colour, scent, taste and sound, ordered by causal laws and explicable only in terms of mathematics, is one that gives little status to the poet. It is one indeed that gives little status to man himself, since, once the process of scientific explanation had started, it was soon seen that man himself, as part of the natural order, could be explained in similar terms. Poetry was not alone in suffering the effect of the new movement; religion itself was its companion.

I take this passage from R.L. Brett's book on Shaftesbury.[1] But Mr Brett is quite right in claiming that observations of this kind have been a commonplace in literary history for several years. And it is for its representative quality that I quote it.

There are several objections to it. In the first place it requires us to

1 R.L. Brett, *The Third Earl of Shaftesbury. A Study in Eighteenth-century Literary Theory* (London, 1951), p. 14.

think in terms of what might have been. It assumes that we are somehow dissatisfied with what poetry we have from the period in question. For such poetry as we have does its best with the materials and in the conditions Mr Brett thinks so unsuitable for it; and it seems to follow that there must be something wrong with this poetry. Instead of declaring, as older writers did, that Pope was no poet or a very limited one (that is, that they got little or no pleasure from reading him), later critics like Mr Brett go to work more deviously and ask, by implication, how Pope could be other than limited when he had such unpromising 'world-pictures' to deal with. Thus it is common nowadays to find the literary historian shaking his head over the poetic insufficiency of Bacon's world-view, or Locke's, or Newton's, or Descartes'. The prevailing tradition in the philosophy of Pope's day, variously described as Baconian, Cartesian, Newtonian, and so on, is generally taken to have been 'bad for poetry'. The chief authority for this view is William Blake, who was never tired of asserting it; and, of course, Blake's authority commands respect. But we have no right to assume that what was bad for Blake is bad for all poets and writers of all sorts at all times. One cannot help suspecting that Blake's view is so attractive today because it chimes in with some hatred and fear of the scientific in ourselves, so that when we attack Locke and Newton as enemies of poetry we are really tilting at Darwin and Herbert Spencer, and reading late-Victorian ideas into Augustan minds.

Secondly, we may object with Mallarmé, that poetry is written, not with ideas, but with words. The truth is surely that many poets listen to philosophers, and philosophize about their own activity, much less than the literary historians of this school imagine. Pope, having wavered towards a near-deism in the *Essay on Man*, recanted it in *The Dunciad*. It may be that this represents a change of heart in Pope, but it may equally well testify to a sort of quite legitimate irresponsibility. He believed in some sense, of course, first the one thing and then the other. But he may have believed as Yeats 'believed' in the extraordinary farrago that he delivered to the world, in *A Vision*, as his 'philosophy'. And these are not, to put it bluntly, the ideas the poets lived by – those presumably, in Pope's case, were the precepts of the Roman Church. These other 'beliefs' seem no more sometimes than a sort of provisional assent or serious play, like Walter Ralegh's 'love' of Queen Elizabeth. When Yeats asked the spirit-medium what it had come for, it replied, 'To give you metaphors for poetry'. Just so may Pope have imagined that the spirits of Bolingbroke and Warburton, Locke and Shaftesbury, came to him.

Historians of ideas are often nowadays solicitous for the poets; and the latter, as often as not, are churlish in their acknowledgements. The truth seems to be that the poet is sturdier, and his attitudes less calculable, than the historians suppose. There is a notion abroad that what is 'organic' is a good thing for poetry; and it follows that what is mechanical is not. The poet, however, takes his metaphors where he finds them, and may choose to extol the Brooklyn Bridge, no less than the meanest flower that blows:

> The familiar contention that science is inimical to poetry is no more tenable than the kindred notion that theology has been proverbially hostile – with the *Commedia* of Dante to prove the contrary.[1]

Mr Brett, it seems to me, is nowhere very clear about the mechanical Limbo, from which, by his account, Shaftesbury the knight errant came to deliver the poets. He nowhere states what it is that poets want from the world-pictures that the philosophers deliver to them. In a way, this is just as well. For on the one hand (and this is the really damning criticism of Mr Brett's position) we know too little for sure about how the mind of the poet works, to be able to say that this 'world-picture' will be good, and that one bad; and, on the other hand, the relations between poet and philosopher are a great deal more complicated than those of purveyor or errand boy and customer. I gather, however, from Mr Brett's passages on the Cambridge Platonists (e.g. pp. 21, 22), that he thinks the poet is happy when the philosopher delivers him a world of symbols, a natural world in which each natural thing 'stands for' something else that is supernatural. This is a common assumption, yet it is surely open to question. Of certain poets, at any rate, it would seem true to say that they look not for symbol, but for metaphor; not for what dissolves on scrutiny into something else, but for what on scrutiny becomes more and more splendidly itself. This, or something like it, seems the point that Professor Willey makes, when he says that Cambridge Platonism was no help to the poets – a contention that Mr Brett disputes.

A book has recently appeared which may make it more difficult henceforward to take up a position like Mr Brett's. This is *The Emperor's Clothes*, by Kathleen Nott,[2] which is fairly described by its sub-title, 'An attack on the dogmatic orthodoxy of T.S. Eliot, Graham Greene, Dorothy Sayers, C.S. Lewis, and others'. Among these 'others' is one of Mr Brett's authorities, Professor Willey.

But Miss Nott will make this sort of thing more difficult, chiefly in the sense that she will make it unfashionable – if, that is, as seems likely from the reception accorded her book, she sets another fashion herself. For it turns out that Descartes and Locke are as much the villains of her literary history as of Mr Brett's, while one of the very few points on which she agrees with Mr Eliot is in a fierce dislike of Thomas Hobbes. She defends the scientist against the attacks of those she calls 'neo-scholastics' or 'Augustinians', only so long as he does not open his mouth. She declares that Professor Willey

---

1   Hart Crane in 1929, quoted by Peter Viereck, *Strike Through the Mask!* (New York, 1950), p. 68.
2   Kathleen Nott, *The Emperor's Clothes* (London, 1953).

confuses the special observations of scientists with the hypotheses and generalizations of philosophers and 'thinkers' which may appear or may claim to be based on these observations.

This second class of 'philosophers and "thinkers"' includes not only Bacon, Hobbes, Locke and Descartes, but also, as she makes clear more than once, a scientist such as Eddington (or, presumably, Newton), when he is on his day off, no longer making his special observations, but philosophizing about his own activity. She admires the scientist and springs to his defence, only so long as he is strong and silent, getting on with the job in the lab. She holds no brief for the 'philosophizer', that is (for Miss Nott, hard as she is on 'loaded words' when she detects them in others, is not above using them herself), for the philosopher of almost any school other than that modern one to which she owes allegiance herself, which understands philosophy as a sort of higher critical semantics.

Thus her objections to Mr Brett's case would boil down to a dark suspicion that he is not really concerned for poetry so much as for the instituted religion which appears, in the last sentence quoted, as a fellow-sufferer; to a further suspicion that he has out-dated ideas of what scientific method is; and – most important – that he fails to distinguish between scientific method and practice on the one hand, and, on the other, philosophizing about it. This last point is very important, and I think Miss Nott is quite right to bring this charge against Professor Willey and his followers. There is certainly something disingenuous about 'accompanied by' in the first sentence quoted from Mr Brett – 'The whole movement of philosophy which ... was accompanied by the vast expansion of scientific inquiry and achievement. ...' Mr Brett plainly means us to understand that the relation between the science and the philosophy was something more intimate than a mere coincidence; these are smear-tactics, guilt by association. And as Miss Nott points out, the confusion is often more flagrant than this – the crime is laid at the door of a hypostatized 'Science', which lumps together Descartes and Robert Boyle. Miss Nott's aim is to rescue Boyle and others like him from this smear, and to assert that a poet's best friend is his scientist. However that may be, it was certainly well worthwhile to distinguish the experimenter from the man who tried to rationalize his findings. After all, the conflict between the experimental empiricists on the one hand and the Cartesian rationalists on the other is a fact of the history of science, and it is a fact ignored in an argument such as Mr Brett's. Miss Nott at this point is shoulder to shoulder with Ernest Fenollosa, who maintained, 'Science fought till she got at the *things*. Poetry agrees with science and not with logic.'

All the same, this objection, weighty as it is, is the only valid criticism Miss Nott has to bring against Professor Willey and his followers. And I think it is hardly sweeping enough to justify her, when she pillories Professor Willey in a chapter-heading, albeit in the distinguished company of T.E. Hulme and Mr Eliot. It is true she makes other criticisms of Professor Willey's procedure, but most of these are either too nicely meticulous or else wrong-headed.[1] Thus it is quite true that we ought not to hypostatize, and treat large abstractions as if they were concrete phenomena; but if Professor Willey does this with 'Science', Miss Nott does it with 'Puritanism', and it seems as if something of the sort is unavoidable in any form of discourse. Elsewhere Miss Nott devotes many pages to a criticism of Professor Willey, this time in company with Maritain, which amounts to this – that he has set out to define the change in men's minds which occurred in the seventeenth century, whereas, according to Miss Nott, he ought to have shown how this change was inevitable. Professor Willey offers to say what happened to men's minds at this period. It is a sufficiently tall order, one would have thought, but it is not tall enough for Miss Nott, who demands that he explain why what happened *did* happen.

To my mind, Miss Nott is unfair to Professor Willey, simply because she is so largely in agreement with him. She agrees with him and with Mr Brett and also Mr Cleanth Brooks, in finding something sadly lacking in the English poetry of the eighteenth century. And she agrees with them further in laying some of the blame for this at the door of Hobbes and Locke. The last thing one can say of her in general is that she pulls her punches, yet in all this it seems to me she is too conservative, and also (what is more to the point) lamentably unscientific. Taking over without question the view that eighteenth-century poetry is on the whole a pretty shabby performance, she offers no evidence beyond a few of the more flagrantly false-poetical locutions of Gray and Collins, torn from their context – it seems a curious procedure for a writer so vociferously in favour of observation and verification as the bases of scientific method.

As for blaming Hobbes and Locke for this, the evidence is all the other way. In one of the extraordinary assertions that turn up on nearly every page, even in the midst of otherwise close and cogent argument, she observes, 'good contemporary scholars do actually know more about the times and conditions in which the dead poets worked than the poets did themselves'. I do not think she would find one good contemporary scholar to agree with her. But it is certainly true that such scholars as Marjorie Nicolson, John Arthos, W.K. Wimsatt and others have discovered and are discovering how much the greatest literary achievements of the eighteenth century owe to, not just the scientists, but the philosophizers about science. Miss Nicolson has shown how the imaginations of

---

1   She is quite right, though, about the passage from Professor Willey on p. 171. And it is important.

Thomson and Edward Young were fired by Locke and Newton together. Mr Wimsatt has shown how Dr Johnson's prose-style is similarly based upon the psychology of Locke – a psychology which, as Miss Nott goes out of her way to say, could not be classed as scientific in her sense, but only as pseudo-scientific philosophizing. This is that same pseudo-scientific psychology of association which, as Wilbur Cross and lately Douglas Jefferson have shown, is the basis of Sterne's comic masterpiece, *Tristram Shandy*, and which, in its later but still unscientific elaboration by David Hartley, is a guiding principle of Wordsworth's *Prelude*, as Beatty pointed out thirty years ago. It is not necessary for Miss Nott to esteem the first version of the *Prelude* so highly as I do, but certainly the onus is on her to prove that it would have been better if Wordsworth had never read David Hartley. Perhaps she will prefer the later, more 'Christian' version – but in view of her militant agnosticism that might be rather hard for her to do.

Miss Nott claims to follow the clue given by Mallarmé, that poetry is written not with ideas but with words. But she does not follow it far enough. If we follow it further, we see the poet as a marauder, who ransacks the speech and written language of his own time and earlier, looking for words which are arresting and suggestive, or for words, dry and inconspicuous in common usage or in the place where he finds them, which can be made remarkable in the different context he envisages for them. When he finds them, he tears them out of the perhaps elaborate structure of meaning in which he finds them, and takes them over for his own purposes. It follows that the poet and the writer of imaginative prose is less interested than other users of language in the stability of the language he uses; indeed, some poets have spoken as if they have a vested interest in instability, conceiving their duty to be the breaking-down of accepted meanings and usual collocations, in order by new combinations to make experience seem once again new and surprising. Swift complained that the language in his time was changing too swiftly, valuable older words continually slipping out of use, as new words shouldered their way in. Now it is probably true that there are periods when the language is too fluid, even for poets, when they must join forces with the writers of functional prose to arrest the too rapid development of the language. (T.S. Eliot has suggested that the present time is such a period.) But the poet will tend to welcome a fairly rapid rate of change in the language of his time, because the old word slipping out of use can be brought back and used to all the more effect because of the slight tinge of quaintness it has already acquired, and the new word can be acclimatized, while retaining something piquant and surprising. T.S. Eliot calls this 'An easy commerce of the old and the new'; and the operative word is 'easy'.

Pope lived at a time when new words were coming into the language in great numbers. Some of these were undoubtedly, as Swift thought, pieces of new-fangled jargon which did not last, but were subsequently, by another change of fashion, discarded. But there is the famous case of 'mob', which Swift condemned as a vulgar abbreviation, to show that there was a place in the language for some of the novel words he would have excluded. Simeon Potter comments:

> All those complex changes and developments, all those adoptions and adaptations which had contributed to the making of English over so many centuries had achieved in the year 1700 a certain balance or equilibrium.[1]

As he goes on to point out, 'equilibrium' in this sense is not the same as that stability for which Swift yearned. It may be defined, perhaps, as that state of the language in which the old and the new can be brought to consort together with some degree of ease. If so, then the poets of Pope's age were perhaps as fortunate as they thought they were, in coming to use the language when they did.

As might be expected, in view of the great expansion of scientific activity at this time and earlier, one of the most fruitful sources of new words in this period was the writing of those scientists who are often taken to have done so much damage to Augustan poetry. John Arthos, for instance, has shown how the adjectives formed by the suffix '-y' ('beamy', 'sluicy', and so on), so often derided as false-poetical, were in fact coined by scientists in the late seventeenth century. If we seek to know how it was that poets could make use of laboratory language in treating of their traditional subject-matter, the human heart, we find that we have to give some credit to just those 'mechanic' philosophers and psychologists who are the *bête-noire* of Professor Willey, Mr Brett, and Miss Nott alike. For once Hobbes and Locke had allowed the possibility that man's mind and heart were subject to the same laws of motion as governed the world of physics, the poets were able to use the new words in writing of the emotions and aspirations of men:

> Through clouds of Passion Pulteney's views are clear
> He foams a Patriot to subside a peer; ...

In these lines, which may be Pope's, the poet is able to use the language of the chemist to describe the character and conduct of a venal politician. He is able to do so because the philosophers have suggested the possibility that the heart of the politician functions in the same sort of way as a chemical in a retort, and it does not matter that the poet may not believe this – whether he believes it or not, the idea is still there for him to play with. Even if he is bitterly opposed to all this aspect of the thought of his

1   Simeon Potter, *Our Language* (London, 1950), p. 60.

time, he can just for that reason push it to an extreme, to make it look silly. In any case, these metaphors, straddling with one foot in and one foot out of the laboratory, are a distinctive feature of Augustan writing, in verse and in some sorts of prose. It is at the bottom of what are by common consent some of the greatest literary achievements of the age. And, in so far as the writers owe it to anyone at all, they owe it to the scientists and to the 'mechanic' pseudo-scientists no less.

The 'mechanic' philosophers, deducing from the findings of the experimenters a crude materialism, stimulated into life another range of metaphors that were shamming dead. These were the puns concealed in etymology – the 'inspiration' that is 'wind', the 'profundity' that is deep and therefore low, therefore to be achieved by bathos or the art of sinking. William Empson has demonstrated how these puns are the basis of *A Tale of a Tub*, on the principle, to which Swift gave perhaps only provisional assent as a *working* principle, 'Everything spiritual and valuable has a gross and revolting parody, very similar to it, with the same name'.[1] 'Spirit' means, among other things, alcohol, and hence, when dissenting enthusiasts claim to be imbued with the spirit, Swift can apply the materialist logic embodied in the very etymology of the word, and suggest that they are drunk. The ambiguity can work equally well in the other optimistic way, as for Berkeley in *Siris*, where, because he finds a beneficial spirit (in the chemist's sense) in tar-water, the writer can conclude that the spirit (the holy spirit now, in the theologian's sense) is infused throughout the created world. Burke uses the same pun when he speaks of 'a sort of flippant, vain discourse, in which, as in an unsavoury fume, several persons suffer the spirit of liberty to evaporate'. Or there is Berkeley again, in *Alciphron*, making his free-thinker declare:

> You may dispute the Matter if you please. But a Man of Parts is one thing, and a Pedant another. Pains and Method may do for some sort of People. A Man must be a long time kindling wet Straw into a vile smothering Flame, but Spirits blaze out at once.

Here again, for this range of punning metaphors concealed in etymology, the writers are indebted, if to anyone, then to such as Boyle in the first place, but to Hobbes and Locke in the second. These necessarily superficial comments suggest a view of the relationship between poet, scientist, and philosopher or philosophizer, which is at odds certainly with Professor Willey's view and Mr Brett's, but with Miss Nott's no less. And I submit that this view is arrived at by ways much nearer to the scientific method of observation and verification than anything Miss Nott has to offer.

---

1   William Empson, *Some Versions of Pastoral* (London, 1935), p. 60.

'A plague o' both your houses' is an easy attitude to take up, but not one that gets us very far. It is not really my attitude to Miss Nott's book, for my sympathies are with her in what she is trying to do, if not in the way she tries to do it. But the slapdash methods that she employs in literary history are just as evident, unfortunately, in those other parts of her book that have attracted more attention. I sympathize with her attack on Mr Eliot's evasiveness in all his prose apart from the strictly literary criticism of his earlier years, and I think there is now a case that he must answer, though I don't think he will. If he should, he would find it anything but difficult, not because Miss Nott's case is a weak one in itself, but because in her conduct of it she lays herself open so continually. Consider the following specimen:

> The point here is that Mr Eliot does not want religions to be scientif-
> ically studied. This gives us the clue to the meaning of his remarks on
> humanism and the experimental. It gives us also the essential explana-
> tion of all his other dislikes, including liberalism, psycho-analysis,
> sexual relations apart from the narrow prescription of the Church,
> freedom of intellectual inquiry, and 'progress'. All these things when
> they are valuable, that is, here, when they lead to increase of happiness
> or contentment, do so in so far as they are the result of an observa-
> tional, experimental, a scientific attitude.

Let us be quite clear. What Miss Nott says is that 'sexual relations apart from the narrow prescription of the Church lead to increase of happiness or contentment in so far as they are the result of an observational, exper-imental, a scientific attitude'. What is the evidence, the body of scientific observation, which gives Miss Nott such enviable assurance in dealing with such a perplexing field of human activity? How many readings did she take on her gauge of human contentment, and what is that gauge? How can she be so sure that a condition of successful sexual relations is not some degree of mutual esteem, or else of affection, between the sexual partners? Is such esteem or such affection, supposing either or both to be necessary, arrived at by observation and experiment?

It would not be hard to find other passages begging just as many ques-tions. Miss Nott, for all her dislike of dogma, is no mean dogmatist herself, though she deals in a different kind of dogma. All the same, it is not often that one comes across such a lively and such a meaty book as *The Emperor's Clothes*. It is the sort of book that continually tempts the reader to pencil exclamation marks in the margin. And in my own case these were expressions of emphatic approval at least as often as of aston-ishment. It is not in the first place a work of literary history, but a polemic. And perhaps in that context one should not expect literary history to be anything but sketchy and dubious. Still, observation, infer-ence, verification – these are just the principles that Miss Nott continually invokes; and her literary history affords one field in which we can judge her own performance in the light of her own principles. I do not think she comes out of the test very well. Still that does not invalidate the principles as such. And no doubt it is silly to expect her to re-write the history of English literature, merely as it were in passing. It was obviously bad strategy on her part even to try, and yet I cannot wish that she had played safe. For it is seldom indeed that one finds a book of this kind that fails through all along trying to do too much. I recommend this book – oh, with endless reservations, but heartily none the less.

The Twentieth Century, CLV (March 1954), pp. 270–80.

V Berkeley and the Style of Dialogue

Soon after *The Principles of Human Knowledge* (1710) had appeared, the still youthful Berkeley (1685–1753) wrote to his friend Percival expressing his disappointment that Samuel Clarke had refused to be drawn into discussion of that work:

> That an ingenious and candid person (as I take him to be) should declare I am in an error, and at the same time, out of modesty, refuse to shew me where it lies, is something unaccountable. ... I never expected that a gentleman otherwise so well employed should think it worth his while to enter into a dispute with me concerning any notions of mine. But being it was so clear to him that I went on false principles, I hoped he would vouchsafe in a line or two to point them out to me that so I may more closely review and examine them.[1]

We do not always understand what a writer of Berkeley's period meant when he says of some one, as Berkeley says here of Clarke, that he is a candid person. For 'candid' and 'candour' are words of much narrower meaning now than in the eighteenth century. The idea of candour was then relevant in fields of experience where the modern reader, used only to the attenuated notion current today, is not at home with it. And this breadth of meaning seems a characteristic of terms which are crucial to the thinking of man in any given time. It is an interesting question whether the breadth of meaning attached to a word is a consequence of that word's standing for something important, or whether it is not the cause of that importance.

At any rate there is little doubt that an understanding of what 'candour' meant for the Augustans is a key to much that seems odd or elusive in their thought; and this is as true of Berkeley as of the rest. To understand Berkeley's idea of candour leads, by way of profitable surmise, into that part of his thought to which he never gave systematic expression – it leads us to his ethics.

No one claimed more for candour than Blifil in *Tom Jones* (1749), when he was arguing that nowhere in Scripture did 'charity' mean giving things away:

---

1   Benjamin Rand, *Berkeley and Percival* (Cambridge, 1914), p. 94.

'The Christian religion,' he said, 'was instituted for much nobler purposes than to enforce a lesson which many heathen philosophers had taught us long before, and which, though it might perhaps be called a moral virtue, savoured but little of that sublime, Christian-like disposition – that vast elevation of thought, in purity approaching to angelic perfection – to be attained, expressed, and felt only by grace. Those,' he said, 'came nearer to the Scripture meaning who understood by it candour, or the forming of a benevolent opinion of our brethren, and passing a favourable judgement on their actions; a virtue much higher and more extensive in its nature than a pitiful distribution of alms, which, though we would never so much prejudice or even ruin our families, could never reach many; whereas charity, in the other and truer sense, might be extended to all mankind.' (II, v)

Berkeley never makes candour mean as much as this. Nor indeed does Fielding; for Blifil of course is a scoundrel, and here he is damning himself out of his own mouth – the passage is heavily ironical. Yet there would be no point to the irony if claims as large as this were not indeed made for candour in the society which Fielding wrote for. And sure enough, the biblical scholar Edward Harwood, reading in the First Epistle to the Corinthians how charity (which he called 'benevolence') 'beareth all things, believeth all things, hopeth all things, endureth all things', translated this by: 'It throws a vail of candour over all things …'[1] When Berkeley gave Clarke the credit of thinking him a candid person, he was expecting him to do more than just speak his mind. And similarly Dryden was asking a great deal of the speakers in his conversation-piece *Of Dramatic Poesy* (1668), when, in his prefatory epistle to Buckhurst, he promised that they would dispute 'like gentlemen, with candour and civility', and not 'like pedants, with violence of words'.

When Berkeley calls Clarke 'candid' he does not mean only what we should mean, that Clarke speaks his mind without fear or favour. He means that and he means more – that Clarke is so concerned to arrive at the truth that he lets nothing stand in the way of helping others to do so. He means even (in the manner of Captain Blifil) that Clarke is prepared to give any man the benefit of the doubt and think him an earnest seeker after truth rather than a whipper-snapper eager to make his mark by dint of outrageous novelty. For I do not think there is anything ironical in Berkeley's letter. If it raises a smile, it is at Berkeley's simplicity, in thinking Clarke could set him right without entering into a dispute with him. And yet perhaps this is not simplicity at all. It takes two to make a

---

1   *A Liberal Translation of the New Testament*, 2 vols. (London, 1768); quoted by James Sutherland, 'Some Aspects of Eighteenth-Century Prose', in *Essays on the Eighteenth Century Presented to David Nichol Smith* (Oxford, 1945), p. 109.

quarrel, and perhaps Berkeley was confident of restraining himself even if he found Clarke's objections of no weight. That would be candid; and Berkeley took candour seriously.

Candour, in any sense, is a virtue that shows itself most plainly in intelligent conversation. And unless we realize the presence of candour in the background, we are at a loss to explain the importance that the Augustans gave to 'polite conversation'. Herbert Davis has pointed out how important this was to Swift.[1] How can we explain that the value of good conversation is one of the few positive values to be found in the writings of that supremely negative and destructive mind? It seems to argue in Swift a disastrous lack of proportion – unless we remember that for the Augustans conversation was the chief opportunity for the exercise of candour, and that candour was to them a virtue sometimes hard to distinguish from charity itself.

Herbert Davis appropriately ends his essay with a tribute to Berkeley for introducing 'qualities of good conversation' into philosophical writing, as Addison had introduced them into the *Spectator's* 'Saturday sermons'. This is nothing new, of course; it is a tribute often paid to Berkeley in particular as to the Augustans in general. But if we take 'candour' into account, then the tribute has an added force. Besides, the qualities of good conversation have an obvious and immediate relevance to a literary form that Berkeley made his own – the dialogue or the conversation-piece. Professor Davis makes his point about Berkeley by quoting from his preface to *Three Dialogues between Hylas and Philonous* (1713). It would have been more elaborate, but also more telling, to illustrate 'qualities of good conversation' from the dialogues themselves, from something that is, however trimmed and elevated, at bottom conversation exemplified.

Berkeley, as a writer of dialogues, has been compared with Plato and Leopardi, and contrasted with Landor, because 'his dialogues embody ideas instead of exhibiting characters';[2] and the same biographers have endorsed Sir Herbert Read's judgement that in Berkeley's hands, as in Plato's, 'the dialogue has been purged of its dramatic nature. ...' But this turns out to rest upon a quibble, for 'if the essential of drama is the portrayal of action, then the essential of dialogue is the creative activity of ideas – ideas in action, one might say'. Indeed one might; and if one did, then, on Sir Herbert's definition of drama, the dialogues of Berkeley would be as dramatic as Landor's.

Berkeley's later dialogues in *Alciphron* (1732) are very different from the *Three Dialogues*, and part of the difference is that there is more 'char-

---

1   Herbert Davis, 'The Conversation of the Augustans', in *The Seventeenth Century: Studies in the History of English Thought and Literature from Bacon to Pope, by Richard Foster Jones and Others Writing in his Honor* (Palo Alto, 1951).

2   J.M. Hone and M.M. Rossi, *Bishop Berkeley* (London, 1931), pp. 79–80.

acter' in *Alciphron*. But this does not mean that *Alciphron* is more dramatic. The essential difference between the two works is stated conclusively by Hone and Rossi: 'In the *Dialogues between Hylas and Philonous*, both interlocutors are well disposed persons and lovers of truth; and if there is conflict, it is the conflict of the slow intelligence and the lively one.'[1] In other words, Hylas is as wrong as Alciphron is; but he is candid, where Alciphron is not. It is in the *Three Dialogues* that we see candour, as it were, in action.

Before showing this by example, it will be well to recall what a large undertaking it was. There is a famous work of literature where the same thing is attempted without much success – and this is Dryden's *Of Dramatic Poesy*. E.M.W. Tillyard once made the point: 'Dryden did not reach perfection of tone at once. There is something rather set and formal about the way he treats Ancients, French, and English in the *Essay of Dramatic Poesy*, as if he were arguing for freedom and impartiality, not taking them serenely for granted.'[2] And Tillyard goes on to show that in later critical writings Dryden deals freely and impartially, with less fuss than in the Essay. But it is surely necessary to take into account, in this connexion, the form of the Essay. By throwing it into the form of a conversation-piece Dryden is trying to fulfil the promise he makes in his prefatory Epistle, to show that controversial subjects can be handled 'with candour and civility' in the society for which he writes. As I have argued elsewhere,[3] and as Tillyard obliquely confirms, Dryden was unsuccessful in this. Who or what is to blame for this, whether Dryden in particular or Restoration society at large, is something we cannot determine; if the society failed its poet, the poet too was at fault in mistaking the temper of his society, and looking to it for models which it could not provide. And if we think that Berkeley in the *Three Dialogues* succeeded where Dryden failed, we should be chary of taking the credit for this from Berkeley himself so as to argue that society under Queen Anne was more civilized than it had been under Charles II.

Oddly enough (yet is it so strange?) the words 'candour' and 'candid' do not appear in the *Three Dialogues*. At times 'ingenuous' is used where it seems that 'candid' is meant:

> *Phil.* ... But, can you think it no more than a philosophical paradox, to say that *real sounds are never heard*, and that the idea of them is obtained by some other sense? And is there nothing in this contrary to nature and the truth of things?
>
> *Hyl.* To deal ingenuously, I do not like it. And, after the conces-

1   Hone and Rossi, loc. cit.
2   E.M.W. Tillyard, 'A Note on Dryden's Criticism', in *The Seventeenth Century,* op. cit., pp. 334–5.
3   See Chapter VIII above.

sions already made, I had as well grant that sounds too, have no real being without the mind.

    Phil. And I hope you will make no difficulty to acknowledge the same of *colours*.

    Hyl. Pardon me: the case of colours is very different. ...[1]

There is a sense in which this is thoroughly theatrical dialogue. As we read we put ourselves into the posture of the speakers, of Hylas in particular; what Hylas says is said in a certain, though always changing tone, which is conveyed to us. 'To deal ingenuously ...' which is rueful; 'I had as well grant ...' (reluctant, without being grudging); 'Pardon me: ...' (suddenly alert and assured). We even supply appropriate gestures, an unwilling rub of the nose or the jaw, the biting of a lip. Hylas is by far the more engaging and attractive of the speakers; and this is because of his candour. Repeatedly embarrassed, always pressed hard, he admits the points made against him and is never near to losing his temper, or to escaping through a deliberate quibble. And Philonous too, though he is less sympathetic because always on the winning side, is fair, and more than fair, to his opponent, letting him take his time, letting the argument circle and eddy and return upon itself.

In short, the dialogues are, among other things, an example of good manners and disinterested behaviour. Yet (this is the real achievement) the effect is not obtained by emasculating controversy. In Dryden the speakers are so careful, each of the other's *amour propre*, that they dare not push their disagreements to a point. Not so Hylas and Philonous; neither of them need pull his punches:

    Hyl. You may draw as many absurd consequences as you please, and endeavour to perplex the plainest things; but you shall never persuade me out of my senses. I clearly understand my own meaning.

    Phil. I wish you would make me understand it too. ... (p. 393)

    Hyl. I know not how to maintain it; and yet I am loath to give up *extension*, I see so many odd consequences following upon such a concession.

    Phil. Odd, say you? After the concessions already made, I hope you will stick at nothing for its oddness. (p. 400)

    Phil. How many shapes is your Matter to take? Or, how often must it be proved not to exist, before you are content to part with it? (p. 433)

There is excellent comedy here, not only the drama of a slow mind and a

---

1 'The First Dialogue between Hylas and Philonous'; *Works,* ed. A.C. Fraser, vol. I (Oxford, 1901), p. 392. Future references to Berkeley are to this edition.

quick one, but the chastening comedy of how the human mind will twist and turn (unconsciously) to evade unpalatable conclusions, to cling to what is familiar. The candour comes with the realization by both speakers that the game has rules which the mind (however unwillingly) must observe. Hence the frequent excursions into logic:

> *Hyl.* You have indeed clearly satisfied me – either that there is no difficulty at bottom in this point; or, if there be, that it makes equally against both opinions.
>
> *Phil.* But that which makes equally against two contradictory opinions can be a proof against neither.
>
> *Hyl.* I acknowledge it. (pp. 468–9)

> *Hyl.* I own myself entirely satisfied for the present in all respects. But, what security can I have that I shall still continue the same full assent to your opinion, and that no unthought-of objection or difficulty will occur hereafter?
>
> *Phil.* Pray, Hylas, do you in other cases, when a point is once evidently proved, withhold your consent on account of objections or difficulties it may be liable to?... (p. 481)

Disputation observes a discipline, an order that the shifty mind continually seeks to evade. To admit the discipline and bring one's own mind into line – this is one aspect of candour.

The sharpest sarcasm is permissible; and at least once the sarcasm becomes something more elaborate, a Swiftian irony:

> *Phil.* But is it not strange the whole world should be thus imposed on, and so foolish as to believe their senses? And yet I know not how it is, but men eat, and drink, and sleep, and perform all the offices of life, as comfortably and conveniently as if they really knew the things they are conversant about.
>
> *Hyl.* They do so: but you know ordinary practice does not require a nicety of speculative knowledge. Hence the vulgar retain their mistakes, and for all that make a shift to bustle through the affairs of life. But philosophers know better things.
>
> *Phil.* You mean, they *know* that they *know nothing*.
>
> *Hyl.* That is the very top and perfection of human knowledge. (p. 443)

On the other hand, a plain admission of confusion deserves a helping hand:

> *Phil.* ... This point I thought had been already determined.
>
> *Hyl.* I own it was; but you will pardon me if I seem a little embarrassed: I know not how to quit my old notions.
>
> *Phil.* To help you out, do but consider. ... (p. 401)

Undoubtedly the disputants, and Hylas in particular, are idealized. We can hardly believe that such self-control and compliance was to be found in the conversations of Augustan London, even in the conclave of the Scriblerus Club. On the other hand, we cannot think that the dialogue has no basis in reality; apart from anything else, the vivid movement of authentic speech is there to prove the contrary – 'But the novelty, Philonous, the novelty!...', '... That is not fair, Philonous ...'. 'Things! You may pretend what you please; ...' In other words, if the conversation is idealized, it is the most useful kind of idealization, near enough to reality to incite men to realize it. And to that extent, the *Three Dialogues* can be thought of as implicitly a treatise in ethics, an exemplification of the virtue of candour.

Ellen Douglass Leyburn, in a valuable essay, has found a striking similarity between what we take to be the ethical views of Berkeley and what we know to be the views of Dr Johnson: 'It is impossible to read *Alciphron* with Johnson in mind without finding there sentiments that almost make us forget relations of time and space and think them echoes of *Rasselas* and *The Rambler*.'[1] However it may displease the Irish admirers of Berkeley, for whom his Irishness is his greatest virtue, I think this comparison is valid and striking. There *is* a similarity between Berkeley's outlook on human conduct and Johnson's. And it seems plain, when we consider Johnson's mostly disparaging comments on Berkeley, that he had probably read none of Berkeley's works, and almost certainly not *Alciphron*. On the other hand, there is one matter on which they plainly part company. There can be little doubt that Berkeley enjoyed disputation, but hardly in the sense in which it was 'Johnson's favourite sport'.[2] And he would surely have disapproved of a conversationalist who disputed to gain the victory at any cost. Berkeley, I fear, would have found Johnson a not wholly candid man.

Berkeley's achievement in the *Three Dialogues* can be valued at the rate it deserves if that work is compared with Shaftesbury's *The Moralists: a Philosophical Rhapsody*. Despite the ominous sound of 'rhapsody' in the title, *The Moralists* is in fact one of the best things in the *Characteristics* (1711). And – what is more surprising – it is, at its best, genuinely expansive and enlivening, precisely in its rhapsodical passages, where Shaftesbury's optimism builds on a Spinozistic basis with most enthusiasm. Though on scrutiny seldom genuinely eloquent, yet these passages are placed in the economy of the whole – and so, to some extent, 'placed'

---

1 'Bishop Berkeley, Metaphysician as Moralist' in *The Age of Johnson: Essays Presented to Chauncey Brewster Tinker* (New Haven, 1949), p. 328.
2 Ibid., p. 321.

in another sense, so as to quell our disquiets about them – by rising out of dialogue. For this is Shaftesbury's own experiment in the manner of dialogue which elsewhere in the *Characteristics* he has recommended as a philosophical and literary form, a recommendation which he here repeats. As the sub-title indicates ('a Recital of Certain Conversations on Natural and Moral Subjects'), *The Moralists* is itself a dialogue, though one in which the conversations are for the most part reported instead of being *oratio recta*. As such, it is by no means unattractive. Particularly interesting is the presence of two shadowy figures, named only as an old gentleman and his younger companion, who – though they say very little – considerably enliven the scene for as long as they are present. There is for instance an admirably contrived situation in which Philocles, one of the principal speakers, explicitly speaks as *advocatus diaboli*, on the side of irreligion. This is a convention which Philocles' antagonist, Theocles, can agree to for the sake of discussion, whereas the old gentleman, continually blurring convention into reality, supposes that Philocles must be truly an infidel. This is a far subtler effect than any contrived by Dryden or, to take another instance, by Mandeville; it looks forward to the use of false-naïveté by one of the speakers in Berkeley's second set of conversation-pieces, his *Alciphron* of 1732. Yet as a whole *The Moralists* is best compared with *Three Dialogues*, Berkeley's earlier attempt at the dialogue form. For Shaftesbury had made it very plain that in his view the Dialogue could give only an idealized image of the common pursuit of truth, since in actuality candour and civility were so wholly lacking in the society of his and Berkeley's time. In *The Moralists* he wrote:

> You know too, that in this academic philosophy I am to present you with, there is a certain way of questioning and doubting, which no ways suits the genius of our age. Men love to take party instantly. They cannot bear being kept in suspense. The examination torments them. They want to be rid of it upon the easiest terms. 'Tis as if men fancied themselves drowning whenever they dare trust to the current of reason. They seem hurrying away they know not whither, and are ready to catch the first twig. There they choose afterwards to hang, though ever so insecurely, rather than trust their strength to bear them above water. He who has got hold of an hypothesis, how slight soever, is satisfied. He can presently answer every objection, and with a few terms of art, give an account of everything without trouble.[1]

The image of the current of reason and the twigs of hypothesis is as good as anything Shaftesbury ever achieved. Hardly less admirable is his comparison of these modish thinkers with geometers ('They are all

---

1 Shaftesbury, *Characteristics,* ed. John M. Robertson, vol. II (London, 1900), pp. 7–8. Future references to Shaftesbury are to this edition.

Archimedeses in their way, and can make a world upon easier terms than he offered to move one'). And the same assurance informs his next paragraph:

> In short, there are good reasons for our being thus superficial, and consequently thus dogmatical in philosophy. We are too lazy and effeminate, and withal a little too cowardly, to dare doubt. The decisive way best becomes our manners. It suits as well with our vices as with our superstition. Whichever we are fond of is secured by it. If in favour of religion we have espoused an hypothesis on which our faith, we think, depends, we are superstitiously careful not to be loosened in it. If, by means of our ill morals, we are broken with religion, 'tis the same case still: we are as much afraid of doubting. We must be sure to say, 'It cannot be', and ''tis demonstrable. For otherwise who knows? And not to know is to yield!'

The attack is rounded off with a backward glance at earlier periods 'when not only horsemanship and military arts had their public places of exercise, but philosophy too had its wrestlers in repute' (we may think, justly enough, of the first page of Sidney's *Apologie*), and the point is made that in such an age as Shaftesbury's the philosophical dialogue could be written only by swimming against the current, by taking few hints from the actual conduct of conversations and disputations and many more from the sense of how they should have been conducted. Accordingly, Shaftesbury's Theocles and Philocles are idealized further than Berkeley's Hylas and Philonous – further, and also less skilfully, less persuasively, for Theocles is pompous and priggish.

Shaftesbury in these passages argues that the difficulty of writing the philosophical dialogue in the early eighteenth century derived from a deep-seated intellectual insecurity in English society of that time – not the sort of thing we are invited to think about the English Augustan Age. Elsewhere, however, and chiefly in the *Advice to an Author*, Shaftesbury finds not psychological but social and historical reasons. *Advice to an Author* is conducted so diffusely, and contains so much of the affected writing which Shaftesbury called 'rhapsody', that it is hard and inconvenient to recognize that what Shaftesbury says about the dialogue is interesting good sense. Though Berkeley was right in *Alciphron* to ridicule the affectation with which Shaftesbury elaborated his idea to begin with, yet his ideal of 'mirror-writing', of the author in dialogue with himself, could be said to contain all Romanticism in embryo. Moreover, Shaftesbury quite justly extends the idea of dialogue to comprehend, as the true end of the noblest literature, the dramatic and the objective. It is thus that he can link together Plato and Homer. And however strangely it may consort with his proto-Romanticism, and still more with the self-regarding affectation of his own style, Shaftesbury's preference for this objective and dramatic manner to the direct wooing of the reader by the writer is a lesson worth learning in an age like the present, when 'tone' in the writer counts perhaps for too much.

As Shaftesbury develops his theme, the dialogue of a writer with himself becomes the dialogue of a writer with his subject, with 'Nature'. It is still opposed to the dialogue of writer with reader:

> An author who writes in his own person has the advantage of being who or what he pleases. He is no certain man, nor has any certain or genuine character; but suits himself on every occasion to the fancy of his reader, whom, as the fashion is nowadays, he constantly caresses and cajoles. All turns upon their two persons. And as in an amour or commerce of love-letters, so here the author has the privilege of talking eternally of himself, dressing and sprucing himself up, whilst he is making diligent court, and working upon the humour of the party to whom he addresses. This is the coquetry of a modern author, whose epistles, dedicatory, prefaces, and addresses to the reader are so many affected graces, designed to draw the attention from the subject towards himself, and make it be generally observed, not so much what he says, as what he appears, or is, and what figure he already makes, or hopes to make, in the fashionable world. (1, 131)

Shaftesbury's conspicuous refusal to write dedications and prefaces suggest that his other affectations, like his waywardness, his launchings into rhapsody and jerkings out of it, are clumsily derived to make the effect dramatic and objective – as a soliloquy overheard, not a speech addressed to the reader, who on the contrary by these means is continually wrong-footed. The dialogue, Shaftesbury goes on to say, excludes all this 'pretty amour and intercourse of caresses between the author and reader':

> ... here the author is annihilated, and the reader, being no way applied to, stands for nobody. The self-interesting parties both vanish at once. The scene presents itself as by chance and undesigned. You are not only left to judge coolly and with indifference of the sense delivered, but of the character, genius, elocution, and manner of the persons who deliver it. ... (1, 132)

Then, after copying the abruptness and lack of ceremony with which at the start of a Platonic dialogue the poor philosopher accords a powerful dignitary, Shaftesbury observes:

> Whilst I am copying this ... I see a thousand ridicules arising from the manner, the circumstances and action itself, compared with modern breeding and civility. – Let us therefore mend the matter if possible, and introduce the same philosopher, addressing himself in a more obsequious manner, to *his Grace*, *his Excellency*, or *his Honour*, without

failing in the least title of the ceremonial. ... Consider how many bows
and simpering faces! how many preludes, excuses, compliments! –
Now put compliments, put ceremony into a dialogue, and see what
will be the effect!

This is the plain dilemma against that ancient manner of writing
which we can neither well imitate nor translate, whatever pleasure or
profit we may find in reading those originals. (1, 133–4)

Though Shaftesbury here seems to mistake the symptoms for the
disease, he puts his finger on that feature of his society which had
distorted Dryden's conversation-piece. And his conclusion – 'Our
commerce and manner of conversation, which we think the politest
imaginable, is such, it seems, as we ourselves cannot endure to see represented to the life' – brings it home to us why Dryden had to fail, and why
Berkeley, in order to succeed with *Three Dialogues*, had to depart from
verisimilitude.

If Shaftesbury had lived to read *Alciphron*, he would hardly have admitted
that these were dialogues in which 'the self-interesting parties both vanish
at once'. For no one will contradict R.L. Brett when he protests that in
Alciphron Berkeley is unfair to Shaftesbury.[1] He is unfair to Shaftesbury,
and to Mandeville too, chiefly because he uses the *argumentum ad
hominem*. These arguments are not philosophical; but then, *Alciphron*,
though it contains much philosophy, is a work of Christian apologetics,
to which the precept which Berkeley observes, 'By their fruits shall ye
know them', is appropriate though 'unfair'. And of course there is
nothing unfair about his procedures if they are seen as procedures of literature. Berkeley plays the game according to the rules not of the philosopher but the dramatist; and his arguments are no less telling for being
embodied in character and situation. For *Alciphron* is an altogether
different affair from the *Three Dialogues*. True, the free-thinkers' arguments are rebutted time and again with strict logic; and if this is philosophical, it is also (as Berkeley does it) intensely dramatic. But over and
above this there is the point, made by drama in a less abstracted sense, that
both the free-thinkers, Lysicles and Alciphron, are uncandid. Berkeley
says, in effect, 'These arguments can be demolished, as I show; but, in any
case, what sort of person uses them?' And he shows that too. Lysicles is a
young puppy; but Alciphron is a more formidable disputant, and a subtler
portrait. In many ways he is a model of good breeding; and yet there is
something wrong about him. It is hard to define this, except in the way
that Berkeley hints at. Briefly, he lacks candour. He is more concerned to

1   R.L. Brett, *The Third Earl of Shaftesbury: a Study in Eighteenth-Century Literary Theory*
    (London, 1951), p. 170.

score a point than to get at the truth; that is one way of putting it. In any situation he prefers to think the worst; that is another.

Probably a score of readers will enjoy *Alciphron* for every one who will enjoy *Three Dialogues*. For we like in prose what we would not approve in conversation, hard-hitting vigour and vividness, sarcasm, bitterness, eloquence, the full battery of rhetorical resources. What we respond to most immediately in Dryden, for instance, are the places where he is fighting hard and remorselessly, arguing with his back to the wall or else in complete confidence about the rightness of his case, and using all the tricks of argument, candid or uncandid, to make his point. In his preface to *The State of Innocence* (1677), for example, Dryden's apology for poetic licence, however right and timely, is conducted by way of blank assertions, ridicule, sarcasm, all the tricks of the rhetorical trade. We would not tolerate it in conversation; it is *not* candid, it is *not* civil – and if it were we should like it much less. Very often, when candour and civility are achieved in literature, they bore us. To the perfect good manners of Addison, or of Berkeley in the *Three Dialogues*, we prefer the relatively uncandid Swift, or Johnson as Boswell reports him, or the Berkeley of *Alciphron*. It is tempting to say that we are right to feel thus; that what we look for in literature, and rightly, is to have our emotions played upon by the rhetorician, not our reasons satisfied by fair and scrupulous argument. But of course, even if literature is a province of rhetoric, not essentially of logic or dialectic, there is abundant ancient precedent for not absolving the rhetorician, however brilliant and resourceful he may be, from responsibility for the truth of what he is saying as well as for the effect of it upon his readers. And when we read works which are eloquent and candid as well, such as the *Three Dialogues* or Johnson's review of Soame Jenyns,[1] it is hard not to think that the literary pleasure these afford, to just the degree that it is less immediate and vivid, is more elevated, more substantial and more refined.

If it is true, as Aubrey Williams has argued in his book on *The Dunciad*,[2] that Pope's lifetime saw a crisis in the status and understanding of the traditional discipline of rhetoric, and in particular a general agreement not to require of the orator truth in his matter as well as winningness in his manner, then the development of the dialogue in this period might seem a particular instance of this crisis. After the relative failure of Dryden's conversation-piece had shown that English society did not after all provide models for candour and civility, two courses were open – to use the dialogue as an image of what should be, or of what was. Berkeley followed the first course in *Three Dialogues;* the second in *Alciphron*.

---

1   *The Literary Magazine,* XIII–XV (1757), reprinted in *Johnson: Prose and Poetry,* ed. Mona Wilson (London, 1950), pp. 351–74.
2   Aubrey L. Williams, *Pope's Dunciad: a Study of its Meaning* (London, 1955).

The second course was perhaps easier than the first. But it required great capacities. If *Three Dialogues* should be compared with Shaftesbury, *Alciphron* earns our respect when it is set beside Mandeville's dialogues in Part 2 (1729) of *The Fable of the Bees*. Mandeville there grumbles:

> When partial Men have a mind to demolish an Adversary, and triumph over him with little Expence, it has long been a frequent Practice to attack him with Dialogues, in which the Champion, who is to lose the Battel, appears at the very beginning of the Engagement, to be the Victim, that is to be sacrifised, and seldom makes a better Figure, than Cocks on Shrove-Tuesday, that receive Blows, but return none, and are visibly set up on purpose to be knock'd down.[1]

This is what Mandeville accuses Berkeley of in A *Letter to Dion* (1732), where he maintains that Lysicles and Alciphron are mere men of straw. Mandeville has a very skilful and amusing parody of Berkeley's style in *Alciphron*. But the very fact that he misses or ignores the sharp distinction between Berkeley's Alciphron and his Lysicles is enough to make Mandeville's criticism wide of the mark. And in Mandeville's own dialogues his Antonio is far more of a man of straw, far less credible, than either Lysicles and Alciphron. Mandeville seems to have grown tired of the dialogue form as he proceeded with it, for the character of Antonio as sketched in the preface, together with some rather clumsy attempts at verisimilitude in the first two dialogues, suggest that Mandeville meant to make of him what Berkeley made of Alciphron, a study in lack of candour; but if that was his original intention he soon wearied of it. Moreover, the colloquialism which the dialogue demands of Mandeville in the second part of *The Fable of the Bees* precludes the eloquence and fanciful imagery which quite often in Part I (1714) dignify his rough and hearty style. Mandeville's Antonio, after a little perfunctory huffing and puffing in the first two dialogues, takes the instructions of Cleomenes even more meekly than Hylas in his dealings with Philonous; and yet, at the same time, at the beginning of each dialogue there is an attempt at tedious and irrelevant verisimilitude which is no more than stage-business. Mandeville's dialogues fall between the two stools of the consciously idealized candour of Hylas and Philonous, and the far more lifelike behaviour of the four speakers in *Alciphron*.

The point of comparing Berkeley with distinguished contemporaries like Mandeville and Shaftesbury is to make it clear that Berkeley, when he wrote his conversation-piece, did not share in a general bounty vouch-safed to all cultivated and energetic men. It was not Augustan society nor

---

1   Bernard Mandeville, *The Fable of the Bees,* ed. F.B. Kaye, vol. II (Oxford, 1924), p. 8.

'the spirit of the age' which wrote *Three Dialogues* and *Alciphron*. James Sutherland, in an essay to which all students of eighteenth-century prose are indebted,[1] quotes an admirable passage from Colley Cibber's autobiography, and then observes:

> Nobody taught Cibber to write like this; he learnt to write this admirable prose by having first learnt to write dialogue for his comedies, and he learnt to write that partly by imitating Congreve, and partly by listening to the conversation of gentlemen, and so in time acquiring it, or something like it, himself.

As a verdict on Cibber this may well be just. Yet the principle is a dangerous one. The Augustans themselves did not have such a high opinion of the conversation of the gentlemen of their day, as Swift's *Tatler* essay 'On Corruptions of Style' may remind us. In the Augustan age as in any other, to deal candidly with oneself, still more to give a lively and edifying image of candour in others – these achievements were won by the lonely and exacting labour of distinguished individuals who were not carried by the current of their times but strove against it.

The English Mind: Essays Presented to Basil Willey, ed. H.S. Davies and G. Watson (Cambridge: CUP, 1964).

---

1   James Sutherland, 'Some Aspects of Eighteenth-Century Prose', op. cit., p. 101.

VI The Language of Science and the Language of Literature, 1700–1740

It is generally agreed that in the first half of the eighteenth century, there is an exceptionally close and significant relationship between the two immense fields of human activity so rashly indicated in my title – between science, that is, and literature. And some writers have offered to define this relationship in the roundest, most uncompromising terms. The example I will take is Professor R.L. Brett, on page 14 of his book on *The Third Earl of Shaftesbury. A Study in Eighteenth-Century Literary Theory*.

> The whole movement of philosophy which started with Descartes and which was accompanied by the vast expansion of scientific inquiry and achievement, has been seen, and no doubt rightly, as producing an atmosphere inimical to poetry. The view of the universe its influence had made the generally accepted one, was that of a mechanism run on mathematical principles and devoid of colour, scent, taste and sound. Science had enlarged the size of the universe, but had turned it into a lifeless machine; which worked by forces that could be expressed in mathematical formulae, but not in poetry. What was real was what could be measured, weighed, and expressed in numbers, not what could be made the subject of poetry. Such writers as A.N. Whitehead, Basil Willey and Douglas Bush have all made the point that the mechanical view of the world is one that does not commend itself to the poet. Its declaration that what is 'really real' is a world of atoms in motion, devoid of all secondary sense qualities such as colour, scent, taste and sound, ordered by causal laws and explicable only in terms of mathematics, is one that gives little status to the poet. It is one indeed, that gives little status to man himself, since, once the process of scientific explanation had started, it was soon seen that man himself, as part of the natural order, could be explained in similar terms. Poetry was not alone in suffering the effect of the new movement; religion itself was its companion.

The distinguished names which Professor Brett cites as his authorities sufficiently justify my quoting him at such length; his statement is representative – in fact, it is not too much to say that he is here the spokesman of a powerful orthodoxy.

Yet it is surely open to several objections, begs a lot of questions. In the first place it requires us to think in terms of what might have been. It assumes that we are somehow dissatisfied with what poetry we have from this period; for such poetry as we have does its best with the materials and in the conditions Professor Brett thinks so unsuitable. It follows from his argument that there must be something wrong with this poetry; and since this poetry includes the poems of Alexander Pope (to go no farther), this seems a very bold assumption – would certainly have seemed so, for instance, to Dr Johnson. Secondly we may object, with Stéphane Mallarmé, that poetry is written not with ideas but with *words*. We cannot be as confident as Professor Brett that we know what is good for poets and what is bad for them; for poets continue to surprise us by finding themes (which is to say, words) to excite them, where we least expected anything of the sort. The truth is surely that many poets listen to the philosophers, and philosophize about their own activity, much less than many people imagine. There is, it may be thought, a particularly telling example of this in this very period – the case of Pope who, having wavered towards a near-deism in the *Essay on Man*, recanted it in *The Dunciad*.[1] It may be that this represents a change of heart in Pope; but equally well it may witness to a sort of quite legitimate irresponsibility. He believed, in some sense, of course, first the one thing and then the other. But he may have believed as some have held that Yeats 'believed' in the extraordinary farrago he delivered to the world in *A Vision*, as *his* 'philosophy'. These are not, to put it bluntly, the ideas that the poets lived by – those in Pope's case, were, presumably, the precepts of the Roman Church. In both poets, these 'beliefs' sometimes seem no more than a sort of provisional assent or serious make-believe, like the love which Walter Ralegh and some other Elizabethans professed to feel for Queen Elizabeth. When Yeats asked the spirit-medium what it had come for, it replied, 'To give you metaphors for poetry.' Just so may Pope have imagined that the spirits of Bolingbroke and Warburton, Locke and Shaftesbury, came to him. I am not asserting that this is so; I am only pointing out the evidence that the relationship between a poet's poetry and his professed beliefs is by no means so direct as Professor Brett, and thinkers of his school, tend to suppose.

Historians of ideas are often nowadays solicitous for the poets; and the latter, as often as not, are churlish in their acknowledgements. The truth seems to be that the poet is sturdier, and his attitudes less calculable, than

1   See Arthur Friedman, 'Pope and Deism', in *Pope and his Contemporaries. Essays presented to George Sherburn* (Oxford, 1949).

the historians suppose. There is a notion abroad that what is 'organic' is a good thing for poetry; and it follows that what is mechanical isn't. The poet, however, takes his metaphors where he finds them, and may choose to extol the Brooklyn Bridge, no less than the meanest flower that blows. As Hart Crane declared, himself the laureate of the Brooklyn Bridge, 'The familiar contention that science is inimical to poetry is no more tenable than the kindred notion that theology has been proverbially hostile – with the *Commedia* of Dante to prove the contrary.[1]

It seems, then, that there are sufficient reasons for taking another look at the relations between science and literature at the beginning of the eighteenth century. And we may begin to do so by glancing at some other books which bear upon the matter.

First, there are a number of books by Professor Marjorie Nicolson, of which the most germane to the present purpose is called *Newton Demands the Muse*. This book establishes that some of Sir Isaac Newton's scientific discoveries, particularly those in his *Opticks*, fired the imagination of a number of writers, of whom the most influential in both prose and verse was Addison, and probably the most substantial, in terms of intrinsic merit, was James Thomson, author of *The Seasons*. I am not aware that Professor Nicolson's case has been seriously challenged. And accordingly we find ourselves in the position of having to maintain (if we agree with Professor Brett) that, when certain considerable writers thought themselves imaginatively excited to poetic purpose by the worlds revealed by science, they were self-deluded.

In fact, this self-delusion is something that the orthodox argument requires us to impute to most of the writers of our period. It is notable that Professor Brett (and in this he is typical) says nothing of how the scientific world-view affected the writers of *prose*. And it's easy to see how this comes about. For it is orthodox to suppose that this period, the age of Swift and Berkeley, Addison and Steele, is a great age – perhaps *the* great age – of English prose; and it's orthodox also to think that some of the credit for this goes to the scientists. One may mention here the work of Richard Foster Jones (see *The Seventeenth Century* by R.F. Jones and others, 1951), which substantiates the familiar argument that the scientists had no sooner instituted the Royal Society (for the furtherance of scientific experiment, and the pooling of its findings), than they began to demand a naked and direct sort of prose appropriate to the lab.-book – a sort of prose handed down as a legacy from Dryden to the prose writers of the age of Queen Anne and the first Hanoverians. Thus we are in the position of congratulating prose writers of this period on their good

---

1   Quoted by Peter Viereck, *Strike through the Mask!* (New York, 1950), p. 68.

fortune, at the same time as we commiserate with the poets for their ill luck, living when they did. Yet this is the very opposite of what these writers thought themselves. For if they were poets, they congratulated themselves on inheriting the language from Denham and Waller and Dryden, who, as they said, 'first gave it regular harmony, and discovered its latent powers'; whereas, if they were writers of prose, we find them grumbling about the vicious styles then current and the unstable condition of the language they had to use – as Swift does, for instance, in his *Proposal for correcting … the English Tongue*. If we follow Professor Brett, we have to tell the poets that they were living in a fool's paradise, at the same time as we tell the prose writers that they didn't know how lucky they were. Yet perhaps the writers themselves recognized their own situation better than we can. What is more, if we argue in Professor Brett's way, we are obliged to adopt some questionable assumptions about the relation of prose to poetry *at any time*. We are committed to supposing that poetry and prose differ not in degree but radically, in kind; so that the conditions favourable to the one may be death to the other; and the grouping of both sorts of writing under the head of 'literature' is at bottom only misleading. This is the assumption of those Victorian critics who, like Matthew Arnold, defined Dryden and Pope as 'classics of our prose, not of our poetry'. And that, we may hope, is a position no longer respectable.

Another book that may be mentioned here is one that created some stir when it came out some years ago – Miss Kathleen Nott's *The Emperor's Clothes*. This is a work of polemic, not of scholarship; and its lack of scholarship seriously impairs its polemical attacks on Mr Eliot, Professor Lewis, Professor Willey, and others. On the other hand, it asks some of the questions that we have seen to be begged by the orthodox statement of the case. And it asks one other, which is of some importance. In that orthodox view, who are the villains of the piece? Who are these allegedly so powerful enemies of poetry? Are they the practising scientists? Or are they not rather the philosophers who philosophize about what the scientists seem to be doing? These are two distinct classes of people, even when, as in the case of Isaac Newton, they happen to come together in one person. Shall we exonerate the humble and dedicated scientist on the job, like Robert Boyle, the great chemist, while casting all the blame instead on a philosopher like Locke, theorizing *about* science – which is what Miss Nott wants us to do? Or do scientist and philosopher line up in an unholy alliance, as Professor Brett seems to suppose? Or can we exonerate them both?

We get nearer to brass tacks with another American work, a research-thesis by John Arthos, published in 1949, called *The Language of Natural Description in Eighteenth-Century Poetry*. The argument of this massive and learned study is summarized as follows (p. 88):

It may very well be that many poets [i.e. of the eighteenth century] accepted the idea of a conventional language for poetry because they considered the interests of poetry and natural philosophy to be the same in many important respects. Scientific writing required a set vocabulary formed according to set principles, and it must therefore follow that poetry's needs were similar. This is the extreme conclusion. It is, of course, truer of some poets than of others. But its general validity seems proved by the fact that so many of the same terms are found in scientific prose and in the poetry of the eighteenth century.

This brings us to the same point as Marjorie Nicolson's research into the poetic influence of Isaac Newton; *we* have to think that the poets went calamitously wrong precisely where *they* were most hopeful – in supposing 'the interests of poetry and natural philosophy' (that is natural science) 'to be the same in many important respects'. But Arthos is more challenging than Professor Nicolson, because he traces the effect of this assumption or delusion, not in what the poets wrote or what they wrote about, but in their very way of writing, in their vocabulary, in their *words*. Two components of eighteenth-century poetic diction are particularly revealing from this point of view. First there is that characteristic trick of adjectives which are formed by adding the suffix 'y' to nouns – words like 'beamy', 'bloomy', 'moony', 'roofy', 'sluicy'. All these examples are from Dryden, and Arthos gives examples of exactly similar coinings from the prose of late seventeenth-century scientists. (It is worth pausing to see the implications of this – it means that when Wordsworth, objecting to this vocabulary, declared that there was no essential difference between the languages of prose and poetry, he was enunciating a principle from which had come the very vocabulary he objected to.) The second feature of eighteenth-century diction which enforces the point is the periphrasis – locutions like 'bearded product' for 'corn', 'loquacious race' (frogs) and 'scaly locks' (fish). All these, again, are from Dryden, and we can see as soon as Arthos points it out that such expressions are formed on precisely the same principle as the classifications of an eighteenth-century scientist like the great Swedish botanist Linnaeus – the name of the genus together with the distinguishing characteristic which defines the species (e.g., the white water-lily, *Nymphaea alba*). Of course, in so far as we agree with Wordsworth that locutions of this kind are a blemish to poetry – I don't think they are, necessarily – we have not exonerated science, in this case in its aspect of classification, from exerting a bad influence on poetry. But at least we are seeing that influence in unexpected places. A scientific, or scientific-and-philosophical, influence is at work on other features of eighteenth-century poetic diction, as we shall see. Much that we object to in eighteenth-century poetry as florid, excessively 'poetical', too far from prose usage, turns out on the contrary to be, if anything, only too prosaic.

The last book I want to mention is more important than any of these, and takes us at once to the heart of our subject. It is again American (I need not point the moral): W.K. Wimsatt's study of the prose style of Dr Johnson, *Philosophic Words*, published in 1948. This is a brilliant and momentous piece of scholarship. By 'philosophic' in his title, Wimsatt means what Johnson meant by it: that is, as describing whatever pertains to 'natural philosophy' or, as we should say, to the natural sciences. Such words as 'acrimony' and 'volatile' are, in this sense, eminently 'philosophic' words, for they have been adopted into the language at large from the special terminology of chemistry. Wimsatt shows, from a close study of Johnson's *Dictionary*, that as a lexicographer Johnson set out quite deliberately to assist this adoption into the language of the erstwhile specialized terminology of the sciences, attracting such words out of the laboratory into the drawing-room. At the same time, in *The Rambler*, Johnson the essayist was doing the same thing by other means, exemplifying in practice what, in the *Dictionary*, he urged as theory. For, as Wimsatt shows, the prevailingly abstract, Latinate, and sesquipedalian character of Johnson's style, especially in *The Rambler*, is brought about very largely by his consistent use of these words which he called 'philosophic'. Now, the essays in *The Rambler* are moral disquisitions, and have nothing to do with the natural sciences, except occasionally for purposes of illustration. How, then, could Johnson use so many scientific words in a non-scientific context? He could do so only by extending their significations, and giving them a metaphorical as well as a literal bearing. So, when 'acrimony' is used, it still means literally what it meant in the laboratory, 'corrosiveness'; but it means metaphorically, in the context of moral disquisition, 'severity, bitterness of thought or language'. We still speak of a person as having an acrimonious temperament, or of an acrimonious debate. In fact, the adoption of such words has been so complete that, unless we are chemists (and perhaps even if we are), we are unaware, when we use the word, that we are using a metaphor. It is for us a dead metaphor, whereas for Johnson and his predecessors and contemporaries it was a very lively metaphor indeed, daringly far-fetched. It is the very completeness of Johnson's success which obscures, for us, his achievement. As Wimsatt says, Johnson's prose, at any rate in *The Rambler*, is very highly figurative; in fact, it is *poetic* prose. One tends to think that a highly abstract style is a style devoid of images, hence unmetaphorical; but what makes Johnson's style abstract is also what makes it highly metaphorical.

Now, it is unthinkable that a whole vast movement like this, inside the language, should come about by the deliberate manoeuvre of one writer. Johnson assisted the shift, the adoption of scientific terminology by metaphorical extension into common usage. But he cannot have inaugurated this development. He only raised to the level of conscious exploitation a change that was happening in the language itself. Indeed, in the examples of 'beamy', 'moony' and 'sluicy' given by Arthos, we have already seen the shift-over happening more than fifty years before, with Dryden. And an hour or so with the *Oxford English Dictionary* will show that the process was general. I have cited as exemplifying this shift in our period the words 'volatile' and 'acrimony'. Let me give two more, the words 'insipid' and 'astringency'. For 'insipid' as an adjective, the OED gives three senses, as follows (1) 'Without taste, tasteless', of which it gives six examples, ranging between 1620 and 1822; (2) a figurative sense, 'Wanting the qualities which excite interest or emotion; uninteresting, lifeless, dull, flat', the earliest citation being from Evelyn's Diary for 1649, while others include one from Swift, 1710–11; and (3) obsolete sense, 'Devoid of taste, intelligence or judgement; stupid, foolish, dull', exemplified from, among others, Baxter in 1651 and Pepys, 1662–5. It is surely clear that the technical sense 'tasteless' ('Water is an insipid fluid'), which antedates the others, in fact produced those others by metaphorical extension from talking about natural substances to talking about human beings or human products ('an insipid person', 'an insipid book'). And this extension takes place, if we may trust the OED, precisely in the span of years between Dryden and Johnson. The case is clinched when we look further in the OED and find 'insipid' as a substantive (as in *The History of the Insipids*), first used in 1700 and thereafter by Defoe in 1727. A very little reading in the early eighteenth century will establish 'insipid' as a favourite word in the period; and it is easy to see why – it was a newish word even in its literal sense, and very new in its figurative meaning, a lively and daring metaphor taken from technical terminology. As for 'astringency', the earliest example given by the OED of a figurative sense (that is, of the sense we give it today) is John Galt's *Entail* of 1823, just as its earliest example of a figurative sense for 'astringent' comes from Byron's *Don Juan*, Book 5, in 1820. I think I have found what amounts to figurative use of both these words, as of the cognate word 'astringe', in William Law in the 1740s – a matter to which I may return. Otherwise 'astringency', in the eighteenth century, had the sense given to it by Johnson's *Dictionary*: 'The power of contracting the parts of the body; opposed to the power of relaxation.' That is to say, 'astringency' was still a technical term of the science of physiology. And accordingly, its use is exemplified in Johnson's *Dictionary* by a quotation from Arbuthnot's *Essay on Aliments*:

> Acid, acrid, austere, and bitter substances, by their astringency, create
> horrour, that is, stimulate the fibres.

One could not wish for a more instructive example of how the English of the early eighteenth century is for us a foreign language. Hardly one of the words in this sentence is used as we should use it today. 'Astringency' and, of course, 'bitter', we are accustomed to think of as having both literal and metaphorical senses, but, as we have seen, if 'astringency' had a figurative sense at all in Arbuthnot's day, or Johnson's, that use of it would be daringly novel. 'Acrid' is a word that we *can* use figuratively ('the essay is written in a rather acrid tone', an 'acrid' controversy), but only in its literal sense has it any wide currency. And 'acid' is rather similar, though it is in common use metaphorically on the lower deck of the Royal Navy, to mean 'sarcastic'. But 'austere' and 'horror' are used nowadays only in their figurative senses, so that only with a shock do we realize how they once had literal (i.e. 'philosophic') senses, as part of the technical vocabulary of physic. Arbuthnot's sense for 'horrour' is close to the image carried by the root word in Latin, the image of hair standing up on the head; we see it in poetry when Dryden writes, in a way to us either nonsensical or ludicrous, of a hillside which is 'horrid with fern'.

When we read the English prose of Milton or Sir Thomas Browne, we are ready to recognize that we have to do some translating of their idiom into our own. And similarly, in a later period, with the prose of Johnson or Gibbon – when Johnson in a famous passage declares that pastoral is 'easy, vulgar and therefore disgusting', we are ready to recognize that no one of these words means just what it means today. But with Dryden's prose we seem to leap suddenly into the modern world. And from Dryden through to something later than 1740, the prose, by its familiar colloquial rhythms, deludes us into thinking that no such scrutiny of vocabulary is called for, that the idiom of that day is simply our own idiom. We have found reason to suppose that this isn't so; that semantic changes are going on at least as rapidly in this period as in any other and must be watched at least as closely; above all, that some of these changes have to do with a relation between scientific terminology and common usage. If so, these changes in meaning have everything to do with the question of how, in this period, science and literature are related.

Our subject, therefore, resolves itself from 'Science and Literature' into 'The Language of Science and the Language of Literature', in the first half of the eighteenth century. By thus cutting down at once to the level of language, we shall be working in the spirit of Mallarmé's truism: 'Poetry is written not with ideas but with words.' We shall also be assuming that the history of literature can be accurately studied only as an extension of the history of the language. This is what the historians of the language have been maintaining for a long time, but in practice this principle hardly ever gets applied except in the periods of Old English and Middle English. For the most part we look in vain to the historians of language for any application of the principle to a period as 'modern' as that of the eighteenth century. Instead, it is the critics and literary historians – Arthos and Wimsatt – who can come to our help. To these names I would add one other, that of Professor Empson, who is almost alone among British scholars in turning his attention in this direction. First in some passages of *Some Versions of Pastoral*, and then in his *Structure of Complex Words*, he has done work of the kind we are asking for. And I shall take as my text for the next stage some comments by him on the prose vocabulary of Swift, which I find in *Some Versions of Pastoral*.

2

W.K. Wimsatt, when he establishes how Dr Johnson in *The Rambler* is continually defining human and moral conditions by metaphors drawn from the natural sciences, goes on to show how every such metaphor derives from, and helps to maintain, one philosophical system, that of John Locke. For to bring over into ethics and psychology the terminology of natural science is to imply that the workings of the mind are precisely analogous to the workings of matter; and this was one of the implications, or one of the assumptions, of Locke's philosophy. The point is taken beautifully, later in the century, by William Blake in his notes to Reynolds' *Discourses*. Reynolds writes, 'My notion of nature comprehends not only the forms which nature produces, but also the nature and internal fabrick and organisation ... of the human mind and imagination.' This is precisely the assumption which underlies Johnson's metaphorical use of terms from natural science. And Blake pounces at once: 'Here is a Plain Confession that he thinks Mind and Imagination not to be above the Mortal and Perishing Nature. Such is the End of Epicurean or Newtonian Philosophy; it is Atheism.'[1] Hence it is not surprising to find, in Wimsatt's words, that 'Locke was evidently the British philosopher chosen to represent his kind in the Dictionary'. Berkeley, for instance, had challenged the Lockean system; but Johnson, it seems, chose to ignore the challenge. This goes along with Johnson's known dislike of Berkeleyan thought as he understood it; and again it is not surprising that Berkeley is quoted in the *Dictionary* only eight times – a marked contrast to the strongly Berkeleyan cast of Ephraim Chambers' *Cyclopaedia*, a work that in other respects was one of Johnson's main sources.[2]

Already here we come near to answering a question that was raised earlier, that of the role played, in the matter of connections between science and literature, by non-scientists, philosophers like Locke. The case of Johnson shows that such philosophers were essential, as middlemen, as the medium through which scientific terms and conceptions became available to writers for use as metaphors. It suggests further that this sort of deliberately ambiguous vocabulary, a range of effects in which, as we have seen, the language of our period was unusually resourceful,

1   Blake, *Poetry and Prose,* Nonesuch edn. p. 807.
2   *Wimsatt, Philosophic Words* (New Haven, 1948), p. 96.

was available only to writers who adopted, consciously or unconsciously, the Lockean or Newtonian 'world-view'.

But this is not so. On the contrary, this range of effects is particularly inviting to writers who are opposed to the Lockean or Newtonian universe. The only difference is that such writers will exploit this vocabulary to comic or satirical effect. And this is a very important point, because a great deal of the finest writing of the period, in verse and prose alike, *is* comic or satirical; just as much of it is produced by men like Swift and Pope, who were bitterly opposed to the whole trend of scientific development in their day.

Berkeley has already been cited as a writer of this kind, an intimate friend of both Pope and Swift, like them a conservative, fighting for a traditional and Christian view of the world in the teeth of the more mechanical and materialist view which a philosopher like Locke was constructing on hints from the scientists. Yet Berkeley's weapon was ridicule, as in the fantasy which he contributed to Steele's *Guardian* (no. 39). This purports to be a visit to the pineal gland of a freethinker, the pineal gland in Cartesian philosophy being the seat of the soul. Berkeley visits first the highest part of this structure, the understanding, which he finds 'narrower than ordinary, insomuch that there was not room for a miracle, prophesy, or separate spirit':

> This obliged me to descend a story lower, into the imagination, which I found larger, indeed, but cold and comfortless. I discover'd PREJU-DICE in the figure of a woman standing in a corner, with her eyes close shut, and her forefingers stuck in her ears; many words in a confused order, but spoken with great emphasis, issued from her mouth. These being condensed by the coldness of the place, formed a sort of mist. ...

This is the joke at its broadest. It consists simply in taking the materialists at their word, and trying to visualize psychological processes in mechanical terms. The mock-solemn account of the forming of delusions in terms taken from physics, 'being *condensed* by the coldness of the place', is not much unlike hypotheses that were advanced in all seriousness by some 'mechanical' psychologists. It prepares the reader to see the absurdity when later on in the essay, in a place called 'the store-house of ideas', he is told of 'corporeal spirits'.

Something like this prepares us for the more subtle and powerful treatment of the scientific metaphor as an anti-mechanist joke, where the whole pun is carried in single words. This is what we find all through Swift's *Tale of a Tub*. Empson has argued that Swift's style in this work is determined by the perception that 'Everything spiritual and valuable has a gross and revolting parody, very similar to it, with the same name. Only unremitting judgement can distinguish between them ...' And he sees Swift as haunted, throughout this work, by the appalling suspicion that the mechanists were right, that 'everything spiritual is really material; Hobbes and the scientists have proved this; all religion is really a perversion of sexuality.' Whether or not Swift was appalled by this possibility – I prefer to think he was just sardonically amused – Empson is certainly right about the way in which Swift exploited his perception:

> The language plays into his hands here, because the spiritual words are all derived from physical metaphors; as he saw again and again how to do this the pleasure of ingenuity must have become a shock to faith. *Spirit* in English is mixed with the chemical sense – 'the profounder chemists inform us that the strongest spirits may be extracted from human flesh' (the fanatics are lustful), and with its special sense of alcohol (intoxicated with the spirit, the fanatics are drunk); and its root derivation is from wind or breath (inspired by the breath of God or the wind of the spirit the fanatics are windbags). In a state of 'enthusiasm' they are possessed by devils or an animal impulse; they ought to possess it. 'Besides themselves' with ecstasy they are mad. When 'profound', being deep, they are low, being dark, they are senseless, or dropping they perform a bathos. When 'sublime', being airy, they are insubstantial (the spiritual is a delusion), being high, they are unsafe or become the mob in the gallery. There was no word with which some such trick could not be played.[1]

With this admirably penetrating and momentous observation, we take a big stride forward. We now see that what we are looking for in the vocabulary of this period is not confined to the new words, like 'acrimony', 'volatile', 'insipid', taken over from the scientists. We have to look just as closely at long-established crucial and familiar words like 'spirit', 'inspiration', 'profundity'. For the process works both ways: if words from physics, chemistry and physiology can be dignified from having a merely material reference into having an immaterial one, words from religion and ethics and aesthetics can be deflated from having a spiritual reference into having a grossly corporeal one. It's easy to see how the perception came about; even as they adopted scientific terms into common usage, by giving them a figurative sense besides their literal sense, the writers were forced to realize that many elevated words in use for centuries had themselves originally been formed in precisely the same way, and the evidence of this was in their etymology, in their Greek and Latin roots. There is another cross-reference here, into poetic diction; for Arthos defines one component of such diction in the eighteenth century as 'words already in good standing in English, but occurring in a construction that is Latin or in a sense that properly belongs to the Latin

---

1   See the passages quoted in the Appendix.

original', as when Dryden writes 'horrid with fern' or 'the morning dew prevents the sun'. A poet later than Dryden could use this device either to bring his poetic observation into line with scientific observation (as Thomson does, often) or else to ridicule the scientific habit by pressing it to an extreme.

The particular range of puns which Empson isolates accounts for a great deal of the wittiest writing in the anti-mechanist tradition. Take the word 'profundity'. By relying implicitly on the truthfulness of etymology, we get an irrefragable chain of logic: 'Profound' is 'deep'; to go deep is to sink; lead sinks fastest; therefore the most profound thinkers are the most leaden. This is the logic behind that elaborate spoof of the Scriblerus Club, *The Art of Sinking in Poetry, or a Treatise of the Bathos*. 'Bathos' represents an extension of the same logic from Latin etymology into Greek, and comes up with the surprising conclusion that the most profound writers are the most bathetic. Conversely, 'elevation'. 'Elevation' is 'rising high'; what rises high is levity; nothing rises so high as balloons, which are bags of wind; therefore the most elevated writers are the biggest windbags or those who display most levity. Once admit that there is no gulf fixed between the material and the immaterial worlds (which was the admission that Locke demanded), and the reasoning is impregnable.

It is doubtless no accident that a moving spirit behind *The Memoirs of Martinus Scriblerus* was Dr John Arbuthnot, the Queen's physician, whom we have met already as the author of an *Essay on Aliments*. The baffling ambiguity in the terminology of contemporary medicine, an ambiguity which we illustrated from that work, would not be lost on a man like Arbuthnot, who combined the physician and the man of letters. Out of the Scriblerus Club, where Pope and Swift were Arbuthnot's associates, and out of *The Memoirs of Martinus Scriblerus*, came both *Gulliver's Travels* and *The Dunciad*. And so it is no surprise that the pun on 'profundity', for instance, is constantly in evidence in Pope's poem. His dunces, you recall, are led to profundity, that is, to the bottom of the Thames, by the leaden weight of their own stupidity:

> Not so bold Arnall; with a weight of skull,
> Furious he dives, precipitately dull.
> Whirlpool and storms his circling arm invest,
> With all the might of gravitation blest.
> No crab more active in the dirty dance,
> Downward to climb, and backward to advance
> He brings up half the bottom on his head,
> And loudly claims the Journals and the Lead.

This is from Book 2; there is the same pun in Book 4, when the dunces are attracted to their mother-goddess, Dulness, by 'strong impulsive gravity of Head':

None need a guide, by sure attraction led,
And strong impulsive gravity of Head;
None want a place, for all their centre found,
Hung to the Goddess, and coher'd around.
Not closer, orb in orb, conglob'd are seen
The buzzing bees about their dusky Queen.

'Gravity' is a particularly good example. Traditionally used to designate the spiritual quality of certain temperaments and personalities, it is forced back, when Newton with learned propriety adopts it to designate a principle of physics, upon its root meaning in Latin. 'Gravity' becomes 'gravitas', becomes 'weight'. And so, once again, a grave thinker becomes a leaden-footed thinker. His weightiness is all in his lack of buoyancy – one sees how the joke could be extended indefinitely. This is a much better pun than the one in Shakespeare about how, when someone is dead, he'll be a 'grave' man. For Shakespeare's pun is a matter of merely accidental likeness of sound, whereas Pope's feels back along the lines of etymological development to a genuine likeness of meanings. It is used to comic effect, yet the comedy has an edge to it. For it is refusing to take seriously a view, of the relationship of the material to the supposedly immaterial, which was being taken very seriously indeed by many of Pope's contemporaries. It is therefore an extremely serious joke. And incidentally, in an age when physics was trying to explain all phenomena without exception by reference to the laws of motion, 'impulsive', the word that goes with 'gravity', partakes of the same crucial ambiguity.

In a very valuable essay, '*Tristram Shandy* and the Tradition of Learned Wit',[1] D.W. Jefferson has shown that when Sterne adopted Lockean psychology as a structural principle in *Tristram Shandy*, he was exploiting contemporary science in a way not very different from what we have just seen in Pope and Swift. To be sure, Sterne cannot be grouped with these writers in the anti-mechanist camp. On the contrary, he has been called, on the strength of these borrowings, a disciple of Locke. But Jefferson shows that this won't do, that Sterne, when he borrowed from Locke, 'exploited his ideas freely as opportunities for wit, playing with them in a manner quite unlike that of their original begetter.' And this is just how one would describe Swift's dealings with the mechanical philosophers in the *Tale of a Tub*, and Pope's in *The Dunciad*.

But Jefferson makes what is for our purposes a more important point when he shows that both Sterne and Swift, when they use science like this, belong in a tradition which goes far back into the sixteenth century. In this 'tradition of learned wit' the most important name is that of

1 *Essays in Criticism* I: 3 (July 1951), pp. 225–38.

Rabelais. We find Rabelais making fun of what Jefferson calls 'intellectual habits belonging to the pre-Enlightenment world of thought'; that is, of such characteristics of medieval thought as the extended catalogue or the appeals to multiple authorities. Jefferson points out that Donne in part belongs to this tradition; for this is the wit we find in Donne's use of Thomist metaphysics in a poem like 'Aire and Angells'. But the crucial point is made when he goes on to point out that 'the ratiocinative inge-nuity which writers of the Renaissance and later inherited from the schoolmen was liable to be applied to all kinds of ideas, *even to those of the new science and philosophy*, ...'[1] As a result, he says, 'although we do not look for jokes among the serious students of Newton and Locke', yet 'a person brought up in the old tradition of wit might well find that some of the ideas of Newton and Locke suited his purpose'. In fact, Jefferson's caution about where we needn't look for these jokes is hardly necessary. For Dr Johnson, as we have seen, was a serious student of Locke, and yet there exists *The Rambler*, no. 117, where Johnson himself makes jokes out of the puns concealed in the idea of 'elevation', arguing that since it's good for an author to have elevated thoughts and style, it is to his advan-tage to live in a garret, at the top of a house. But the centrally important point remains; that the new philosophy, the new words and ideas which came out of the laboratories of the Royal Society, didn't inaugurate, by reaction, a new tradition of comic writing, but, rather, refreshed and gave new impetus and opportunities to an old tradition. This was the tradition of Rabelais. And Jefferson points out that the English tradition of the later parts of Rabelais did not appear until 1693 and 1694. 'It is noteworthy', he remarks, 'that the completed work was a new book when Swift began to write his early satires.' It is indeed.

We speak of the *Tale of a Tub* and *The Dunciad* as 'satires', yet I have been placing them both, following Jefferson, in a tradition I call 'comic'. But C.S. Lewis has warned us that we tend to underestimate the amount of sheer comedy in a great deal of Augustan writing:

> It is true that they regarded satire as a 'sacred weapon', but we must not so concentrate on that idea as to forget the sheer *vis comica* which brightens so much of their work. *Gulliver* and *The Dunciad* and the whole myth of Scriblerus have missed their point if they do not some-times make us 'laugh and shake in Rabelais' easy chair'. Even their love of filth is ... much better understood by schoolboys than by psychoanalysts: if there is something sinister in it, there is also an element of high-spirited rowdiness.[2]

1   Jefferson, op. cit. My italics.
2   C.S. Lewis, 'Addison', in *Essays presented to D. Nichol Smith*, p. 1.

Both Swift and Berkeley were first and foremost devout and militant churchmen; as such, they saw the threat to the Church involved in the doctrines of the mechanic philosophers, and they took care to swim against that current in the thought of their time. But even so, they saw this movement as only one among several, all hostile to the cause they were pledged to defend – there were the deists, for instance, vowed to the teachings of Toland and Shaftesbury. And in any case, to the extent that they were both artists, they would feel rather a sort of glee at this weapon put into their hands, the puns uncovered which asked for comic elaboration. The conservative Augustan writers played with the mechanic philosophies, and they amused themselves by drawing upon them, and upon the scientists behind them, for metaphors. Swift and Sterne, of course, and Pope in *The Dunciad*, amused themselves to some purpose; comedy is not irresponsible. But I find little evidence that Hobbes and Descartes and Locke cast a black shadow over them all, as R.L. Brett and William Empson seem to think. The question is how far the poets and prose writers were alarmed and affronted by the mechanical world-view, how far just amused and intrigued. Where they are amused, the punning metaphors go into comedy: where they are alarmed, the metaphors go into satire. And because our sense of humour is less robust than that of the Augustans, we often mistake for satire what in fact is comedy.

But this, for us, is a side issue. If we follow the clue provided by Mallarmé, his reminder that poetry is made not of ideas but of words, we see the creative writer as a marauder, who ransacks the language of his own time and earlier, looking for words which are arresting and suggestive, or for words, dry and inconspicuous in common usage or in the place where he finds them, which can be made remarkable in the different context he envisages for them. When he finds them, he tears them out of the perhaps elaborate structure of meaning in which he finds them, and takes them over for his own purposes. It follows perhaps that the poet is less interested than the prose writer in the 'stability' of the language he uses; indeed, some poets have spoken as if they had a vested interest in instability, conceiving their duty to be the breaking-down of accepted meanings and usual collocations, in order by new combinations to make experience seem once again new and surprising. Swift complained that the language in his time was changing too rapidly, valuable older words continually slipping out of use as new words shouldered their way in. And it is probably true that there are periods when the language is too fluid, even for poets, when they must join forces with the prose writers to arrest the too rapid development of the language. But the poet will tend to welcome fairly rapid change in the language of his time, because the old word slipping out of use can be brought back and used to all the more effect because of the slight tinge of quaintness it has already acquired, and the new word can be acclimatized, while retaining something piquant and surprising. In *Four Quartets*, T.S. Eliot calls this 'An easy commerce of the old and the new'; and the operative word is 'easy'.

Pope, then, lived at a time when new words were coming into the language in great numbers. Some of these were undoubtedly, as Swift thought, pieces of new-fangled jargon which did not last but were subsequently, by another change of fashion, discarded. But there is the well-known case of the word 'mob', which Swift condemned as a vulgar abbreviation, to show that there was a place in the language for some of the novel words he would have excluded. In his Pelican book, *Our Language*, Simeon Potter remarks 'All those complex changes and developments, all those adoptions and adaptations which had contributed to the making of English over so many centuries, had achieved in the year 1700 a certain balance or equilibrium.'[1] As he goes on to point out, equilibrium in this context is not the same as that 'stability', a condition of impossible stasis, for which Swift yearned. It may be defined, perhaps, as that state of the language in which the old and the new can be brought to consort together with relative ease. And if so, the poets of Pope's age may have been as fortunate as they thought they were, in coming to use the language when they did.

As we have seen, one of the most fruitful sources of new words (and of new senses for old ones) was the writing of those scientists who are often taken to have done so much damage to Augustan poetry. On this showing, it seems, on the contrary, that they helped poets, by opening up new ranges of vocabulary. When we look at Potter's examples of words for which the scientists were responsible ('centrifugal' and 'centripetal', from Newton; 'corpuscle', 'intensity', 'pathological', 'pendulum', from Boyle), we may feel that only one of these, 'intensity', was adopted to any purpose by literature. But as we have seen, not all such words had to wait long before they were adopted. And if we want to know how it was that the poets, for instance, could make sure of this vocabulary so soon, we find that the credit has to go to Brett's other *bête-noire*, the 'mechanic' philosophers. For once Hobbes and Locke had allowed the possibility that man's mind and heart were subject to the same laws as governed the world of physics, the poets were able to use the new words in writing of what was their traditional subject, the emotions and aspirations of man:

> Through clouds of Passion Pulteney's views are clear,
> He foams a Patriot to subside a peer; ...

In these lines, which have been ascribed to Pope, the poet is able to use the language of the chemical laboratory to describe the character and conduct of a venal politician. He is able to do so because materialistic

1   Simeon Potter, *Our Language* (London, 1950), p. 60.

philosophers have envisaged the possibility that the heart of a politician may function in the same sort of way as a chemical in a retort. It does not matter that the poet may not believe this; whether he believes it or not, the idea (and the words, the words – 'subside') are still there for him to make play with. Even if he is bitterly opposed to all this aspect of the thought of his time, he can, just for that reason, push it to an extreme, to make it look silly. In fact, this pun or this metaphor (the device partakes of both), straddling with one foot in, one out of the laboratory, is a distinctive feature of Augustan writing, in verse and in some sorts of prose; and it is at the bottom of some of the greatest literary achievements of the age. The writers owe it to the scientists and the philosophers.

I shall turn next to some writings in which such devices are used, not to deflating effect in the comic or satiric modes, but affirmatively, seriously, even in the mode that the age itself called 'sublime'. And my examples will centre around, not one of the new words, but the word 'spirit', an ancient aristocrat of the language which became infected, as William Empson has seen, from rubbing shoulders with the *parvenus*.

3

There is a point in *Alice in Wonderland*, where Alice speculates about diet:

> 'When *I'm* a Duchess', she said to herself (not in a very hopeful tone, though), 'I won't have any pepper in my kitchen *at all*. Soup does very well without – Maybe it's always pepper that makes people hot-tempered', she went on, very much pleased at having found out a new kind of rule, 'and vinegar that makes them sour – and camomile that makes them bitter – and – and barley-sugar and such things that make children sweet-tempered. I only wish people knew *that:* then they wouldn't be so stingy about it, you know…'

Alice's 'new kind of rule' isn't new at all, but ancient. And this logic, which for us belongs in Wonderland, or else in childishness, in the past was the logic of science. What is the relation between hot pepper and hot temper, sweet sugar and sweet temper, camomile and a bitter tongue, vinegar and a sour look? We reply, I suppose, that the relationship is metaphorical, or, as we say, *only* metaphorical. But it is indisputable that in the past the relationship was one not of metaphor but of identity, as it is for Alice. What was the relationship for scientists and for laymen, in the early eighteenth century? I shall suggest that if the relationship then was metaphorical, the metaphors were very lively ones, whereas for us they are dead; and that the relationship of identity had been so recently discredited in that period that simple people still believed in it, and more sophisticated people were fairly often trapped by their own metaphors into forgetting that it was metaphors they were using, and so relapsed into the more primitive way of thinking, by which to make yourself sweet-tempered you ate sweet things.

This is only another way of putting Empson's insight about the ambiguity of, for instance, the crucial word 'spirit' in *A Tale of a Tub*. We can see Alice's Wonderland logic operating with the word 'spirit', when we turn to another nineteenth-century example Charles Lever's novel of 1841, *Charles O'Malley*. Captain Power, a character in the novel, recommends the punch he has prepared:

> 'Eh, doctor? you advise it yourself, to be taken before bedtime; nothing inflammatory in it; nothing pugnacious; a mere circulation of the better juices and more genial spirits of the marly clay, without arousing any of the baser passions; whiskey is the devil for that.'

Whiskey is a spirit; and it raises *your* spirits, if you drink it. What is the relation between that spirit and those spirits? Again we answer: Metaphorical. But Captain Power talks as if they were identical. Also, the spirit of Scotch whisky, is a distillation of the spirit of barley. What is the spirit in barley, and how does it get there? When Captain Power speaks of the 'genial spirits of the marly clay', do we not follow that other ambiguous word 'genial' into thinking of genie or djinns, or into 'the genius of place', so that the spirit becomes at one point an embodied phantom, like a dryad? What do we mean, or what do we think we mean when we say, 'The very spirit of the Highlands is in this whisky'? Can we be absolutely sure that we aren't ourselves trapped by the multiple ambiguities in this word, into envisaging an identity when our rational minds will countenance only a comparison or an analogy?

Only by raising these questions do we put ourselves in the right frame of mind for a passage such as this, from Bernard Mandeville's famous *Fable of the Bees* (1714):

> ... I shall prove, that, ... what the greatest Hero differs in from the rankest Coward, is altogether Corporeal, and depends upon the inward make of Man. Whan I mean is call'd Constitution; by which is understood the orderly or disorderly mixture of the *Fluids* in our body: That Constitution which favours Courage, consists in the natural Strength, Elasticity, and due Contexture of the finer Spirits, and upon them wholly depends what we call Stedfastness, Resolution and Obstinacy ... That some People are very much, others very little frightened at things that are strange and sudden to them, is likewise altogether owing to the firmness or imbecillity in the Tone of the Spirits ...
>
> That Resolution depends upon this Tone of the Spirits, appears likewise from the effects of strong Liquors, the fiery Particles whereof

crowding into the Brain, strengthen the Spirits; their Operation imitates that of Anger, which I said before was an Ebullition of the Spirits. It is for this reason that most People when they are in Drink, are sooner touch'd and more prone to Anger than at other times, and some raving Mad without any Provocation at all. It is likewise observ'd that Brandy makes Men more Quarrelsome at the same pitch of Drunkenness than Wine; because the Spirits of distill'd Waters have abundance of fiery Particles mixt with them, which the other has not. The Contexture of Spirits is so weak in some, that tho' they have Pride enough, no Art can ever make them fight, or overcome their Fears; but this is a Defect in the Principle of the *Fluids*, as other Deformities are faults of the *Solids*.[1]

You notice here one of the 'philosophic words' like 'insipid'. It is 'imbecillity', still used to refer only to a material condition, not to an immaterial condition, a condition of the mind, as in the modern sense of the word. Thus later in the eighteenth century, the naturalist Gilbert White remarks, 'The imbecility of birds seems not to be the only reason why they shun the rigour of our winters ...' And he doesn't mean that birds are weak-minded but that they are weak-bodied. Similarly Mandeville, elsewhere in *The Fable of the Bees* (Remark (N)), declares, 'The firmness and Imbecillity of our Hope depend entirely on the greater or lesser degree of our Confidence, and all Hope includes Doubt ...'

Mandeville is a particularly interesting case for our purposes, because, like Arbuthnot, he was a practising physician and published treatises of medicine. That is, like Arbuthnot, he united in his own person the scientist and the man of letters. His modern editor notes that in his *Treatise of the Hypochondriack and Hysterick Passions*, a medical treatise which he published in 1711, Mandeville (edn of 1730, p. 163) recognized the physiology of the fluids as perhaps only a convenient hypothesis. However this may be, in the passage quoted Mandeville is assuming that this physiology is not hypothesis but fact.

Physiology, of course, was one science which had been entirely materialistic since long before Newton and Descartes, Hobbes and Locke, indeed since the time of the ancients. Most readers of literature know vaguely about the role of the four humours in the materialistic physiology of the Elizabethans. No less important to Elizabethan medicine, and no less material, were the 'spirits', which were distinct from the 'humours', though conveyed, like them, in the blood. When Donne writes, 'As our blood labours to beget / Spirits, as like souls as it can', he is referring to the *animal* spirits which are so called by reference not to the brute creation

1   *The Fable of the Bees*, Remark (R), in *Works,* ed. F.B. Kaye (Oxford, 1924), I, pp. 211, 212.

but to *anima* (soul); thus animal spirits are something very near to soul, though distinct from it – and hence the point of Donne's lines. The animal spirits (located for some authorities in the liver, for others in the head) were distinguished by sixteenth-century physiologists from the *vital* spirits, those again from the *nutrimental* spirits, and those in turn from the *generative* spirit; which last is the 'spirit' of Shakespeare's line, 'The expense of spirit in a waste of shame / Is lust in action'.[1]

While Mandeville may no longer believe in this complicated classification, his talk of 'fluids' and 'spirits' shows him still thinking in Elizabethan terms. And indeed his contemporary John Locke still speaks of 'the animal spirits' quite unmetaphorically. Our emancipation from this world of thought is signalized in the distinction we make between 'spirituous' (used of spirits like alcohol, which are material) and 'spiritual' (used of spirits which are immaterial). But our emancipation is partial, for we haven't two nouns to correspond to these adjectives, but only one, 'spirit'. And what do we mean when we speak of a horse or a young person as 'spirited'? Is the spirit in question material or not? At any rate, our distinction between 'spirituous' and 'spiritual' was unthinkable for the eighteenth century, as this passage of Mandeville shows. It is a distinction – not a very efficient one – designed to cope with the awkwardness of using the same word for alcohol and for the Third Person of the Trinity. We find we need some word to distinguish between those spirits which are methylated and those which are angelic. For Mandeville and his contemporaries no such distinction existed, nor is it clear that they yet felt the need for it. Some of them, indeed, as we shall see, built great hopes and much eloquence on *not* having it, for this permitted them to believe in a single principle actuating all forms of life, from the basest to the most ethereal.

One of these, rather surprisingly, was Berkeley. It is surprising because Berkeley, as a friend of Swift and Pope, belongs rather with the men unsympathetic to scientific and materialist thought, who exploited this ambiguous vocabulary to comic or ironical effect. In the sixth dialogue of his *Alciphron, or the Minute Philosopher* (1732), he makes one of his four speakers declare,

> To inspire, is a Word borrowed from the *Latin*, and strictly taken means no more than to breathe or blow in: nothing therefore can be inspired but what can be blown or breathed, and nothing can be so but Wind or Vapour, which indeed may fill or puff up Men with fanatical and hypocondriacal Ravings. This sort of Inspiration I readily admit.

---

1   See Patrick Cruttwell, 'Physiology and Psychology in Shakespeare's Age', *Journal of the History of Ideas*, XII: I (January 1951), pp. 75–89

But the speaker here is a representative of the freethinkers whom Berkeley is writing to expose. And he immediately calls on one of his own spokesmen to counter this argument by in the same way reducing the word 'discourse' to its Latin root-meaning, 'running about', thus uncovering the futility of all such arguments from etymology. And in the same Dialogue, when another of the freethinkers manipulates the ambiguity of words like 'spirit', 'unctuous' and 'volatile', to deduce the nature of the human soul from the behaviour of vegetables, Berkeley has his other spokesman retort with the unanswerable question, 'But what relation hath the Soul of Man to Chymic Art?' Yet in his last work, *Siris* (1741), Berkeley, at the end of his life, falls into all these traps which in earlier books he had guarded against so carefully.

It is interesting to see how this comes about: *Siris* is a very peculiar little book, which has for its sub-title, *A Treatise of Tar-Water*. Berkeley, by this time residing in his Irish bishopric, had been concerned about a bad epidemic of cholera in his diocese, and had found, or thought he found, an effective medicine, tar-water. When he tried to account for this and to put it on record, he found himself in the field of pharmacy and botany – in other words, in that scientific area of language where, as we have seen, the ambiguities in a word like 'spirit' were particularly rife and particularly misleading. One other consideration should be taken into account. In the last quotation, one notices the word 'hypocondriacal'. And we have encountered the same word in the title of Mandeville's medical text-book, his *Treatise of the Hypochondriack and Hysterick Passions*. 'Hypochondria' and its derivatives, 'hypochondriac' and 'hypochondriacal', are very common words in this period, just as the peculiar conditions to which they refer were a feature of the life of the time. Ian Watt, in his *Rise of the Novel*, gives evidence of this, and speculates plausibly about the causes of it. 'Hypochondria' was so much in people's minds and mouths that it was abbreviated into 'the hyp'; and I have heard old-fashioned and provincial persons in my own lifetime say, 'Oh, you give me the hyp', where we should say, 'You give me a pain in the neck.' 'The hyp', as the eighteenth century used the term was sometimes not far from what the present century has learned to call *Angst*. It has even more to do with what we call 'nervous debility'. In other words, it is a malady which belongs bafflingly in a sort of no-man's-land between mind and body; and the eighteenth-century usage represents a first groping towards the territory of psychosomatic medicine. Berkeley is convinced that tar-water is a good medicine for this ailment, as indeed for all others, for it soon appears that for him tar-water is a panacea.

Berkeley's diction, in *Siris*, is based upon a choice of terms which are throughout nicely ambiguous. We speak of a 'mild' purgative as we speak of a 'mild' disposition; and 'mild' therefore can be used so that the reader feels, in the word, an identity of physical and spiritual. Berkeley recommends tar-water (§105) as 'a cordial, not only safe and innocent, but giving health and spirits as surely as other cordials destroy them'. We should not describe a medicine as 'innocent'; for just as we distinguish between 'spirituous' and 'spiritual', so we distinguish between 'innocuous' and 'innocent' keeping 'innocent' to refer (outside of the law courts) exclusively to a spiritual state, immaterial where 'innocuous' is material. But this distinction was unknown to Berkeley, as it was to Donne when he wrote, 'The trepidation of the spheres, / Though greater far, is innocent'; there, both 'trepidation' and 'innocent' have for us the force of learned Latinate puns, though they would not have had that force for Donne's first readers. On the other hand, 'cordial' retains, for us, both its senses, and, as a noun, refers to a medicine having certain properties, while, as an adjective, it describes human temperament and human behaviour. Accordingly this word implies, if we scrutinize it closely, an identity between the world of physical medicine and the world of the human spirit. But of course we do not scrutinize it closely – which only means that the ambiguity of the word can work upon us all the more powerfully.

Again, when we learn (§92) that 'the animal salts of a sound body are of a neutral, bland, and benign nature', it would be wrong to say that the physical properties of the salts are defined by analogy from the moral properties of a virtuous human character. 'Bland' and 'benign' are suspended between the physical order and the moral, partaking equally of both, and implying that the two orders are not ultimately to be distinguished.

We know better than to suppose that this ambiguous vocabulary was Berkeley's creation, any more than it was Johnson's. Some ambiguities were crucial to the thinking of the alchemists, for whom a metal, for instance, could be noble or ignoble, and could have, as plants still have for the herbalist, a specific 'virtue'. (Somewhere hereabouts there is the crucial ambiguity of the one English word, 'virtue', standing for moral worth on the one hand, and on the other for the Renaissance Italian *virtù* – the ambiguity which in our period leads Shaftesbury to say, in his *Advice to an Author*, 'thus the science of virtuosi and that of virtue itself become, in a manner, one and the same.'[1]) But the range of such ambiguities was greatly extended when the scientists of the Royal Society, finding the need of new concepts, with learned propriety constructed their names for these concepts out of Latin roots which had already produced English words, of ethical rather than scientific bearing. The *Shorter Oxford English Dictionary* finds 'bland' first applied to inanimate things in 1667. To call them 'inanimate' begs the question which such words as 'bland' successfully evade. So, too, the dictionary finds 'innocent' first used as opposed to 'malig-

---

1   Shaftesbury, *Characteristics,* ed. John M. Robertson, I (London, 1900), p. 217.

nant' by a pathologist of 1662; and 'benign' used of medicines in 1735.

These usages have an interesting history. Some – 'bland', 'benign' and 'innocent', as applied to medicines – have simply disappeared. Others have been pruned of their ambiguity by dividing into two, as the seventeenth-century 'melancholy' is now shared between 'melancholy' and 'melancholia', having caused many confusions in the process.[1] Others retain their metaphorical power; for what layman, hearing of a person afflicted by a 'malignant' growth, does not feel a tug in the word, towards the idea of possession by evil spirits?

Berkeley, in *Siris*, exploited this field of ambiguity with exceptional thoroughness and consistency:

> The balsam or essential oil of vegetables contains a spirit wherein consist the specific qualities, the smell and taste of the plant. Boerhaave holds the native presiding spirit to be neither oil, salt, earth, or water, but somewhat too fine and subtle to be caught alone and rendered visible to the eye. This, when suffered to fly off, for instance, from the oil of rosemary, leaves it destitute of all flavour. This spark of life, this spirit or soul, if we may so say, of a vegetable departs without any sensible diminution of the oil or water wherein it was lodged.
>
> It should seem that the forms, souls, or principles of vegetable life subsist in the light or solar emanation; which in respect of the macrocosm is what the animal spirit is to the microcosm – the interior tegument, the subtle instrument and vehicle of power. No wonder, then, that the *ens primum* or *scintilla spirituosa*, as it is called, of plants should be a thing so fine and fugacious as to escape our nicest search. It is evident that nature at the sun's approach vegetates, and languishes at his recess: this terrestrial globe seeming only a matrix disposed and prepared to receive life from his light; when Homer in his Hymns styleth earth the wife of heaven, αλοχ' οὐρανοῦ ἀοτερόεντος.
>
> The luminous spirit which is the form or life of a plant, from whence its differences and properties flow, is somewhat extremely volatile. It is not the oil, but a thing more subtle, whereof oil is the vehicle, which retains it from flying off, and is lodged in several parts of the plant, particularly in the cells of the bark and m the seeds. This oil, purified and exalted by the organical powers of the plant, and agitated by warmth, becomes a proper receptacle of the spirit: part of which spirit exhales through the leaves and flowers, and part is arrested by this unctuous humour that detains it in the plant. It is to be noted this essential oil, animated, one may say, with the flavour of the plant, is very different from any spirit that can be procured from the same plant by fermentation. [§§ 42, 43, 44.]

---

1   Cf. Amy Reed, *The Background of Gray's Elegy* (New York, 1962).

Despite the careful disclaimer in the last sentence, it is clear that the 'spirit' named there, which is alcoholic, differs from the 'spirit' of the first sentence only in being fermented. That first 'spirit' is immediately qualified as 'too fine and subtle to be caught alone and rendered visible to the eye'. Yet this is not the immaterial spirit which equals 'soul'; for Berkeley guards against this by explaining against his normal practice, that this identification is 'only metaphorical' – 'This spark of life, this spirit or soul, *if we may so say* ...' However, this is an old trick. The writer takes the precaution of 'if I may say so', but he knows very well that that disclaimer hardly weakens the metaphorical force at all; so he has it both ways. And so he is able to move at once to 'forms, souls, or principles' (with no disclaimer this time), to *ens primum* or *scintilla spirituosa*. By this time, the spirit of vegetables is for the reader a spirit as an angel is a spirit; and this is cunningly reinforced by the 'luminous spirit' who soars into the last paragraph. Berkeley is safe. He 'means', logically, the spirit derived from sunlight; but all the force of the locution derives from the disreputable, illogical part of the meaning, by which the 'spirit' is bright and shining as angels are. Finally, in a casual parenthesis, Berkeley returns to the 'spirit', as of wood alcohol. And so, in the end, the reader has been inveigled into accepting an ambiguity as a meaning. The writer is not using the language to think with; he is permitting the language to do his thinking for him.

This is a way of using language which is legitimate in poetry. If it occurs in philosophy more often than philosophers suppose, it isn't anything that they can feel comfortable about. In *Siris* all is metaphorical. What is to be made, for instance, of that nature which 'at the sun's approach vegetates, and languishes at his recess'? Does it 'really' languish? Or is the expression 'figurative'? Truly, we cannot say. For in this world where 'spirit' is something like wood alcohol, yet also a soul, subsisting in the light, we cannot be sure about the languor in nature. Most readers will feel, at any rate, that when Berkeley speaks of nature languishing, he means something less metaphorical, more nearly literal, than a modern speaker would mean; much more literal (for a further example) than if that same speaker were to say of a person that he 'vegetates'. And languor, too, it will be noted, belongs in the ambiguous territory of hypochondria, where a moral and spiritual condition seems open to diagnosis by physicians.

Again and again, tar-water is described in terms which strike the modern reader as applicable only to moral and psychological conditions. It is 'unctuous', 'subtle', 'active'. It is (§49) 'gentle, bland and temperate'. And (§72) 'it is of so just a temperament as to be an enemy of all extremes' – phrasing which one could think to find in Hume, describing a moral man. So too, 'There is a lentor or smoothness in the blood of healthy strong people; there is often an acrimony and solution in that of weakly morbid persons.' And we cannot, perhaps we should not, dismiss the human and moral connotations of 'acrimony' from a passage which purports to be scientific observation. The truth seems to be that for Berkeley here, as for his age in general, the distinction which we make between the scientific and the moral was unnecessary, positively unwanted. For this is what *Siris* is about, at least in its highest reaches – about a divine activity and presence which gloriously informs the whole of created nature, from lowest to highest.

There is an even more rhapsodic treatment of these linguistic muddles in *An Appeal to All that Doubt* (1740), by the famous saint of the English Church, William Law;

> If a delicious, fragrant *Fruit* had a Power of separating itself from that rich *Spirit*, fine *Taste*, *Smell*, and *Colour* which it receives from the Virtue of the Sun, and the Spirit of the *Air;* or if it could in the *Beginning* of its Growth, turn away from the *Sun*, and receive no Virtue from it, then it would stand in its own first Birth of *Wrath*, *Sourness*, *Bitterness*, and *Astringency*, just as the *Devils* do, who have turned back into their own dark Root, and rejected the *Light* and *Spirit* of God: so that the hellish Nature of a Devil is Nothing else, but its own *first Forms* of Life, withdrawn, or separated from the heavenly Light and Love; just as the *Sourness*, *Astringency*, and *Bitterness* of a Fruit, are Nothing else but the *first Forms* of its own vegetable Life before it has reached the Virtue of the Sun, and the Spirit of the *Air*.[1]

Besides the muddles we are by now familiar with, in the word 'light' and in the 'virtue' which is also *virtù*, we perceive the full range of the bewildering shifts inside the word 'spirit' – from the 'rich Spirit' of a fruit, through 'the Spirit of the *Air*' to 'Spirit of God' and back to 'the Spirit of the *Air*'.

This passage from Law is of peculiar interest because in it, as very often elsewhere, Law is following very closely the doctrines of the German mystic, Jacob Boehme. Now, Isaac Newton himself had read Boehme, and Law asserted most strenuously that it was from Boehme that Newton got the hint for formulating his laws of motion. And Caroline Spurgeon, in the *Cambridge History* of *English Literature* (vol. 9, p. 208), agrees with Law in thinking it 'almost certain that the idea of the three laws of motion reached Newton through his eager study of Boehme'. Others disagree, and the case resolves itself into scrutinizing the ambiguous meanings, in Newton's work, of 'spirit', as well as of some other words like 'attraction' itself (to which Law gives a mystical meaning), and 'tincture' (another ambiguous word, alchemical in origin, very common in the period, in Berkeley, for instance). Stephen Hobhouse, for instance, challenging Spurgeon's assertion, declares, of 'spirit' as used by Newton:

---

1   William Law, *An Appeal to All that Doubt,* ch. 1, §12.

The conceptions of aether and of aethereal spirit or spirits as used by Gilbert, Descartes, Boyle and other physicists, have a long and varying history. Though the terms have at times theological and mystical, or perhaps we should say animistic, associations, it seems to me clear that in Newton's mind there was nothing properly metaphysical or 'spiritual' (as God and thought are spiritual) about 'aethereal spirit', which was merely an extremely thin, elastic, penetrating, wavelike medium, allied not to thought but to matter, even if apparently different from it in some of its properties.[1]

Hobhouse hedges carefully, putting quotation-marks around 'spiritual', and an explanatory parenthesis after it – 'as God and thought are spiritual'. One respects him for this caginess, as one respects Spurgeon, on the opposite side of the argument, for finding the connection between Boehme and Newton *'almost* certain'. For the truth seems to be that terms like 'spirit', 'tincture', 'attraction' are so slippery in this period that there can be no certainty about their meaning in any context whatever. If so, then the question which Hobhouse and Spurgeon are debating, or (to take another example) the much-debated problem of how to square *Siris* with the rest of Berkeley's thought – these are questions which, in so far as they can be answered at all, can be answered only by the historical semanticist, the student of changing meanings in language. It is my argument that the whole enormous question of the relation between science and literature in this period – perhaps in any period – must be referred to the same authority, and handled only by his tools.

4

As we have seen, the influence of science upon literature in this period is so pervasive and so protean that the only way to grasp and handle it is through close and particular analysis of vocabulary. Moreover, we have seen that we need to look out, not so much for new words borrowed by literature from the sciences (vast and important as that territory is), as for old words which scientific pressure causes to take on new meanings. An easily definable and very important area of the language, in which this process can be observed, is the vocabulary of political theory. And it's from this area that I shall now produce a few examples.

One cannot read Shakespeare or any of his contemporaries without realizing how important for the sixteenth and seventeenth centuries was the habit of regarding the political community of the nation by analogy

---

1   Stephen Hobhouse, 'Isaac Newton and Jacob Boehme: An Enquiry', reprinted as Appendix 4 of his *Selected Mystical Writings* of William Law (1948), pp. 416–17.

with the human body. This habit of thought has left indelible traces on our own vocabulary, as when we speak of the National Coal Board or of the House of Commons or of the Privy Council as 'a properly constituted *body*', when we speak of our monarch as 'the *Head* of State', or of whomever it is as the *'head'* of the Coal Board. Sometimes indeed we still speak of the whole bunch of us, in our political aspect, as 'the body politic'. For us these are dead metaphors, which we use (with quite unjustified confidence) as if they were not the highly figurative expressions which they are. For Shakespeare, on the other hand, as we know or must be made to see, they were very lively metaphors indeed; so lively, in fact, that he almost seems to fall, sometimes, into the opposite error from our own, and to regard the analogy between human and political body not as just a manner of speaking, nor even as a manner of thinking, but as a provable fact, on which arguments may be based.

If we ask how the eighteenth century used these metaphors, we should by now be prepared for the answer: Halfway between Shakespeare and ourselves, they think now in his way, now in ours; they start thinking our way and then, without realizing it, relapse into Shakespeare's way; they start thinking his way and then without knowing it slip into our way. The tools they had to use, the vocabulary, were so slippery (because at such a crucial state of transition) that they continually failed them.

Here, for instance, is a good writer we have already considered in other connections, the physician, cynical philosopher and wit Bernard Mandeville:

> ... I would compare the Body Politick (I confess the Simile is very low) to a Bowl of Punch. Avarice should be the Souring and Prodigality the Sweetning of it. The Water I would call the Ignorance, Folly and Credulity of the floating insipid Multitude; while Wisdom, Honour, Fortitude and the rest of the sublime Qualities of Men which, separated by Art from the Dregs of Nature, the fire of Glory has exalted and refin'd into a Spiritual Essence, should be an Equivalent to Brandy.[1]

It is easy to say that Mandeville, of course, can't be serious. Certainly he isn't serious, in the Shakespearean way, about the metaphor he starts with, that of the body politic. For if the nation is in all seriousness like a human body, how can it at the same time be like a bowl of punch? Plainly at this point 'the body politic' is as much of a dead metaphor for Mandeville as it is for us. But what then, about the alternative analogy, with the bowl of punch? I think it is probably safe to say (I wouldn't like to be any more definite) that Mandeville doesn't *mean* to be serious in

---

1   *The Fable of the Bees*, Remark (K), in *Works*, I, pp. 105–6.

this, either. But it's a very dangerous game he is playing. Sooner or later he is sure to cut himself with his own double-edged tools; the slipperiness of his own vocabulary is going to throw him off balance. For his words are ambiguous throughout. Consider, for instance, 'sublime' – that word which was so momentous in the eighteenth century. No less than moralists and poets, and in our day psychoanalysts, chemists can 'sublimate', just as in the eighteenth century they could (and did continually) 'exalt' and 'refine'. We have already noticed 'insipid' as one of the crucial 'philosophic words', taken over from scientific terminology and given a figurative extension. And so, when Mandeville speaks of 'the floating insipid Multitude', we do well to remember a piece of political jargon of our own day, 'the floating vote'. The floating vote stands for those people who Labour and Conservative alike fear may vote Liberal. And alike on the Left and Right we hear of 'milk-and-water Liberalism'. That 'milk-and-water' is our substitute for Mandeville's 'insipid'. Can we be quite sure that we shall at all times remember how this imputed connection between a certain political programme and an infantile diet is no more than figurative? The propagandists and advertisers who put such expressions into circulation are banking on the probability that we shan't remember this. And in the same way we may bank on the probability that Mandeville has forgotten, or will forget, how the connection between the fire of glory and the fire under the chemist's crucible or under the pot with the punch in it, is only a fanciful connection.

Accordingly we cannot be surprised to find Mandeville writing elsewhere:

> Lucre is the best Restorative in the World, in a literal Sense, and works upon the Spirits mechanically; for it is not only a Spur, that excites Men to labour, and makes them in love with it; but it likewise gives Relief in Weariness, and actually supports Men in all Fatigues and Difficulties.[1]

'In a *literal* Sense ...', it '*actually* supports ...' I do not need to point the moral: the writer is trapped by his own metaphors.

This is to take the metaphor of 'the body politic' all too seriously – to the point of forgetting that a metaphor is what it is. Yet for Mandeville in general, as we have seen, this is a dead and discredited metaphor; and consciously he thinks rather in that mechanical metaphor which was a creation of his own age – that other metaphor for the political community which we use when we speak of 'the balance of power' or of the constitution as 'a system of checks and balances'. There is, for instance, a passage in the sixth dialogue of part II of *The Fable of the Bees*, where there

---

1   *The Fable of the Bees*, sixth dialogue, in *Works*, II, pp. 354–5.

is an elaborate treatment of government precisely as a machine of weights and counterweights, explicitly compared with, first, a knitting-frame for the weaving of stockings, second, a clock. And yet, had not physiologists advanced the hypothesis that the human body was itself a machine, to be ultimately explained, as knowledge accumulated, in terms of mechanics? Indeed they had:

> Man never exerts himself but when he is rous'd by his Desires: While they lie dormant, and there is nothing to raise them, his Excellence and Abilities will be for ever undiscover'd, and the lumpish Machine, without Influence of his Passions, may be justly compared to a huge Wind-mill without a breath of Air.[1]

Here, the air which is to move the sails of the wind-mill is that mere puff or gust to which physics and etymology combined have reduced the idea of 'spirit'. And thus:

> ... the Legislature ought to resolve upon some great Undertakings that must be the Work of Ages as well as vast Labour, and convince the World that they did nothing without an anxious regard to their latest Posterity. This will fix or at least help to settle the volatile Genius and fickle Spirit of the Kingdom ...[2]

Here the ambiguity of 'volatile' – that 'philosophic' word – and of 'spirit', is no longer treacherous. For if it be true that 'volatile'. can be used literally only in chemistry and biochemistry, and be applied to political behaviour only by figurative extension, still there is no risk in not remembering this, since 'spirit' in both cases operates mechanically.

In other words, in Mandeville and others of his period, the metaphor of 'the body politic' was not at odds with the other metaphor of society as a machine. Both could remain live metaphors and yet be reconciled. For if the human body was itself a machine, then society could preserve its analogy with the human body, at the same time as it worked by checks and balances. So far from being mutually irreconcilable, the two metaphors could seem to support and corroborate each other. Hence, when we seem to find – as we do frequently – a mixed metaphor for political society, when we want to ask, 'Do they conceive of society organically or mechanically?' the writers can only reply with perfect consistency that since for them the organic is mechanical, they never regard society as an organism so thoroughly as when they describe it in terms of mechanics. This is what we find, for instance, in Mandeville (to come back to him for the last time):

1   *The Fable of the Bees*, Remark (Q), in *Works*, I, p. 184.
2   Mandeville, 'Essay on Charity and Charity Schools', in *Works*, I, p. 321.

… Those who immediately lose by the Misfortunes of others are very sorry, complain and make a Noise, but the others who get by them, as there always are such, hold their Tongues, because it is odious to be thought the better for the Losses and Calamities of our Neighbour. The various Ups and Downs compose a Wheel that always turning round give motion to the whole Machine. Philosophers, that dare extend their Thoughts beyond the narrow compass of what is immediately before them, look on the alternate Changes in the Civil Society no otherwise than they do on the risings and failings of the Lungs; the latter of which are as much a part of Respiration in the more Perfect Animals as the first; so that the fickle Breath of never-stable Fortune is to the Body Politick, the same as floating Air is to a living Creature.

Avarice then and Prodigality are equally necessary to the Society. That in some Countries, Men are more generally lavish than in others, proceeds from the difference in Circumstances that dispose to either Vice, and arise from the Condition of the Social Body as well as the Temperament of the Natural …[1]

Here Mandeville can adapt or translate into his own materialistic terms a metaphor even more ancient in political thought than that of 'the body politic' − the image of the Wheel of Fortune, turning as there is blown upon it 'the fickle Breath of never-stable Fortune'. And the translation is complete. We may regret the impoverishment of the metaphor in terms of imaginative resonance. We might even feel a sort of wry melancholy at the confidence and buoyancy of this materialism whose hopes or pretensions we have since seen exploded. But we cannot here, as we may elsewhere, point to Mandeville as his own dupe, trapped by metaphors starting to unforeseen life in his own language.

This is so, however, only because we know from the whole tenor of Mandeville's writings that he was − so it appears − a Hobbesian materialistic cynic, by conviction. The case is quite different when we are dealing with a writer whose conscious intention appears to be to refute the whole materialistic thesis. Swift is such a writer. And when we discover in him the image of the body politic and the image of checks and balances used indiscriminately or interchangeably of the political order, we have no recourse but to diagnose a genuine and betraying mixture of metaphors, even to find − dangerous as this is, with a writer such as Swift − a man duped by his own language. We are speaking here not of the ironical Swift of *The Tale of a Tub* or *A Modest Proposal*, but of Swift of *The Conduct of the Allies* or of *A Discourse of the Contests and Dissentions of the Nobles and Commons at Athens and Rome*. One may find Swift's prose

1   *The Fable of the Bees*, Remark (Y), in *Works*, I, p. 250.

much more enjoyable and bracing in such plainly polemical pieces as these, than in the pieces of elaborate irony like the *Argument to prove that the Abolishing of Christianity in England may ... be attended with some Inconveniences*. And it is permissible to think that the present age may prefer the squirming ironies chiefly because of our predisposition towards 'complexity', and because, unable ourselves to believe anything with conviction, we cannot sympathize with statements of conviction or with the argument of a straightforward case. Nevertheless it turns out that the irony is a notably effective self-defence – that may indeed be just what is wrong with it – and Swift, shorn of his irony, looks a very vulnerable thinker, shut out by his own intemperance from recognizing the powerful currents of his age (like the revolution of scientific method) and equally incapable therefore of guarding against the intellectual and linguistic quicksands which those new currents created.

In a commentary which Yeats wrote on his own play about Swift, *The Words on the Window Pane*, Yeats declared that in *A Discourse of the Contests and Dissentions of the Nobles and Commons at Athens and Rome*, Swift's political theory so clearly foreshadows Burke's that between them, he thought, they made of the political philosophy of English conservatism an Anglo-Irish creation. But of course Burke's use of language in political theory is not open to the same objections as Swift's. In particular, he belongs to a later generation when the Christian view of life, and the materialistic or mechanical are – if still at odds – no longer so overtly and inescapably posed one against the other; Burke's enemies are the radical doctrinaires in politics, who may indeed be the heirs of the materialists, but equally often derive from quite other sources – Deistic rationalism for instance. Burke, because he belongs to a later generation, cannot be fitted into the present scheme. Yet because he is so plainly, by any account, the man in the eighteenth century who most conspicuously combined a genius for language with a genius for political thought, it is worth considering how he avoided or else exploited the ambiguities which, as we have seen, infested the language of political theory for his predecessors. We remember him, of course, as the great champion of the political society conceived as an organism; it is from him, indeed, that we have learned to think of an organic view of society as irreconcilably opposed to a mechanistic view of it. It is his constant contention that a political society grows and changes as a tree grows and changes, according to its own rhythms and its own inherent laws; and that it is dangerous lunacy, therefore, to design for the state a blue-print in the shape of a written Constitution, as one may or must create a blue-print for a machine. It is hardly too much to say, therefore, that Burke spent his lifetime fanning into renewed life the dead or dying metaphor of the state as 'the body politic'. Yet in Burke too, the scientific analogy is never far off:

When I see the spirit of liberty in action, I see a strong principle at work; and this, for a while, is all I can possibly know of it. The wild *gas*, the fixed air, is plainly broke loose: but we ought to suspend our judgment until the first effervescence is a little subsided, till the liquor is cleared, and until we see something deeper than the agitation of a troubled and frothy surface.[1]

This is the old pun extricated by Empson from *The Tale of a Tub*, by which 'spirit' in the language of the divinity school is identified with 'spirit' in the language of the chemist's laboratory. The difference, I suspect, is that the chemistry to which Burke appeals is a chemistry which has asserted its independence of mechanics. M.H. Abrams, in *The Mirror and the Lamp*, has pointed out how the analogy with chemistry recommended itself to Burke's contemporaries who were literary critics, at least one of them – Coleridge – being also a political theorist, and of Burke's organicist persuasion. It seems that of all the natural sciences chemistry was the one which the Romantics embraced as an ally against a mechanistic view of things. But it would need a historian of science, more learned than I am, to confirm my suspicion that this came about because of the changed status of chemistry itself, in relation to the other sciences.

What can be said with some assurance is that when Burke uses the scientific analogy, he does so with a different tone from Swift or Berkeley, Mandeville or William Law, or any of the writers earlier in the century. When Burke writes of 'a sort of flippant, vain discourse, in which, as in an unsavoury fume, several persons suffer the spirit of liberty to evaporate',[2] the metaphor again is the old metaphor of Swift and Berkeley, gone dead in common parlance, into which Burke breathes new life. He remakes the metaphor in a new mould. For the argument of the metaphor in Burke is neither Berkeley's in *Siris* – 'Liberty is a spirit as alcohol is a spirit, for all things are spiritual'; nor Swift's in *The Tale of a Tub* – 'Liberty is a spirit as alcohol is a spirit, for all things are material.' The tone is not exultant, as with Berkeley, nor sardonic, as with Swift. It is sober. The old metaphor is used, but given a new lease of life.

And this, as we have said, is Burke's usual practice: he takes old political metaphors like the Shakespearean metaphor of grafting and gardening[3] and gives them new life:

Our political system is placed in a just correspondence and symmetry with the order of the world, and with the mode of existence decreed to a permanent body composed of transitory parts; wherein, by the disposition of a stupendous wisdom, moulding together the great and

1 *Reflections on the French Revolution*, pp. 6, 7 (Everyman edition).
2 *Reflections*, p. 27.
3 *Reflections*, p. 29.

mysterious incorporation of the human race, the whole, at one time, is never old, or middle-aged, or young, but, in a condition of unchangeable constancy, moves on through the varied tenor of perpetual decay, fall, renovation, and progression. Thus, by preserving the method of nature in the conduct of the state, in what we improve, we are never wholly obsolete. By adhering in this manner and on these principles to our forefathers, we are guided not by the superstition of antiquarians, but by the spirit of philosophic analogy. In this choice of inheritance we have given to our frame of polity the image of a relation in blood; binding up the constitution of our country with our dearest domesticities; adopting our fundamental laws into the bosom of our family affections; keeping inseparable, and cherishing with the warmth of all their combined and mutually reflected charities, our state, our hearths, our sepulchres, and our altars.[1]

This relation which Burke calls 'philosophic analogy' is related to that which Johnson made when he spoke of 'philosophic words'. In both contexts, I think, 'philosophic' means 'of natural philosophy', that is to say, scientific. It was not for nothing that Burke was a younger associate of Johnson and Reynolds. But the analogy with science is now pursued under other patronage than that of John Locke; for it was not for nothing that Burke lived to see Wordsworth's and Coleridge's *Lyrical Ballads*.

But 1798 is a year far outside the limits I have set myself. And for an example which will draw together as many as possible of the threads I have unravelled, I shall do better to withdraw into the period I defined. This, then, is from Berkeley again – not from the elated and innocent Berkeley of *Siris*, but from *Alciphron*, his dialogues of 1732:

The Wheels of Government go on, though wound up by different Hands: if not in the same Form, yet in some other, perhaps a better. There is an endless Variety in things: weak Men, indeed, are prejudiced towards Rules and Systemes in Life and Government: and think if these are gone, all is gone: But a Man of a great Soul and free Spirit, delights in the noble Experiment of blowing up Systemes and dissolving Governments, to mold them anew upon other Principles, and in another Shape. Take my Word for it: there is a plastic Nature in things that seeks its own End. Pull a State to pieces, jumble, confound, and shake together the Particles of Humane Society, and then let them stand a while, and you shall soon see them settle of themselves in some convenient Order, where heavy Heads are lowest, and Men of Genius uppermost.[2]

1 *Reflections*, pp. 31, 32.
2 *Alciphron*, dialogue 11.

The speaker is Lysicles, one of the freethinkers; and so, of course, these are not the views of Berkeley himself. On the contrary, the passage is heavy with irony, as Lysicles damns himself out of his own mouth. It is this that gives the writing such a Swiftian note. Moreover, the style is much more figurative than is usual with Berkeley; and just for that reason it would be hard to find elsewhere, in such short compass, so many of the characteristic and crucial Augustan metaphors. There is first the image of society as a machine ('the Wheels of Government'). Then there is science seen by the Tory, Berkeley, as disruptive and irresponsible ('the noble Experiment of blowing up Systemes ...'). 'Plastic Nature' is a concealed gibe at Shaftesbury and the Cambridge Platonists behind him; Brett quotes examples of the phrase used by Cudworth and Norris.[1] Science is narrowed to the specific science of chemistry (the 'particles' are left to 'stand' and 'settle'). And finally comes the old joke of the bathos ('where heavy Heads are lowest'). By implication (since Lysicles is a fool) there is present another, Burkean image of the State as something which, if blown up, dissolved, remoulded, pulled to pieces, jumbled, confounded, shaken together, and allowed to stand, will be harder to replace than the speaker realizes.

This other society, present by implication, may be in the image of 'the body politic'; we shall tend to think so, if we pick up the echoes (unintended, I am sure) to two famous passages of Shakespeare:

> though the treasure
> Of Nature's germens tumble all together
> Even till destruction sicken; answer me ...[2]

and

> Smite flat the thick rotundity o' the world!
> Crack Nature's moulds, all germens spill at once ...[3]

But it won't do. Berkeley is sincerely appalled at the thought that one should 'jumble, confound, and shake together the Particles of Humane Society'. But his vision of what happens if one does, is not so precise as Shakespeare's,[4] nor so appalled. His metaphors for doing violence to nature in this way are snatched right and left from various fields of activity, which are not co-ordinated into one total picture; when Shakespeare takes an image from science, that image locks into place, not only in that one field but in one impressive structure of human thought over all.

1   R.L. Brett, *The Third Earl of Shaftesbury* (London, 1951), pp. 25, 26.
2   *Macbeth* IV, i. 58–60.
3   *King Lear*, III: ii. 7–8.
4   For the meaning of 'germens' see Walter C. Curry, *Shakespeare's Philosophical Patterns* (Baton Rouge, 1959), ch. II; and cf. *Macbeth*, ed. J.D. Wilson, pp. 149–50.

Thus it is time to admit that the role of the metaphor in Augustan writing, whether of verse or prose, is different from its role in Elizabethan literature. It is not, I think, that there are less metaphors for the Augustans to play with, nor that science and philosophy in their time provided less, or less attractive, metaphors than Elizabethan science and philosophy. But the Augustans are more eclectic. They take their metaphors where they find them, sometimes in Hobbes, sometimes in the alchemists, sometimes in Boyle or Newton, Shakespeare or Milton, Virgil or Homer, often in Latin and Greek etymology. The metaphors of Shakespeare, however apparently diverse, add up to one comprehensive scheme of man's nature and his destiny – this is true at least, by comparison with the Augustans. The Augustan metaphors refer to several 'world-pictures' in turn, the Hobbesian picture among them; and all of these pictures cannot be equally true.

Of this eclecticism it is once again Berkeley's *Alciphron* that provides an example:

> Men are too apt to reduce unknown Things to the Standard of what they know, and bring a Prejudice or Tincture from Things they have been conversant in, to judge thereby of Things in which they have not been conversant. I have known a Fidler gravely teach that the Soul was Harmony; a Geometrician very positive that the Soul must be extended; and a Physician, who having pickled half a Dozen Embryos and dissected as many Rats and Frogs, grew conceited and affirmed there was no Soul at all, and that it was a vulgar Error.

With an unpleasant shock we realize that for Berkeley (this is spoken by Crito, one of his spokesmen against the freethinkers), the idea that the soul is harmony is neither more nor less ridiculous than the idea that it is extended. As he dismisses them together here, so elsewhere he will use them together, or use one or other as he pleases, for metaphors. He can do so because for him a metaphor is merely a figure of speech, not a figure of thought. Here is certainly a contraction not in the field of metaphor, but in man's notions of its validity. There is some evidence that scientists, and still more, scientific philosophers, are at least partly to blame for this contraction; but to explore this would be another story.

Appendix

'Here it may not be amiss to add a few words upon the laudable practice of wearing quilted caps; which is not a matter of mere custom, humour, or fashion, as some would pretend, but an institution of great sagacity and use; these, when moistened with sweat, stop all perspiration, and by reverberating the heat, prevent the spirit from evaporating any way, but at the mouth; even as a skilful housewife, that covers her still with a wet clout, for the same reason, and finds the same effect.

'... upon these, and the like reasons, certain objectors pretended to put it beyond all doubt, that there must be a sort of preternatural spirit possessing the heads of the modern saints; and some will have it to be the heat of zeal working upon the dregs of ignorance, as other spirits are produced from lees by the force of fire.

'... I am apt to imagine, that the seed or principle which has ever put men upon visions in things invisible, is of a corporeal nature; for the profounder chemists inform us, that the strongest spirits may be extracted from human flesh. Besides, the spinal marrow, being nothing else but a continuation of the brain, must needs create a very free communication between the superior faculties and those below: and thus the *thorn in the flesh* serves for a spur to the spirit. I think, it is agreed among physicians, that nothing affects the head as much as a tentiginous humour, repelled and elated to the upper region, found, by daily practice, to run frequently up into madness.'

Swift, *A Discourse on the Mechanical Operation of the Spirit* (1704)

The Language of Science and the Language of Literature 1700–1740 (London & New York: Sheed & Ward, 1963).

VII The Deserted Village:
Poem as Virtual History

Mrs Susanne Langer has written a sequel to her brilliant and momentous *Philosophy in a New Key*. The new book, *Feeling and Form*,[1] is explicitly (see the sub-title) a theory of art developed from the earlier work. And this puts me in a queer position. For, discussing *Philosophy in a New Key* in these pages,[2] I tried to draw out the implications of that book for aesthetics, in particular for literary theory. Now Mrs Langer has done the job herself, and has done it much better. It seems that I underrated Mrs Langer, and that *Philosophy in a New Key* can be made to yield an aesthetics altogether more respectable than I thought.

There is, after all, some excuse for my mistake. It was unexpected enough, as I said at the time, to find a philosopher with a real grasp of what it feels like to listen to a sonata and to read a poem. I could surely be forgiven for supposing that she would not have as firm a grasp of the difference between reading a poem and listening to a sonata, as she had of what was common to these two activities. Forgivable or not, that was the mistake I made. Supposing that Mrs Langer was more at home with music than with the other arts (I think I'm right about that still, but am no longer so sure), I supposed that the flaw in her literary theory would come from confusing poetry with music. I was wrong. But then, who would have bargained for a philosopher-musician, who, turning to poetry, could produce a whole chapter full of admirably rapid yet subtle analyses of very various poems? Yet so it is. And there are equally illuminating chapters on painting, on sculpture, architecture, the dance, the novel and the drama. Mrs Langer is a prodigy. I can only withdraw all my earlier criticisms and proceed, in all humility, to expound her thesis.

Aesthetics has for long been the poor relation of philosophy and only an embarrassing distraction for the specialist critics of each of the arts. Mrs Langer redeems it, and chiefly by putting first things first. Instead of asking 'What is the function of the work of art for the artist who produces it?' or, on the other hand, 'What is the effect of a work of art on those

1   Susanne K. Langer. *Feeling and Form* (London, 1953).
2   Davie, 'Syntax in Poetry and Music', *The Twentieth Century*, CLIII (February 1953), pp. 128–34.

who respond to it?' she asks 'What *is* it? What *is* a work of art?' She answers herself by saying that every artefact is an abstraction:

> All forms in art, then, are abstracted forms; their content is only a semblance, a pure appearance, whose function is to make them, too, apparent – more freely and wholly apparent than they could be if they were exemplified in a context of real circumstance and anxious interest. It is in this elementary sense that all art is abstract. Its very substance, quality without practical significance, is an abstraction from material existence; ...
>
> But abstract form as such is not an artistic ideal. To carry abstraction as far as possible, and achieve pure form in only the barest conceptual medium, is a logician's business, not a painter's or poet's. In art forms are abstracted only to be made clearly apparent, and are freed from their common uses only to be put to new uses: to act as symbols, to become expressive of human feeling.
>
> An artistic symbol is a much more intricate thing than what we usually think of as a form, because it involves *all* the relationships of its elements to one another, all similarities and differences of quality, not only geometric or other familiar relations. That is why qualities enter directly into the form itself, not as its contents, but as constitutive elements in it. Our scientific convention of abstracting mathematical forms, which do not involve quality, and fitting them to experience, always makes qualitative factors 'content'; and as scientific conventions rule our academic thinking, it has usually been taken for granted that in understanding art, too, one should think of form as opposed to qualitative 'content'. But on this uncritical assumption the whole conception of form and content comes to grief, and analysis ends in the confused assertion that art is 'formed content', form and content are one. (pp. 50, 51)

It is here, in her use of 'symbol' that Mrs Langer leans most heavily on her earlier book; for 'symbol' is her 'new key'. When she says that art forms 'act as symbols, to become expressive of human feeling', not only 'symbol' but also 'expressive' and 'feeling', have rather special meanings. A symbol does not express a feeling, as a signal expresses what it stands for, or as a symptom expresses what causes it. In fact, normal usage balks at using 'expression' in these latter cases:

> When we say that something is well expressed, we do not necessarily believe the expressed idea to refer to our present situation or even to be true, but only to be given clearly and objectively for contemplation. Such 'expression' is the function of symbols: articulation and presentation of *concepts*. Herein symbols differ radically from signals. A signal is comprehended if it serves to make us notice the object or situation it bespeaks. A symbol is understood when we conceive the idea it presents. (p. 26.)

Hence what is expressed by an artefact conceived as a symbol in this sense is *a concept of feeling*. This lifts art out of the trough of the 'emotive' where the positivists would leave it, and it makes the feeling expressed in the artefact something distinct from the emotions of the artist in creating it, and from the emotions of the perceiver in responding to it. It also enables Mrs Langer to adopt Clive Bell's notion of 'significant form' while leaving behind his 'aesthetic emotion'.

The arts, according to Mrs Langer (and this is where I under-rated her), are distinguished one from another not by the different media they employ, but by the different abstractions they make from actuality. The first advantage of this is that she evades the pit-fall of purity ('pure poetry', 'pure music'), which I had envisaged as yawning in her path. The peculiar illusion or 'semblance' which each art creates is determined by the abstraction it makes. Thus all the plastic arts create the semblance of *virtual space*. Among the plastic arts, painting creates a semblance of virtual space in the form of *virtual scene;* sculpture in the form of *virtual kinetic volume*; and architecture, in the form of *virtual place*, or, as Mrs Langer calls it, *an ethnic domain*. These formulae, of course, mean little by themselves. The sculptural semblance of virtual volume for instance, differs from actual volume in several ways, notably:

> It is more than the bulk of the figure; it is a space made visible, and is more than the area which the figure actually occupies. The tangible form has a complement of empty space that it absolutely commands, that is given with it and only with it, and is, in fact, part of the sculptural volume. The figure itself seems to have a sort of continuity with the emptiness around it, however much its solid masses may assert themselves as such. (p. 88.)

Or consider Mrs Langer's very apt and compelling example of how, in architecture, virtual place is abstracted from actual place. A Gypsy encampment is on the site of what was once a Red Indian encampment. Is it the same place, or different? It is the same *actual* place, but a different *virtual* place, for a Gypsy camp is a different place from a Redskin camp. It is place in this second sense with which architecture deals, and it is such virtual place of which it creates semblances, 'ethnic domains'.

Music creates the semblance of *virtual time*. I found this difficult, but only I think because music is the art in which I feel least at home. In distinguishing virtual time from actual time Mrs Langer sometimes sounds like Mr J.B. Priestley and sometimes like Bergson. Her criticism of Bergson is very telling just because it is informed with sympathy: his notion of *la durée pure* she considers an invaluable discovery, but his prejudice against any 'spatializing' concepts forced him to maintain that *durée* could be expressed only formlessly, as mere flow, whereas music expresses the passage of time (the movement from tick to tock which clock-time cannot express) in highly articulated symbolic forms.

Dance creates the semblance of *virtual powers*. Mime is not essential to it. Gesture, normally a vehicle of self-expression more intimate even than language, is used by the dancers to express a feeling that they only imagine or conceive themselves as experiencing. The powers which seem to hold two dancers in tension, now drawn together, now flung apart, are not any actual powers, erotic or other, but virtual powers abstracted from these.

'Poesis' creates the semblance of *virtual experience* or *virtual events*, which differ from actual experience or actual events in that every item of the experience presented is an emotional factor, having emotional value. At this point occurs the chapter to which I referred, made up of analyses of 'Tyger, tyger, burning bright', of a poem by Li Ts'ao translated by Witter Bynner, of Herrick's 'A Sweet disorder in the dress', and of other poems by Blake, Mr De La Mare, and Goldsmith. I quarrel only with the last of these, a passage from *The Deserted Village*, to which I will return.

Within 'poesis', different literary forms are distinguished largely in terms of their governing tense. Lyric occurs in a virtual present, narrative (whether in verse or prose – the distinction is unimportant) in a virtual past, drama in a virtual future. If this seems queer, how do we account for the fact that, in telling over to another person the plot of a novel or a narrative poem, we invariably cast the narrative in the present tense? According to Mrs Langer this is our acknowledgment that the artistic shaping, the abstraction, comes with the casting of the whole into the past tense, in the form of *virtual memory*, which differs from actual memory in that every item remembered has a quality of relevant feeling. Again, the tense of drama is the future because every situation presented in drama is big with ominous consequence; so that 'the future appears as already an entity, embryonic in the present'. In comedy the future appears in the image of Fortune: the comic hero, continually thrown off balance by chance events, always regains his equilibrium and in doing so follows the rhythm of all organic life. In tragedy, however, the future appears in the image of Fate: the tragic hero, however often he regains his balance, is fated to be unbalanced for good and all eventually, and in thus riding for an ultimate fall, he follows the rhythm of specifically human life, conscious of the death that ends every career.

What is so striking about this ambitious structure is not so much its symmetrical neatness, as the way in which every distinction on which it rests, like the one quoted about sculptural volume, is informed with sensibility. The symmetry, in fact, is suspect: as each new distinction comes up, one expects the theorist to show her hand and fall to schematizing, but in fact each one justifies itself as defining more nearly what we ourselves have felt in responding to sculpture, to comedy, to whatever else.

In literary criticism at any rate – and it is with literary theory that I shall now concern myself – I think there is no one of the current procedures which escapes unscathed from Mrs Langer's analysis. If we argue from origins ('drama evolved from dance, and dance from ritual; therefore drama at bottom is rite'), she tells us brusquely that drama as we now have it, dance as we now have it, is something *sui generis*, and that to unearth origins and trace developments is at best history, at worst antiquarianism, and in either case wholly irrelevant to criticism. The same holds for all our tracing of images to archetypes in folklore and mythology; having done that, we have still only assembled the raw materials – what matters is the use made of them. But the other wing of literary-critical opinion is under fire no less. However the followers of I.A. Richards may differ from the followers of William Empson and those again from the disciples of F.R. Leavis, all practise a method that will not do for Mrs Langer:

> Whatever our integrated organic response may be, it is a response not to cumulative little verbal stimuli – a precariously sustained progress of memories, associations, unconscious wishes, emotions – but a response to a strongly articulated *virtual experience*, one dominant stimulus. (p. 215.)

Yet if this embarrasses the American New Critics, those who have lately arisen to challenge the New-Critical procedure (e.g. Mr J.V. Cunningham[1] or Miss Rosemond Tuve[2]) get even shorter shrift. Miss Tuve, for instance, asks us, in dealing with seventeenth-century poetry, to make a distinction between 'the thoughts a man had' and 'a man having thoughts'; but there is no room for this distinction in Mrs Langer's theory, when she says of reflective poems, 'Essentially they create the *semblance* of reasoning; of the seriousness, strain and progress, the sense of growing knowledge, growing clearness and conviction – the whole experience of philosophical thinking.' As she says, 'it is not a proposition, but the entertainment of one, which necessarily involves vital tensions, feelings.'

Like any other critic, I have invested too heavily in some of these disciplines to be able to see Mrs Langer's alternative for what it is worth. The re-orientation she demands is too complete to be made on the spur of a moment. I do not myself know where I stand, and any criticisms I offer will be attempts to explore some implications which, until I explore them, are no clearer to me than to anyone else.

In the first place, as might be expected perhaps of a philosopher, Mrs Langer seems to give little credit to the historical approach. Her own historical perspective is that of her master, Ernst Cassirer, and of Owen Barfield. She sees the history of the human mind in terms of its gradual

1 J.V. Cunningham, 'Logic and Lyric', *Modern Philology* (August 1953), pp. 33–41.
2 Rosemond Tuve, *Elizabethan and Metaphysical Imagery* (Chicago, 1947).

evolution from mythic thinking, which determines the form of language, is supported and furthered by language (in the shape of metaphor) and yet is ultimately driven out by language, as syntax gradually begets discursive thought and so supersedes mythic thinking by scientific thinking. This shift, she says, is probably never complete, and is more nearly complete for some persons and groups of persons than for others. This is all very well; but it could be argued that this is too long a perspective to be of much practical use to the literary historian, who requires to know rather how far the shift has gone for certain groups of persons at certain times. As literary historians and as critics of any past literature, we need to know the history of language in far more detail than Mrs Langer allows for. Thus Miss Tuve might maintain, against Mrs Langer, that for Philip Sidney and John Donne alike the shift to discursive reason had gone so far that their poems move right outside of what Mrs Langer takes to be poetry. And so too Mr F.W. Bateson's case about 'A sweet disorder in the dress', which Mrs Langer dismisses in a footnote, rests on a verifiable observation about the connotations, in Herrick's time, of the word 'precise'.

In the same way, when Mr I.A. Richards treats the reading of a poem as an infinitely delicate and hazardous operation, we may agree with Mrs Langer that this view of the correct response is just as precious as Clive Bell's 'aesthetic emotion' which it was designed to laugh out of court, and we may further agree with her that, other things being equal, a poem should command our attention quite imperiously. But in *Practical Criticism*, it may appear, Mr Richards presented nearly unimpeachable evidence that at the present day other things are not equal, that our culture is at a stage of its history when – never mind for what reasons – the accurate reading of a poem is, for most people, a very hazardous and delicate business indeed. The class-room and lecture-hall techniques now most in use for the teaching of literary appreciation (outlined in Leavis and Thompson's *Reading and Discrimination*, for instance) were evolved in the light of Mr Richards' findings. Many teachers know by this time that the theoretical assumptions on which they are based are rather shaky, and that this limits their effectiveness. But they are still the best available, however weak their theoretical foundations, just because they take into account the many obstacles (pulp-literature, noise, advertising, background music, and so on) which the untutored person today has to surmount before he can learn to respond to a poem. We may hope for new techniques based on Mrs Langer's better theory. But anyone concerned with the teaching of literature will smile wryly at any technique based on the contention that a good poem will (nowadays) impose itself on the reader, demanding imperiously just the sort of attention it wants, and no other.

If I now take issue with Mrs Langer on the score of Goldsmith's 'Deserted Village', it is not so much for the sake of that poem in itself (though certainly I esteem it more highly than she does), as for the chance of thus seeing, in a specific instance, how her theory works out in practice. Mrs Langer is led to consider this poem because she is taking up the challenge of Dr Tillyard in his *Poetry Direct and Oblique*, where he contrasts eighteen lines from Goldsmith's poem with Blake's 'The Echoing Green'. For him Goldsmith's poetry is direct, in that the poet 'wants the reader to think primarily of villages when he talks of Auburn', whereas Blake's is oblique, in that the poet, though he writes of a village, wants the reader to think, not primarily of villages, but of something illuminated by them, the whole idea of fruition. Mrs Langer will have none of this, since for her there can be only one kind of poetry. For her both poems are equally 'oblique', since both are *created virtual histories*. Just as the import of 'The Echoing Green' is not some idea standing apart from and oblique to the literal sense, so the import of *The Deserted Village* is not exhausted by the literal sense. Each poem presents village life as a virtual history, and the import of each is created in the process of abstraction by which the actual history becomes virtual. Many readers, I suspect, will have been dissatisfied with Dr Tillyard's argument here, though they may not phrase their dissatisfaction in Mrs Langer's terms; and in fact Dr Tillyard himself seems apologetic about his own distinction. I am not concerned to vindicate Dr Tillyard, but rather to argue that a better case can be made for *The Deserted Village* in Mrs Langer's own terms.

The passage immediately in question is as follows:

> How often have I loitered o'er thy green,
> Where humble happiness endeared each scene!
> How often have I paused on every charm,
> The sheltered cot, the cultivated farm,
> The never-failing brook, the busy mill,
> The decent church that topt the neighbouring hill,
> The hawthorn bush, with seats beneath the shade,
> For talking age and whispering lovers made!
> How often have I blessed the coming day,
> When toil remitting lent its turn to play,
> And all the village train from labour free
> Led up their sports beneath the spreading tree,
> While many a pastime circled in the shade,
> The young contending as the old surveyed;
> And many a gambol frolicked o'er the ground,
> And sleights of art and feats of strength went round;
> And still as each repeated pleasure tired,
> Succeeding sports the mirthful band inspired.[1]

---

1   Mrs Langer has 'youthful' for 'mirthful' in the last line.

According to Mrs Langer, the green is here established as the dancing-place to which the brook, the mill, the cot, the farm, and the *decent* church (giving 'social sanction' and 'divine chaperonage' to the dance) are related, not as contiguous in actual space, but symbolically. The references, 'beneath the shade', 'in the shade', 'beneath the spreading tree', draw the Magic Circle of the dancers, and the dance itself is enacted in such phrases as 'lent its turn', 'circled', 'frolick'd o'er the ground', 'went round', *'repeated* pleasure', *'succeeding* sports'.

Mrs Langer goes on:

> The alternating partners are youth and age, the dance is the Dance of Life, and Goldsmith's village is the human scene. As such, the fragment Professor Tillyard chose to treat as 'statement poetry' is only one half of the contrast which is the guideline of the whole poem: element for element the dance is opposed to the later scene, wherein the green is overgrown, the brook choked and marshy, the church unvisited, the farms abandoned. Had Goldsmith limited the description of Auburn revisited to this antithesis, and given the reason – the encroachment of an irresponsible aristocracy on the sober, balanced, rural economy – in a few striking words, he would have written a strong poem. The moral would have been an artistic element, the shadow of unfeeling and brute force dispelling the natural rhythm of human life. But the poem is longer than his poetic idea; that is why it ends up 'moralizing', and gets lost in weak literal appeal. (pp. 232, 233.)

In venturing this judgement Mrs Langer goes outside her own brief, since she has declared in her Introduction that her book 'does not offer criteria for judging "masterpieces", nor even successful as against unsuccessful lesser works – pictures, poems, musical pieces, dances, or any other'. Plainly such criteria are offered here, but on the whole Mrs Langer observes the limitations she imposes. This passage on Goldsmith is exceptional.

I am not clear about the complementary 'later scene' to which Mrs. Langer refers, for I do not find a reference in the poem to 'the church unvisited'. But the green is overgrown, the brook choked, and the farms abandoned, already by line 50; and the reason for this, encroachment on the rural economy, is given by line 75. The remaining 355 lines of the poem are therefore, according to Mrs Langer, superfluous. This is to lop it back with a vengeance! But in any case the whole argument about 'the intricacy of a group dance' in or behind the lines quoted is surely a clear case of misplaced ingenuity, of reading into the poem, not reading out of it. Mrs Langer focuses on the green and makes it the focus of the village because it is at the end of the first line quoted and also, I suspect, because it certainly is the focus of the poem by Blake with which the Goldsmith passage is compared. Coming where it does in the poem, at the end of the

seventh line, it draws no attention to itself, and is only one item, no more
and no less important than church, mill, farm, brook, and cot. Hence the
church looks down from its hill not on the green but on the village as a
whole – it may even be on the opposite side of the village from the green.
As for 'lent its turn', 'went round', *'repeated* pleasure', *'succeeding* sports',
their dancing pattern of turning, circling, alternating, and so on, would
not be apparent to the eighteenth-century reader, for whom they were
part of the current small-change of poetical expression. But the conclusive argument against Mrs Langer's interpretation appears if we extend
the quotation for a further six lines:

> The dancing pair that simply sought renown,
> By holding out to tire each other down;
> The swain mistrustless of his smutted face,
> While secret laughter titter'd round the place;
> The bashful virgin's sidelong looks of love,
> The matron's glance that would those looks reprove.

This makes it plain that for Goldsmith dancing is only one in a catalogue
of several activities (others are flirtations, and horseplay with smutty
faces), which take place on the green.

It is worth considering what would happen if, having disposed of Mrs
Langer's case for the poem, we should revert to Dr Tillyard's. Mrs Langer
could still find a place for it, though not under poetry. It would come, on
Dr Tillyard's showing, into what Mrs Langer calls applied art, discursive
writing such as the essay, the biography, historical and philosophical
exposition, all of which, she agrees, can become art. The fact of its being
cast in verse form should not keep it out of this category any more than
Johnson's *Rasselas* or Berkeley's or Plato's dialogues should be kept out of
it simply by being cast in the form of fiction. (*Rasselas* is plainly not fiction
in the semblance of *virtual memory*, which is Mrs Langer's name for the
primary abstraction of the true novel and the narrative poem.) The odd
thing is that *The Deserted Village* would make a better showing as excellent discursive writing in verse than as the very imperfect poem that Mrs
Langer conceives it to be. For having (rightly, I think) discarded the false
criterion of 'purity', Mrs Langer sets up no hierarchy among her categories; and so there is no implication that 'applied art', whether in literature or in plastic design, is in any way inferior to 'fine art'. Moreover Mrs
Langer herself encourages such fast work in the slipping of awkward cases
from one genre to another; it may take some readers' breath away to find
her, for instance, classing all the plays of Racine and Corneille as heroic
comedies. (Incidentally one would like a fuller account or a more elaborate system of literary genres: could not comedy, for instance, here treated
solely as a dramatic form, be made to cover some non-dramatic works?
The very suggestive account of the nature of laughter makes me want to

include under 'comedy' such poems as Louis MacNiece's 'Bag-Pipe Music' or some of Cleveland's brilliant bravura-pieces of heartless wit.)

But there is no need to take *The Deserted Village* on Dr Tillyard's terms. We can agree that it is a virtual history like 'The Echoing Green' without the help of Mrs Langer's unacceptable fantasy about the dance and without rejecting, as she does, most of the poem as it stands. As a virtual history of village life Goldsmith's poem differs from Blake's only in presenting a different semblance and so a different feeling. 'The Echoing Green' confidently expresses the rhythm of fruition, generation succeeding generation, as something robust and hardy; *The Deserted Village* expresses it as frail and thoroughly vulnerable. The cycles of unflurried fruition to which Goldsmith looks back are, in line 69, 'Those gentle hours that plenty bade to bloom'. As fugitive and temporary as a flower or as the bloom on the skin of a fruit (line 128: 'But all the blooming flush of life is fled'), they required special conditions in which to flourish and could be blasted with ease:

> Princes and lords may flourish, or may fade;
> A breath can make them, as a breath has made:
> But a bold peasantry, their country's pride,
> When once destroyed, can never be supplied.

'Bold' in these famous lines is the sturdiest, most militant epithet applied in the poem to what is more frequently called 'gentle' or 'harmless'. Yet even here the effect is thoroughly ambiguous, for if princes and lords can be made by a mere breath, there is no implication that they can be got rid of so easily; perhaps a bold peasantry, that cannot be made so easily, can be unmade with no trouble at all. And what *is* certain is that lords and princes are always in good supply, where peasants aren't. The whole drift of the passage is towards presenting the peasants, who embody the rhythms of fruition, as altogether more difficult to maintain than the gentry and the merchants who encroach on them.

This feeling is first announced in the second couplet:

> Where smiling spring its earliest visit paid,
> And parting summer's lingering blooms delay'd.

A floating petal comes to rest – what could be more fugitive? (That logically the petal has nothing to do with the village life does not matter; it is the emotional timbre of the image which counts.) It is important to notice that rather oafish horseplay is to be found on the green as well as dancing (and anyway the dancing itself is rather oafish – 'By holding out to tire each other down'). Goldsmith's swains differ from Blake's in being, from one point of view, yokels, clodpoles – 'And the loud laugh that spoke the vacant mind'; that is part of their vulnerability when once the more knowing tradesmen get among them. For this reason the vicar, good as he is, is made 'unskilled', eminently gullible, ineffectual in worldly matters like the Vicar of Wakefield; so too the pedagogue's absurd pretensions to learning, and the ease with which he impressed his gaping audience. The first passage ends with 'all these charms are fled' (there is an overtone of timorousness in 'fled'), to be echoed almost at once,

> Thy sports are fled, and all thy charms withdrawn:
> Amidst thy bowers the tyrant's hand is seen,
> And desolation saddens all thy green!

One snatch of a muscular hand, and the whole way of life crumbles. And the villagers, of course, offer no resistance:

> And, trembling, shrinking from the spoiler's hand,
> Far, far away thy children leave the land.

The encroaching powers are seen in terms of bulk and weight:

> Along the lawn, where scatter'd hamlets rose,
> Unwieldy wealth, and cumbrous pomp repose;

The hamlets, and their way of life, are crushed like flowers under a dead weight laid upon them. 'Cumbrous pomp' becomes 'long pomp' in line 259, and 'long-drawn pomp' in line 317. To sustain this pomp, in line 269, 'Proud swells the tide with loads of freighted ore', and even in its fall, the power of commercial luxury is presented in terms of mass:

> Kingdoms by thee, to sickly greatness grown,
> Boast of a florid vigour not their own;
> At every draught more large and large they grow,
> A bloated mass of rank unwieldy woe;
> Till sapp'd their strength, and every part unsound,
> Down, down they sink, and spread a ruin round.

(The word 'rank', incidentally, links this domain of luxury to the domain of fearful luxuriance in the tropics to which the dispossessed emigrants flee.) To set against this mass and weight, the rural way of life can provide only 'innocence' and 'sweet confusion', sounds 'soften'd' by distance and carried on the 'whispering wind', 'murmurs' that 'fluctuate in the gale', an alehouse that is a 'tottering mansion', a cottage (line 329) that shelters its inhabitants only as a thorn shelters a primrose, and

> The breezy covert of the warbling grove,
> That only shelter'd thefts of harmless love.

Where only such poor defences are available, well may the poet ask:

> Where then, ah! where shall poverty reside,
> To scape the pressure of contiguous pride?

No wonder that when the poet recollects the hopes he once entertained
of ending his days in Auburn, he should think of it in terms of husbanding
out a taper, nursing a dying flame, of a hare returning to its form pursued
by hound and horn, and of a gentle gradient into death, smoothed by
resignation. (That the taper refers logically to the ebbing life, again makes
no difference; the emotional timbre of the image contributes to the total
symbolic form.) No wonder, finally, that the poet applauds the man who
'since 'tis hard to combat, learns to fly', and that, at the end of the poem,
'sweet Poetry' should be celebrated as 'Still first to fly where sensual joys
invade'.

The upshot of this analysis, which is not of course exhaustive, I take to
be this: that *The Deserted Village* is a virtual history like 'The Echoing
Green', and a symbol articulated more closely and intricately than Blake's.
Blake's poem is perfect in its narrow compass as Goldsmith's on its much
larger scale. And the only part of the poem that will not fit this interpretation consists of the four last lines, splendid in themselves but in
emotional tenor out of keeping with the rest; and, sure enough, Boswell
records that these lines were supplied by Johnson.

I believe that the import of this poem, considered as one symbolic
form, had been borne in upon me long before I chose to confirm it and
bring it into consciousness for myself, by subjecting it to analysis. I agree
with Mrs Langer, in other words, that my understanding of the poem was
not a process of response to successive verbal stimuli, though that is up to
a point how I have had to deal with it in presenting my analysis. Hence,
though my interpretation differs radically from Mrs Langer's, I can regard
it as some sort of vindication of her theory. Yet if Mrs Langer's interpretation satisfied her, presumably for her the virtual history had a different
import. So perhaps a poem does not impose its import quite so imperiously as she supposes, on even a very alert and sensitive mind. We can
hardly afford, it seems, however much we applaud her theory, to abandon
our working assumption that nowadays the proper reading of a poem is a
very risky and delicate operation indeed.

VIII Dramatic Poetry: Dryden's Conversation-Piece

For all the syllabus-makers may say, the *Essay of Dramatic Poesy* is not a masterpiece of our criticism. Its strongest claim on our attention is not as criticism but as conversation-piece – meaning by that, what it has meant to some painters, an idealized picture of ideally civilized social behaviour. And even from that point of view, one may object either that the society is not idealized enough, or else that the society in question does not deserve what Dryden claims for it.

To say that the piece as a whole is not great criticism, not criticism at all, is not to deny, of course, that great criticism is to be found in it. There is, for instance, the examen of *The Silent Woman*, still an excellent introduction to a neglected play; there are the rapid firm delineations of Shakespeare, Beaumont and Fletcher, and Jonson; and there are excellent things in the last few pages, about the use of rhymed verse on the stage. But it can hardly be denied that these are the plums in what is sometimes very suety pudding. No one can be much interested in the issues of Ancient versus Modern drama, or the French tradition versus the English. These questions are 'dated' of course; but that is not the whole of it. Many issues raised in Sidney's *Apologie* are dated; yet a sympathetic reader can re-phrase those issues in terms more suitable to the present day, and can find that they are of living, because perennial, interest. He cannot do this with Dryden's essay. There the issues are dated in another way, more seriously; we are bored not only by the questions themselves, but by the way they are debated. The discussions, as Dryden presents them, are unavoidably inconclusive, because they are so nebulous.

Dryden could have asked, or implied, the questions: Am I, in my next play, to observe the unities? Am I to take Corneille for my model, or Shakespeare? Posed in this fashion, the question of French versus English drama could have come to life; for it would have taken account of the poet's peculiar temperament, his personal aptitudes and limitations, the sort of actors for whom he wrote, the expectations of his audience. And it is obvious that this is how these questions presented themselves to Dryden; but he chose to present them to his reader in a way that drained them of all this vitality. One begins to think that Dryden had not decided what it was he sought to do. If this was to be a conversation-piece, why make the talk about literature? Or else, if Dryden wanted to talk about literature, why do so at the level of the dilettante? As it stands, the essay is neither one thing nor the other. The two halves pull away.

The non-critical aspect of the Essay is announced in the Dedication:

> And yet, my Lord, this war of opinions, you well know, has fallen out among the writers of all ages, and sometimes betwixt friends. Only it has been prosecuted by some, like pedants, with violence of words, and managed by others, like gentlemen, with candour and civility.

Dryden intends to show that literary debates can be conducted with candour and civility. It cannot be said that he succeeds. In his endeavours to be a gentleman, he forgets not to be dull. And the experiment worked no better in life than in literature; for Sir Robert Howard, the Crites of the *Essay*, took offence at the only passage where Dryden speaks with a certain warmth and force. And because they could not agree about rhyme in dramatic verse, Howard and Dryden not only argued the point in later writings but were barely civil to each other when they met.

The first pages of the essay show the conversation-piece at its best. Everyone remembers the setting of the scene, as the four gentlemen row out to a place where they can hear the sound of the naval engagement at the river's mouth:

> and then, every one favouring his own curiosity with a strict silence, it was not long ere they perceived the air to break about them like the noise of distant thunder, or of swallows in a chimney: those little undulations of sound, though almost vanishing before they reached them, yet still seeming to retain somewhat of their first horror, which they had betwixt the fleets.

What is less often remembered is that this is not just a setting of the scene, a sort of ornamental frame. This is not just a prelude, announcing a pretty theme not picked up again before the end. One convention governs the whole, or nearly the whole; and if the reader forgets that he is listening to gentlemen conversing on a boating-excursion, the writer does not forget. The prose is as firmly controlled when Eugenius extols the Moderns, as before the talk has started. Dryden never forgets that he can discuss French or Greek drama only in the terms and at the temperature of a gentlemanly relaxation. That is why, when we look for critical penetration, we are for the most part disappointed.

Almost from the start the talk takes a literary turn. This is beautifully handled, and the transition, from the supposed victory to the panegyrics upon it, is admirably smooth. This gives Dryden a chance to comment upon verse in general, before the discussion is narrowed to dramatic verse. The exercise of wit, by Lisideius and Crites, upon the two 'extremities of poetry', illuminates, of course, Dryden's problems in *Annus*

Mirabilis, which he was writing at the same time as the *Essay*. All the same, that is just what this is — an exercise of wit, the pleasantry of an intelligent amateur, not the analysis of a practising poet. Already Dryden is in trouble with the convention he has chosen; for what he wants to say about the decadence of the 'metaphysical' tradition is not exhausted by Lisideius' epigrams about Clevelandism. Later in the essay he manoeuvres into a position from which he can return to the theme and Eugenius is made to digress from Plautus, so as to compare him with Cleveland, and then wander further into comparing Cleveland with Donne. The digression is anything but natural, and the manoeuvre is clumsy. This later passage, in fact, is one of the points where the essay cracks up in the stress of conflicting intentions.

A more obvious, yet more complicated example of this strain occurs early in Crites' speech for the Ancients against the Moderns:

> Dramatic Poesy had time enough, reckoning from Thespis (who first invented it) to Aristophanes, to be born, to grow up, and to flourish in maturity. It has been observed of arts and sciences that in one and the same century they have arrived to great perfection; and no wonder, since every age has a kind of universal genius, which inclines those that live in it to some particular studies: the work then, being pushed on by many hands, must of necessity go forward.
>
> Is it not evident, in these last hundred years, when the study of philosophy has been the business of all the Virtuosi in Christendom, that almost a new Nature has been revealed to us? That more errors of the school have been detected, more useful experiments in philosophy have been made, more noble secrets in optics, medicine, anatomy, astronomy discovered, than in all those credulous and doting ages from Aristotle to us? — so true it is, that nothing spreads more fast than science, when rightly and generally cultivated.

This is flagrant. If Dryden needed or wanted to pay a compliment to the Royal Society, he could have done so more gracefully and plausibly at almost any other point. Crites does not even pursue his observation by evoking the 'universal genius' of Athens, of which literary achievement is only one aspect. The notion of 'universal genius' is pulled in by the ears; it is not merely irrelevant, it is at odds with all that Crites is trying to maintain, and it plays into the hands of his antagonist, as Eugenius is quick to note:

> I deny not what you urge of arts and sciences, that they have flourished in some ages more than others; but your instance in philosophy makes for me: for if natural causes be more known now than in the time of Aristotle, because more studied, it follows that poesy and other arts may, with the same pains, arrive still nearer to perfection …

There is, I conceive, only one explanation of Dryden's clumsiness in giving to Crites such obviously inappropriate sentiments. Feeling the want in the supposed discussion of any cut and thrust, he attempts to supply it by deliberately giving to one speaker an argument which can be turned upon him by another. But he does so most inefficiently, revealing the whole contrivance to the least attentive reader. And if we pursue the question a stage further, and ask why he was so clumsy, the most likely explanation appears to be that he knew he was giving to his conversationalists a disinterested agility that they did not possess. I think he felt uncomfortably that in reality the cut and thrust would not have been verbal only.

In other words, Dryden, in trying to show that gentlemen could argue with candour and civility, was going beyond the pattern that the society of his time could furnish. It is true that there is some evidence for just such urbanity in Charles II himself, who could, it seems, take a joke against himself. But after all the Addisonian reformation of manners had not yet taken place,[1] and there is some reason for supposing that in reality the Buckhursts, Sedleys and Howards modelled themselves on the older pattern of gentility:

> greatly to find quarrel in a straw
> When honour's at the stake.

If this explanation is correct, it explains why all the set discussions in the *Essay* are so dull. For if Sedley and Howard could not brook contradiction, Dryden, when he involved them in argument, had to phrase the argument so vaguely that no one of these touchy gentlemen should ever need to reach for his sword. (He had to do so, that is, if he was to keep in touch with the social reality at all.) It has been pointed out for instance that the only principle all four speakers have in common is that of 'Nature', and yet when they appeal to 'Nature' they do not all mean the same thing. The point is made by a pair of recent editors:

> It soon becomes apparent in reading these arguments that the chief terms of the disagreement result from two conceptions of the word 'Nature'. The first, which gives Crites and Lisideius their backing, is that Nature teaches restraint, preciseness, that the artist must imitate the generality of Nature, that is to say, he must present aspects which represent the essence or the class of the feature described. Minor variations are not allowed room, for these peculiarities and individual differences are not a part of the eternal truth that the poet must imitate in Nature. The opposite view is supported by Neander, who follows

1   See C.S. Lewis, 'Addison', in *Essays on the Eighteenth Century presented to David Nichol Smith*, p. 7.

the idea that Nature teaches variety and copiousness. The poet, in this view, must present Nature in all her aspects, her infinite variety on the single pattern.[1]

The editors do more than justice to Crites and Lisideius. The speakers are at all times much further than this would suggest from defining the terms they use. They had to be. If they had offered definitions, disagreement among them would have been sharper than anything Dryden could risk. Only one definition is offered in the essay, and that by Lisideius, who defines a play as *'A just and lively image of human nature, representing its passions and humours, and the changes of fortune to which it is subject, for the delight and instruction of mankind.'* There is a show, but only a show, of disagreement:

> This definition, though Crites raised a logical objection against it – that it was only *genere et fine*, and so not altogether perfect, was yet well received by the rest ...

We are left to take the speech as being merely in character, remembering that Crites is 'a person of a sharp judgement, and somewhat too delicate a taste in wit, which the world have mistaken in him for ill-nature'. But in fact his objection has substance; since the missing logical term, the *differentia*, is not one that we can do without. Without it, the definition offered by Lisideius comprises the novel no less than the drama. But this is typical of the whole essay; Dryden has to sidestep the crux of any argument. It is only shadow-boxing after all.

It is true enough, however, if we allow ourselves to supply the missing crux (as we have to), that we find it in the notion of 'Nature'. And it is true enough, as the editors say, that the speakers differ in their interpretation of following Nature, according as some take it to mean making Nature stand out in clean unfettered lines, by cleaning her of individual accidents and generalizing the instance, while others, notably Neander-Dryden himself, suppose it to mean preserving as many as possible of such accidents, by copiousness. But this is not the only range of disagreement. The speakers differ, as it were, in another dimension, according as some suppose art more natural the more it seems to be artless, while others, notably Neander-Dryden himself, suppose it more natural the more artificial it is. This last contention, which seems only a tiresome paradox to the modern mind, is of course at the bottom of all Renaissance poetic theory. It seems something more than paradox if one argues as follows: human nature is a part of 'Nature', and indeed a specially important part, since man has potentialities, for good and evil, beyond any other creature;

1   H.H. Adams and B. Hathaway, *Dramatic Essays of the Neoclassic Age* (New York, 1950), p. 39.

it follows that man is following nature most faithfully, and revering her most, when he does most to realize his nobler potentialities; artistic creation is one of the noblest of his potentialities, since in it he approaches the divine creativity; hence a poet is more natural the more he is creative, the more he can make his creations stand free from himself, elaborate and self-sufficient. This is the Renaissance argument, and it is Dryden's.

As usual the allegiance is nowhere explicit. It is most nearly so in the last pages where Neander-Dryden disputes with Crites-Howard about the use of rhyme. This argument, the third and last, is conducted on a much higher level than the others. Both Crites and Neander, for instance, take into account the expectations of the audience for which they write:

> And this, Sir, calls to my remembrance the beginning of your discourse, where you told us we should never find the audience favourable to this kind of writing, till we could produce as good plays in rhyme as Ben Jonson, Fletcher and Shakespeare had writ out of it. But it is to raise envy to the living, to compare them with the dead. They are honoured, and almost adored by us, as they deserve; neither do I know any so presumptuous of themselves as to contend with them. Yet give me leave to say thus much, without injury to their ashes; that not only we shall never equal them, but they could never equal themselves, were they to rise and write again. We acknowledge them our fathers in wit; but they have ruined their estates themselves, before they came to their children's hands. There is scarce an humour, a character, or any kind of plot, which they have not used. All comes sullied or wasted to us: and were they to entertain this age, they could not now make so plenteous treatments out of such decayed fortunes. This therefore will be a good argument to us, either not to write at all, or to attempt some other way.

The passage is justly famous. It is, on the one hand, a beautiful example of tact and tactics, the most graceful of compliments, the most engaging sort of modesty. This is its appeal in the convention of the conversation-piece, which here, perhaps because this is Dryden speaking, is suddenly impressive. Yet in another way the passage is out of the convention altogether; these are the facts of the case, after all. The argument is not only graceful, but immediate and compelling. This is the voice of the professional, though it speaks with the tact of the amateur. Literary traditions are seen no longer as so many different modes, each with its peculiar pleasure for the discriminating palate, but seen as the poet sees them, pen in hand – as a rich legacy, certainly, but also as a range of treatments no longer practicable, of things that no longer need to be done, that no longer *can* be done, because they have been done consummately well already. Howard and Dryden in fact are criticizing as poets criticize, no longer as dilettanti.

'Nature', accordingly, gets here a more searching scrutiny than anywhere else in the *Essay*. This is seen most clearly, perhaps, when Howard replies to one of Dryden's arguments for rhyme:

> But verse, you say, circumscribes a quick and luxuriant fancy, which would extend itself too far on every subject, did not the labour which is required to well-turned and polished rhyme set bounds to it. Yet this argument, if granted, would only prove that we may write better in verse, but not more naturally. Neither is it able to evince that; for he who wants judgement to confine his fancy in blank verse, may want it as much in rhyme: and he who has it will avoid errors in both kinds.

As soon as Howard has allowed himself to distinguish between writing well and writing naturally, he draws back and contradicts himself – 'Neither is it able to evince that'. The distinction seems reasonable enough to the modern mind, but it would not seem so to the mind of the Renaissance; for (so Sidney might argue) the better one writes, the more nearly one fulfils the potentialities of human nature, and hence the more 'natural' one is. This is the point at issue between Dryden and Howard – Dryden can agree with Sidney, where Howard cannot.

This does not appear, when Dryden replies to this particular argument. His reply is interesting and impressive for other reasons. It is a good example of what, I tend to think, is Dryden's most enduring contribution to criticism – his practice of using, for the operations of the human mind, a metaphor from corporate human activity. He speaks of the making of a poem as of the mason's building of a house. And as elsewhere he speaks of it as a hunt, with Invention as the spaniel, so here 'Judgement is indeed the master-workman in a play; but he requires many subordinate hands, many tools to his assistance'. It is a range of metaphor which may be preferred to the mechanical metaphors of Locke or the chemical metaphors of Coleridge, when they cover the same field. Again Dryden's reply is interesting because from it we may infer that in his own estimation, Dryden had himself 'a quick and luxuriant fancy', needing discipline rather than stimulus.

But, to return to 'Nature', Dryden's view of it appears most plainly when he defends rhyming repartee:

> But you tell us, this supplying the last half of a verse, or adjoining a whole second to the former, looks more like the design of two, than the answer of one. Suppose we acknowledge it: how comes this confederacy to be more displeasing to you, than in a dance which is well contrived? You see there the united design of many persons to make up one figure: after they have separated themselves in many petty divisions, they rejoin one by one into a gross: the confederacy is

plain amongst them, for chance could never produce anything so beautiful; and yet there is nothing in it that shocks your sight. I acknowledge the hand of art appears in repartee, as of necessity it must in all kind of verse. But there is also the quick and poignant brevity of it (which is an high imitation of Nature in those sudden gusts of passion) to mingle with it; and this, joined with the cadency and sweetness of the rhyme, leaves nothing in the soul of the hearer to desire. 'Tis an art which appears; but it appears only like the shadow-ings of painture, which being to cause the rounding of it, cannot be absent; but while that is considered, they are lost: so while we attend to the other beauties of the matter, the care and labour of the rhyme is carried from us, or at least drowned in its own sweetness, as bees are sometimes buried in their honey. When a poet has found the repartee, the last perfection he can add to it, is to put it into verse. However good the thought may be, however apt the words in which 'tis couched, yet he finds himself at a little unrest, while rhyme is wanting: he cannot leave it till that comes naturally, and then is at ease, and sits down contented.

Given the fact that Dryden and his contemporaries have to write in rhyme, because Shakespeare has done all that can be done with blank-verse, Dryden has only to point out (as he does) that any convention, however stilted, can be made to serve verisimilitude, so long as it is managed well enough to make the audience accept it. Howard is answered, and the argument is closed – or could be. But Dryden goes beyond this, and in the last two sentences he is arguing not that rhyme can do as well as blank-verse, but that, other things being equal, it will always do better. Ballet is not only as natural as drama; potentially, at any rate, it is more natural, and the more nearly drama approaches the dance, the more natural and better it will be.

It is here that Dryden is most the Elizabethan, and the key to his atti-tude is in the phrase, 'high imitation of Nature'. The notion that there can be high imitation and low imitation is as queer to the modern reader as it was (presumably) to Howard. Howard is no fool; he does not think, with some late-Romantic critics, that art is more artistic the more artless ('spontaneous') it is. He knows that artifice is always a part of art; he only thinks that the less the artifice appears in the art, the more natural it is. For him it is all a question of degree: and this is how the question is seen today. But Dryden thinks in another dimension altogether, in terms of 'high' and 'low', as well as 'near' and 'far'. So he can say 'heroic rhyme is nearest Nature, as being the noblest kind of modern verse'. Art must be 'wrought up', geared to its highest pitch, to get near to Nature. It is not a question of slackening a convention until it can accommodate a natural untidiness; it is not even true that between a lax convention and a strait one there is nothing to choose; the convention must be made tighter, more exacting, more austere than ever. And if *ars est celare artem*, then the more artificial the art, the more it deserves credit for concealing itself.

In the histories of literature Dryden figures as an innovator; and rightly so. Yet to his contemporaries, as the man who admired the old-fashioned Shakespeare, and found something to say for the old-fashioned Donne, he may well have seemed rather a conservative. It is probable that he spent more time and energy trying to keep in touch with older native traditions than in breaking free of them to adapt his art to novel conditions. His greatness, from one point of view, is in his knowing how far to give way to the pressure of his age, and where to resist it. Because his age was so different in so many ways from what had gone before, he had to make striking innovations; and naturally these are what impress us most forcibly in his work. But no less striking, perhaps, is the extent to which he was able to conserve older procedures and adapt them. In particular, Dryden's poetry is usually regarded as the first considerable embodiment in practice of the novel Hobbesian poetic theory; and of course this is right. But in theory as in practice he looked back to masters far older than Hobbes – to Sidney and the Renaissance, from whom he learnt more important things than the Three Unities.

Cambridge Journal, 5 (June 1952), pp. 553–61.

IX The Critical Principles of William Cowper

After Ben Jonson, Cowper is the most neglected of our poets. It was Hayley's *Life and Letters* that set the fashion; ever since, no poet has been surrendered so frequently, and with so little compunction, to the tender mercies of the biographer. Such criticism as there is has labelled Cowper 'Romantic precursor'; and it seems that we read his poems only to discover in them things that have been done better since, by Wordsworth or some other. No one will deny that the Wordsworthian and other potentialities are there, but they are surely not the most important things in Cowper's poetry. His work is far more the consummation of one tradition than the prelude to another. 'What is salt in Cowper you can taste only when you have detected that by a stroke of madness he missed, or barely missed, being our true English Horace, that almost more nearly than the rest he hit what the rest had been seeking.'[1] He was very consciously and deliberately a neo-classical poet.

He was, if anything, a defiant rearguard. Already, by the time he wrote, the neo-classical austerity was rare, and the taste was all for florid diction, the sublime, a syrupy metrical smoothness, and melting sensibility. His critical conservatism is apparent enough in the poems that are not read, such as 'Truth', 'Table-talk' and 'Retirement'. It is also apparent in the letters, along with the famous (and genuine) charm; but criticism in the letters is sparse and scattered, and it is only when a number of random judgements are put together, that one sees the consistency of Cowper's conservatism.

For a first exhibit, we may take the lines on Johnson:

> Here Johnson lies – a sage by all allow'd,
> Whom to have bred may well make England proud;
> Whose prose was eloquence, by wisdom taught,
> The graceful vehicle of virtuous thought;
> Whose verse may claim – grave, masculine, and strong,
> Superior praise to the mere poet's song;

---

1 Sir Arthur Quiller-Couch, 'On the Lineage of English Literature' in *On The Art of Writing*, (Guild Books edn), p. 127.

The word 'strong' is not there just for the rhyme; it means something exact. Jeffreys was to say, of some 'very sweet verses' by Rogers, 'They do not, indeed, stir the spirit like the strong lines of Byron'. Going along with 'grave' and 'masculine', Cowper's 'strong' cannot mean anything like that; it means, in fact, 'the strength of Denham', which Johnson had himself described, writing of that poet. By way of proof, one need only point to another complimentary poem, Cowper's stanzas 'To Dr Darwin, author of *The Botanic Garden*':

> We, therefore, pleas'd, extol thy song,
>   Though various, yet complete,
> Rich in embellishment as strong,
>   And learn'd, as it is sweet.

For here, very neatly, Darwin is complimented on his 'strength' in lines which echo most plainly just those hackneyed lines from 'Cooper's Hill' which were taken by Johnson, and indeed by the whole eighteenth century, as the model of that strength.

If there is a master-key to the principles of Augustan poetry (still so little understood), it is Johnson's 'Life of Denham'. There Johnson's description and illustration of 'strength' is masterly; and it would be presumptuous to offer a paraphrase. 'Strength' is a name given to a certain quality of 'compactness' in expression. 'Compactness' is Cowper's word, and we do well to adopt it instead of 'concentration', which is more familiar. Concentration of expression is a form of words which we commonly use when meanings lie one upon another in layers, or sail one above another on different planes. This is the world of William Empson's ambiguities and Cleanth Brooks' ironies. Their characteristic metaphors – meanings in 'layers', meanings on 'levels' – are valuable. But they are not much use when we deal with the Augustans. 'The Castaway' is probably the only poem by Cowper which will respond to treatment in these terms; and it is no coincidence that 'The Castaway' is probably read today far more than any other poem by Cowper, except perhaps 'John Gilpin'. It is a great poem; but it stands alone in Cowper's work. It is in 'a class by itself', but not because it shows Cowper excelling himself, only because it shows him writing in an unusual mode. Layers and levels are not much use, in reading the rest of Cowper; there are only two layers ('tenor' and 'vehicle'), and only one level. His poetry like Denham's is uni-vocal. Its characteristic virtue is the saying one thing at a time as succinctly as possible; not the saying of many things at once. The metaphor here is of a more or less rigid metrical box, into which, by syntactical expertness, an astonishing number of things can be lodged – all of them distinct, all inter-locking. This is the meaning of 'strength'.

By showing that Cowper appeals to 'the strength of Denham', we place him in the tradition not of Johnson alone, but of Pope and Dryden, both of whom appealed back to Denham in the same way. In fact of course the tradition was much older; Carew, long before, had extolled Donne as 'masculine', and Suckling had told Godolphin 'not to write so strong'. Strength did not appear with Denham; he only displayed it precociously, in a form suited for the things Dryden wanted to do. At any rate, for Dryden and for Pope, as is well known, this aspect of their art, represented by Denham, went together with another, represented by Waller, who stood for metrical correctness. In their view, the Denham element was a complement to the Waller element, and vice-versa. Not that the one led naturally into the other; on the contrary, there was tension between them. It was difficult to follow both of them at once, and so, in trying to do so, the poet generated the energy which could give his writing grit and force. Waller stood for the rigidity of the metrical box; the more rigid the metrical frame, the harder it was to pack it as full as Denham did. Conversely it was easy to be as smooth as Waller so long as one was diffuse; the one model counteracted the other.

The lines to Darwin show Cowper taking just these bearings, as Dryden and Pope had done; for 'sweet' stands for Waller, just as 'strong' stands for Denham. It is true, however, that Cowper's view of metre was not Pope's. In passage after passage,[1] he deplored the vicious taste of his time for a cloying smoothness in cadence, and insisted on a certain rough-ness in metre, a redundant syllable or a reversed foot. So, although no poet (not even Hopkins) was more an admirer of Milton, he deliberately rejected the Miltonic model for his own blank-verse.[2] Similarly, in a well-known passage in 'Table Talk' he censures Pope for reducing English versification to a mechanical technique. On the other hand (what is less often remembered) he has just implied that this worked for Pope precisely because he was so 'compact'. In other words, Pope could afford to be smooth in a rather obvious way, just because he was so 'strong'; Cowper and his contemporaries, he says, have to make their music less obvious because they can't rival Pope in closely packing their matter. The two criteria are always linked together for Cowper, balancing and checking against each other; but his interpretation of the one criterion, the model of Waller, is nearer to Dryden's view than to Pope's – and in fact he admired Dryden the more.[3]

1   E.g., *Letters*, ed. Hayley (1806), IV, 43, III, 279, II, 341.
2   Ibid., II, 279.
3   Ibid., II, 289, 290. cf. 'English Bards and Scotch Reviewers' (Dryden compared with Pope).

> Like him great Dryden pour'd the tide of song
> In stream less smooth, indeed, yet doubly strong.

To Cowper, Pope's excessive smoothness is redeemed by his incomparable 'strength'; to Byron, Pope is smoother but Dryden stronger. But Byron means by 'strength' what Jeffreys means, not what Cowper has in mind. It is a revealing illustration of how Byron's pretensions to belong to the neo-classic tradition are really quite empty gestures, trailings of a coat.

Strength in the sense of compactness and closeness is nearly always the first gauge that Cowper applies; but 'harmony' or 'music' is nearly always the second. The clearest examples of this two-fold standard occur in the many comments on Homer, when Cowper is occupied with his Homeric translations:

> A story-teller, so very circumstantial as Homer, must of necessity present us often with much matter in itself, capable of no other embellishment than purity of diction, and harmony of versification can give to it. *Hic labor, hic opus est.* For our language, unless it be very severely chastised, has not the terseness, nor our measure the music of the Greek.　　　　　　　　　　　　　　　　　　　　　　*(Letters,* III, 13)

A critic who sees in poetic diction no more than a 'certain traditional decorum of language, a necessary convention (and a necessarily changing one) about the use of words in poetry',[1] will be at a loss to understand how the purity of such a diction can be associated with 'terseness'. Indeed, the notion of 'purity' in such a case will seem meaningless, unless it means what the Elizabethans called 'decorum', the proper maintaining of a convention once established. That, indeed, is part of what Cowper and Johnson meant by 'purity'; and another part of their meaning, the part associated with terseness, is, as I have suggested, their concern for 'strength'. But neither of these exhausts the meaning of the term in their criticism. To be 'pure' a diction must maintain the decorum of the convention chosen for a given poem (and, beyond that, decorum also dictated what conventions were proper to different kinds). To be pure, a diction must also sustain comparison, in respect of compactness, with Denham and (later) with Pope. But it must satisfy other requirements; and these others were concerned with the relation between the poet's selected language and the language spoken about him in what was agreed to be the best society.

This is the aspect of the matter acknowledged by Cowper when he says that English, the spoken language, must be 'severely chastised' before it is equal to the task of reproducing Homer. This too will strike us as strange. It seems to us that the spoken language was not so much chastened as heightened, in order to produce the Augustan diction. In consequence it is inconvenient to find Cowper admiring Homer for his 'majestic plain-ness':

> I am truly happy, my dear, in having pleased you with what you have seen of my Homer. I wish that all English readers had your unsophisticated, or rather unadulterated taste, and could relish simplicity like

---

1　G.S. Fraser, 'Some Notes on Poetic Diction', *Penguin New Writing,* Number 37 (1949), p. 116.

you. But I am well aware, that in this respect, I am under a disadvantage, and, that many, especially many ladies, missing many turns and
prettinesses of expression, that they have admired in Pope, will
account my translation in those particulars defective. But I comfort
myself with the thought, that in reality it is no defect, on the contrary
that the want of all such embellishments as do not belong to the original will be one of its principal merits with persons indeed capable of
relishing Homer. He is the best poet that ever lived for many reasons,
but for none more than for that majestic plainness that distinguishes
him from all others. As an accomplished person moves gracefully
without thinking of it, in like manner the dignity of Homer seems to
cost him no labour. It was natural to him to say great things, and to say
them well, and little ornaments were beneath his notice. *(Letters*, II,
362)

He strikes this Wordsworthian note more than once:

Simplicity is become a very rare quality in a writer. In the decline of
great kingdoms, and where refinement in all the arts is carried to an
excess, I suppose it is always rare. The latter Roman writers are
remarkable for false ornament, they were yet no doubt admired by the
readers of their own day; and with respect to authors of the present
era, the most popular among them appear to be equally censurable on
the same account. Swift and Addison were simple. (Letters, II, 146)

Yet in calling this Wordsworthian, it is easy to blur distinctions. It is
easy to argue that Cowper certainly is plain by comparison with Pope,
but ornate by comparison with Wordsworth, that he stands in an interesting half-way house. This is to make him a Romantic precursor all over
again, and it is necessary to insist that while Cowper differs from Pope
only in degree, he differs radically from Wordsworth. His Homer is
compared with 'an accomplished person', whose ease and simplicity seem
natural just because they have been so assiduously worked for. There is no
question of dignity and simple eloquence being innate. For Wordsworth,
on the other hand, to be genuine these things had to be innate.

In this matter Johnson was more Wordsworthian than Cowper, and
Cowper took him to task for it. The occasion was Johnson's 'Life of
Prior', a poet whom Cowper much admired:

His reputation as an author, who, with much labour indeed, but with
admirable success, has embellished all his poems with the most
charming ease, stood unshaken 'till Johnson thrust his head against it.
And how does he attack him in this his principal fort? I cannot recollect his very words, but I am much mistaken indeed, if my memory
fails me with respect to the purport of them. 'His words', he says,
'appear to be forced into their proper places. There indeed we find

them, but find likewise, that their arrangement has been the effect of constraint, and that without violence, they would certainly have stood in a different order.' By your leave, most learned Doctor, this is the most disingenuous remark I ever met with, and would have come with a better grace from Curl, or Dennis. Every man conversant with verse-writing, knows, and knows by painful experience, that the familiar stile, is of all stiles the most difficult to succeed in. To make verse speak the language of prose, without being prosaic, to marshal the words of it in such an order, as they might naturally take in falling from the lips of an extemporary speaker, yet without meanness; harmoniously, elegantly, and without seeming to displace a syllable for the sake of the rhyme, is one of the most arduous tasks a poet can undertake. He that could accomplish this task was Prior; many have imitated his excellence in this particular, but the best copies have fallen far short of the original. And now to tell us, after we and our fathers have admired him for it so long, that he is an easy writer indeed, but that his ease has an air of stiffness in it, in short, that his ease is not ease, but only something like it, what is it but a self contradiction, an observation that grants what it is just going to deny, and denies what it has just granted, in the same sentence, and in the same breath?

(Letters, I, 294)

There can be little doubt that Cowper is right; the 'Life of Prior' shows Johnson the critic at his least impressive. It seems likely that the critic was put on edge by Prior's charming licentiousness, in 'Henry and Emma', for instance, which shocked the High-Churchman Johnson, as it did not shock Cowper, the evangelical Calvinist At any rate, it can hardly be doubted that on Prior Johnson was not just severe, in fact not just at all, but querulous. If we agree as to Prior, with Johnson rather than Cowper, so much the worse for us; it is time we realized that Prior was not just the Austin Dobson-*de-son-jour*, and I think he deserves all Cowper claims for him – but that is by the way.

The passage is of interest in several ways, apart from presenting Johnson in a careless moment as more of a Romantic precursor than ever Cowper was. In the first place, Cowper's admiration of Prior's ease sets him back, once again, in the strictest neo-classical tradition, along with Dryden. As Cowper stands with Dryden in esteeming 'strength' (for Dryden, Denham; for Cowper, Denham and Pope), and 'correctness' (for Dryden, Waller; for Cowper, Dryden himself); so, with him, he values 'ease', and as Dryden admired Suckling, Cowper admires Prior. Ease should not be identified with metrical smoothness, though smoothness is often an aspect of it. At bottom, the 'ease' esteemed by neo-classical writers is as old as Castiglione; it is a sort of urbane *insouciance*, almost insolence, an attribute of tone in addressing the reader. It is something more stable and more discreet than the raffishness of 'Don Juan', which was the best the Romantics could put in its place. And of course it was something for which Wordsworth, that provincial by conviction, could find no room at all.

The Wordsworthian reference is inevitable, for it is another feature of Cowper's comments on Prior that he here comes as near as ever he does to the Wordsworthian principle that 'There neither is, nor can be ... any essential difference between the language of prose and of metrical composition'. Cowper admires Prior for having shown, among other things, how 'To make verse speak the language of prose, without being prosaic'. This is an aspect of the neo-classical attitude to literature which is hardly ever understood, indeed seldom noticed. Johnson, no less than Cowper – in fact, the Augustans in general – insisted, as Wordsworth insisted, that the poet had a duty to the spoken language. And, again like Wordsworth, they meant, by 'the spoken language', no Audenesque colloquialism, but the sort of speech to be found reflected in informal prose. But for them this requirement, this duty laid upon the poet, was one among many, others being the observance of decorum, the need for compactness, and metrical felicity. Cowper, for instance, takes account of decorum when he congratulates Prior on his prosaicism at the same time as he distinguishes his style as 'familiar'. Wordsworth, in his criticism, elevated the one criterion at the expense of all others, and in so doing broke down, not only for his own readers but for succeeding generations, a critical mechanism of far greater delicacy, attempting and promising a finer discrimination. Perhaps the mechanism was delicate to no end, ingenious, intricate and ineffective. If so, it is a monument to the pedantry of not the eighteenth century only, but of the sixteenth and seventeenth also. The reader of poetry who is honest with himself must decide, by deduction from his own readings, whether the writing of poetry is an affair of massive simplicity, or a province where nicety of taste and sureness of judgement is as important as integrity of purpose. In any case there can be no question where Cowper stands. He stands for taste and judgement. In his own eyes, at any rate, he was nobody's precursor, but a poet coming late in an old tradition rich in achievement and based on principles tested in the practice of two centuries.

Cambridge Journal, 7 (December 1953), pp. 182–8.

X Christopher Smart:
Some Neglected Poems

Smart's translations of the Psalms do not constitute one of his main claims
to fame or to our attention. And Father Devlin is right when he says of
this work that 'its main interest lies in its being an unintentional rehearsal
for the *Song to David*.[1] But this in itself is a notable claim on our atten-
tions, and we sharpen it if we say that the Psalm versions make a bridge
to the *Song to David* from *Rejoice in the Lamb*. For this is the chronology –
Rejoice in the Lamb was begun and pushed forward in the first half of 1759,
when Smart, having been discharged as incurable from one madhouse,
enjoyed an interval at liberty before being committed to another about
August of that year; the further fragments which Bond calls B1 and B2
were written in confinement once again, up to about August 1760, fragment C belongs to March, April, and May 1761; and fragment D, the
latest section, runs from July 1762 through to the end of January 1763,
the eve of his release.[2] But these later sections of *Rejoice in the Lamb* are
not much more than Smart's therapeutic device for keeping himself
occupied, and for counting off on the calendar the days remaining before
the release which he knew was being negotiated. The grandiose liturgical
design which Smart had in mind when he composed the A and B fragments of *Rejoice in the Lamb* has quite disappeared from the later sections
of that manuscript; for its place had been taken by the work on the
Psalms, to which Smart refers excitedly in the later parts of the other
poem. Moreover, since Smart set about as soon as he was released to
solicit subscribers and arrange publication for his Psalms, it appears that
not only the bulk of the voluminous *Rejoice in the Lamb* but also most of
the more than 50,000 words of his Psalter derive from the period 1759 to
1763 – that is, to the second and longer stretch of his confinement, in
which he was allowed pen and paper (which on his first stretch had been
denied him). In other words, the work on the Psalms went on concur-
rently with the writing of at least the D fragment of *Rejoice in the Lamb;*
but because so much of this later work on *Rejoice in the Lamb* is perfunctory or private, it is legitimate to regard the Psalms as having to all intents

---

1 Christopher Devlin, *Poor Kit Smart* (London, 1961), p. 139.
2 W.H. Bond (ed.), *Jubilate Agno* (London, 1954), Introduction.

and purposes *succeeded Rejoice in the Lamb*. For it seems clear that not later than 1762 the energy of Smart's principal concern and dedication shifted from the one to the other.

The psalms in Smart's version are not true translations of the Hebrew poems, but rather quite loose paraphrases. One likes them a great deal less, once one compares them with any true translation, such as those in the Authorized Version, in the Prayer Book, or even among the freer versions of the Sidney Psalter made by Philip Sidney and his sister Mary and members of their circle. And yet every time that Smart departs from his original, as he does frequently and widely, this departure was intended to *tell* – and to tell not as a matter of literary decorum, but as a matter of doctrine.

In the first place, like many sincere Christians since his own day but like few of his own time, Smart was disturbed and shocked by the barbarous ferocity of many of the Hebrew psalms, especially those which are martial exhortations or morale-builders for the ancient Jewish nation in its struggle to survive among the heathen; and so Smart consistently emasculates the Psalms, converting the often barbarous morality of the Old Testament into the sweeter tone of the New.[1] The name of Christ is invoked as often as possible. Moreover, and more interestingly, Smart exploits to the utmost any chance of connecting Christ with the natural creation – and this, once again, not because he was at bottom 'a nature-poet' (which is what Father Devlin comes near to suggesting), but for reasons of Christian doctrine. Throughout all his sacred poems Smart directs his praise not in the first place to God the Redeemer, nor to God the Judge, nor to God the Protector of His faithful (which last is the char-acteristic emphasis of the Hebrew psalms), but to God the Creator. God as Christ, as the Son rather than the Father; and yet God as Creator rather than Redeemer – these are the emphases which Smart wants, and his wish to make these emphases is what lies behind nearly all the liberties he takes.

This severely doctrinal and moral purpose cannot be distinguished from a purpose which may be called liturgical. The particular form which religious mania took with Smart was a fervent wish that the Church of England should supplant the Church of Rome as the cardinal and catholic church of Christendom. This is a wish which many Anglicans have enter-tained and doubtless still entertain. But they held by it, or they hold by it, only as a pious hope; Smart espoused it as a deliberate programme, and one which might be speedily implemented, since he believed that God had called him to implement it. Apparently he thought it quite feasible

---

1   Brittain points out that precedents for such 'evangelical interpretation' are Archbishop Parker's versions of 1557(?), John Patrick's of 1679, Isaac Watts' of 1719. Brittain's example from Smart is Psalm 7, where God's bow bent to shoot the arrow of vengeance becomes the rainbow, emblem and pledge of God's mercy. See *Poems by Christopher Smart*, ed. R. Brittain (Princeton, 1950), pp. 279–80.

that St Paul's in London might supplant St Peter's as the metropolitan cathedral of international Christendom – hence the line in his 'Hymn for the Day of St Philip and St James', 'In the choir of Christ and WREN'. And certainly when he planned first *Rejoice in the Lamb*, and later the Psalms along with the Spiritual Songs, as a form of liturgy for Anglicanism rejuvenated and thus made supreme, he thought there was a real possibility that the Church of England might accept a form of service built around these compositions of his.[1] Smart's hopes crashed about him in 1765 when so far was the Church of England from recognizing him that Anglican opinion solidly preferred before his version of the Psalms the paraphrases of an old rival, James Merrick. Merrick's versions got into print before Smart's, and it was particularly galling that Merrick's publisher was John Newbery, Smart's father-in-law. (Smart's marriage is an enigma; Robert Brittain blames Smart's wife and his father-in-law for a great deal that went wrong with Smart's life, whereas Father Devlin pleads strenuously that they be acquitted.) What is important is to realize that in his paraphrase of the Psalms Smart had invested a great deal; it was not intended merely to take its place among the many metrical versions of the Psalter (such as Merrick's), but on the contrary to equip the Church of England for the vastly enhanced role which Smart unrealistically thought that she was to play. The motives behind it are not in any usual sense literary; and if we describe it instead as a work of piety, we must understand that what informs it is something far more ambitious and urgent than what is usually connoted by that word.

And yet there is no hope of our reading Smart's psalms in this way, in the spirit and with the sort of attention which he hoped for. We owe it to him to know what his intentions were. But the way to read these pieces with enjoyment is to take them as eighteenth-century devotional poems in their own right, pausing to check them by other versions only when, as often happens, they seem so wholly of the eighteenth century that one cannot conceive how they have any relation to the world of ancient Israel; there is much instructive amusement to be got from comparing Smart's versions at such points with the Prayer Book or the Authorized Version. Often one will be disappointed; in Psalm 147 for instance, such splendidly quaint expressions as 'The blessings of a social mess', or the ice 'Like vitreous fragments o'er the field', turn out to have little or no warrant from the original. But it is not always so. In Psalm 78, while enumerating the mercies of God to the Children of Israel in the wilderness, Smart writes:

---

1   At least he may have hoped for such recognition as George Wither received for his *Hymns and Songs of the Church* (1623), for which Wither got a royal patent directing that these original poems be bound up with Wither's *Metrical Psalter* for the use of the Church. See Brittain, p. 286.

He rained flesh upon them thick
 As dust upon the ground,
And fowls he lavish'd, quill'd and quick,
 Like sand beside the sound

Unless we have the Scripture at our fingertips we may well think that the idea of 'raining flesh', when God sent fowls falling on the Israelite tents, was possible only to the witty and bizarre imagination of eighteenth-century rococo. But it is there in the Prayer Book: 'He rained flesh upon them as thick as dust: and feathered fowls like as the sand of the sea.' Even the typically unsubtle but splendid alliteration of 'quill'd and quick' is only half redundant to the original; for Smart's delightful discovery 'quill'd' corresponds exactly to the Prayer Book's 'feathered'. If we care to compare the Sidney Psalter version we find that it is the seventeenth-century wit which is quaint and cumbrous, and elaborates on the original, for it speaks here about 'rain of admirable kind', about 'The dainty quails that freely wont to fly', and later (delightfully but redundantly) of how the Israelite encampment 'With feath'red rain was wat'red every way'.

For my next example, three verses from Psalm 139, it will be confusing if I do not give the Prayer Book version first:

14. My bones are not hid from thee: though I be made secretly, and fashioned beneath in the earth.
15. Thine eyes did see my substance, yet being imperfect: and in thy book were all my members written;
16. Which day by day were fashioned: when as yet there was none of them.

This is an astonishing penetration by the imagination of the psalmist into the mysteries of embryology. Smart's version runs tamely at first but rises to a fine concentration:

The substance of each nerve and bone
To thee are intimately known,
 And at my hour of birth
Thou didst thy quick'ning spirit breathe,
Though I be taken from beneath,
 And but refin'd from earth.

Thine eyes review'd th'imperfect sketch
Ere yet my limbs began to stretch
 And were for action ripe;
Before my members were of age
For birth, thou wrote them in thy page,
 And with the fairest type,

Which day by day assay'd to live,
And as thou didst conception give,
    Were warm'd with gradual heat;
When flesh and vital moisture both
Slept in the burial of their growth,
    And none were yet compleat.

Smart, as it seems at first, gives, for 'though I be made secretly, and fashioned beneath the earth', 'Though I be taken from beneath, / And but refin'd from earth'. And this is disappointing: 'taken from beneath' has a disconcertingly constrictive literal sense to it; and for 'refin'd' ('refin'd from earth') there is no warrant in the original's 'fashioned beneath in the earth'. But Smart like all great translators disperses his effects, and this is no more than a stop-gap measure; the translation of 'fashioned beneath in the earth' is completed two stanzas later with the splendid expression 'Slept in the burial of their growth'. Again, 'thou wrote them in thy page', which seems at first like the tired use of a stock conceit, turns out to be as close as possible to 'in thy book were all my members written'; as for the redundant elaboration of this, 'And with the fairest type', it is impossible to read this in the context of the Psalms and Spiritual Songs as a whole without seeing a serious pun, on the type set by the printer and on the type which we encounter in words like 'prototype' and 'archetype', for Smart uses the word continually in this latter sense, being vowed to the sort of scriptural exegesis which sees for instance David as a type of Christ.

But now hear what the Sidney Psalter makes of this passage:

Thou, how my back was beam-wise laid,
    And raftering of my ribbs dost know:
        Know'st ev'ry point
        Of bone and joynt,
    How to this whole these partes did grow,
In brave embrod'ry faire arraid,
    Though wrought in shop both dark and low.

Nay, fashionless, ere form I tooke,
    Thy all and more beholding eye
        My shapeless shape
        Could not escape:
    All these tymes fram'd successively
Ere one had being, in the booke
    Of thy foresight enrol'd did ly.

'Raftering of my ribbs' and 'wrought in shop both dark and low' – these murky splendours lie outside Smart's range altogether; but they are out of Coverdale's range also, and indeed out of range of the psalmist himself.

The original gives no warrant for them. Yet who would wish them away? This I take as evidence that in translation redundancy is not the unforgiveable sin – not if the redundant material is sufficiently splendid.

And this shall be my cue for a last example, from Psalm 118, where 'This is the Lord's doing: and it is marvellous in our eyes' becomes, in Smart:

> It is the work of God direct,
> For he himself is architect,
>   So beautiful and bold;
> 'Tis elevated to surprize,
> Beyond our thought, before our eyes.
>   Believe ye, and behold.

This is redundancy with a vengeance! And yet, given that the image of the architect is not gratuitous (for just before has come the famous image of the corner-stone – 'The same stone which the builders refused: is become the head-stone in the corner'), then the expressions 'beautiful and bold' and 'elevated to surprize' – taken as they are from the vocabulary in which the eighteenth century characteristically appreciated architecture – may very justly be taken as necessary to a fresh and vivid, and therefore true translation of the Prayer Book's single word, 'marvellous'.

I turn now to the *Hymns and Spiritual Songs*, bound up with the Psalms on their first publication in 1765. For these higher claims have been made, and must be made, than for the versions of the Psalms, interesting and often beautiful as those are. Father Devlin says (p. 159), 'the best of his hymns have a quality all their own, austerely tender, as if the baroque had developed gently and easily from the medieval, skipping the doubt and the passion and the grandeur that lay between …' This seems to be penetrating and just, and yet it is difficult to make use of this formulation as a starting point for reflections and explorations of our own. For the term 'baroque', though it has proved useful in relation to some of the other arts in England, has never proved itself useful in relation to our literature; and when we look at the confusions it seems to have provoked in the French in relation to French literature, we may well be grateful that it is one category we do not have to deal with. Yet in relation to Smart's *Hymns* it certainly *feels* right. One way of taking it is offered by Brittain when he asks us to see, as a crucial element in the *Hymns*, the influence of English baroque music, as Smart knew it and responded to it in the work of such composers as Arne and Boyce. However Brittain's remarks on this, though they are certainly illuminating about how each of the Hymns requires the context of all the others, being interlinked and interwoven, otherwise leave the analogy with eighteenth-century English music as no more than a tantalizing suggestion.

What we are looking for, in order to make use of Devlin's word 'baroque', is some precedent in English for the sort of thing we find in Smart's *Hymns*. It may be of course that no even partial precedent is to be found. What we have, thanks chiefly to Brittain's very distinguished work, are precedents for Smart's style in foreign languages – in Horace, and also in Hebrew poetry. And Devlin makes the further suggestion that interesting precedents may be found in medieval Latin, a matter which I wish that students of medieval Latin would investigate. But all of this leaves us as far as ever from finding English precedents for Smart. Very early in his career Smart translated into Latin Pope's 'Ode for St Cecilia's Day', and won Pope's approval for it; and undoubtedly that side of Pope's achievement (one to which nowadays we give rather little attention) left its mark on Smart's style of writing in Odes and ceremonial Hymns. Devlin suggests that Smart's first and most influential English model was Marvell, but he does not argue this case nor give any external evidence of it; and in default of such evidence and argument, I am inclined to think that where Smart seems to strike a Marvellian note (as he certainly does) this is because the same qualities in Horace appealed to Smart as to Marvell, and that what looks Marvellian is really Horatian. But one further possibility presents itself, among three works which Brittain (p. 286) interestingly notes as partial precedents for at least the *genre* of poetry which the *Hymns and Spiritual Songs* represent. These are Herbert's *The Temple* (1633), Crashaw's *Steps to the Temple* (1646), and Herrick's *Noble Numbers* (1647). One of these names in particular should make us pause, when set beside the word 'baroque' which we take from Father Devlin. This is the name of Crashaw. For Crashaw, as the one notable English poet of the counter-Reformation, is the one poet in English to whom the term 'baroque' can be applied with proper strictness. And it might be instructive to compare the *Hymns and Spiritual Songs* with Richard Crashaw's *Steps to the Temple*.

One interesting thing about both the poets just proposed as furnishing Smart with English precedents of a sort – Crashaw, that is, and Pope – is that they are Roman Catholics. Smart on the other hand is militantly anti-Roman, as was inevitable, given his hope that St Paul's should supplant St Peter's. And yet in order to do this Smart's Protestantism had to take on some of the colouring of that which it hoped to supplant; and not just in Smart's concerns for saints and especially angels does he seem near to Romanism, but also his attempt to conceal some of the ferocity of the Old Testament behind the New seemed to some of his contemporaries, and may seem to us if we think about it, to smack of the Roman Church. It is Father Devlin who has brought this out, and has pointed out also, as no previous biographer has done, that Smart's wife was a Roman Catholic. It is too soon to say that Devlin is right in his theory about the connection between Smart's queer and unsuccessful marriage, and the liturgical and doctrinal implications of his poems; but some connection there must be, and the clue to much that is still baffling about Smart must lie in this area and have to do with his very complicated attitude towards the Roman Church.

As for Richard Crashaw, one of the things characteristic of Crashaw's poetry is a disparity between the complexity of the surface and the simplicity beneath. This is what distinguishes Crashaw from the so-called 'metaphysicals' with whom he is often grouped – the extreme ingenuity of his poetic wit and the elaboration of his poetic structures do not, as with Donne, testify to a divided or tormented, self-doubting or self-questioning attitude in the writer. And the same is true of Smart, particularly in the *Hymns and Spiritual Songs*. Smart's poetry is unsubtle, but this does not mean either that Smart was simple-minded, or that the structure of his poems is straightforward. It is the attitude behind the poems which is simple, impressively simple, naïve in the very best, most valuable sense. For it is the attitude of praise, praise undertaken from a position of unshakeable and unquestioning conviction. On the other hand Smart, like Crashaw, deploys in the service of this single-minded purpose a very elaborate and copious rhetoric indeed. In both poets the local effects are often of a very subtle kind, and the means employed to this end are very subtle means; yet the total effect is not subtle, but simple.

A good example is the Hymn on the Nativity:

Where is this stupendous stranger,
    Swains of Solyma, advise,
Lead me to my Master's manger,
    Shew me where my Saviour lies.

O Most Mighty! O MOST HOLY!
    Far beyond the seraph's thought,
Art thou then so mean and lowly
    As unheeded prophets taught?

O the magnitude of meekness!
    Worth from worth immortal sprung;
O the strength of infant weakness,
    If eternal is so young!

If so young and thus eternal,
    Michael tune the shepherd's reed,
Where the scenes are ever vernal,
    And the loves be love indeed!

See the God blasphem'd and doubted
    In the schools of Greece and Rome;
See the pow'rs of darkness routed,
    Taken at their utmost gloom.

Nature's decorations glisten
  Far above their usual trim;
Birds on box and laurel listen,
  As so near the cherubs hymn.

Boreas now no longer winters
  On the desolated coast;
Oaks no more are riv'n in splinters
  By the whirlwind and his host.

Spinks and ouzles sing sublimely,
  'We too have a Saviour born',
Whiter blossoms burst untimely
  On the blest Mosaic thorn.

God all-bounteous, all-creative,
  Whom no ills from good dissuade,
Is incarnate, and a native
  Of the very world he made.

Here the total effect is the characteristic Smart effect – a full-throated
paean of praise, whole-hearted simple gratitude to God, unconditional,
without qualifications or reservations or doubts or questionings. And this
full-throatedness, this absence of complications, is faithfully mirrored – as
always in Smart, notably in the *Song to David* – in the firmness with which
the poem hammers out its metrical beat, in the emphatic alliterations
('stupendous stranger'), and in the reverberating richness of the rhymes,
especially the rhymes on two syllables: 'stranger'/'manger', 'Holy'/
'lowly', 'meekness'/'weakness', 'eternal'/'vernal'. It is easy to get so
caught up in this resonance that one does not notice how witty the poem
is; that is, how strenuous the thinking is. Consider only the third quatrain:

  O the magnitude of meekness!
    Worth from worth immortal sprung;
  O the strength of infant weakness,
    If eternal is so young!

Alliteration binds 'magnitude' with 'meekness', so as to bring out how
unusual it is for these two qualities to go together – they are not quite
incompatible, yet 'magnitude' usually points one way, 'meekness'
another. After a line which lets down the tension, it is screwed up again
to 'the strength of ... weakness', which is *oxymoron;* that is, the two qualities crammed together *are* in normal usage incompatible, blank opposites
indeed – and the implication is that for an occasion so abnormal as the
Incarnation of a God normal usage is inadequate, its values are all
reversed, its categories confounded. And now, instead of letting down the
tension again, it is screwed up further still; and the poem soars – not just
into more fervent feeling, but intellectually, into paradox – 'If eternal is

so young!' This means, literally, 'if God is a new-born infant'; but it means also, imaginatively, 'if the divine is unchangeable, inexhaustible vigorous and creative'. To take 'eternal', which means by definition 'outside time', and ram it up against 'young', which has meaning only within the dimension of time – this expression ought to be meaningless, nonsensical; but we discover to our astonishment that it isn't meaningless at all, though the mind at full stretch can only just grasp the meaning and can only with great difficulty formulate the meaning to itself.

'If eternal is so young' is deftly re-arranged then into 'If so young and thus eternal' – which is the sort of effect that Brittain would want to analyse by way of analogies from contrapuntal baroque music. And 'young' is not taken away from the human timespan into that of the seasons: 'young' now means 'the youth of the year', i.e. 'spring'. Hence 'vernal', and the identification naturally and wittily follows of the archangel Michael with the pastoral poet piping a spring eclogue. And yet the birth was at Christmas in the depth of winter, when 'the pow'rs of darkness' (Satan of course but also the long nights and short days of December) are 'Taken at their utmost gloom'. With 'Nature's decorations glisten', we hear an aggressively anti-Wordsworthian string such as Smart plucks very often – for instance, in the 'painted beauties' of the Hymn to St Philip and St James. But here the artificiality is even more deliberate and necessary. This is to represent the natural as unnatural? But of course! Spring in midwinter *is* unnatural. How can it not be, since it is supernatural? The language is artificial? But of course! It is speaking of a divine artifice disrupting the natural order.

The whole conceit and paradox of Boreas (who *is* winter) no longer 'wintering' (the use of the verb is masterly) is clinched in the penultimate stanza. Here, as Brittain acutely points out, Smart telescopes two legendary stories – the story of the Glastonbury thorn which is supposed to bloom at Christmas, being sprung from the staff of Joseph of Arimathea; and the rod of Aaron, which in Numbers XVII bloomed in the tabernacle to approve the elevation of the Levites to the status of a hereditary priestly caste. By thus telescoping a story of the apostle in Britain with a story of divine sanction for a chosen priesthood, Smart implies the possibility and the rightness of regarding the Church of England (rather than of Rome) as God's chosen church.

And one paradox remains, the most astonishing and profound of all – the gloss on the word 'incarnate' by which, in a way that ought to be nonsensical but astoundingly isn't, God who created the world is said to be himself a creature of that world – 'a native / Of the very world he made'.

Smart's translations from Horace should be better known. There are two of them: a prose translation of the 1750s and a verse translation which appeared in 1767. Whereas the painstaking prose-crib was often reprinted and used by generations of schoolboys, the verse-translations have never been reprinted after the first edition; not only are they almost unknown, but copies are very hard to find. And yet the Preface which Smart wrote for these translations is the only document we have in which Smart explains, or hints at explaining, his own poetic practice.

Unfortunately, this is not so useful as it sounds. For it is hard to agree with Christopher Devlin that the Preface, no less than the translations themselves, shows 'his complete sanity and urbanity in everything that did not probe the one secret obsession'. On the contrary, it seems to me that the Preface, though it is certainly not the product of a deranged mind, no less certainly comes from a mind that is seriously disoriented – a mind which, to say the least, has lost its sense of proportion. (See for instance Smart's gratuitous footnote to the effect that Stonehenge was the work of giants.) The Preface touches in disconnected fashion on three topics, and two of these – Smart's remarks on the 'curious felicity' of Horace, and his observations on what he calls 'impression' – are of imme-diate importance; but Smart's treatment of both these matters is glancing and general, and the most we can make of them is tantalizing and tenta-tive, not solidly helpful.

Smart begins his Preface by speaking of 'the lucky risk of the Horatian boldness'. And he elaborates:

> Horace is by no means so much an original in respect to his matter and sentiments (which are rather too frequently borrowed) as with regard to that unrivalled peculiarity of expression, which has excited the admiration of all succeeding ages.

Then, after some distracting digressions, he returns to the topic:

> Mr *Pope* himself, however happy in taking off the spirit and music of *Horace*, has left us no remarkable instance, to the best of my memory, of this kind. In truth this is a beauty, that occurs rather in the Odes, than the other parts of Horace's works; where the aiming at familiarity of style excluded the curiosity of choice diction.

Robert Brittain, who alone has wrestled so far with the problem of what Smart meant by this, has some enlightening and sensible pages, suggesting how, not just in these translations but in all his poems, Smart strove for the Horatian 'curious felicity' by following the instructions given in the *De Arte Poetica* about the tactful use of archaic words and neologisms. I think Brittain is right about this, though he does not sufficiently recog-nize how much which he presents as peculiar to Smart was common to eighteenth-century poets in general: for example, the use of English words in the sense of their Latin roots, as when Smart uses 'vague' to mean 'wandering'. But I suspect that curious felicity in Smart has less to do with artful choice of words than with artful arrangement of them:

Smart goes on to specify those of his translations of the Odes in which he believes he has attained to this felicity, and very few of those he specifies exemplify the curiosities of vocabulary to which Brittain draws attention. Moreover, my own experience has been that in the Second Book of the Odes, for instance, those by which Smart on this basis lays most store are by and large those which are least to my taste.

It seems important, therefore, to consider the possibility that often when Smart essays 'the curiosity of choice diction', he is striving for something which we would rather he had never achieved. A little thought will reveal how this may well be so. For from the remarks by Smart which I have quoted already, meagre as they are, we gather at least one thing quite definitely – that Horace's 'curious felicity', as Smart sees it, is attainable only in an elevated style. This is implied when Smart says that in Horace's poems other than the Odes this felicity should not be looked for since 'the aiming at familiarity of style' excluded it. And there is a footnote which tells the same story, in which Smart concedes that in the first Ode of the first book (in which he believes that he has managed curious felicity in many places) he has made the style more lofty and less conversational than in the Latin. Because twentieth-century taste is for the most part still Wordsworthian enough to prefer eighteenth-century poetry at its least ornate, when it is most conversational, it may well be that we shall prefer Smart's less ornate versions of the epodes and satires to his version of the Odes, though he laid most store by these.

It is worth dwelling on this for a little, for it affects Smart's poetry as a whole. Except for his youthful and admirable *vers-de-société*, and the poems which he wrote for children, Smart's diction is characteristically very ornate indeed, and his tone is very lofty. Moreover one effect which is peculiar to him, which is very valuable and moving, the effect which one commentator has called his 'piercing naïveté', is possible only because his style is thus choice and elevated. The naïveté pierces only because it strikes at us suddenly out of a body of language which in general is not naïve at all, but on the contrary very sophisticated and polished. The Hymn on the Nativity provides an example:

> Boreas now no longer winters
>   On the desolated coast;
> Oaks no more are riv'n in splinters
>   By the whirlwind and his host.
>
> Spinks and ouzles sing sublimely,
>   'We too have a Saviour born',
> Whiter blossoms burst untimely
>   On the blest Mosaic thorn.

When the spinks and ouzles are made to speak with childlike simplicity,

the effect is indeed piercingly childlike and not childish, infantile or
mawkish, only because they speak to us out of a context defined by the
stilted artifice of 'Boreas', and the no less deliberate grandeur of 'the blest
Mosaic thorn'. The effect is earned, it is not at all a cheap gimmick which
loses its value as soon as we see through it. For the naïveté of language in
the one case witnesses to a real directness of apprehension, just as the elaboration of language in the other cases reflects a genuine complexity.
Smart's distinction is in the rapidity and lack of fuss with which he can
switch from extreme indirectness to extreme directness and back again. It
is probably impossible to say whether this characteristic effect is part of
what Smart intended by 'curious felicity', or whether it came about as a
lucky by-product of Smart's striving after something else.

However that may be, in Smart's translations of Horace's Odes the
efforts at 'curious felicity' rather often end unhappily. Book I Ode 4 is a
fair example:

Solvitur acris hiems grata vice veris et Favoni:
　　Trahuntque siccas machinae carinas.
Ae neque iam stabulis gaudet pecus, aut arator igni;
　　Nec prata canti albicant pruinis.
Iam Cytherea choros ducit Venus, imminente Luna:
　　Iunctaeque Nymphis Gratiae decentes
Alterno terram quatiunt pede: dum graves Cyclopium
　　Vulcanus ardens urit officinas.
Nunc decet aut viridi nitidum caput impedire myrto
　　Aut flore, terrae quem ferunt solutae.
Nunc et in umbrosis Fauno decet immolare lucis,
　　Seu poscat agnam, sive malit haedum.
Pallida mors aequo pulsat pede pauperum tabernas,
　　Regumque turres, ô beate Sexti,
Vitae summa brevis spem nos vetat incohare longam.
　　Iam te premet nox, fabulaque manes,
Et domus exilis Plutonia, quo simul mearis,
　　Non regna vini fortiere talis,
Nec tenerem Lycidam mirabere, quo caret juventus
　　Nunc omnis, et mox virgines tepebunt.

A grateful change! Favonius, and the spring
　　To the sharp winter's keener blasts succeed,
Along the beach, with ropes, the ships they bring,
　　And launch again, their watry way to speed.
No more the plowmen in their cots delight,
　　Nor cattle are contented in the stall;
No more the fields with hoary frosts are white,
　　But Cytherean Venus leads the ball.

> She, while the moon attends upon the scene,
>   The Nymphs and decent Graces in the set,
> Shakes with alternate foot the shaven green.
>   While Vulcan's Cyclops at the anvil sweat,
> Now we with myrtle shou'd adorn our brows,
>   Or any flow'r that decks the loosen'd sod;
> In shady groves to Faunus pay our vows,
>   Whether a lamb or kid delight the God.
> Pale death alike knocks at the poor man's door,
>   O happy Sextius, and the royal dome.
> The whole of life forbids our hope to soar,
>   Death and the shades anon shall press thee home.
> And when into the shallow grave you run,
>   You cannot win the monarchy of wine,
> Nor doat on Lycidas, as on a son,
>   Whom for their spouse all little maids design.

It is not just an unreasoning preference for the colloquial which makes us (surely) pick out as the best things in Smart's verse translation the two points where he is most conversational – that is to say, the exclamatory opening, 'A grateful change, Favonius!', and, at the close (corresponding to lines now rejected from the Latin text), the delightful discovery of the 'little maids', 'Whom for their spouse all little maids design'. In between, we are repeatedly aware of loss if we look from Smart's prose translation to his verse. There is a loss in moving from the sturdy word 'hale' in Smart's prose ('hale from shore the dry ships') to the weak alternative 'bring'; the single word 'dry' in the prose is worth infinitely more than the redundant 'their watry way to speed'; 'the royal dome' is similarly more stilted for the Latin *turres* than is 'towers of kings'; and 'forbids our hope to soar' quite loses the suggestion of a balance-sheet which there is in the original and, faintly, in Smart's prose. And when we turn from these matters of choice of words, to the question of their arrangement, the case is even clearer. It will be recalled that this is the ode with which in a famous essay T.S. Eliot compares Marvell's 'To His Coy Mistress', in respect of the introduction of death into both poems. J.V. Cunningham has argued, persuasively I think, that the comparison Eliot proposes does justice to neither poem. And Cunningham remarks, of Horace's poem:

> Death occurs in this poem with that suddenness and lack of preparation with which it sometimes occurs in life. The structure of the poem is an imitation of the structure of such experiences in life. And as we draw from such experiences often a generalization, so Horace from the sudden realization of the abruptness and impartiality of death, reflects *vitae summa brevis spem nos vetat incohare longam*

The brief sum of life forbids our opening a long account with hope
But the proposition is subsequent to the experience; it does not rule
and direct the poem from the outset. And the experience in Horace *is*
surprising and furnishes the fulcrum on which the poem turns.[1]

Cunningham's point is that in Marvell's poem the experience is *not*
surprising and does *not* provide a fulcrum; because it isn't that kind of
poem. But if Horace's poem is the sort that does have a fulcrum, then
Smart's treatment of it will be crucial. And Cunningham indicates what
the fulcrum is; it is the famous line and a half,

> Pallida mors aequo pulsat pede pauperum tabernas,
>   Regumque turres ...

What does Smart make of this? –

> Pale death alike knocks at the poor man's door,
>   O happy Sextius, and the royal dome

He pulls back the renewed address to Sextius from the succeeding
sentence where it belongs (as his own prose acknowledges), and rams it in
as an interjection between 'poor man's door' and 'royal palace', where it
is crucially important that these two should go closely together. The
rearrangement only weakens and distracts because the run of the line
persuades us to look, at first reading, for a connection between Sextius
and 'royal dome', as if the latter too were being addressed. Unhappy
re-arrangements of this kind, producing pointless ambiguities and obscu-
rities, are not uncommon in Smart's versions; and if these, as I suspect,
came about by his efforts after 'curious felicity', so much the worse for
him and for that principle which he espoused. For another example I take
four lines from Ode 10 of the first book, addressing Mercury:

> Thee when a boy, with threads injoin'd
> To bring the steers you had withdrawn,
> Apollo laugh'd aloud to find
>   His quiver also gone.

These lines are incomprehensible until we turn to Smart's prose translation, where we find: 'While Apollo in threatening voice terrified you,
then but a boy, unless you should restore the oxen conveyed away by
your artifice, he laughed, being deprived of his quiver into the bargain.'
And even when we have thus learned what Smart's verses mean, or are
intended to mean, we still cannot make sense of the grammar of his lines.
What we have in a case like this is English being treated, particularly in

---

1   J.V. Cunningham, *Tradition and Poetic Structure* (Denver, 1960).

the matter of word-order, as if it were a highly inflected language like the Latin Smart is translating from. This is a charge which is habitually levelled at the Milton of *Paradise Lost*, but the charge sticks on Milton much less than on a later Latinist, Walter Savage Landor; and such unfortunate effects as this recall nothing more insistently than some of the more congested passages of Landor.

In all of this I am not suggesting that these forgotten translations of Horace are deservedly forgotten; on the contrary they are frequently delightful. And I put before you the example of Ode XI from Book I, to show how graceful and surprising Smart's versions can be:

> Seek not, what we're forbid to know,
>   The date the Gods decree
> To you, my fair Leuconoe,
>   Or what they fix for me.
> Nor your Chaldean books consult,
>   But cheerfully submit,
> (How much a better thought it is?)
>   To what the Gods think fit.
> Whether more winters on our head
>   They shall command to low'r,
> Or this the very last of all,
>   Shall bring our final hour.
> E'en this, whose rough tempestuous rage
>   Makes yon Tyrrhenian roar,
> And all his foamy breakers dash
>   Upon the rocky shore.
> Be wise and broach your mellow wine,
>   Which carefully decant,
> And your desires proportionate
>   To life's compendious grant.
> E'en while we speak the moments fly,
>   Be greedy of to-day;
> Nor trust another for those pranks
>   Which we may never play.

Here we must applaud the wholly eighteenth-century and yet compact and accurate lines – 'And your desires proportionate / To life's compendious grant'. But it remains true that Brittain's claims for this part of Smart's work, just and generous as those claims are, have to be treated with caution.

As for the other principle which Smart enunciates in his Preface – the principle of 'impression' – his remarks on this unfortunately are even more cryptic and elusive than his treatment of the Horatian *curiosa felicitas*. He speaks of:

another poetical excellence, which tho' possessed in a degree by every great genius, is exceeding in our Lyric to surpass; I mean the beauty, force and vehemence of *Impression:* which leads me to a rare and entertaining subject, not (I think) any where much insisted on by others.

    Impression then, is a talent or gift of Almighty God, by which a Genius is impowered to throw an emphasis upon a word or sentence in such wise, that it cannot escape any reader of sheer good sense, and true critical sagacity. This power will sometimes keep it up thro' the *medium* of a prose translation; especially in scripture, for in justice to truth and everlasting pre-eminence, we must confess this virtue to be far more powerful and abundant in the sacred writings.

That last sentence necessarily brings to mind Longinus on the Sublime; for 'Longinus' not only makes a point of praising Hebrew poetry for its sublimity (and, of the confusingly many examples which Smart proceeds to give, the first three are in Hebrew), but 'Longinus' also, by implication, indicates that sublimity can persist through translation. Moreover Smart himself, introducing a later example from Homer, speaks of how the lines he quotes from Homer 'are worked up to … a pitch of sublimity'. Out of 'Longinus' the passage which seems most nearly to correspond to Smart's idea of 'impression' comes in Section X when the ancient critic is commenting on some lines from (again) Homer, and on lines moreover which, like the lines in Smart's example, describe a storm at sea. 'Longinus' says that Homer in this place 'has stamped, I had almost said, upon the language the form and features of the peril' (A.O. Prickard's translation). Unfortunately we look in vain in Smart's remarks for what the ancient critic so remarkably gives us – an analysis of the sublime effect in terms of particular use of particular words:

> Yet again, by forcing together prepositions naturally inconsistent, and compelling them to combine [and 'Longinus' then quotes the specific Homeric phrase he has in mind], he has so strained the verse as to match the trouble which fell upon them; has so pressed it together as to give the very presentment of that trouble; has stamped, I had almost said, upon the language the form and features of the peril …

This passage of ancient criticism suggests quite precisely, as a modern analogue to the ancient effect he so much admires, something like some passages from Hopkins' 'Wreck of the Deutschland'. And only some of the passages which Smart cites as examples seem to be passages in which Hopkinsian or Homeric liberties are taken. All the same, as has been remarked by others, the principle of 'impression' was for Smart an important one, a constantly guiding principle – as one sees from *Rejoice in the Lamb* several years before: 'For my talent is to give an impression upon words by punching, that when the reader casts his eye upon 'em, he takes up the image from the mould which I have made.' Plainly 'impression' is not used by Smart loosely, but is a word which seems to draw behind it a complicated metaphor from die-casting, a metaphor which indicates what Smart conceived himself to be doing when he wrote. And yet this metaphor is not to be found in 'Longinus', (whose treatise Smart studied when attending Bishop Lowth's lectures on Hebrew poetry), but in Horace's *Ars Poetica* (I. 59). It is a puzzling business, and deserves further study.

If anything has emerged from this consideration of Smart, I hope it is this – that whether he writes poems of ecstasy and wonder, or poems of a more worldly cast, he does not fit into the category that is sometimes called 'pre-Romantic'; he is not 'a Romantic precursor', but wholly a poet of the eighteenth century. This appears in nothing so clearly as in his verse for children, to which I now turn all too briefly; to the *Hymns for the Amusement of Children*, Smart's last work, not published until 1775.

It may seem, from a point made earlier, that since in these poems Smart abandoned 'the high style', he might here have fallen into that mawkishness from which in general his lofty tone and style rescued him even when he was dealing in effects of piercing simplicity. This is not so, however. In the first place, though the Hymns for Children may be said to be in a low style, this is true only relative to the unusually high style which Smart employed in his other devotional poems; the style is not so low as what Wordsworth and Blake after him were to employ in children's verse, or what Isaac Watts had employed before him in writing for children. In fact, our first impression is likely to be of surprise at how few concessions Smart made to his audience of children, how much he demands of his young readers, in width of vocabulary particularly. The matter to which Brittain draws attention, Smart's artifice of *recherché* archaism in diction, can be illustrated from these poems as from the poems Smart wrote for adults. For example, in Hymn V:

> And still peculiar on my side,
>   Keep me from rigour free;
> Make me forgive, in manly pride,
>   All that exact on me.

Here the use of 'peculiar' is by no means a straightforward one. It is so much a favourite word of Smart that it becomes an idiosyncratic mannerism. As Father Devlin says (p. 173), '"Peculiar" is Smart's favourite adjective for subtleties …, as "stupendous" is for mysteries.' The children who have wrestled with this special meaning in the first line of the quatrain are faced in the last line with the archaic oddity of 'exact on' instead of 'exact from'. Or there is Hymn XXVIII:

> Then pray with David, that the Lord
>   Wou'd keep himself the door;
> And all things from the lips award,
>   That make thy brother sore

(where 'award' is used in the strictly Latinate sense of 'ward off'). Thus Smart is not 'coming down to the child's level' at all so much as most writers for children think they have to do. And this in itself saves him from seeming either mawkish or patronizing.

But more important is the fact that behind these poems there lies a wholly non-Romantic idea of what a child is. Smart is as far as possible from seeing the child in the Wordsworthian way as 'mighty prophet, seer blest'; there is no sign of the Romantic conviction which lies behind some of Blake's *Songs of Innocence* as well as behind Wordsworth's 'We are Seven' – the conviction that the child has access to sources of wisdom and insight which are closed to the adult. Smart on the contrary seems to believe, as perhaps all centuries before the nineteenth believed, that the child is a small and incomplete adult; that his lack of adulthood is a misfortune, though an inevitable one – a privation, which must be remedied as soon as possible, in his own interests; that the duty of the adult towards the child was to feel compassion for him in his incompleteness, to protect him from the perils which this brought upon him, and to assist him to complete himself. The best thing an adult can do for a child is to help him to grow up as quickly as possible – hence the awesome precocity of many children in earlier literature, which we as post-Romantic readers find disconcerting and unpleasant though the writers plainly felt nothing of the sort. Smart's *Hymns for the Amusement of Children* are meant to help the children to stop being children. When they are set in the mouth of a child (many of them are not spoken by the child but addressed to him by an adult), we are not to take it that the child is speaking out of his own resources but is repeating back words which the adult has put into his mouth, and made him learn. Since we are all more or less like children in our imperfect grasp of eighteenth-century values, many of these poems are highly instructive for the twentieth-century reader – especially those many hymns which have for title a single word, like Taste, Learning, Elegance, Honesty, Moderation, Temperance, Prudence; for these are in effect versified definitions of what these crucial terms meant for an eighteenth-century adult mind. Here is Hymn XV, 'Taste':

> I
> O guide my judgment and my taste,
>   Sweet SPIRIT, author of the book
> Of wonders, told in language chaste
>   And plainness, not to be mistook.

II

O let me muse, and yet at sight
 The page admire, the page believe;
'Let there be light, and there was light,
 Let there be Paradise and Eve!'

III

Who his soul's rapture can refrain?
 At Joseph's ever-pleasing tale,
Of marvels, the prodigious train,
 To Sinai's hill from Goshen's vale.

IV

The Psalmist and proverbial Seer,
 And all the prophets sons of song,
Make all things precious, all things dear,
 And bear the brilliant word along.

V

O take the book from off the shelf,
 And con it meekly on thy knees;
Best panegyric on itself,
 And self-avouch'd to teach and please.

VI

Respect, adore it heart and mind.
 How greatly sweet, how sweetly grand,
Who reads the most, is most refin'd,
 And polish'd by the Master's hand.

What this is about is 'immediacy' – a matter which is clearly very much to the point of what Smart meant by that cardinal principle of his, 'Impression'. 'Taste', he implies, is the capacity to recognize immediacy; not an ability to weigh pros and cons, but the capacity to bypass or anticipate that process of reasoned judgement by responding vividly and at once to the artistic experience. It is astonishing and melancholy that the only poem by Smart which has evoked that vivid response at all generally is the *Song to David;* I am convinced that this happens only because so few readers ever look at Smart's other poems.

Eighteenth-Century Studies III: 2 (winter 1969), pp. 242–64.

XI Yeats, Berkeley and Romanticism

'Romanticism', of course, is by this time quite unmanageable. By itself it gets us nowhere. When a reviewer of Yeats' *Collected Poems* (in *Adelphi*, November 1950) sees the volume as striking a blow for 'the franker, simpler, more intelligible, and often, even to the end, romantic ways of poetry', there is no way of rebutting him: since, among the unmanageably many meanings that have been given to 'romantic' and 'romanticism', there is doubtless one that does indeed relate it to frankness and simplicity. And I have no doubt that there are other meanings of 'romantic' in terms of which one could quite properly regard all Yeats' poetry, first and last, as romantic. On the other hand I shall argue that there is another sense of 'romantic', by which Yeats can be seen, in the 1920s, to break quite deliberately with the romanticism of his youth. This again is not disputed; no one is likely to deny that in one sense 'Among School Children' is a less romantic poem than 'The Lake Isle of Innisfree'. But I shall argue that this change in the poet goes deep; that the obvious and commonly recognized change in style testifies to a far-reaching and permanent change in a philosophic attitude. And this, I think, is less generally acknowledged.

There is obviously a connection here – or at least the possibility of a connection – with Yeats' interest, at the time he wrote 'Among School Children', in the thought of Berkeley. For Berkeley too, until twenty or thirty years ago, was regarded as a proto-Romantic philosopher, one of the fathers of subjective idealism; and Yeats became interested in him at just about the time when Berkeleyans began to challenge this reading of him, and to take seriously his own claim to be a philosopher of common sense. I shall argue, to buttress my claim for an anti-Romantic Yeats, that the poet's enthusiasm for the philosopher was not just a trailing of his Anglo-Irish coat (such as we find, for instance, in the Berkeleyan stanza of 'Blood and the Moon'), but that it came out of a real grasp of Berkeley's significance as something other than what Coleridge, for instance, supposed.

The romanticism, then, that I am talking about, is the romanticism that Yeats explicitly discards in the last stanza of 'Among School Children':

> Labour is blossoming or dancing where
> The body is not bruised to pleasure soul,

Nor beauty born out of its own despair
Nor blear-eyed wisdom out of midnight oil.
O chestnut-tree, great-rooted blossomer,
Are you the leaf, the blossom or the bole?
O body swayed to music, O brightening glance,
How can we know the dancer from the dance?

In the second, third, and fourth lines the poet rejects three kinds of
more or less deliberate self-division, willed mutilation or sickness, as ways
toward beauty and wisdom. For instance 'the body... bruised to pleasure
soul' is surely a sort of shorthand not just for the flagellations and mortifi-
cations of religious asceticism, but also for that Romantic tradition of
sexual passion which comes from the Courtly Love of the Middle Ages
through the *Vita Nuova* and the Platonism of Sidney's 'Astrophel and
Stella'. For to delay carnal consummation indefinitely, or to exclude it
altogether, so as to screw up sexual desire into something 'purer', more
intellectual and spiritual, is a clear case of mortifying the flesh. And yet
this was precisely the traditional spiritual discipline by which Yeats had
schooled himself throughout his early life, in his wilfully exacerbated
hopeless passion for Maud Gonne (who is, of course, much in evidence
in earlier stanzas of this poem).

Again 'beauty born out of its own despair' can refer, not only once
again to Maud Gonne (if the poet's love for her had not been despairing,
it would not have been beautiful, nor produced beauty in poems), but
also to the 'terrible beauty' that was born in 1916 out of the despair of a
foredoomed enterprise. It can also be taken to describe the whole of
Yeats' earlier practice of quarrelling with himself, in mask and antimask,
calling up his own opposite, adopting a pose and then forcing himself to
live up to it – in poetry, if not in life.

As for 'blear-eyed wisdom out of midnight oil', the most revealing
commentary on this was surely written by a great contemporary, Thomas
Hardy, in his portrait of Clym Yeobright in *The Return of the Native*:

> The face was well shaped, even excellently. But the mind within was
> beginning to use it as a mere waste tablet whereon to trace its idiosyn-
> crasies as they developed themselves. The beauty here visible would in
> no long time be ruthlessly overrun by its parasite, thought, which
> might just as well have fed upon a plainer exterior where there was
> nothing it could harm. Had Heaven preserved Yeobright from a
> wearing habit of meditation, people would have said, 'A handsome
> man'. Had his brain unfolded under sharper contours they would have
> said, 'A thoughtful man'. But an inner strenuousness was preying upon
> an outer symmetry, and they rated his look as singular.
>
> Hence people who began by beholding him ended by perusing
> him. His countenance was overlaid with legible meanings ... He

already showed that thought is a disease of flesh, and indirectly bore
evidence that ideal physical beauty is incompatible with emotional
development and a full recognition of the coil of things. Mental lumi-
nousness must be fed with the oil of life, even though there is a physical need for it; and the pitiful sight of two demands on one supply was
just showing itself here.

When standing before certain men the philosopher regrets that
thinkers are but perishable tissue, the artist that perishable tissue has to
think.

Yeats in this place is plainly Hardy's artist who regrets 'that perishable
tissue has to think'. And his thought is Hardy's thought – 'thought is a
disease of flesh'. Behind them both, as often behind another contemporary, Thomas Mann, lies the conception of the artist or the thinker as an
individual carrying the curse of a society, his gifts a sort of sacred sickness;
and this is, as a fact of literary history, a conception thrown up by the
Romantic movement in Europe.

Yeats in all three lines is probing that aspect of Romanticism mislead-
ingly labelled 'introspection'. It is not Romantic to be capable of self-
consciousness and hence of introspection; of making one part of the
personality regard what some other part is thinking and feeling, even as it
quite 'sincerely' thinks and feels. Romanticism takes the further step from
self-regarding to self-manipulating; and by harnessing the will to one half
of the divided personality it induces the other half to think and feel as it
wants to feel. Hence, ever since *Le Neveu de Rameau*, the Romantic fascination with the hypocrite, the actor, and the double; and its ever more
frantic attempts to surprise itself into feeling what it is not prepared to
feel. Hence too its search for primitive minds in which the vicious circles
of self-consciousness have not yet appeared – the noble savage, the idiot,
the naïf, the good and simple peasant. (But all this of course is just a
dogmatic aside.)

Where does Berkeley stand in relation to this? Oddly enough he can
be detected in at least one place considering the issue in just the home-
made, unphilosophical terms I have adopted here. This comes in the fifth
dialogue of the relatively late work, *Alciphron*, where Berkeley is attacking
Shaftesbury. Berkeley's spokesman, Crito, is made to read from
Shaftesbury's *A Soliloquy, or Advice to an Author*, mocking Shaftesbury's
Ciceronian style by reading it as if it were loose and irregular dramatic
verse. Euphranor, Crito's ally, carries on the joke by pretending that it is
a play or a poem that is being read. And the freethinker Alciphron,
Shaftesbury's apologist, falls into the trap:

> You are mistaken, it is no Play nor Poetry, replied Alciphron, but a
> famous modern Critic moralizing in Prose. You must know this great
> Man hath (to use his own Words) revealed a *Grand Arcanum* to the

World, having instructed Mankind in what he calls *Mirrour-writing, Self-discoursing Practice, and Author Practice* and shew'd 'That by virtue of an intimate Recess, we may discover a certain Duplicity of Soul, and divide our *Self* into two parties, or (as he varies the Phrase) practically form the Dual Number'. In consequence whereof he hath found out that a Man may argue with himself and not only with himself, but also with Notions, Sentiments, and Vices, which by a marvellous Prosopopoeia he converts into so many Ladies: and so converted, he confutes and confounds them in a Divine Strain. Can anything be finer, bolder, or more sublime?

Here Berkeley by implication condemns and derides the attitude behind Yeats' famous dictum that out of quarrels with others the poet makes rhetoric; out of quarrelling with himself, poetry. As I should prefer to say, he stands with the later Yeats against the earlier. Berkeley derides proto-Romanticism in Shaftesbury, in the interests of Augustan common sense; the later Yeats, I think, also rejects Romanticism – and partly at least (in view of his enthusiasm at this period for Anglo-Irish Augustanism) in the interests of the same Berkeleyan ideal.

It would be disingenuous to take this passage of *Alciphron* (relaxed as it is, and wholly directed to scoring off an opponent) as a considered statement of the philosopher's central position. Yet it is thoroughly in line with the bearing of his thought as a whole. Notoriously, Descartes drove a wedge between that part of the personality which knows the world through the senses, and that other part which knows, as he maintains more reliably, by cogitation, deducing which of the reports made by the senses can be trusted. Locke drives the wedge a little deeper, deducing the existence of 'matter', as to which, since it is colourless, scentless, soundless, tasteless, the senses give us no reports at all. The old-fashioned view of Berkeley was that he drove the wedge a little deeper still, and so took his place in the line of succession from Locke through Hume to Kant. But the modern reading is that Berkeley's criticism of Locke was more radical; that he refused as a psychological impossibility the Lockean and Cartesian view that the self which knows through perception and the self which knows through cogitation can be distinct and at variance in their findings. This revised view of his significance seems preferable on many counts – not only because it is, as Dr Luce and others have shown, consonant with the argument of Berkeley's *Principles*; but also because it is consonant with the tone of his writing there, which is the tone of a man who believes himself to be irritably clearing away unnecessary refinements and false subtleties. Moreover this anti-Cartesian conservatism is what one would expect of a friend of Pope and Swift.

It is not easy to determine which view of Berkeley was held by Yeats. When he writes, in 'Blood and the Moon', of 'God-appointed Berkeley that proved all things a dream', he seems to lean towards the older view. Yet Dr Luce himself (*Berkeley's Immaterialism*, Preface p.viii) contends that Yeats had 'met the true Berkeley', when he wrote: 'Descartes, Locke, and Newton, took away the world ... Berkeley restored the world. Berkeley has brought back to us the world that only exists because it shines and sounds.'

For our purposes, I believe, Yeats' position is made sufficiently clear by the characteristically wayward but often profound introduction he wrote, in 1931, to Hone's and Rossi's *Bishop Berkeley. His Life, Writings, and Philosophy*. Yeats here declares, 'The romantic movement seems related ... to Locke's mechanical philosophy, as simultaneous correspondential dreams are related, not merely where there is some traceable influence but through their whole substance.' This may be to say no more than I have argued, that the split in the Romantic personality, between the part that feels and the part that manipulates itself feeling, is at bottom the split made by Descartes and widened by Locke. Yeats goes on, in a well-known passage,

> The romantic movement with its turbulent heroism, its self-assertion, is over, superseded by a new naturalism that leaves man helpless before the contents of his own mind. One thinks of Joyce's *Anna Livia Plurabelle*, Pound's *Cantos*, works of an heroic sincerity, the man, his active faculties in suspense, one finger beating time to a bell sounding and echoing in the depths of his own mind. ...

That Yeats was certainly wrong about Pound, and may have been no less wrong about Joyce, is here beside the point. We find him distinguishing his own attitude from theirs, in that he refuses to split himself into two halves, the one part listening to and recording what happens in the other. He claims Berkeleyan authority for this refusal and this claim is vindicated by the view of Berkeley which has gathered ground steadily since Yeats wrote. It is Berkeley he appeals to, along with Swift, Goldsmith, and Burke, when he protests further, 'And why should I, whose ancestors never accepted the anarchic subjectivity of the nineteenth century, accept its recoil; why should men's heads ache that never drank?' We may, if we like, retort that not his ancestors but Yeats himself had joined in the Romantic bottle party; but his attitude now seems to be that his doing so was an aberration, that the Romantic phase was part of the logic of historical events for an English mind, but not for an Irish mind such as his own. At any rate, it seems clear that Yeats in 1931 was so far from considering himself a Romantic, that he thought of his escaping Romanticism (and its consequences) as part of his very Irishry.

And yet it is the poem that must have the last word. I have said that the last stanza of 'Among School Children' rejects the characteristically Romantic ways toward wisdom and beauty. But how should we understand this 'rejection'? What are the alternative ways that are accepted? It is easy to reply: the Berkeleyan, the Anglo-Irish Augustan ways. And no doubt when Yeats asks (rhetorically):

> O chestnut-tree, great-rooted blossomer,
> Are you the leaf, the blossom or the bole?

– he is invoking a way of life in which the self is not divided against itself, in which art and life attain, in his own phrase (again from the introduction to Hone and Rossi), 'swiftness, volume, unity'. But if we put the stanza back in its place at the end of the poem we have to see that the tree is growing, 'Labour is blossoming or dancing', not under any circumstances that man can bring about, but only in some realm of the ideal. For 'Among School Children' is largely a poem about what it is like to grow old. And Yeats in the poem sees that the knowledgeable will, probing to perjure the candid sense ('The body ... bruised to pleasure soul'), is not the product of any human perversion, but an inescapable condition of life on any terms. For what is old age but the decrepitude of sense defaced by informed will? – if not by man's will, then by will of that power which set him his course to run, which, in the course of perfecting a few souls, mutilates all bodies. Thus Yeats, like Hardy in the passage I have quoted, saw that the setting up of soul or mind against body was a law of life, whether we like it or not. There remains, I suppose, only the question whether we should adopt this law for ourselves, furthering and hastening the progress, aggravating the sickness to which we are born; or whether we should (however vainly, in the last resort) resist it. Yeats' early thought goes all by contraries: Robartes and Aherne; man and mask; primary and antithetical tinctures. This shows him taking for granted the self-division caused by the introverted will, abetting it and embracing it as a technique for dealing with experience. I have argued that the later Berkeleyan Yeats resented this law and protested against it, as Hardy declares that the artist should.

Irish Writing 31, Yeats special number, ed. S.J. White (summer 1955); reprinted in *English Literature and British Philosophy*, ed. S.P. Rosenbaum (Chicago, 1971).

XII Augustan Lyric

I

Chronology

This anthology is concerned, not quite but almost exclusively, with one kind of poetry written in England between the death of Dryden in 1700 and the appearance in 1790 of William Blake's *Songs of Innocence*. The second of these dates hardly needs to be justified; for whatever we take 'lyric' to mean, we know that it describes the *Songs of Innocence*, and yet whatever we take 'Augustan' to mean, we know that it does not describe William Blake. On the other hand 'Augustan' certainly fits, as has been widely acknowledged (not least in the eighteenth century), poems written by Dryden and others in the last thirty or forty years of the seventeenth century; and some of those poems, by explicitly offering themselves as 'Song' or 'Ode' or 'Hymn', demand to be categorized as 'lyric'. It has to be explained why these poems have been excluded.

To explain, we have to go outside strictly literary history. There is a current tendency to decry what the eighteenth century called 'the Glorious Revolution' of 1698, which effectively though not immediately ousted the Stuart dynasty; and to present instead, as the only *true* revolution that the English have experienced (or at least as the nearest that they ever came to that allegedly rejuvenating experience), the Civil War of 1642–49, together with the Cromwellian interregnum which succeeded it. If we measure in terms of blood spilled, or of emotional temperature, this may well be right. But if we measure in terms of *consequences*, we must think that the eighteenth century was right in regarding the Revolutionary Settlement of 1698 as much more momentous than the regicide of 1649. At the risk of simplifying grossly, it may be said that the Revolutionary Settlement acknowledged that England had become or was fast becoming, a bourgeois and mercantile society. And the writers of the Restoration period were only fitfully aware of this; for the most part their writings assume a society which is aristocratic, and monarchical in the thoroughgoing sense that the monarchy is taken to be naturally and essentially absolute. Both assumptions were challenged, and in effect overthrown, by the Revolutionary Settlement.

Accordingly, whereas in Restoration comedy and lyric the merchant figures largely as potential cuckold, his wife and daughters appearing only to be seduced by the aristocratic rake, in post-revolutionary literature the merchant (Addison's Sir Andrew Freeport) is on the contrary a figure of great consequence, and his womenfolk must be treated with flattering attention and civility. And this is an accurate reflection of what seem to have been the facts of economic and political life: the land-owning aristocrat could survive and keep his privileges only if he allied himself with the mercantile interests – an alliance which is the basis of the Whig hegemony throughout most of the eighteenth century. The monarch, so far from being absolute, could survive only so long as he acknowledged that the effective power rested with this allegiance between the landed and the commercial interests. And the code of manners, by which the Duchess of Newcastle and the wife of the lately knighted London merchant could when necessary communicate on stately terms without embarrassment, was worked out and disseminated in *The Spectator* by those journalists of genius and social responsibility, Addison and Steele. It is not a mere change in the ruling dynasty, but on the contrary this momentous switch from a predominantly aristocratic to a predominantly middle-class society, which requires us for our purposes to take as starting-point 1700 or 1698 rather than 1660.

And at the other end of our span, it is not until 1790 that English imaginations, like William Blake's or Joseph Priestley's, began to conceive, faced with the spectacles of first the American and then the French revolutions, that the liberties ensured by the Glorious Revolution were not altogether real, or not altogether comprehensive; to conceive the possibility of an industrial rather than a mercantile economy, and of a popular rather than a bourgeois democracy.

II

'Lyric'

We get a slanted image of the English eighteenth century when we approach it by way of the greatest literary imaginations of the period. For it so happens that what are arguably the most intense and passionate writers of the century – Pope and Swift in the first half, Johnson and Goldsmith in the second – were profoundly reactionary minds. All four were, in different degrees, out of sympathy with the Whiggish England that they were born to – commercial as that was, expansionist, dynamic, technologically inventive and confident. Tories in a world of Whigs, they were in the strictest sense 'radicals' – though of the Right; their criticisms of their society went to the roots, asking *why* social mobility, *why* territorial and commercial expansion, *why* conspicuous consumption, should be accepted as self-evident symptoms of national health and vigour. And so it is not surprising, though it is ironical, that the twentieth-century radical of the Left should find it relatively easy to sympathize with, and admire, an eighteenth-century radical of the Right such as Johnson; both are critics of capitalist imperialism, one before the fact, the other after it.

In the nature of the case, however, these could not be *lyrical* imaginations. For the profoundly radical and reactionary imagination, the natural mode and vehicle is the critical mode of attire. And precisely because, in the satirist, imagination is in this way not so much active as *re-active*, old-fashioned readers at least since Matthew Arnold have found it hard to allow to satire anything but an inferior status among the exertions and endeavours of poetry. Where the eighteenth century is concerned this prejudice, though it persists more widely than we care to acknowledge, has come under so much fire from leaders of opinion that it has largely gone underground. There are many more people who think that Pope is not truly a poet at all, than there are people prepared to stand up and say so.

What has been taken for granted, by both parties to this muffled argument, is that the case for our eighteenth-century poetry must rest upon a recognition not just, right enough, that the satire (along with related kinds like the epistle) is an honourable and noble form; but also that the reader whose ideal of true poetry is Shelley or Gerard Manley Hopkins or George Herbert must cast aside such prejudices and expectations when he engages with the poetry of the eighteenth century. In other words, whatever the virtues of the poetry of that century, it is assumed that they cannot be lyrical virtues.

And yet how can that be? If, as I have argued, the characteristic temper of the English eighteenth century is expansive and confident (everything that Pope and Swift, Johnson and Goldsmith, were not), how can it be that this temper is not expressed in its poetry? Were *all* the poets Tories, not a Whig among them? Once the question is put in that form, it will be seen that there was, there *must have been*, lyrical poetry in the eighteenth as in any other century. And in fact, if we take 'lyrical' in this extended sense to comprehend whatever is sanguine, positive and excited, the century has a great lyrical poet in James Thomson (1700–48), author of *The Seasons*, of *Liberty*, and of 'Poem to the Memory of Sir Isaac Newton'. For Thomson's was an imagination which responded with elation and wonderful vividness to the enlarged horizons opened up by maritime expansion and traffic on the one hand, on the other hand the discoveries and applications of Newtonian science.

However, I have tried to take 'lyric' in a narrower sense, to mean *a poem composed either to match an existing piece of music, or in the expectation and hope of a musical setting being contrived for it.* And this rules out all of Thomson's important poems except 'Rule, Britannia' (which last, however, reads very differently in the context I have just sketched for it than when it is taken to be a piece of patriotic sabre-rattling, heartlessly produced to order).

I have excluded also the poet whom a reader in 1788 declared to be 'the greatest lyrist the world has produced'. This was Thomas Gray. His incautious admirer was the poetess Anna Seward, and the performances by Gray which she had in mind were undoubtedly his Pindaric Odes. The Pindaric Ode, a form much practised throughout the century and particularly in its later decades, is without doubt one kind of lyric, and for mostly excluding such poems I can plead only practical considerations: the more famous examples, by Gray and others, are readily available elsewhere; they require a frame of mind not appropriate to poems I'm more concerned the reader should respond to; and finally, they would have taken up too much room.

For, so far from eighteenth-century lyrics being hard to find, there is an embarrassment of riches. 'Rule, Britannia', 'Hearts of Oak', 'Rock of Ages', 'Guide me, O Thou great Jehovah', ''Twas when the seas were roaring', 'When I survey the wond'rous cross', 'Gentle Jesus, meek and mild', 'Here's to the maiden of bashful fifteen', 'All in the Downs the fleet was moor'd', 'God moves in a mysterious way', 'Here, a sheer hulk, lies poor Tom Bowling', 'How doth the little busy bee', 'Let dogs delight to bark and bite', 'Jesu, lover of my soul' – each of these (and the list could be three times as long) turns out to be an eighteenth-century lyric, as I have defined it. And that Englishman or Englishwoman has had a deprived childhood, who does not remember one or two out of this list as somehow familiar. Not all of them by any means, once the words are abstracted from the catchy tune that comes to mind along with each of them, stands up as a poem in (as we oddly say) 'its own right'. And accordingly not all of them appear in these pages. Yet 'its own right' is a strange conception when applied to poems that are, in the strictest sense, lyrics; for, almost by definition, such a poem asks to be judged as only one half of a total experience of which the other half is the tune that we sing it to. Moreover, in cases where we know the tune (or *some* tune), abstracting the words from the tune, if it is legitimate, is not always in practical experience possible. And it varies greatly from one reader to the next – not just because of native aptitudes, but because of different experience.

Take the case of the congregational hymn. The eighteenth century is the great age of English hymn-writing, the century of Watts and Wesley, Newton and Cowper. A reader who is used, in church or chapel, to sing 'Christians, awake!' or 'Glorious things of thee are spoken', will find it much harder to consider the hymns as poems, as exclusively verbal constructions, than will the reader who never worships. (On the other hand, presumably, the Christian reader will be more in sympathy with what the hymns, as poems, *say*.) I have tried to get round this difficulty, and to let all readers start equal, by printing mostly hymns that are seldom sung.

III

'Augustan'

But with an anthology where, as now appears, the hymns of the Christian churches must figure largely, what happens to the promise implicit in the word, 'Augustan'? Surely the point the hymns enforce is that, in this century which we call unthinkingly 'neoclassical', the imagination of the English of all ranks is peopled by figures and events from the Hebrew scriptures at least as much as by personalities and stories from Graeco-Roman mythology, history and literature. True enough; and it is hard to think of a point that is more worth making. Yet the truth is that the most influential and famous hymn-writers – Watts, the Wesleys, Cowper – were very good and cultivated Latinists; and that the precedent of Horace above all was as compelling for them as for the secular poets their contemporaries.

It is Horace above all who matters; the Horace of the *carmina*. For the pre-Augustan Catullus, the eighteenth century as a whole had less liking than the seventeenth century before it or the nineteenth century after. And though Thomson and others at mid-century imitated Tibullus, as others imitated Anacreon and Pindar, it is the Horace of the *carmina* (the 'odes') who stands for most of the eighteenth century as the type of the lyric poet.

It is just here that it becomes important to take the measure of Matthew Prior who, not at all by accident, stands first in this anthology. For the eighteenth century, and we must suppose for Prior himself, his most important poem was his most ambitious, *Solomon on the Vanity of the World*, of which Charles Wesley in 1778 required his daughter Sally to get the first book by heart. Henry Bett has shown that *Solomon* was so constantly in the minds of the Wesleys that it is literally impossible to account for every turn of phrase which Prior's poem contributes to the Wesleys' hymns. However *Solomon* is in no sense a lyrical poem, and so Prior as a religious or devotional poet is represented here by his Ode, *On Exodus iii.14*, which the Wesleys esteemed not much less than *Solomon*. (See the notes to this poem for a demonstration that the disrepute into which Prior has fallen as a religious poet – he does not figure in Dame Helen Gardner's *Book of Religious Verse* – is undeserved.) Nevertheless, the Horatian Prior whom the eighteenth-century poets esteemed, sacred and secular poets alike, is not the religious poet but the author of, for instance, 'A Better Answer to Cloe Jealous'. This poem is printed in one anthology after another, yet no one undertakes to explain what claim it has on our attention, so manifestly trivial as it is in subject-matter. It is prudent and proper not to break butterflies on wheels; yet it will not do to label this poem 'charming', and leave it at that. Nearly forty years ago F.R. Leavis in his *Revaluation* showed how to account for the distinction of not dissimilar pieces of bantering gallantry by Thomas Carew and Andrew Marvell. Their value and their achievement, Leavis said, was in their tone; though what the voice said was trivial, by its tone the voice in the poem displayed *urbanity*. And urbanity, the Horatian virtue, was a very serious matter for these poets and their first readers, as it should be for us; for it is neither more nor less than tact and sympathy and sureness in the handling of human relations within the decorous proprieties insisted on by a civilized society. Leavis showed how the touch was lost, how good breeding coarsened into mere raffishness, in poems of gallantry written after the Restoration. What can be claimed for Prior is that at his hands the valuable urbanity was regained – yet with a difference, all the difference involved in passing from an aristocratic to a bourgeois society. This is to claim for Prior in verse what has been often claimed for Addison and Steele in prose. Women's Liberation may prefer the 'Madam' or 'Lady' of aristocratic address to Prior's 'child' and 'girl'; undoubtedly in the transition certain finenesses were lost, and it may indeed be true that privileged women in the upper orders of Elizabethan and Caroline society enjoyed more equality *vis-à-vis* their menfolk than did the wives and daughters and mistresses of the eighteenth-century middle class (though those women sought and achieved more equality as the century wore on). Yet a poem like 'A Better Answer' or 'To a Lady: She Refusing ...' certainly affords a valuable model of how to handle relations between the sexes with civility and finesse. If we look at Prior's Horatian poems as so many model performances in the conduct of human relations, in using social conventions so as to steer and enrich such relations rather than stifle them, we cannot fail to be impressed by Prior's range; not just how a man should behave towards his wife or his mistress, but how a grown man should treat a girl-child, how a bachelor should treat his housekeeper (as in the admirable and surprising 'Jinny the Just', too little known since its first publication in 1907), how a man should treat his colleague, his drinking-companion, his patron – these are the problems, if that is the word, to which Prior addresses himself. The more trivial the overt subjects or occasions, the more the lesson goes home, for what is involved is precisely *nuance*, a nicety of human attention for which no occasion (a tiff, a fit of the sulks, an awkwardly discontinued conversation) is too trivial to be worth taking care about. And thus, at the end of the 'Better Answer', the explicit appeal to Horace is intended seriously, for all that it is touched upon so lightly; there are sides to Horace in the *carmina* which are outside Prior's range altogether, but Horace's urbanity is what Prior can respond to very acutely, and can emulate with great resourcefulness.

Intimately related, and even more to the point if we are concerned with Prior's legacy to his successors, is the line:

Let us e'en talk a little like folks of this world.

Much more than is commonly acknowledged, eighteenth-century poetry *does* talk 'like folks of this world'; and indeed a main intention of this anthology is to show how much of it does so. Of poets not represented here, Swift almost throughout, and Pope much of the time, use a language that is conversational, not to say colloquial; and one can only suppose that those people have not read Pope who declare confidently to the contrary. As the century wore on, however, the language of poetry became more divorced from the language that was spoken; though there are striking exceptions like Cowper, and one has to distinguish between Johnson and Goldsmith, who admitted spoken usage as a relevant consid-eration, and poets like Gray, who did not. To hymn-writers like Watts and the Wesleys and Cowper, themselves learned and sophisticated men who sought for their hymns a diction meaningful to unlearned con-gregations, Prior's precedent in talking 'a little like folks of this world' was momentous. And this explains why Cowper should have exploded in indignation at Johnson's treatment of Prior in his *Lives of the Poets*, and why John Wesley should have printed in his *Arminian Magazine*, though to the scandal of some of his followers, Prior's ballad, 'Henry and Emma', which Johnson the High Churchman thought improper. It explains why Isaac Watts, not much less than the Wesleys and Cowper, drew on Prior's precedent; and why John Wesley towards the end of his life should have sprung to Prior's defence with his *Thoughts on the Character and Writings of Mr Prior*. The devotional poets recognized their debt to Prior, and repaid it in admiration. And since Prior in his secular poems quite often skirts impropriety, we begin to see that the eighteenth-century hymn-writers were not such blinkered and inflexible dogmatists as we tend to suppose.

IV

Ballads

A very different matter is the other body of popular poetry which I have tried to represent. In church or chapel the unlettered eighteenth-century Englishman could be nourished, at least some of the time, by a poetry like the poetry of Horace; by language that was clean, solid and intellectually sinewy, as well as forcefully melodious. In the theatre or the taproom, though Boreas and Amphitrite and Gallia and Albion swirled neo-classical draperies about the patriotic words that he sang or had sung to him, these were excrescences upon a form, the ballad, which owed nothing to precedents in Latin or Greek. In the eighteenth century the ballad was understood to be at least as much lyric as narrative, as we see when John Gay calls his masterpiece 'a ballad-opera'. However *The Beggar's Opera* is in English a unique achievement; and it would be generally agreed that the street-ballad of the eighteenth century is a sadly degenerate relative of those ballads of the Anglo-Scottish border which we think of as the classics of this form. One can always be asked to imagine that in the eighteenth as in any other century, in field or market or at the quay-side, the 'people' was composing, and singing or reciting, poems more truthful and affecting than the poems of the literate *élite* which we read from the printed page. But the trouble is that on this argument any example of this poetry which is put before us has to be inferior, because it has to be had corrupted into print before we can look at it. Accordingly we have a duty to be sceptical; the naval ballads which I have chosen to represent the popular ballad in general turn out to be not *by* 'the people' but *for* them; or else, if some of them had a source that was genuinely of the people, like the 'fore-bitters' that we know were composed and sung on the men-o'-war, that original has been transformed and dressed up to please a wider audience, before ever the piece comes down to us. This is not to say that they are all of a piece; on the contrary, David Garrick's 'Hearts of Oak' is seen for the humane and true if modest achievement that it is, when set beside John Wignell's 'Neptune's Resignation', which I have rescued from oblivion chiefly so as to show how bad an eighteenth-century lyric could be.

What this material can cure us of is the not uncommon self-pitying supposition that ours, 'the TV age', is the first in which the media of communication have been manipulated so as to feed us, 'the people', with entertainment that is manifestly insulting to us, trashy and dishonest. The printed page is a medium no less than the television network, and indeed when print takes the form of 'broadsides', as it commonly did for the topical ballads (see Pinto and Rodway, *The Common Muse*), we may say that it is a *mass*-medium. Charles Dibdin (1745–1814) had a career as a purveyor of mass-entertainment such as we too readily suppose has been possible only in our own times or in the past hundred years. In the eighteenth century as in ours what is offered as 'art of the people' turns out to be that very different thing, art directed at the populace by promotors who seek a wide sale, or else art wished on the populace by those who have a recruiting-sergeant's interest in offering themselves as 'the people's' spokesmen.

A much more respectable name than Dibdin's is smirched by this sort of imputation; for 'Sweet William's Farewell' by Gay is rather plainly, when we look at it, heartlessly patronizing. Gay's talent was for the burlesque; and just as his *Shepherd's Calendar* fitfully achieves the pastoral note by setting out to be mock-pastoral, so *The Beggar's Opera* achieves the heroic while intending only the mock-heroic. Thus it may be that 'Sweet William's Farewell' was intended to burlesque certain genuine ballads, on much the same lines as Gay's broader and less interesting burlesque, 'Twas when the seas were roaring'. But in either case we surely have to say that the burlesque was misconceived and cheap, in a way that no incidental felicities ('So the sweet lark, high-pois'd in air/ Shuts close his pinions to his breast') can compensate for. And more generally, when Horatian urbanity is thus reduced to an ironical formula for eating one's cake and having it (the manoeuvre is practised by twentieth-century poets as well), we have a duty to refuse the bargain. I am confessing to a distrust of Gay's motives which will explain why, accomplished and sensitive as he is, he figures in this collection less largely than might have been expected.

Gay's failure is excusable and symptomatic. Though in earlier periods there had been literature directed at the mercantile or artisan middle-class – for instance, in the Jacobean period, Thomas Deloney's romances and Dekker's plays – the social revolution registered by the Revolutionary Settlement demanded a rethinking of artistic categories so wholesale that such precedents were hardly helpful. Literary theory since the Renaissance had assumed that the middle and lower classes in society could figure in the national literature, except in specially class-oriented *genres* like Deloney's narratives, only under the aegis of *comedy*. 'Sweet William's Farewell' shows Gay trapped in this assumption, struggling to overcome or circumvent it, but ultimately defeated. It's in the light of this defeat that the mid-Victorian anthologist, F.T. Palgrave, was splendidly right to single out for posterity 'Sally in Our Alley' by the obscure and unhappy Henry Carey, as succeeding where the infinitely more gifted poet, Gay, had failed – in giving a touching and unaffected image, without condescension, of how human sentiments and relations worked out among the lower orders. Carey's poem has been anthologized many times since, seldom with any sense so sure as Palgrave's of what its claim on our attention consists in. Because it is thus readily available, I have omitted it.

The Beggar's Opera represents not a solution of this problem but an evasion of it; for by setting his action in the criminal classes (among whom the class-structure of law-abiding society is kaleidoscopically mingled, rather than inverted), Gay brilliantly circumvented the problem of how to make artisans and merchants as much the objects of human concern as were fine lords and ladies. And accordingly, as William Empson and others have shown, *The Beggar's Opera* – suavely central though it is to English Augustan literature – in fact finds its progeny in Romantic literature, in a literature which assumes that honesty and humanity are to be found not anywhere in the interstices of the social order but only outside that order, among the outlaws, the 'cop-outs'.

V

Four Poets

Rather than represent non-lyrical poets by uncharacteristic lyrical effusions (Pope by the 'Ode: on Solitude' and the 'Universal Prayer'; Swift by 'The Day of Judgment'; Johnson by 'A Short Song of Congratulation'; Goldsmith by a song from *The Vicar of Wakefield*), I have chosen to devote space rather to certain eighteenth-century poets whose genius was indeed lyrical, to a degree that I think is still unacknowledged. I name four such poets: Watts, Smart, Cowper, John Newton. (A fifth, Charles Wesley, certainly deserves no less of me and of my readers; but Wesley's claims must await another time and another hand.)

ISAAC WATTS

The English puritan, that figure which, however we apprehend it, must figure so largely in any account that we give of our seventeenth century – what happens to him when the seventeenth century becomes the eighteenth? If we asked ourselves that question (it seems we seldom do), we should collide at once with the massive figure, and the formidably single-minded career, of Dr Isaac Watts.

We may say that the puritan became respectable – less by acceding to the standards of society, than by making those standards bend to his. But this is inadequate. With Watts the English puritan became not just respectable, but (the more pregnant and momentous term that the eighteenth century set store by) he became *civil*. He contrived, in Watts' time and with Watts' help, to enter into, and take his share of, Augustan secular culture – and all without bending the rigour of his principles.

It's important to realize that many puritans remained within the Church of England. John Norris for instance, who helped to form Watts' literary opinions (see Norris's *Collection of Miscellanies*, 1706), was rector of Bemerton. And later in the century, if the Evangelical movement was a puritan movement (as it surely was), most of its leading figures – John Newton, Toplady, the Wesleys themselves – remained inside the Established Church. The puritan is not to be identified with the dissenter or, as we mostly call him today, the nonconformist. But because dissenters were, like the Papists, debarred by law from many areas of the national life (for instance from the universities – the dissenters in consequence created their own alternative educational establishment, in many ways more liberal than Oxford and Cambridge), it is among the dissenters like Watts that we get the strongest sense of a culture within a culture, distinct from the national culture yet not insulated from it.

The process was traced by Max Weber and later R.H. Tawney by which the Puritan principles (frugality, regularity, sobriety, diligence), since they were also the requirements for commercial success, in due

course and in many cases brought worldly rewards to those whose hopes
were set (so they would have said, and no doubt sincerely) upon another
world altogether. By Watts' time the fruits of this happy coincidence
were there for the gathering in; and by 1700 a great deal of the commerce
and finance of the City of London, as of provincial centres like Bristol,
Hull and King's Lynn, was in the hands of the dissenters. But this is due
not solely to the puritanism which the dissenters shared with many anglicans, but to the statecraft which had deliberately diverted into commerce
the dissenting talent and energy which might have gone into government. At any rate, these dissenters were among those merchants with
whom the Whig landowners had to combine if they were to keep their
privilege and status. The dissenters were the implacable though sober
zealots for whom maintaining the Whig hegemony was a matter of life
and death; who would have plunged England into renewed civil war
rather than see a Tory administration, just as some of Swift's associates in
the brief Tory administration of 1712–13 were prepared to deal with the
Pretender, as their only hope of regaining the power that they lost with
Queen Anne's death. Each knew his enemy: Swift, whose whole career
makes sense only if we see it directed at such as Watts; and Watts, whose
loyal poem of 1705 to Queen Anne was given a vicious 'Palinodia' in
1721, because the Queen had let in the Tories ten years before.

It would be charitable to say that Watts as poet has been the victim of
his own success; that we take so much for granted the rhetoric of the
English congregational hymn that we never pause to wonder who created
that rhetoric. (Watts did, almost singlehanded.) But we ought not to be
so charitable, not to ourselves nor to our mentors of this and of preceding
generations. For the curiously ambiguous status of Isaac Watts as poet –
his figuring modestly in all respectable anthologies and a great deal more
largely in our oral tradition, yet never remembered as one in the succession of our illustrious poets – reflects, one cannot help but think, a similar
ambiguity in the official or received version of English culture when it
comes to assessing the contribution to that culture of puritanism in
general and of nonconformists in particular. The roundheads of
Cromwell are remembered as the iconoclasts who defaced the sculpture
of our churches; Watts and his associates are thought of as comically illiberal because they supported (as Prior did also) Jeremy Collier's successful
protest against the licentiousness of the Restoration theatre; dissenters of
a later day are remembered as Matthew Arnold's 'philistines'; and in our
own day the nonconformists are said to have influenced, for good or ill,
far more than Karl Marx the cast of mind of the British Labour Party.
Particularly puerile are attempts to explain English nonconformity, along
with brass bands and whippet-racing, as a product of something called (if
you please) 'working-class culture'. One looks in vain for any general
recognition that the artistic culture of the nation, so far from being repu-

diated by nonconformists as the product of a ruling class or an alien caste, has been embraced by the best of them in every generation, and enriched (though also at times valuably purged) by their efforts. Isaac Watts is the unavoidable representative of that embrace and that enrichment.

When A.E. Housman, in *The Name and Nature of Poetry* (1933), quotes four lines of Watts and comments, 'That simple verse, bad rhyme and all, is poetry beyond Pope', this is worse than useless. It suggests, and is meant to suggest, that there is an artless tradition represented by Watts, which is a superior alternative to an artful tradition represented by Pope. No such thing! Watts is a very artful poet, and his simplicity is the product of art. (It is also the product of a heroic abnegation by this poet of the splendours and artifices which he could deploy, and had, in his earliest pieces – see his 'Few Happy Matches'.) Isaac Watts is a great poet by precisely those standards that make Pope a great poet. This is not to say he is as great as Pope; that would be absurd. But it does mean that, hymn-writer as he mostly though not exclusively is, Watts represents not an alternative tradition but the one unavoidable tradition of English poetry. In his hymns and out of them he writes solidly, cleanly and sparely. This is what we say of Pope; and it is what we have to say, if we are honest, of Watts.

This point must be emphasized, and not just in relation to Watts. In Henry Bett's admirably learned and indispensable book, *The Hymns of Methodism*, perhaps the single wrong note is struck when, discussing the importance of Prior for the Wesleys, Bett says, 'It was his influence that saved them from the monotonous antithesis of the "correct" style of Pope.' There is a letter from John Wesley (to the Reverend Mr Furley, 15 July 1764) which shows that Wesley could hardly have agreed with this:

> If you imitate any writers, let it be South, Atterbury, or Swift, in whom all the properties of a good writer meet. I was myself once much fonder of Prior than Pope; as I did not then know that stiffness was a fault. But what in all Prior can equal, for beauty of style, some of the first lines, that Pope ever published? –
>
> > Poets themselves must die, like those they sung
> > Deaf the praised ear, and mute the tuneful tongue;
> > E'en he whose heart now melts in tender lays,
> > Shall shortly want the generous tear he pays.
> > Then from his eyes thy much-loved form shall part;
> > And the last pang shall tear thee from his heart:
> > Life's idle business at one gasp be o'er
> > The Muse forgot, and thou beloved no more.
>
> Here is style! How clear, how pure, proper, strong; and yet how amazingly easy! This crowns all; no stiffness, no hard words; no apparent art, no affectation; all is natural, and therefore consummately beautiful.

Go thou and write likewise.

(Wesley, Works, vol. xiii, 417)

This passage is not at odds with what Wesley was to write eighteen years later in his *Thoughts on the Character and Writings of Mr Prior*, for there Pope is attacked not at all for his style but for the 'exquisitely injudicious' subject and sentiment of his 'Verses to the Memory of an Unfortunate Lady'. And if it seems odd to have Prior considered as 'stiff' by contrast with Pope, he certainly is so in for instance the pindarick 'Ode to the Memory of Colonel Villiers', which Wesley singles out as one of three pieces 'which he has taken the pains to polish'. Insist as we must on the importance of Prior for the lyrical poets who came after him, there can be no question of tracing from him a 'tradition' which is an alternative to Pope's. And enthusiasts for Watts or for the Wesleys do their subjects no service at all when they set them up in competition with the greatest poet of their age.

CHRISTOPHER SMART

Fifteen years ago, in *The Late Augustans*, I proposed: 'It is not impossible that when Smart is judged over the whole range of his various production – conventional in form as well as unconventional, light and even ribald as well as devotional, urbane or tender as well as sublime – he will be thought of as the greatest English poet between Pope and Wordsworth.' In the years since, this suggestion has been treated with at best respectful incredulity; and although Smart has attracted rather more scholarly attention in the interim, I see little sign that he is now regarded otherwise than as he was then, as the author of one poem of inexplicable genius, *Song to David*, and another of fascinatingly deranged imperfection, *Jubilate Agno*. Particularly significant, and to my mind lamentable, is the decision of Dame Helen Gardner, when she assembled *A Book of Religious Verse* (1972), to follow a bad and hoary precedent in printing a mutilated version of *A Song to David*, thus denying herself space for more than one of the *Hymns and Spiritual Songs for the Festivals of the Church of England*. So far as I am concerned my fifteen-year-old claim for Smart still stands; it awaits either vindication or rebuttal.

   To my sorrow I've not been able to represent Smart 'over the whole range'. Being pressed for space, I've chosen to represent him by his secular rather than devotional pieces, selecting however for his 'divine' poem one of the *Hymns* not readily available elsewhere. Of the pieces that I give, two, it should be noted, come from the very beginning of Smart's career; his 'Morning Piece' and 'Noon Piece' appeared in a university magazine as early as 1750. And indeed it seems, to judge from these two incomparable performances, that if Smart's talent increased in power thereafter, it suffered in delicacy and refinement – as indeed one might expect, in view of the ravages which a misery, largely but not wholly self-inflicted, later subjected him to.

The achievement of 'A Morning Piece, Or an hymn for the hay-makers' can best be seen by comparing it with John Cunningham's 'Morning'. Cunningham's poem is delightful: fresh, uncluttered, authen-ticating itself at every step as it cleaves true to one immediate experience after another. How wasteful, we rightly think, the time spent by other poets (by Cunningham himself in other poems) on invoking rhetorical or mythological figures to mediate between them and a sensed experience which ('See the chattering swallow spring;/Darting through the one-arch'd bridge') was all the time available to them in memory, if only they had stayed still long enough to attend to it! And a taste in poetry such as ours will be, if we have schooled ourselves on the post-Imagist poetry of our own time, will reasonably enough see in Cunningham's modest but solid and refreshing piece a vindication of such a post-Imagist slogan as the late William Carlos Williams' 'No ideas but in things'. This is surely a right and valuable response, so far as it goes. But to turn to Smart's poem is to move into a realm that post-Imagist poetics has never dreamed of. In 'A Morning Piece' one of the traditional rhetorical figures, *prosopopoeia* (or personification), so far from mediating between the poet and his expe-rience, is a way of lifting that experience to a new power. By means of it, each item of sensuously registered and remembered experience becomes, while retaining its itemized integrity, a sign and manifestation of an energy abroad in the waking world. 'Strong Labour got up with his pipe in his mouth / And stoutly strode over the dale' – so misread, in his excitement, Oliver Goldsmith, adding, 'There is not a man now living who could write such a line'. And what did Goldsmith mean, if not that the real labourer smoking real tobacco in a real pipe ('He lent new perfume to the breath of the south') is also, by this way of putting it, an instance and a proof of the energy altogether more generally called 'labour' (for instance the labour of bees in the flower or the hive), of which the perfume might as readily be sweat or honey as tobacco? By contrast, John Cunningham's 'Philomel' is the merest inert short-hand for 'nightingale'.

And the proof that this indeed was Smart's vision (which is to say, his experience) is in that aspect of his writing which is least controvertible as it is least demonstrable – in his 'ear', in the sureness and promptness with which he switches rhythms. Rhythm – this is how an energy manifests itself, and when we switch rhythms we are discriminating among energies (energies abroad outside us, and within us only if we choose to invite them in, as it is the poet's glory to do). Smart's switching of rhythms, so much in contrast with Cunningham's solid trochees (themselves an achievement in a century so tuned to the iambic), was what the Pindaric ode required of its poets, as did the operatic aria. Smart's changes of gear strike me as manifestly superior to Gray's laborious and creditable attempts at the same effect, as also to such a bravura-piece as Dryden's 'Alexander's Feast', where each change of rhythm simulates the entry of a musical instrument. And Smart achieves it all without raising the key of his speech above the Horatian, 'Let us e'en talk a little like folks of this world'.

When Smart moves from his 'Morning Piece' to his 'Noon Piece', he does more than move through the hours of the forenoon. A perception announced in the 'Morning Piece' ('Sweet Society the bride ...') is now permitted to parade in its full disconcerting grandeur: 'energies' are created or given substance by nurture as well as nature. Even before we get to 'Sidney's high-wrought stories', the allusions to pastoral convention ('Colin Clout and *Yorkshire* Will') have made us realize that 'nurture', which we might as well call 'culture', if it has not actually *produced* energies (and perhaps it has), has at all events so radically transformed energies (for instance the energies of human sexuality) that it deserves to be ranked on a level with Nature herself. And thus it is in a garden ('Where Flora's flock, by nature wild/To discipline are reconcil'd,/And laws and order cultivate,/Quite civiliz'd into a state') that the human agents can with decency and self-respect surrender to the urgent promptings of their sexual appetites. What light this context throws back on to the ambiguous dangerousness of that salient image – 'Their scythes upon the adverse bank/Glitter 'mongst th'entangled trees' – would be a study in itself. Let it be said at least that this mid-eighteenth-century pastoral escapes as certainly as seventeenth-century pastorals like Marvell's, from the socio-political reading that William Empson has found so rewarding in respect of less ambitious pastorals, like Gay's *Beggar's Opera* or Gray's *Elegy*. Smart's poems claim to have a metaphysical import; their rhythms and their *prosopopoeia* claim as much; and only if the claim is granted, can those dimensions of their panoply be justified.

The ode 'To Admiral Sir George Pocock' is certainly an inferior performance, and notable more for astonishing eccentricities than for secure achievement. And yet, what extraordinary audacities there are –

> When Christ, the seaman, was aboard,
> Swift as an arrow to the *White* ...

And in any case I could not miss the chance of showing how Smart, no less than the other distraught devotional poet Cowper, has his connections with the quite other side of eighteenth-century lyrics represented by the naval ballads.

The hymn for the day of St Philip and St James was chosen from among many, which deserve attention no less, chiefly for two reasons: first, 'In the choir of Christ and WREN' captures more completely than any other line in Smart's poetry what seems to have become his governing preoccupation or obsession (much complicated apparently by his having married a Papist), his wish to make St Paul's in London supplant St Peter's in Rome as the metropolitan church of Christendom; secondly, because

> And the lily smiles supremely
> Mentioned by the Lord on earth ...

merits John Middleton Murry's comment, 'This is the true, the strange Christian *naïveté*' – to which one need only add that, within the universe of poetic rhetoric, this simplicity pierces, and counts for so much, precisely because it strikes into a fabric that is not simple at all, but on the contrary elaborately patterned. The marching power of Smart's rhythms, in these hymns that he envisaged sung by massed congregations, is as evident here as in the hymn on the Nativity, or in *A Song to David* itself. And appropriate as it undoubtedly is to the full-throated unqualified celebration that Smart intended in these poems, the loss of fineness and variable flexibility since the 'Morning Piece' and 'Noon Piece' ought to be noted.

WILLIAM COWPER

On 19 November 1787 Cowper was visited by the clerk of the parish of All Saints, Northampton, who asked him to compose some verses which could be printed at the foot of the Bill of Mortality, i.e. the list which the parish clerk published each Christmas, of the parishioners who had died during the year. In a letter written eight days later Cowper described the dialogue which ensued between him and John Cox, the clerk:

> To this I replied; – 'Mr Cox, you have several men of genius in your town, why have you not applied to them? There is a namesake of yours in particular, Cox the statuary, who, everybody knows, is a first-rate maker of verses. He surely is the man of all the world for your purpose.' 'Alas! sir, I have heretofore borrowed help from him, but he is a gentleman of so much reading that the people of our town cannot understand him.'

Accordingly Cowper composed verses not just for 1787, but also for 1788, 1789, 1790, 1792 and 1793. Each poem was published anonymously as a broadside and can thus be considered as in the strictest sense *popular* literature. the poem for 1788, with significantly an epigraph from Horace, is particularly fine.

The point of the anecdote is that Cowper was even more 'a gentleman of ... much reading' than Mr Cox the sculptor; but that, as a poet of genius rather than 'a first-rate maker of verses', he could, when he wanted to, write so that 'the people of our town' might understand him. This was a point of pride for Cowper, and he reverts to it often in his letters. When he undertook to translate Homer, for instance, he wanted to surpass

previous translators by bringing out what he took to be the heroic plain-
ness of Homer's language. And it should come as no surprise that
Cowper, like the Wesleys, took Prior to be the model and master, for the
eighteenth century, of such a plain and popular style as he needed for the
Bills of Mortality, for other broadsides that he wrote, and for his hymns.

(The relationship with the Wesleys may be close. In the poem for the
Bill of Mortality in 1788 appears the stanza:

> Sad waste! for which no after-thrift atones:
> The grave admits no cure of guilt or sin;
> Dew-drops may deck the turf that hides the bones,
> But tears of godly grief ne'er flow within.

And this may owe something to the mockery which six years before John
Wesley had heaped on Pope's couplet from 'Verses to the Memory of an
Unfortunate Lady':

> Yet shall thy grave with rising flowers be dress'd,
> And the green turf lie light upon thy breast.

'Who would not,' says Wesley, 'go to hell, to have the green turf grow
upon his grave? Nay, and primroses too! For the poet assures her, –

> There the first roses of the spring shall blow!')

Cowper is a poet of very wide range indeed, and he was as much the
master of elevated and florid diction as of the plain and popular. In particular, as a man with a very lively sense of humour (which he valued all the
more, from being recurrently a victim of insane melancholia), Cowper in
many poems – repeatedly, for instance, in *The Task*, or in that masterpiece of barely controlled hysteria, the 'Ode on the Death of Mrs
Throckmorton's Bulfinch' – exploited to comic effect the disparity
between elevated diction and humble or apparently trivial subject matter,
or else calculated switches and transitions from one level of diction to
another. In the anthologies Cowper's achievement with these techniques
inevitably, and quite properly, bulks large; the more narrowly focussed
concern of this collection permits us to represent him by pieces in which
he is plain and forceful. If this means that his flair for verbal comedy gets
rather little showing, it brings out on the other hand his masculine trenchancy, whether he is commenting on Admiral Keppel's court-martial or
on how 'God moves in a mysterious way'. Cowper uses the same
straightforward, hard-hitting style, whether he is addressing his friends
and neighbours as members of the same congregation, or as fellow-
citizens perturbed by public affairs like the Gordon riots or the slave-trade
or the war with revolutionary France.

And not only in style are the secular and the religious poems at one.
For God's ways of moving are never more mysterious than when He

brings about those events for which even today our lawyers can find no better explanation than to call them Acts of God; when for instance he sends the Royal George with all her complement to the bottom, not when she is in action against the enemy nor in heavy weather on the high seas, but when she seems to be securely moored by the harbour-wall; or when (to take the case never explicit in these poems but behind all or most of them) he singles out for the curse of intermittent insanity the humane and cultivated poet, who cannot avoid his doom though he withdraws from public life into a well-cushioned provincial retirement. To Cowper, a Calvinist as Watts had been, as the Wesleys very deliberately were not, this aspect of God – His omnipotence, which is to say His total freedom to act as He chooses in ways that seem to human reason unjust and unaccountable – was something borne out by every moment of waking life. The marvel is that this constant awareness did not paralyse the poet, nor did it hypnotize him so that he could not take a lively and partisan interest in the public happenings of his time.

JOHN NEWTON

There are few nowadays to whom the Reverend John Newton is even a name. And among those few there are some, I fear, for whom the name conjures up a grotesque image, both comic and horrifying, of a Pecksniffian hypocrite who walked the planks of his slave-ship in the South Atlantic, reflecting aloud, for the sake of the human cattle chained to their gratings below, 'Glorious things of thee are spoken/Zion, city of our God'; a monster of complacency who later, after a well-publicized 'conversion', harried into insanity his parishioner William Cowper, by hell-fire sermons expounding Calvinist doctrine at its most rigid and ferocious.

In fact Newton, as the captain of a slave-ship, was as humane as possible by the standards, and given the conditions, of the slave-trade in his day. His conversion was publicized, much later, precisely to give ammunition to those who wanted the slave-trade outlawed. The records of the Evangelical Movement show that, far from being an extremist, Newton continually tried to mediate between the Calvinist and the Arminian wings. And as for Cowper, he had known suicidal fits of insane melancholia before he ever met Newton, and the seeds of it were in congenital hypochondria. But all this, it will seem, is to plead no more than mitigating circumstances. By the standards of his day, both in his first profession and his second one, John Newton was temperate and enlightened – very well; but then (it will be said) the standards of his day were abominable. It is better to take the bull by the horns and admit that Newton was a remarkably simple, even an obtuse man. This at least saves him from the charge of hypocrisy. He was sincere within his limits, which were narrow.

Long before humanitarian feeling and the political genius of William Wilberforce made the slave-trade a burning issue of social morality, men like James Thomson and William Shenstone had perceived the monstrous anomaly of Sunday services at sea for the crews of slave-ships. But Newton, self-educated, represents a much less sophisticated level of society than Thomson or Shenstone or his own friend, Cowper. And for the historian, just that is his irreplaceable value. Newton on his last voyage committed to his diary his fears of an insurrection among his slaves:

> We have not been wanting in care to keep it out of their power, yet (as the best mere human precaution is insufficient to guard against everything) they had found means to provide themselves with knives and other dangerous weapons and were just ripe for mischief. So true it is that except the Lord keep the city the watchman watcheth in vain!

We find it hard to credit a simplicity which could in all good faith subscribe that last pious reflection. Yet it's just this naïveté which, later in Newton's life, produced his best hymns:

The prophet's sons, in times of old,
  Though to appearance poor,
Were rich without possessing gold,
  And honour'd, though obscure.

In peace their daily bread they eat,
  By honest labour earn'd;
While daily at Elisha's feet
  They grace and wisdom learn'd.

The prophet's presence cheer'd their toil,
  They watch'd the words he spoke,
Whether they turn'd the furrow'd soil,
  Or fell'd the spreading oak.

Once, as they listened to his theme,
  Their conference was stopp'd;
For one beneath the yielding stream,
  A borrow'd Axe had dropp'd.

'Alas! it was not mine,' he said
  'How shall I make it good?'
Elisha heard, and when he pray'd,
  The iron swam like wood.

If God, in such a small affair,
  A miracle performs,
It shows his condescending care
  Of poor unworthy worms.

Though kings and nations in his view
   Are but as motes and dust,
His eye and ear are fix'd on you,
   Who in his mercy trust.

Not one concern of ours is small.
   If we belong to him
To teach us this, the Lord of all
   Once made the iron swim.

This disconcerting *literalness* in the reading of the Christian Revelation was something that more complex and self-conscious writers like Isaac Watts and George Herbert (they were Newton's favourite poets) strove to attain by strenuous moral and artistic discipline. Those who know Newton from his logs and diaries, from his 'Authentic Narrative' (of his own conversion), from his innumerable letters, will realize that for him on the contrary this naïveté was natural. The absence of conscious intention and strategy, the lack of pressure and strain behind the ultimate transparency, certainly makes Newton's hymns inferior, as poems, to the poems of Herbert and the best hymns of Watts and Cowper. Yet the product speaks for itself. Its poetic virtues are minimal perhaps, yet real and rare, and moral as much as literary. For it is honesty, the refusal to slip anything over on the reader or the congregation, which pins down the miracle at its most literal, by *rhyme:*

'Alas! it was not mine,' he said,
   'How shall I make it good?'
Elisha heard, and when he pray'd
   The iron swam like wood.

And it is the same wide-eyed concern to get the point home at its most astounding which justifies what seems at first sight a clear case of that bane of eighteenth-century poetry, the superfluous because 'stock' epithet:

For one beneath the yielding stream
   A borrow'd axe had dropp'd.

It is of the nature of streams to 'yield'. This one didn't – and that's just the point; simple enough in all conscience, but in its very simplicity massively disconcerting.

The tang of colloquial idiom is everywhere in Newton:

The Manna, favour'd Israel's meat,
   Was gather'd day by day;
When all the host was serv'd, the heat
   Melted the rest away.

In vain to hoard it up they try'd,
   Against tomorrow came;
It then bred worms and putrify'd,
   And proved their sin and shame.

'Twas daily bread, and would not keep,
   But must be still renew'd;
Faith should not want a hoard or heap,
   But trust the Lord for food.

The truths by which the soul is fed,
   Must thus be had afresh;
For notions resting in the head
   Will only feed the flesh.

However true, they have no life
   Or unction to impart;
They breed the worms of pride and strife,
   But cannot cheer the heart.

Nor can the best experience past
   The life of faith maintain;
The brightest hope will faint at last,
   Unless supply'd again.

Dear Lord, while we in pray'r are found,
   Do thou the Manna give;
Oh! let it fall on all around,
   That we may eat and live.

''Twas daily bread, and would not keep …', 'Must thus be *had* afresh …'
– this is the language of the eighteenth-century small shopkeeper and
thrifty housewife, an idiom which has not got into English poetry at all,
except through the hymn-book. Perhaps Newton's most audacious and
brilliant use of the colloquial is, on an off-rhyme, at the end of 'By the
poor widow's oil and meal':

Then let not doubts your mind assail,
   Remember God has said,
'The cruse and barrel shall not fail,
   My people shall be fed.'

And thus, though faint it often seems,
   He keeps their grace alive;
Supply'd by his refreshing streams,
   Their dying hopes revive.

Though in ourselves we have no stock,
   The Lord is nigh to save;

> The door flies open when we knock,
>   And 'tis but ask and have.

The people who spoke this language – and John Newton who wrote for them, because he was one of them – are much stranger to us than their social betters whom we encounter in poetry so much more often. They were, for instance, much more callous, in a way which our humanitarianism finds hard to forgive, which is however easy to understand when we consider that they were only one defaulting creditor away from Gin Lane or the Debtor's Prison, only one press-gang away from the floating slums that were the British warships. They had, in any case, compensating virtues. In particular they saw piety and religious observance in terms of history which was literally true, and doctrine that was to be explained, and then accepted or rejected, not explained away or allowed to dissolve behind a mist of emotional indulgence. At their most fervent, their fervour was always related to the literally true and the doctrinally exact. As a result they produced a body of religious poetry which is the least *religiose* of any that one can think of.

Introduction to *Augustan Lyric* (London, 1974).

XIII Trevenen

I *His Return* (Christmas, 1780)

Winds from Cook's Strait cannot blow
Hard enough to lift the snow
Already comfortably deep
Where Roseveare and Treyarnon sleep;
Knit to the centre from the far
Fastness of their peninsula,
The Cornish dream that distance can
Deliver their young gentleman
Unaltered to his mother's arms,
To be in rectories and farms,
Assembly-rooms and markets, shown
As the great Cook's and yet their own.
          Camborne's as certain as St James
That vocabulary tames
The most outlandish latitude;
That, at a pinch, to speak of rude
Hardihood will meet the case
And teach a Bligh to know his place;
And 'gallant' and 'ingenious' will
Confine their irrepressible
Midshipman who murders sleep,
Sprung from the London coach to heap
His hero-worship of the dead
Hero on each doting head.
          It would be years before he knew
Himself what it had brought him to;
What it had meant, his profiting
By the good offices of King
And Bligh, the mote-dance in the air
Of their vacated cabins where
Sea-glitters pulsed above his head
Bent to his books. And loving dread
Of his commander's furies taught
Lessons of another sort

If he could trust to having seen
How far from rational and serene
Command might be. When, at the oar
Under Cook's marginally more
Indulgent but still beetling eye,
He clawed a cutter round the high
Northwestern overhang, it meant
The profile of a continent.
So much he knew, and knew with pride;
And yet he was not satisfied,
Not now, nor later. But for now
He chatters to his mother how
Captain King he can instate
As the dead Cook's surrogate:
King, with his connections; King
In Ireland now and finishing
The narrative of the fatal cruise
(Awaited, though no longer news);
King, and his kindness (Bligh, the spurned,
Unconnected patron, burned
With a jealousy that seared
King's account, when it appeared,
With marginalia ...); King, whose eyes
Smiled on skill and enterprise
Such as young Trevenen knew
He could boast, and ardour too;
Sweet James King, whom more than one
Hawaiian wanted for a son;
King, then (and so the plaudits end)
At once a mentor and a friend,
Rare composite of gall and balm,
Skilful to command and charm.
        Thus, mixed with talk of azimuth
And quadrant, to confound Redruth,
Trevenen, merrily enough,
Talks of how it merits love,
Some men's authority; and some
Clerical auditors keep mum,
Shocked to know how near they come
To greeting (so enthralled they are)
With an impious 'huzzah'
Such a sublime condition as
They've pressed on their parishioners
As more than human. 'Well, but no,'

They tell themselves, 'the boy don't know
How near he grazes Gospel-truth.
Brave spirit of ingenuous youth!'
And so they huff and puff it home
With (to their wives) 'Come, madam, come!'
Their wives and daughters half aware
Dear Papa has an absent air.
          It troubles him, as well it might,
To see in such resplendent light
Mortal redeemers crowd upon
A stage that should be cleared for One,
That One, Divine. There was some doubt
Whether Cook had been devout;
Though as to that one could not feel
Happy with excess of zeal,
Remembering saintly Wesley whose
Vexatiousness had emptied pews
Down all the stolid Duchy, packed
Gwennap Pit, and loosed in fact
Who knew what furies in deluded
Tin-mine Messiahs? So he brooded,
The honest rector. As for that,
He thought, there's worse to wonder at:
Wrong principles inflame and spread
When they aureole a head
Rank has exalted more than those
Who merely by their talents rose.
Thus, nothing's more alarming than
That too warm Christian gentleman,
Lord George Gordon, the inspired
And loved authority that fired
Prison and church, and did not spare
Lord Mansfield's house in Bloomsbury Square ...
'Bah!' he thought, 'what has all this
To do with young men's loyalties?'

II *Life and Contacts* (1784–1787)

The poet Crabbe, with whom he shared
Burke as patron, never cared
(It appears) to throw a frame
Round the poems that made his fame.
There, as if through window-glass,

Men like James Trevenen pass
Plain and unflattered. Never mind
Asking what poetic kind
Crabbe's tales belong to; they escape
Any predetermined shape,
Comic, heroic, or whatever.
Pointing morals was, however,
Crabbe's substitute. Subtitled 'Or
Hero-worship,' would a more
Rationally pleasing piece,
With less of oddity and caprice
In the conduct of it, come
Of this that we're embarked upon?
Hardly: morals underlined
Outrage our taste. Besides, my mind
Is far from made up in this case
About what moral we should trace
In a story that is more
Painful than I've prepared you for.
– First, the untimely death of King.
His malady was lingering,
And yet did not take very long
Once it attacked the second lung.
Then, the death of brother Matt
At twenty-three, beleaguered at
Okehampton in the inn, who trolled,
'Unlike the ladies of the old
Times,' his song; 'their hue unfaded
That needed no calash to shade it ...'
The light young tenor 'of the old
Times, the old ancient ladies' told,
Echoing in a brother's head
Cracked gaiety, the singer dead.
        A man, thus severally bereaved,
Labours not to be deceived
By smiling seas of Life, nor Art's
Flattering pledge to furnish charts.
And no such suave commitment mars
Crabbe, the realist *sans phrase* ...
Perhaps had Johnson lived, whose pen
Tinkered with *The Village*, then
Some one had upheld the claims
Of spectacles defined by frames,
Or songs like Matthew's, set to airs

Traditional at country fairs;
But Johnson died, unwept by most,
And left, to rule the sprawling roost,
Crabbe's earnest, just, unfocussed page
As prolix model to an age
Which, fed on ornament, would brook
Pindaric Odes to Captain Cook
And, stretched on Ossian, did not shirk
Orations paced by Fox and Burke:
Splendid, sublime and fervent, strong
In argument, but long, but long.
    Apart from that, it can be shown
To have been an age much like our own;
As lax, as vulgar, as confused;
Its freedoms just as much abused;
Where tattle stole a hero's thunder,
His death a thrill, and nine days' wonder;
Where personalities were made,
And makers of them plied a trade
Profitable and esteemed;
Where that which was and that which seemed
Were priced the same; where men were duped
And knew they were, and felt recouped
By being town-talk for a day,
Their Gothic follies on display;
Where (and here the parallel
Comes home, I hope, and hurts as well)
Few things met with such success
As indignant righteousness.
Burke's the paradigm of this,
Hissing at enormities
In India, at Westminster-hall
(Holy debauch, a free-for-all);
A man of principle, not able
(Like Fox, who had the gaming-table
To share his heart with politics)
To guard against the squalid tricks
That Tender Conscience and Just Rage
Play, when on a public stage;
Not keeping, in his fevered heart,
Passion and Principle apart;
But purchasing his never too
Much honoured sense of what was due
To private merit and indeed

Domestic virtue, by a need
To compensate for his serene
Privacies by public spleen …
      To King, the friend of Irish friends,
Burke gives a bed, and Jane Burke tends
His hopeless case. And King's release
Comes in that same year, in Nice,
Whither Trevenen had, with one
Other, conveyed him, to the sun.
      The Burkes had sent him; and he rode
Back to them, slowly, overshadowed
Thenceforward, always, by a sense
Of human life's inconsequence.
      No man more worthy of his trust,
It might be thought – nor, if he must
Still worship, of his worship – than
The great, good Anglo-Irishman,
Edmund Burke. Secure within
That circle, guest of Inchiquin
At Cliefden, or else entertained
At Gregories itself, he gained
Dubious information how
Iniquitous were Pitt and Howe;
How unregarded was the merit
Of Cook, of King; how to inherit
Their mantle meant he must not hope
For advancement of much scope.
At other times their conversation
Was a liberal education
In men and manners; how Lord George
Gordon, once again at large
(Though, some years before, expelled
From this circle) was impelled
By honour when for the disbanded
Mariners he had demanded,
The year before, some action such
As could have shipped them for the Dutch;
How Cowper, in *The Task*, confessed
To remaining unimpressed
By the reasons given for
Incursions on Tahiti's shore;
How fractious Barry must be borne with,
Painting lineaments of myth
For all his tantrums, the antique

Burning his style down to the Greek;
How Nollekens had little sense
Of decency, yet could dispense
With it, to mould a *busto*; how
Cagliostro made his bow;
How civil good Sir Joshua was,
And Admiral Saunders; how, across
A field from where they sat, was found
The plot of venerable ground
Where slippery Waller lay; and how
Illiberal was Pitt, was Howe ...
      Small wonder if his head was turned,
If a renewed resentment burned
In him to sell his rusting sword
Wherever sovereigns could afford
Ensigns announcing to the gale
Citizens of the world in sail.
      Bligh gets the *Bounty*, and not he;
He's pledged himself to Muscovy.

III *His End* (The Battle of Viborg, 21 June 1790)

Long, splendid shadows! Cornwall, lit
Bronze in the evening, levels it
Off, and pays all; the yea or nay
Of switched allegiance, as the day
Dies on the old church-tower, seems
A dilemma of our dreams
Which, however urgent once,
Awake we need not countenance.
The gilding beams that reconcile
This antique issue, can for mile
On cloud-racked mile slant on, to reach
Amber on a Baltic beach ...
Apollonian, reconciling
Art, that is drenched in tears, yet smiling!
Persuading us to think all's one,
Lit by a declining sun.
      Not for George Crabbe! His it is
To give untinged veracities;
And, though it's Christian, this indeed
Our baffled heroes seem to need,
Moving to their wasteful ends,

Betrayed by principles and friends –

> Cold and pain in the breast,
> Fatigue drives him to rest.
> Rising, 'to open a new
> Source of comfort to you'
> (Writing to his wife
> The last night of his life),
> Captain Trevenen, sick,
> Wears on no other tack,
> Aware man's born to err,
> Inclined to bear and forbear.
> Pretence to more is vain.
> Chastened have they been.
> Hope was the tempter, hope.
> Ambition has its scope
> (Vast: the world's esteem);
> Hope is a sickly dream.
> And seeking, while they live,
> Happiness positive
> Is sinful. Virtue alone –
> This they have always known –
> Is happiness below.
> Therefore, she is to know,
> Whatever is, is right.
> That solid, serious light
> Shall reconcile her to
> Candidacy below
> For where his sails are furled,
> Far from fame and the world.

Camborne's rector would have seen
Comfort in the ghastly scene,
There in the British burial-ground
In summery Kronstadt, had he found
His son so firm, and yet so meek.
So truly Christian, truly bleak
The sentiments a man should speak,
Meeting his Maker! In our eyes
A man we cannot recognize
As Burke's or King's accomplished friend,
Cowed mumbler from the sealed-off end
Of Celtic England, glares and points;
And this raw difference disjoints

Our and Elegy's specious frame,
Framing all our deaths the same
(Our loves, our worships, levelled in
The eyes of Art, that Jacobin).
     Lord George Gordon! he was found
Worshipful, the country round,
Some years before. Now no one hears
His civilly enounced ideas
Without reserve. But when, as host,
He gives his Radicals their toast,
'Mr Burke! who has afforded
Grounds for discussion,' he's applauded.
And, sure enough, we well may find
Burke and the Jacobins of one mind,
One self-same ruinous frame, unless
We recollect that Burke could bless
Those death-bed words from one whose head
He may have turned, whom he misled:
        'Though Will finds worldly scope,
        We have no earthly hope.'
Edmund Burke had cried, 'Amen!'
And James King, and most other men.

Author's note: For Trevenen, see Revd John Penrose, *Lives of Vice-Admiral Sir Charles Vinicombe Penrose and Captain James Trevenen* (London, 1850) and *A Memoir of James Trevenen*, ed. Christopher Lloyd and R.C. Anderson (Navy Records Society, 1959). Burke's tributes to Trevenen and James King are in 'Edmund Burke's Character of his Son and Brother,' Appendix I in *The Correspondence of Edmund Burke*, vol. VII, ed. P.J. Marshall and John A. Woods (Cambridge and Chicago, 1968). I also consulted *Letters of Anna Seward, written between the Years 1784 and 1807* (Edinburgh, 1811); James Prior, *Memoir of the Life and Character of the Right Hon. Edmund Burke* (1st ed., London, 1824); *The Life of George Crabbe, by his Son;* Percy Colson, *Their Ruling Passions* (London, n.d.), pp. 39–90; and various volumes of *The Correspondence of Edmund Burke*. These materials and others were assembled in the thought that I might write a closet-drama; but finding, not much to my own surprise, that I had no talent for that sort of composition, I threw the subject into the only form of writing that I know about and am practised in.

Editors' note: The publication of 'Trevenen' in this issue does not represent a radical change in editorial policy. The Editors believe that if this poem were translated into academic prose it would be a distinguished scholarly article, and are happy to let readers have the benefit of the poetry as well as the scholarship. A sketch of the life of James Trevenen (1760–1790) may be found in the *Dictionary of National Biography*. Readers who are interested in Donald Davie's other poetic interpretations of the eighteenth century should turn to his recently published *Collected Poems 1950–1970*.

XIV Politics and Literature:
John Adams and Doctor Johnson

Professor Oakeshott has argued that poetry makes an irreplaceable contribution to the conversation of mankind; but that it can be seen to be irreplaceable only if the conversation of mankind is understood as something distinct from, because more comprehensive than, the sustained enquiry of the human mind into 'ourselves and the world we inhabit'.[1] Poetry, he argues, is irreplaceable in the conversation of mankind to just the degree that it does *not* contribute to that enquiry.

Although Professor Oakeshott conducts this argument with wonderful grace and amenity, and although his essay is directed mainly against the crass philistine who believes that poetry is ultimately (or sooner) replaceable, yet in my view no serious devotee of the poetic can afford to accept his civil compromise. For such a devotee of poetry (a term which, as Professor Oakeshott uses it, comprehends all literature and all the finer arts), it is essential to maintain that the poetic activity contributes not just to the conversation of mankind but to its enquiry also, that the poetic is a mode of that enquiry, and that a devotion to poetry entails 'a belief in the pre-eminence of enquiry, and of the categories of "truth" and "reality"'.[2]

In respect of this disagreement, a crucial case is the large class of writers who conceived of themselves, and are conceived by others, as contributing to an established field of enquiry; who nevertheless can be seen to be 'making images of a certain kind and moving about among them in a manner appropriate to their characters'[3] – that is to say, acting poetically in the very course of their enquiries. Certain enquirers into politics are particularly interesting from this point of view, if only because, as Professor Oakeshott reminds us, 'in ancient Greece ... "politics" was understood as a "poetic" activity in which speaking (not merely to persuade but chiefly to compose memorable verbal images) was pre-eminent, and in which action was for the achievement of "glory" and "greatness" – a view of things which is reflected in the pages of Machiavelli.'[4]

1 Michael Oakeshott, *The Voice of Poetry in the Conversation of Mankind* (London, 1959).
2 Ibid., p. 35.
3 Ibid., p. 31.
4 Ibid., p. 15n.

I propose to consider, as a political writer of this kind, John Adams, the second President of the United States. And I shall suggest, first, that Adams indeed combines perceptiveness in politics with poetic activity, in the same way, if not to the same degree, as a Bacon or a Burke; secondly, and more immediately to the point, that there is a limit to his political sagacity as to his poetic capacity, a limit which appears when we compare him with Doctor Johnson, an author who (it turns out) meant more to him than he ever cared to acknowledge; and thirdly that his fallings short in political sagacity and in poetry are related, so that we may vindicate common sense and common usage, and speak simply of a single failure of imagination. By this stage of my argument I shall be suggesting that properly to read John Adams as an ornament of American literature is not different from reading him as a shrewd observer of the political arena; and this is to reject, as untrue to the experience of reading John Adams vigilantly and with sympathy, the distinction which Professor Oakeshott asks us to make between 'conversation' and 'enquiry'.

The work by Adams which I shall consider is his *Discourses on Davila*. These appeared at intervals through the year 1790, in the *Gazette of the United States*, a federalist periodical published in Philadelphia. They appeared between hard covers in Boston in 1805, and when C.F. Adams a half-century later reproduced them in Volume VI of the *Life and Works* of Adams, he incorporated some valuable marginalia, dating from as late as 1812–13, found in John Adams' library copy. The Davila whom Adams is discoursing upon, is Enrico Caterino Davila, whose *Historia delle guerre civili di Francia*, published in Venice in 1630, was known to Adams not in the English translation by W. Aylesbury (1647), though that folio was in Adams' library, but in the French translation of 1757 by the Abbé Mallet. Adams may well have been led to the work in the first place by Bolingbroke's commendation of it in the fifth of his *Letters on the Study and Use of History*.

Zoltan Haraszti, in his invaluable *John Adams and the Prophets of Progress*,[1] says of those parts of the *Discourses* which are not straight translations from Davila (as are eighteen out of the thirty-two papers), 'The papers are striking, and reading them one has at first the feeling of having discovered a literary treasure.' Unfortunately, he goes on, this feeling cannot be trusted, since 'the entire group is based upon a single chapter of Adam Smith's *Theory of Moral Sentiments*'. The logic of this is unacceptable unless we have very simple-minded and mechanical ideas of plagiarism on the one hand, originality on the other. Shakespeare himself would not scape whipping if we counted all his borrowings against him. And Mr Haraszti allows that Adams' phrasing is often more powerful than

Smith's, and that 'his passion for stringing together epithets and metaphors makes his presentation particularly vivid'.

However, it is worth examining in some detail Haraszti's case that Adams is heavily indebted to Adam Smith, if only because this will bring us to what interests us more – Adams' indebtedness to Dr Johnson. We find to begin with that Section II of the *Discourses*, with epigraph from Voltaire, though it is not at odds with anything that Smith says, is a genuine elaboration of it – and in a direction (hence in a tone) quite alien from Smith's:

> Of what avail are all these histories, pedigrees, traditions? What foundation has the whole science of genealogy and heraldry? Are there differences in the breeds of men, as there are in those of horses? If there are not, these sciences have no foundation in reason; in prejudice they have a very solid one.

There is nothing in Smith's chapter to approach this implication that if the philosopher's reason permits him to do nothing with such a deep-rooted prejudice but merely deplore it, *so much the worse for him, and especially for his politics.* (This section quotes Young's 'Love of Fame', and aptly.)

Section III, with epigraph from Voltaire, begins with a passage which, as Haraszti shows, has a parallel on the first page of Smith's Chapter. But it soon changes. One may usefully compare a passage about the poor man in Adams (a passage, incidentally, which is much wrenched by Hannah Arendt in her *On Revolution*)[1] with the no less good but quite different development by Smith. And what follows, beginning, 'Is there in science and letters a reward for the labor they require?' has no source in Smith; it recalls rather Dr Johnson's

> When first the college rolls receive his name,
> The young enthusiast quits his ease for fame;
> Through all his veins the fever of renown
> Burns from the strong contagion of the gown;
>
> (*Vanity of Human Wishes*, ll. 135–8.)

At the end Adams shifts from the learned profession to the military, just as Johnson does in his poem.

And sure enough, Section IV has an epigraph from the *Vanity of Human Wishes* about martial glory (of which Smith says nothing):

---

1 New York, 1963. Miss Arendt quotes the passage with long *lacunae*, and this alters the force of it, since Adams allows as Miss Arendt does not that the emulous appetite can be satisfied *socially* (e.g. by the man who keeps a dog to 'look up to him') as well as *politically*. Miss Arendt ignores the source in Adam Smith.

Such bribes the rapid Greek o'er Asia whirl'd,
For such the steady Romans shook the world

Compare Johnson's versions of these 'bribes' ('The festal blazes, the triumphal show') with Adams' taunting interrogations: 'A ribbon? a garter? a star? a golden key? a marshal's staff? or a white hickory stick?' After a remarkable passage on death-beds, and a grandly eloquent paragraph on marks of distinction in the Roman republic (entirely his own), Adams approaches Smith only in his last paragraph, with the example of the triumph of Paulus Aemilius.

Section V has a four-line epigraph from *The Vanity of Human Wishes*, ll. 177–8 conjoined with ll. 183–4 (with no acknowledgement of a *lacuna*). But it is in respect of this paper that comparison with Smith is most in order, and most damaging to Adams. Smith writes:

> To those who have been accustomed to the possession or even to the hope, of public admiration, all other pleasures sicken and decay. Of all the discarded statemen who, for their own ease, have studied to get the better of ambition, and to despise those honours which they could no longer arrive at, how few have been able to succeed! The greater part have spent their time in the most listless and insipid indolence, chagrined at the thoughts of their own insignificancy, incapable of being interested in the occupations of private life, without enjoyment, except when they talked of their former greatness, and without satisfaction, except when they were employed in some vain project to recover it. Are you in earnest resolved never to barter your liberty from the lordly servitude of a court, but to live free, fearless, and independent? There seems to be one way to continue in that virtuous resolution; and perhaps but one. Never enter the place from whence so few have been able to return; never come within the circle of ambition; nor ever bring yourself into comparison with those masters of the earth who have already engrossed the attention of half mankind before you.

And Adams:

> Ministers of state are frequently displaced in all countries; and what is the consequence? Are they seen happy in a calm resignation to their fate? Do they turn their thoughts from their former employments, to private studies or business? Are they men of pleasant humor, and engaging conversation? Are their hearts at ease? Or is their conversation a constant effusion of complaints and murmurs, and their breast the residence of resentment and indignation, of grief and sorrow, of malice and revenge? Is it common to see a man get the better of his ambition, and despise the honors he once possessed; or is he commonly employed in projects, intrigues after intrigues, and

manoeuvres on manoeuvres, to recover them? So sweet and delightful to the human heart is that complacency and admiration, which attends public offices, whether they are conferred by the favor of a prince, derived from hereditary descent, or obtained by election of the people, that a mind must be sunk below the feelings of humanity, or exalted by religion or philosophy far above the common character of men, to be insensible, or conquer its sensibility. Pretensions to such conquests are not uncommon; but the sincerity of such pretenders is often rendered suspicious, by their constant conversation and conduct, and even by their countenances.

Adam Smith is much superior to Adams here, for Adams, once he has committed himself to rhetorical questions, seems unable to break the habit; and Johnson is not in the picture at all. He can be brought into it if we recall that the disappointed statesman probably in Smith's mind as well as in Adams' was *Bolingbroke*, whom Jefferson and Adams both admired (though not uncritically). Johnson had written, in his review of Soame Jenyns' *Free Enquiry*, of 'the contemptible arrogance, or the impious licentiousness of Bolingbroke'.

Section VI has an epigraph from Juvenal and also from Johnson's imitation of him, in a couplet from *London* that was never far from Adams' lips, nor from the tip of his pen:

This mournful truth is everywhere confess'd,
Slow rises Worth, by Poverty depressed.

This section owes nothing to Smith (if only because it is wholly and specifically *political*) and it owes nothing to Johnson, though it has one curious parallel with him:

The Romans allowed none, but those who had possessed curule offices, to have statues or portraits. He who had images or pictures of his ancestors, was called noble. He who had no statue or pictures but his own, was called a new man. Those who had none at all, were ignoble.

Compare Johnson, *The Vanity of Human Wishes*, ll. 83–90.

From every room descends the painted face,
That hung the bright Palladium of the place,
And smoak'd in kitches, or in auctions sold,
To better features yields the frame of gold;
For now no more we trace in ev'ry line
Heroic worth, benevolence divine:
The form distorted justifies the fall,
And detestation rids th' indignant wall.

The similarity here is presumably a matter of Johnson and Adams having a common source in Juvenal.

Section VII appears to owe little to Smith and nothing to Johnson. It has an epigraph from Pope's Moral Essays:

> Tis from high life high characters are drawn,
> A saint in *crape* is twice a saint in *lawn*.

And in Section VIII, which is given up almost entirely to a barely acknowledged verbatim quotation from Smith, the epigraph is again from Pope:

> Wise, if a minister; but if a King,
> More wise, more learn'd, more just, more everything

Section IX however has an epigraph from Johnson:

> Heroes, proceed! what bounds your pride shall hold?
> What check restrain your thirst of pow'r and gold?
>
> (*London*, ll. 61–2)

Adams begins: 'The answer to the question in the motto ...' And this prepares us for the Section to stay quite close to Johnson. So it does, in a curious way; when Adams says, 'Consider the story of the ambition and the fall of Cardinal Wolsey and Archbishop Laud; the indignation of the world against their tyranny has been very faint; the sympathy with their fall has been very strong', he can hardly *not* be reproaching Johnson, or urbanely sneering at him, for treating both these characters in just this way – not in *London* however, but in *The Vanity of Human Wishes*:

> For why did Wolsey near the steeps of fate,
> On weak foundations raise th' enormous weight?
> Why but to sink beneath misfortune's blow,
> With louder ruin to the gulphs below?
>
> (ll. 125–8)

and

> Rebellion's vengeful talons seize on Laud.
>
> (l. 168)

And Adams indeed could claim, when he goes on to quote and praise from Juvenal's Satire III and from Johnson's imitation of it in *London* ('Although the verse, both of the Roman and Briton, is satire, its keenest severity consists in its truth'), that the poet of *London* castigates in others just that thoughtless veneration for eminence which the poet of *The Vanity of Human Wishes* fell into himself when he wrote so mournfully of Wolsey and of Laud. It would be no more than natural for Adams to applaud the young firebrand Johnson, friend of the reprobate Richard

Savage, who wrote *London* against the establishment of Walpole, and to deplore the older and mellower or perhaps more politically timorous Johnson who write *The Vanity of Human Wishes*.

In the four papers which remain of the *Discourses on Davila* I detect no traces of Doctor Johnson, unless indeed it was Johnson, in his capacity as editor and commentator on Shakespeare, who brought to Adams' attention the passages from Shakespeare's *Troilus and Cressida* which make up Section X of the *Discourses*. It is at any rate quite impossible to accept Zoltan Haraszti's insinuation that the 70 lines of Shakespeare, to which of course there is no parallel in Adam Smith, are merely 'padding', an embellishment or amplification of the source only in this discreditable sense. On the contrary Adams' citation of Ulysses' speech on Degree is perhaps the most astonishing and admirable thing in all the *Discourses*. It is common form nowadays to take this as the key passage in the understanding of Shakespeare's political philosophy (the understanding in particular of how undemocratic Shakespeare is); but the passage was first given this central importance only thirty years ago, by the late E.M.W. Tillyard and the late Theodore Spencer. Adams' citation of it thus has the force of a startling anticipation of modern opinion, which that opinion has vindicated.

And yet this ought not to startle us. Twenty-five years ago Alfred Van Rensselaer Westfall in his *American Shakespearean Criticism 1607–1865*,[1] quoted an entry in Adams' Diary for 1772, which consists of a comment on some lines from *The Merry Wives of Windsor*, and declared: 'What may be called the first American Shakespearean comment, if not criticism, began with this man who became the second president of the United States.' Adams in fact was quite exceptional among men of affairs of his age, not just in the United States but in Britain also, in having a mind stocked with literary experience, and in drawing upon that experience not just for flowery embellishments but as a repository of moral and political wisdom. We are accustomed to think of the Founding Fathers as representing, not just a high level of social responsibility and political astuteness, but as representing also, more generally, a high level of civilization. And this is surely right. But when we think in this way we think pre-eminently of Jefferson, and of his sensibility to pictures, statuary, music, architecture. Jefferson read widely in the classical literatures, and undoubtedly he had the best library of all the early Presidents. But of all the Presidents, with the possible exception of Lincoln, the only one to outstrip John Adams as a Shakespearean was his son John Quincy Adams, 'who read the plays on his mother's table when he was twelve years old'. The conclusive evidence of the literary civilization of the elder Adams is

1   New York, 1939, pp. 193–5.

not after all in such a full-dress instance as this use of Shakespeare in the *Discourse on Davila* but in the extent to which Shakespeare and Milton, Prior and Pope, Swift and Young, are ever present in his prose on whatever subject, in the fully assimilated aspect of submerged and unacknowledged quotation and allusion. And Johnson is there too, in just the same way.

In this matter, as in much else, John Adams was at pains to obscure his own tracks. In his old age at least he was ready to blow many a blast on a Philistine trumpet. To Jefferson in 1816 he declared:

> Style has governed the Empire. Swift, Pope and Hume have disgraced all the honest Historians. Rapin and Burnet Oldmixon and Coke, contain more honest truth than Hume and Clarendon and all their disciples and Imitators. But who reads any of them at this day? Every one of the fine Arts from the earliest times has been inlisted in the service of Superstition and Despotism. The whole World at this day Gazes with Astonishment at the grossest Fictions because they have been immortalized by the most exquisite Artists, Homer and Milton, Phidias and Raphael. The Rabble of the Classic Skies and the Hosts of Roman Catholic Saints and Angells are still adored in Paint and Marble, and verse.[1]

In the next year he is still haranguing Jefferson on the same score:

> Eustace is a Supplement to Dupuis; and both together contain a compleat draught of the Superstition, Credulity and Despotism of our terrestrial Universe. They show how Science, Litteratur, Mechanic Arts, and those fine Arts of Architecture, Painting, Statuary, Poetry, Musick and Eloquence: which you love so well and taste so exquisitely, have been subservient to Priests and Kings Nobles and commons Monarchies and Republicks. For they have all Used them when they could, but as the rich had them oftener than the poor, in their power, the latter have always gone to the Wall.[2]

And less than three weeks later he asks another correspondent:

> Is it possible to inlist the 'Fine Arts', on the side of Truth, of Virtue, of Piety, or even of Honour? From the dawn of History they have been prostituted to the Service of Superstition and despotism. Read Herodotus, Pausanias, Plutarch, Lucian, and twenty others, not forgetting several of the Christian Fathers and see how the fine Arts have been employed. Read Eustace's classical Tour of Italy.[3]

1   *The Adams–Jefferson Letters,* ed. Lester J. Cappon (Chapel Hill, 1959), II, 502–3
2   Ibid., p. 507.
3   *Statesman and Friend. Correspondence of John Adams with Benjamin Waterhouse, 1784–1822,* ed. W.C. Ford (Boston, 1927).

But this is rather different, is it not? The question is neither rhetorical nor frivolous; and we know the answer to it no better than Adams did. Certainly I cannot answer it, who would never have read Adams at all, nor Jefferson either, but for the recommendations of that frequently exquisite and always honest poet, Ezra Pound, Fascist and anti-Semite. *Is* it possible to enlist the Fine Arts? We know how to do so no more than Doctor Johnson when he deplored, in the finest of all tributes to Shakespeare, that Shakespeare's plays did not uniformly punish wicked characters and reward the virtuous.

And this is Adams' dilemma. It is not that he does not know what the arts are about, or that he cannot respond to them; what puzzles him, as it puzzled Johnson and puzzles all of us in some degree, is how to square with his conscience the fact that he does respond to them, intensely. This is very clear from another letter written to Waterhouse twelve years earlier:

> I have heard, as you insinuate, that Sterne was a wicked man; and there are traits of a false Character, in his Writings: yet Benevolence, Generosity, Simpathy and Humanity that fill the Eyes and bosoms of the readers of his Works, will plead forever for their immortality. Virtues and Vices, Wisdom and Folly, Talents and imbecility, Services and demerits are so blended in most of the distinguished Sons of Men, that there is no knowing what Judgment to form of them, or what to do with them. Julian, in that ingenious Fable, The Caesars, throws headlong into the gulph of Tartarus, all the Tyrants; Alexander, Caesar, Augustus, Trajan and Constantine, are made to acknowledge that Fame, Power, or Pleasure were their Objects; Marcus Aurelius alone was confessed to have aimed Singly at the good of the People. I know not whether the number of pure Characters among Mankind in general will bear a greater proportion. The Number of unexceptionable Romances is not greater. Most of the fashionable ones, deserve to be slighted more than Sterne. Yet I own myself to be childish enough to be amused with their fictions. ... [1]

'Virtues and Vices, Wisdom and Folly, Talents and imbecility, Services and Demerits are so blended in most of the distinguished Sons of Men, that there is no knowing what Judgment to form of them' – because Adams believed this, we need not be surprised to find that Johnson, some of whose writings were never far from the surface of Adams' mind, should nevertheless never be spoken of by Adams except with marked hostility.

For instance, in Mr Cappon's admirable edition of the *Adams–Jefferson*

1   Ibid., pp. 29–30.

Letters there are two entries in the index under 'Johnson, Samuel, lexicographer'. One of them sends us to Adams declaring in 1815, 'Johnson and Burke were more of Catholicks than Protestants at Heart and Gibbon became an Advocate for the Inquisition'. The other, no more amiable, of date 1813, is much more interesting:

> The fundamental Principle of all Phylosophy and all Christianity is REJOICE ALWAYS IN ALL THINGS. Be thankfull at all times for all good and all that We call evil.' Will it not follow, that I ought to rejoice and be thankful that Priestley has lived? Aye! that Voltaire has lived? That Gibbon has lived? That Hume has lived, though a conceited Scotchman? That Bolingbroke has lived, tho' a haughty arrogant supercilious Dogmatist? that Burke and Johnson have lived, though superstitious Slaves or self-deceiving Hypocrites both. Is it not laughable to hear Burke call Bolingbroke a superficial Writer? To hear him ask 'Who ever read him through?' Had I been present I would have answered him 'I, I, myself, I have read him through, more than fifty Years ago, and more than five times in my Life, and once within five Years past. And in my Opinion, the epithet "Superficial" belongs to you and your Friend Johnson more than to him.' I might say much more. But I believe Burke and Johnson to have been as political Christians, as Leo 10th.

The interesting name here is that of Bolingbroke. For Mr Haraszti has confirmed that the influence of Bolingbroke on Adams was as great as it is here asserted to be. (It was even greater on Jefferson.) Yet Adams finds no inconsistency – nor, given his view of human nature, is there any – in declaring Bolingbroke 'a haughty arrogant supercilious Dogmatist'. But the letter goes on to more interesting matters:

> I return to Priestley, though I have great Complaints against him for personal Injuries and Persecution, at the same time that I forgive it all, and hope and pray that he may be pardoned for it all, above. Dr Broklesby an intimate Friend and convivial Companion of Johnson told me, that Johnson died in Agonies of Horror of Annihilation, and all the Accounts We have of his death corroborate this Account of Broklesby. Dread of Annihilation! Dread of Nothing? A dread of Nothing I should think would be no dread at all. Can there be any real substantial rational fear of nothing? Were you on your deathbed, and in your last moments informed by demonstration or Revelation that you would cease to think and to feel at your dissolution, should you be terrified? You might be ashamed of yourself for having lived so long to bear the proud Mans Contumely.

('The proud man's contumely' – a good example of how intimately Adams' mind is impregnated with Shakespeare.)

You might be ashamed of your Maker, and compare him to a little
Girl amusing herself her Brothers and Sisters by blowing Bubbles in
Soap Sudds. You might compare him to Boys sporting with Crakers
and Rocketts: or to Men employed in making more artificial Fire
Works; or to Men and Women at Farces and Operas, or Sadlers Wells
Exploits; or to Politicians in their Intrigues; or to Heroes in their
Butcheries; or to Popes in their Devilisms. But what should you fear?
Nothing. E mori nolo Sed me mortuum esse nihil estimo.

'I have no wish to die, but that I be dead I consider as nothing.' Brave
words! But what have they to do with the piously barbed hope in the
same paragraph that Joseph Priestley, for his injuries to Adams, 'be
pardoned for it all, above'? At any rate, one of several other places where
Johnson figures in Adams' letters (but unnamed and unacknowledged in
the index), reveals Adams not quite so stoical at the approach of death.
This is in 1814:

I am sometimes afraid that my 'Machine' will not 'surcease motion'
soon enough; for I dread nothing so much as 'dying at top' and
expiring like Dean Swift 'a driveller and a Show' or like Sam. Adams,
a Grief and distress to his Family, a weeping helpless Object of
Compassion for Years.[1]

Swift comes into Adams' head out of Johnson's *Vanity of Human Wishes*:

In life's last scene what prodigies surprise,
Fears of the brave, and follies of the wise?
From Marlb'rough's eyes the streams of dotage flow,
And Swift expires a driv'ler and a show.

As the latest editors austerely explain, 'Swift was intermittently insane
before his death in 1745. Servants are said to have shown him to tourists
for a fee.'

At this point we have reached the inflammatory question of how far
either Adams or Jefferson died a Christian. There seems to be little doubt
that the two old men conceived themselves to be in some sort Christians,
though aware that their Christianity was too sceptical and conditional for
them to afford to be frank about it, except to each other. But Adams at
least, with his ferocious anti-clericalism, was quite incapable of understanding how Johnson, particularly in such a work as *The Vanity of Human
Wishes*, rested his whole view of life on a very bleak and agitated but
unshakeable faith in the Christian God. Adams and Jefferson, in their
letters, are still locked into historical time – Adams like his later admirer
Pound convinced that only sinister destruction of records has lost the clue

1 *The Adams–Jefferson Letters*, II, 435.

which lies somewhere in the historical past; Jefferson, more sanguine and with a more successful career behind him, looking still, though with chastened eyes, for fulfilment in the future. In each case the deistic approval of the Christian ethic simply overlooks the great claim of Christianity – to have redeemed history, and made it meaningful once and for all, by the historical event of the Incarnation. No unitarianism, not any Jeffersonian admiration for Jesus as a great moral teacher, could come near to satisfying what a mind like Johnson's in *The Vanity of Human Wishes*, weary of mere historical process and iteration, looked for in Christian faith.

And this is why, to speak for myself, Adams in his Letters pleases more after a hundred pages than after five hundred. At first one is delighted by his tough-minded and humorous cordiality, his unflagging curiosity, the strong savour as well as the flexibility of his writing. But the suspicion grows that Adams' scepticism is not after all tough-mindedness but the product of a conspiracy theory of history (whence, too plainly alas, some of Ezra Pound's liking for him); the curiosity is (Adams almost admits as much) the running wild of a still hungry intelligence, operating irresponsibly because his conspiracy theory has got him to the stage where every speculation has as much and as little point as any other; and the humour even is irresponsible and after a while leaves a bad taste. A scepticism so thorough as Adams' was by 1812, even if it had firmer bases than it has, leaves a man nothing with which to face the future; and of course Adams was so old by this time that, as he acknowledges, he has really no future to face. It is his age – that is, the age he grew up in, which formed him, the age of the Enlightenment – which gives to all this the unexpected, and undoubtedly quite genuine, good humour.

The Discourses on Davila are another matter. And I hope I have shown that when Zoltan Haraszti had 'the feeling of having discovered a literary treasure', he ought to have trusted that feeling. His discovery that the *Discourses*, when they depart from Davila, rest on a chapter of Adam Smith which Adams amplifies out of Johnson and Shakespeare and others – this, which Haraszti thinks reveals the treasure as fool's gold, in fact does nothing of the kind. He is misled by a mistaken and out-dated notion of what originality is, in literature. The *Discourses on Davila*, at least the fourteen essays of useful reflections embedded in them, are a literary masterpiece. One is tempted to enforce this judgement by quoting a sustained passage, for instance the paragraph from Section IV beginning, 'Has there ever been a nation who understood the human heart better than the Romans …?' But it is better to avoid giving any impression that great literature is a matter of detachable purple passages. On the contrary, what makes the *Discourses* an achievement of the literary imagination is something much more nearly connected with what makes them also a penetrating and perennially relevant examination of political behaviour.

Accordingly, Adams' limitations as an observer of politics are also his limitations as a writer; for in both cases what we have is a failure of imagination. If we now define the place where that failure comes, it is by no means to deny that the *Discourses* are a great imaginative achievement; it is on the contrary to define that achievement by setting bounds to it.

In the *Discourses* Adams is arguing for political institutions as a way of harnessing the allegedly universal passion of emulation. In fact I believe we have to deny that this passion *is* universal: for there are cultures of the unprivileged which elevate 'solidarity' as the highest value, and condemn as betrayals of that principle the distinctions achieved by individuals. Such is the culture of the Trade Unionist, which Adams had no opportunity to observe. But I find that his argument fails in another way, for instance in Section V:

> Emulation really seems to produce genius, and the desire of superiority to create talents. Either this, or the reverse of it must be true; and genius produces emulation, and natural talents, the desire of superiority; for they are always found together, and what God and nature have united, let no audacious legislator presume to put asunder.

The concession which Adams makes here – when he envisages 'the reverse' proposition – reaches much farther than he seems aware of. For if it is only talented men who are emulous, then emulation and the desire for distinction are not such universal appetites as he elsewhere in his treatise supposes. But in any case there is a more horrifying possibility, which Adams does not envisage. What if the *un*talented are emulous? An apparition like Lee Oswald, or other pathetic killers who seem to kill only so as to be caught and 'get their names in the papers' – these suggest that the wish to be distinguished, while not universal, is distributed at random, among talented and untalented alike.

Adams is saved from envisaging this because he still confides in a providentially determined harmony between the desire for distinction and the deserving of distinction – 'what God and nature have united'. And this is characteristic. Although it seems to be true that for Adams 'nature' as a providentially ordained order is less tightly organized than for Jefferson,[1] still he shares with him the conviction that there is such a providential order in nature, and that human reason can discern it. This is indeed the force of the epigraphs he takes from Pope, particularly the motto on Section XIII:

> First follow nature; and your judgment frame
> By her just standard, which is still the same.

For Adams as we might expect seeks authority from the Pope of *Essay on Man* and *Moral Essays*, from the poet whose horizons are bounded by the

---

1   See Daniel J. Boorstin, *The Lost World of Thomas Jefferson* (New York, 1948).

precepts of Bolingbroke, not from the greater poet who in *The Dunciad* envisaged all providential order swept away and chaos come again.

Now Johnson on the other hand could share the experience behind the last lines of *The Dunciad* no less than the experience behind the *Essay on Man*. It is Johnson the devout Christian of Augustinian temper (also Pope the Roman Catholic) who can envisage that God moves in mysterious ways, above and perhaps athwart the natural order which He ordained; it is Adams the sceptic who cannot afford not to believe that God guarantees a beneficent harmony in Nature and human nature. There is one more place where Johnson appears in the *Discourses on Davila*, which brings this out clearly. In section XV, where Adams is in effect denying the contention of the Declaration of Independence that 'all men are created equal', he declares:

> Nature, which has established in the universe a chain of being and universal order, descending from archangels to microscopic animalcules, has ordained that no two objects shall be perfectly equal.

And in the marginalia which Adams subsequently wrote to his own work, he notes against this passage:

> This is not a chain of being from God to nothing; *ergo*, not liable to Dr Johnson's criticism, nor to the reviewer's.

The reviewer is identified by Zoltan Haraszti as Arthur Maynard Walter (1780–1807), and his review appeared in the *Monthly Anthology*. Johnson's criticism of the alleged 'great chain of being' appeared in his review in 1757 of Soame Jenyns' 'Free Enquiry into the Nature and Origin of Evil' – a review which is one of Johnson's greatest works:

> The scale of existence from infinity to nothing, cannot possibly have being. The highest being not infinite must be, as has often been observed, at an infinite distance below infinity …
>
> Between the lowest positive existence and nothing, wherever we suppose positive existence to cease, is another chasm infinitely deep; where there is room again for endless orders of subordinate nature, continued for ever and for ever, and yet infinitely superior to non-existence.
>
> To these meditations humanity is unequal. But yet we may ask, not of our Maker, but of each other, since on the one side creation, wherever it stops, must stop infinitely below infinity, and on the other infinitely above nothing, what necessity there is that it should proceed so far either way, that beings so high or so low should ever have existed? We may ask; but I believe no created wisdom can give an adequate answer.

Adams, it may be, *does* just escape by the skin of his teeth from Johnson's unanswerable objection. But Johnson goes on to explode the whole image of 'the great chain'. In famous words, which have been vindicated by A.O. Lovejoy in his standard work on this topic, Johnson declares:

> This scale of being I have demonstrated to be raised by presumptuous imagination, to rest on nothing at the bottom, to lean on nothing at the top, and to have vacuities from step to step through which any order of being may sink into nihility without any inconvenience, so far as we can judge, to the next rank above or below it.

And Adams cannot escape the charge of 'presumptuous imagination'. In the *Discourses on Davila* Adams is a very great writer. But Johnson is greater – not by virtue of greater facility in the management of language but simply because Johnson's imagination could comprehend abysses and exaltations beyond the compass of that Enlightenment culture which Johnson transcended whereas Adams, restive and sceptical though he was, remained in the end bounded by its assumptions.

Politics and Experience. Essays presented to Professor Michael Oakeshott on the occasion of his retirement (Cambridge, 1968).

XV Edward Taylor and Isaac Watts

I am very well aware of, and I appreciate very much, the charming anomaly by which, to inaugurate this series of essays to commemorate the Bicentenary, the sponsors have invited me, who am not a citizen of the Republic but a subject of Queen Elizabeth. And I'm the more anxious to explain why I've chosen to write of the American poet Edward Taylor not in isolation but in company with his British contemporary, Isaac Watts. My intention is not in the least to minimize Taylor's Americanness; on the contrary I hope to emphasize it and define it, by showing how different the American is from the Englishman, despite the many things that these two had in common – not least, the fact that Edward Taylor passed the first twenty-five years of his life in his native England.

I am not without precedent in this. In particular, my colleague Albert Gelpi, in his book of last year, *The Tenth Muse: The Psyche of the American Poet*, introduced the name of Isaac Watts into his discussion of Taylor, being I believe the first historian to do so; and most of what I have to say can be regarded as the teasing out of implications that are pregnantly hinted at by Professor Gelpi, to whom accordingly I am much beholden. And indeed I can appeal further back, to twenty-six years ago, when Louis Martz wrote his Foreword to that splendid monument of American literary scholarship, Donald Stanford's edition of *The Poems of Edward Taylor*. For Professor Martz there and then hazarded the observation that 'poetry with Taylor's peculiar quality could not, I think, have been written at all in England, even by Taylor himself'. I am sure that Louis Martz was right; and insofar as such propositions can be proven, I hope to prove him right. It's with just that end in view that I propose to approach Taylor by way of Watts, a poet of equal seriousness, equally gifted, very similarly placed as regards doctrinal principle and political circumstance, whose poems however are as different as can be conceived from the poems that Taylor was writing at just the same time on the other side of the Atlantic.

Martz's testimony is particularly valuable because of course it was he, the learned author of *The Poetry of Meditation*, who defined conclusively Taylor's relationship with his English predecessors:

the last heir of the great tradition of English meditative poetry that arose in the latter part of the sixteenth century, with Robert Southwell

as its first notable example, continued on through the religious poetry
of John Donne (and also in those of his secular poems that have
powerful religious elements), reached a fulfilment in the *Temple* of
George Herbert, went abroad to include the baroque motifs of
Richard Crashaw, found another home in Henry Vaughan's uneven
but inspired meditations on the 'creatures,' strengthened the fiber of
Andrew Marvell's slender muse, and, so far as England was concerned,
died at the death of Thomas Traherne in 1674, with both his prose
meditations and their companionate poems unpublished. But as
Crashaw had gone abroad to preserve and extend his Catholic allegiance, so, at the end of the line, in 1668, Edward Taylor sailed for
New England, and there, surrounded by the rude and dangerous life
of the frontier, composed his Puritan and meditative poems.

There may be details here that are worth quarrelling with – I wouldn't
myself, for instance, describe Marvell's talent as 'slender' – but it would
be rash to dispute that this indeed is the line that Taylor was 'at the end
of'. And no reader of Donald Stanford's edition can have failed to notice
how constantly George Herbert's *Temple* in particular is in Taylor's mind,
and in his inward ear, over most of the more than forty years – from 1682
to 1725 – during which he composed the two series of his *Preparatory
Meditations Before My Approach to the Lords Supper.*
  On the other hand we are here concerned not with the line of poetic
achievement that ends in Taylor, but with another line that we take him
to have inaugurated – a line of poetry in English that is distinctively
American rather than British. Moreover it is quite wrong to suppose that,
just because Taylor's debt to George Herbert is manifest, Herbert is the
English poet with whom he must inevitably be compared. On the
contrary, the historical contexts are so different that to compare Taylor
with Herbert serves rather little purpose. George Herbert, aristocratic
scion of an ancient and powerful family of Marcher Lords, Episcopalian,
ornament and admired prodigy of the Stuart court until his pastoral
calling called him away from it – what has this resplendent figure in
common with the obscure provincial Englishman whom the 1662 Act of
Uniformity, imposed by the restored Stuart, drove across the Atlantic to
Harvard College and thence to the frontier outpost of Westfield? Well!
They had something in common after all: Christian piety and pastoral
vocation; and also certain trained and temperamental habits of heart and
mind which account for the similarities of poetic style. But we must
surely beware, as students of literature, of making these similarities
conceal from us the unbridgeable gulf created by the events of history.
Taylor himself, if we may trust the testimony of his grandson Ezra Stiles,
was the last to minimize such historical conditioning. 'He was,' says Stiles,
'a vigorous Advocate for Oliver Cromwell, civil and religious Liberty. A

Congregationalist in opposition to Presbyterian Church Discipline ...
[He] greatly detested King James ...: gloried in King William and the
Revolution of 1688: felt for the dissenters in all their apprehension in
Queen Anne's reign.' George Herbert was dead before any of these
propositions could have meaning for him; but Isaac Watts, thirty years
younger than Taylor, a Dissenting minister as Taylor was, would have
concurred in every one of these sentiments and would have understood
them to mean precisely what Taylor and Ezra Stiles meant by them.
Theologically, politically, socially, above all chronologically, there is so
much common ground between Watts and Taylor that it is astonishing
how far apart they are in poetic style. And that distance between them
must be instructive – as instructive about what poetry in English was to
become, as the stylistic similarities between Taylor and Herbert are
instructive about what that poetry had been.

It is time to remind ourselves what a poem by Watts sounds like. And
I give you one that was quoted also by Professor Gelpi:

The Church the Garden of Christ

We are a Garden wall'd around,
Chosen and made peculiar Ground;
A little Spot inclos'd by Grace
Out of the World's wide Wilderness.

Like Trees of Myrrh and Spice we stand,
Planted by God the Father's Hand;
And all his Springs in Sion flow,
To make the young Plantation grow.

Awake, O heavenly Wind, and come,
Blow on this Garden of Perfume;
Spirit Divine, descend and breathe
A gracious Gale on Plants beneath.

Make our best Spices flow abroad
To entertain our Saviour-God:
And faith, and Love, and Joy appear,
And every Grace be active here.

Let my Beloved come, and taste
His pleasant Fruits at his own Feast.
I come, my Spouse, I come, he crys,
With Love and Pleasure in his Eyes.

Our Lord into his Garden comes,
Well pleas'd to smell our poor Perfumes,
And calls us to a Feast divine,
Sweeter than Honey, Milk, or Wine.

Eat of the Tree of Life, my Friends,
The Blessings that my Father sends;
Your Taste shall all my Dainties prove,
And drink abundance of my Love.

Jesus, we will frequent thy Board,
And sing the Bounties of our Lord:
But the rich Food on which we live
Demands more Praise than Tongues can give.

It's easy to mistake just what this poem is saying. For the 'we' of the first line does not mean mankind as a whole, nor Christian mankind as a whole; nor even Christian Englishmen as a whole. 'We' means 'We English Dissenters'. This has to be the case. For what sense would it make to speak of the Church of England as 'A little Spot ... Out of the World's wide Wilderness'? How could this be said of a Church whose head is the reigning monarch, whose bishops sit as Lords Spiritual in Parliament? The Church of England is the national Church, that is what is meant by calling it the Established Church. By maintaining the strenuous and transparent fiction that the religious community is coterminous with the national community, the English Anglican, even today, must hope to shame the fiction into becoming fact, thus sanctifying or spiritualizing the entire secular order within the state. Isaac Watts, like Edward Taylor, refused to maintain that fiction or to entertain that hope. And thus the 'we' of Watts' poem includes Taylor and his church in Westfield but not the Archbishop of Canterbury nor the congregation in St Paul's Cathedral. The point is obvious; yet experience tells me that it is best to make it thus explicit.

The history, and the polemics, of post-Revolutionary Russia supply us with two expressions that at this point may be useful – from the point of view of the English crown, if Taylor and his fellow New Englanders were *emigrés*, Watts and his fellow English Dissenters were *internal emigrés*. And once the American colonists began to challenge the Crown, the logic worked itself out as one might have expected: Benjamin Franklin wrote home from England in 1770, 'The Dissenters are all for us'; and when hostilities had started, the English Baptist minister John Collett Ryland (1723–92) expressed himself, with bloodcurdling ferocity, thus: 'Were I General Washington, I would call together all my brother officers. I would bare my arm and bid every man bare his, that a portion of blood might be extracted and mingled in one bowl, and swear by Him that sitteth on the Throne and liveth for ever and ever not to sheath the consecrated blade till the freedom of his country was achieved. ... And if after this any one should turn coward or traitor, I should feel it a duty, a pleasure, a luxury, to plunge my weapon into that man's heart.'

However, the situations of the *internal emigré* and of the *emigré* are very different. To be blunt about it, Edward Taylor had no Established

Church to contend with; whereas within perhaps half a mile of the meeting-house in London or Southampton where Dissenting congregations sang this hymn by Watts, there stood a parish church celebrating just that nationally instituted Protestant Christianity which Watts and his fellows had repudiated and opted out of – a repudiation which continued to cost them dear, in civil disabilities and often enough in social ostracism, long after the last of the hated Stuarts, Anne, had been succeeded by the princes of the House of Brunswick. Thus the Calvinist 'elect' of Watts' church were necessarily far more immediately aware of the non-elect from which they had been (to use their own word) 'gathered', than the elect of Westfield could be. And it is this, I think, which accounts for the sensation of mutual comfort and compactness, positively of *cosiness*, which breathes from Watts' beautiful quatrains.

The contrast is striking when we look at one of the poems by Taylor that is derived from just the same place in Scripture as Watts' hymn:

> Oh! that my Chilly Fancy, fluttering soe,
> > Was Elevated with a dram of Wine
> The Grapes and Pomegranates do yield, that grow
> > Upon thy Gardens Appletrees and Vines.
> > It shouldst have liquour with a flavour fraight
> > To pensil out thy Vines and Pomegranates.

> But I, as dry, as is a Chip, scarce get
> > A peep hole through thy garden pales at these,
> Thy garden plants. How should I then ere set
> > The glory out of its brave Cherry trees?
> > Then make my fancy, Lord, thy pen t'unfold
> > Thy Vines and Pomegranates in liquid gold.

> Whence come thy garden plants? So brave? So Choice?
> > They Almugs be'nt from Ophirs golden land:
> But Vines and Pomegranates of Paradise
> > Spicknard, Sweet Cane, and Cynamon plants here stand.
> > What heavenly aire is breezing in this Coast?
> > Here blows the Trade winde of the Holy Ghost.

> Thy Pomegranates that blushly freckles ware
> > Under their pleasant jackets spirituall frize,
> And Vines, though Feeble, fine, and flourishing are
> > Not Sibmahs, but Mount Zions here arise.
> > Here best of Vines, and Pomegranates up hights,
> > Yea Sharons Rose, and Carmels Lillies White.

> These trees are reev'd with Gilliads balm each one
> > Myrrh trees, and Lign Aloes: Frankincense,
> Here planted grow; heres Saffron Cynamon

> Spicknard and Calamus with Spice Ensenc'd.
> Oh fairest garden: evry bed doth beare
> All brave blown flowers whose breath is heavenly aire.
>
> Make me thy Vine and Pomegranate to be
>   And in thy garden flowrish fruitfully
> And in their branches bowre, there then to thee
>   In sweetend breath shall come sweet melody.
>   My Spirit then engrapd and pomegranat'de
>   Shall sweetly sing thee o're thy garden gated.

What we are likely to register first, as something in Taylor to which Watts offers no parallel, may be isolated in the delightful couplet:

> What heavenly air is breezing in this Coast?
> Here blows the Trade winde of the Holy Ghost.

The 'trade wind of the Holy Ghost' manifests *wit*: the peculiar virtue and felicity of those seventeenth-century poets whom Louis Martz has listed for us, those that we call 'the metaphysicals', whom the present century – instructed by T.S. Eliot – has come to esteem once again, after two hundred years of relative neglect. In Watts, in fact, that 'wit' is to be found. For instance when he says

> And all his Springs in Sion flow,
> To make the young Plantation grow,

'plantation' means the gardener's new plantings of trees or shrubs, but it also means – inevitably, given the date and historical context – Plymouth Plantation, or the Plantation of Ulster: a topical and dangerously resonant allusion, which a poet like Donne (or Taylor) would have teased out and made salient, which Watts on the contrary subdues and submerges, particularly by the smooth firmness of his meter. The same wit, deliberately subdued in the same way, is to be found in Watts' great contemporaries, Dryden and Pope; and much might be made of the fact that Taylor left England in 1668, just before the great genius of Dryden had showed itself, drastically modifying the 'metaphysical' tradition so as to make out of it a new style appropriate to the mercantile and scientific and bourgeois England that Dryden sensed as in the offing. Watts, beginning to write in the 1690s, had to take account of Dryden's precedent, as Taylor didn't need to. And Watts' earliest poems in fact, like Dryden's earliest, are exercises in the 'metaphysical' style, from which each of the two poets gradually weaned himself. We may regret that they did so; but in both cases it was deliberate.

Another difference between Taylor and Watts is more far-reaching. In Watts' case, the Church of the elect, conceived of as a garden planted by Christ the gardener, is treated as something that the poet and his hearers are securely *within*, a refuge achieved and occupied, whereas Taylor much more strenuously sees it as something that has to be re-achieved each time that the Sacrament is approached; for at the start of the poem he is *outside* the garden, wistfully peering in:

> But I, as dry, as is a Chip, scarce get
> > A peep hole through thy garden pales at these,
> Thy garden plants.

And this surely gives us, all over again, the distinction between what I have called the emigré and the internal emigré. Watts' English Dissenters, *internal emigrés*, form an almost conspiratorial subculture within the national culture, held tautly distinct at every point against the enveloping culture which tolerates but suspects them. And hence 'election' has for them a social dimension, as it could not have for Taylor and his flock at Westfield. For both poets the election of the elect is of course a spiritual state; but over and above that, for Watts it is a social state, embodied as a society within the larger society, whereas for Taylor it is imaginative and psychological, and above all *individual*.

Hence arises a most striking feature of Taylor's *Preliminary Meditations* – the absence, from these poems in and by which the pastor prepares himself for administering the sacrament, of any consideration of the fellow-worshippers to whom he will administer the sacrament, and with whom he will partake of it. The most disconcerting instance of this is not in *Preliminary Meditations* at all, but in a different sequence, *Gods Determinations*, where there is a piece entitled 'The Soul admiring the Grace of the Church Enters into Church Fellowship'. What must be our astonishment, after such a title, to find that 'fellowship' is precisely what the poem does *not* celebrate, any more than the *Meditations* do! One wonders what Taylor's relations with his fellows were, in the Westfield church, and whether indeed there was anyone there whom he would recognize as 'a fellow'. One recalls him writing to Samuel Sewall in 1696 about 'the Foggy damps assaulting my Lodgen in these remotest swamps from the Heliconian quarters, where little save Clonian Rusticity is …' And there can be little doubt that Taylor in Westfield was starved of congenial company, as Isaac Watts in London was not. Nevertheless, congenial company is one thing, union in Christ is something else; and a modern Christian cannot help but find forbidding the way in which Taylor's emphasis on that union takes no notice, or very little, of the several identities of those who are thus united.

Just this indeed may account for the attractiveness to Taylor of that nuptial allegory by which the eroticism of the Book of Canticles – the Song of Solomon, or the Song of Songs, as we more commonly call it – is made to yield the drama of Christ the Bridegroom calling his Bride the Church to sport in His garden. Through the last twelve years of his work on the *Preliminary Meditations* Taylor very rarely meditated on any text that was not from the Book of Canticles, and these include such unpromising texts as 'His belly is as bright ivory overlaid with sapphires', and 'His legs are as pillars of marble, set upon sockets of fine gold' – of which the best we can say is that Taylor's treatment is no worse than that of his English contemporary, the Baptist Joseph Stennett. But in fact all these Meditations toward the end of the Second Series are poor, grotesque, and frigid – all too patently, and pathetically, the work of an old man. Indeed it is fairly plain that what we have in them, very often, is only early and imperfect drafts. (The failure however is not just at the level of technique and taste – see PM 2.136, written 1717, where the text 'Turn away thine eyes from me, for they have overcome me' is astonishingly taken as addressed by the Bridegroom Christ to his Bride the Church, rather than the other way round.) By consistently identifying the Church, the body of the Elect, with one being, the Bride, Taylor is saved from ever having to regard the Church as composed of its several members, so many individuals. This is as much as to say that Taylor never envisages the Church as a human *society;* and in nothing else is there so wide a gulf between him and Watts, who deliberately and consciously subdued or (as he said) 'sank' his style, so that his poems should be sung with full understanding by unlettered congregations, whereas Taylor wrote for no eye but his own and his God's. After 1738, when George Whitefield induced Jonathan Edwards to introduce Watts' hymns to his congregation in Northampton, Watts was sung as widely in New England as in Old, so that more than a century later his hymns made up the body of poetry most insistently and threateningly present to the Amherst spinster, Emily Dickinson. What a difference it would have made, if American congregations had been singing Edward Taylor instead! But the very idea is unthinkable – not just in their form and diction, but in their substance, Taylor's poems are quite unsuited for any sort of communal rendering.

If Taylor's poetry is thus profoundly unsociable, and therefore painfully lacking in any of the feelings that a man may have for his neighbours, on the other hand Taylor is capable of profound fellow-feeling with other and as we think 'lower' forms of life than the human. The example that springs to mind is the justly well-loved, intricate and tender occasional poem, 'Upon a Wasp Child with Cold'. But the same extraordinary sympathy for nonhuman creatures – insects and birds and even vegetable creatures like nuts – enlivens some of the *Meditations* based on the imagery of the Bridegroom's Garden, out of the Song of Songs. One example out of many is *PM* 2.63, written in 1704:

> Oh that I was the Bird of Paradise!
>   Then in thy Nutmeg Garden, Lord, thy Bower

Celestiall Musick blossom should my voice
  Enchanted with thy gardens aire and flower.
This Aromatick aire would so enspire
  My ravisht Soule to sing with angells Quire.

What is thy Church, my Lord, thy Garden which
  Doth gain the best of Soils? Such spots indeed
Are Choicest Plots empalde with Palings rich
  And set with slips, herbs best, and best of seed.
    As th' Hanging Gardens rare of Babylon
    And Palace Garden of King Solomon.

But that which doth excell all gardens here
  Was Edens Garden: Adams Palace bright.
The Tree of Life, and Knowledge too were there
  Sweet herbs and sweetest flowers all sweet Delight
    A Paradise indeed of all Perfume
    That to the Nose, the Eyes and Eares doth tune.

But all these Artificiall Gardens bright
  Enameled with bravest knots of Pincks
And flowers enspangld with black, red and White
  Compar'd with this are truely stincking sincks.
    As Dunghills reech with stinking sents that dish
    Us out, so these, when balanced with this.

For Zions Paradise, Christs Garden Deare
  His Church, enwalld, with Heavenly Crystall fine
Hath every Bed beset with Pearle all Cleare
  And Allies Opald with Gold, and Silver Shrine.
    The shining Angells are its Centinalls
    With flaming Swords Chaunting out Madrigalls.

The Sparkling Plants, Sweet Spices, Herbs and Trees,
  The glorious Shews of aromatick Flowers,
The pleasing beauties soakt in sweet breath lees
  Of Christs rich garden ever upward towers,
    For Christ Sweet Showers of Grace make on it fall.
    It therefore bears the bell away from all.

The Nut of evry kinde is found to grow big,
  With food, and Physick, lodgd within a tower
A Wooden Wall with Husky Coverlid,
  Or Shell flesht ore, or in an Arching bower
    Beech, Hazle, Wallnut, Cocho, Almond brave
    Pistick or Chestnut in its prickly Cave.

These all as meate, and med'cine, emblems choice
    Of Spirituall Food, and Physike are which sport
Up in Christs Garden. Yet the Nutmeg's Spice
    A leathern Coate wares, and a Macie Shirt,
    Doth far excell them all. Aromatize
    My Soule therewith, my Lord, and spirituall wise.

Oh! Sweet Sweet Paradise, Whose Spiced Spring
    Will make the lips of him asleep to tune
Heart ravishing tunes, sweet Musick for our King
    In Aromatick aire of blesst perfume
    Open thy garden doore: mee entrance give
    And in thy Nut tree garden make me live.

If, Lord, thou opst, and in thy garden bring
    Mee, then thy little Linet sweetly Will
Upon thy Nut tree sit and sweetly sing
    Will Crack a Nut and eat the Kirnell still.
    Thou wilt mine Eyes, my Nose, and Palate greet
    With Curious Flowers, Sweet Odors, Viands Sweet.

Thy Gardens Odorif'rous aire mee make
    Suck in, and out t'aromatize my lungs.
That I thy garden, and its Spicie State
    May breath upon with such ensweetend Songs.
    My Lungs and Breath ensweetend thus shall raise
    The Glory of thy garden in its praise.

In the first half of this poem Taylor treats the Bridegroom's Garden in a way that is, for him, characteristic. He was never tempted, as we surmise that Watts must have been, to locate the Garden in the physical actuality of the meetinghouse or in the human actuality of those met there to worship. Instead, as here, he identifies it first with the lost paradise of Eden, and second with the hoped-for paradise of the Heavenly Jerusalem, Zion, the City set upon a Hill. (And incidentally I find that the hard metallic surfaces of the latter – its beds of pearl, its alleys 'opalled' – effectively prevent any of the insistent though ambiguous eroticism of the Song of Songs surviving into Taylor's treatments of it. Watts' softer textures are potentially more erotic; by the 1740s John Wesley was complaining of this, and some years earlier Watts – in a note to his tenth edition – had begun apologizing for having drawn on the Song of Songs so heavily.) However, in this poem, after the walled Zion has been duly invoked, Taylor is led by his text – 'I went down into the garden of nuts to see the fruits of the valley' – into an absorbed sympathy with varieties of nut and their various ways of being, with 'Pistick or Chestnut in its prickly Cave', and with the nutmeg's spice that 'a leathern Coate wares,

and a Macie Shirt'. After this astonishing and delightful feat of imagination, Taylor can easily manage the less difficult exertion of sympathizing
with a bird, and so he can without any risk of mawkishness identify
himself with 'thy little Linet' that 'sweetly will / Upon thy Nut tree sit
and sweetly sing'. These imaginative exertions are quite outside Watts'
range, and indeed in the long run nothing has so damaged Watts' reputation as his ill-advised attempts, in poems for children, to sympathize with
ant and emmet and bee – performances which survived on British and
American nursery bookshelves through many generations, until hilari-
ously and lethally parodied by Lewis Carroll.

We need not doubt that there are other points of comparison between
these two poets, which it would be instructive to ponder. But there is no
space at my disposal on the present occasion, and I must do the best I can,
on the broad contrasts that have so far emerged, to divine, with the
advantage of hindsight, what were to be the subsequent developments of
American poetry on the one hand, British poetry on the other. And one
thing it seems that we might safely prophesy, after looking at Taylor and
Watts together: British poetry, we might predict, is thereafter to be social,
American poetry is to be unsociable, if not indeed positively antisocial.

This is by no means a novel contention. It may seem to be no more
than Louis Martz was saying when, still comparing Taylor with Herbert,
he declared: 'the writer in England, wherever he may be living, works
within a certain conditioning imposed by the context of that intimate
island's culture: he knows the ways of other learned, literary men; he
senses the current modes of writing; and even though he believes in
freedom of language ... the writer is nevertheless tacitly and unconsciously influenced by the accepted conventions of public speech and
writing in that culture.' But there is a possible implication here that I find
unacceptable. Since it is one that bears more heavily on me than on you,
I shall merely notice it and pass on. It is the implication that the British
poet can be only as good as the state of British culture allows him to be,
that he cannot go against that culture when he perceives it in decline, nor
go more than a little in advance of it when he finds it sluggish or stagnant.
Whatever we mean by calling British poetry 'social', I hope we do not
mean that it can only reflect the state of British society, vigorous at some
times, torpid or depraved at others. The British poet may not want to
claim as much freedom as the American poet; but he certainly aspires to
more freedom than *that*!

Again, Professor Gelpi is plainly saying that British poetry is *social*,
when he declares: 'Taylor's poems bespeak a vigorous, passionate, and
learned mind shaping its apprehensions and speech without the chastening refinements which a sophisticated society of poets and readers
would have bred in him: a society open to and assumed by both Herbert
and Watts.' In fact to a Dissenter like Watts that sophisticated society of

which Professor Gelpi speaks was 'open' only on very stringent conditions; the door to it was not wide open, but at best ajar, and Watts was the first Dissenting leader to push it open for himself and his fellows, as Dr Johnson realized when in *The Lives of the Poets* he remarked of Watts, 'He was one of the first authors that taught the Dissenters to court attention by the graces of language. Whatever they had among them before, whether of learning or acuteness, was commonly obscured and blunted by coarseness and inelegance of style. He shewed them that zeal and purity might be expressed and enforced by polished diction.' More to the point, Watts as we have seen availed himself of his indeed great sophistication only so far as his mostly *un*sophisticated public, his Dissenting congregations, would permit. And this I think is what we should mean when we say that British poetry is social: not that it is sustained by society and social usage, nor that it is inescapably restricted by society and its usages, but that it is *addressed* to society, or rather to some identifiable group within society.

And this, which is plainly not true of Taylor's poetry, seems to be equally untrue of many American poets since Taylor. When I read their poems – I think for the moment of a poet so widely read and widely publicized as Robert Lowell – I get the vivid impression that I am eavesdropping, that the speech I hear is addressed not to me but to someone else, often to the poet's own self or to his God. A generation ago, something similar though not quite the same was said of American prose fiction: that its characteristic mode was not strictly speaking 'the novel' (which is a social form), but 'the romance' (which is not). And the advantage of bringing prose fiction into the discussion is that ever since Henry James' study of Hawthorne, it has been recognized that the difference between the British and the American developments is rooted in quite definable differences between the structure of British and of American society – which is a great deal better than positing some magically elusive sea-change that transforms the Englishman when he becomes American, as Edward Taylor did. Britain, we are used to saying – and it seems to be as true as any thumping generalization can be – is not a social democracy, but a hierarchy. And when we turn to Watts after looking at Taylor, hierarchy is precisely what we find. The Church of England stands higher in the hierarchy than the Congregationalist Church or the Baptist Church – so it was in Watts' day, so it is in ours. This is not a question of opinion, nor of deserts, still less of fatuous snobbery. The Establishment of the Established Church in England is a fact, political in the first place, a social fact in consequence. I have argued that this is the very substance of Watts' 'We are a garden wall'd around', and that there is not – nor could there be – anything similar or analogous in Taylor. The nearest we can come to an analogy – and it is not very near – is the distinction that Taylor makes between church-members and church-attenders, between, in the terms of his poem, 'The Joy of Church Fellowship rightly attended', the elect who ride to heaven in a coach and the humble members of the congregation who trudge that way on foot. Moreover, since the Episcopal Church in America stands on a level with every other church, what divided the two poets in 1700 must still divide a British from an American poet today.

What's more, addressing everyone is the same as addressing no one. The widest possible audience is no audience at all, precisely because it has no lineaments and no contours. One might as well be speaking to one's self or to one's God, as Taylor did. And that indeed is what happens – or so it must seem to an Englishman: the poet of a social democracy is in effect, since he speaks to so many, speaking only to himself or to his God.

And I hope it is clear that that possibility which I have several times allowed for – 'or to his God' – is something more than a form of words. If the poet in the act of writing cannot believe that he is engaged in *a social* activity, it is hard to see how he can describe that activity except as 'religious'. This will be as true of American poets who are strenuous Unbelievers, as of Edward Taylor who was a strenuous Believer. And I am ready to think that it is very generally true of American poets, or of such of them as need to be remembered: they experience the call to write as a religious calling, a *vocation* in the strictest, most elevating and demanding sense. Rather few British poets, today or for the past three centuries (since John Milton in fact), have regarded their calling as anything so exalted and exacting – though certainly some have, and those among the best.

And yet 'religion', as mere etymology tells us, implies a binding together, a tying up in bundles. How then explain our suspicion that American poetry is not just unsociable but positively antisocial? How should that which is supposed to bind up, in fact cleave apart? Where Edward Taylor is concerned I'm reminded, as Louis Martz was, of William Carlos Williams' perception of what a very special kind of religion it was, that New England fostered: 'its *inhuman* clarity, its steel-like thrust from the heart of each isolate man straight into the tabernacle of Jehovah without embellishment or softening.' 'Each isolate man' – that certainly gives the quality of Taylor's religion. All one needs to add is that, while it certainly isolated the believer from his human fellows, it did not isolate him from – on the contrary, it bound him in with – his nonhuman fellows like frozen wasps and hard-shelled nuts and piping linnets, just as it bound Jonathan Edwards to his lovingly and intently observed spiders. Even so, the individualism of Taylor is uncompromising, indeed terrifying. And did this die with him, or was it transmitted as a legacy to the American poets, his successors? That is a question that others must answer, not I. I do however remember that we have been led to that question by William Carlos Williams, one American poet whose religious sense of his vocation *did* lead him to celebrate fellowship, a fellowship between suffering human beings, rather than between the human being and the wasp or the spider, the mountain or the wilderness. Did American poetry have to wait for the twentieth century for that to be possible? And is that why devoted American readers love Dr Williams so dearly? These are questions that I am content to leave in the air.

The Yale Review (summer 1976), pp. 498–514.

XVI Old Dissent, 1700–1740

I want to begin by reading a poem. And since I shall rather seldom in these lectures be able to do this, let us enjoy together while we may the *presence* of poetry, as distinct from more or less impertinent prattle about it. The poem is called 'Man frail, and God eternal', and it will be familiar to most of you, though probably not under that title.

I

O God, our help in ages past,
　　Our hope for years to come,
Our shelter from the stormy blast,
　　And our eternal home.

II

Under the shadow of thy throne
　　Thy saints have dwelt secure;
Sufficient is thine arm alone,
　　And our defence is sure.

III

Before the hills in order stood,
　　Or earth receiv'd her frame,
From everlasting thou art God,
　　To endless years the same.

IV

Thy word commands our flesh to dust,
　　'Return, ye sons of men':
All nations rose from earth at first,
　　And turn to earth again.

V

A thousand ages in thy sight
　　Are like an evening gone;
Short as the watch that ends the night
　　Before the rising sun.

VI

The busy tribes of flesh and blood,
　　With all their lives and cares,

Are carry'd downwards by thy flood,
  And lost in following years.

VII

Time like an ever-rolling stream
  Bears all its sons away;
They fly forgotten as a dream
  Dies at the opening day.

VIII

Like flowering fields the nations stand
  Pleas'd with the morning light;
The flowers beneath the mower's hand
  Lie withering ere 'tis night.

IX

Our God, our help in ages past,
  Our hope for years to come,
Be thou our guard while troubles last,
  And our eternal home.

Those to whom this poem is not wholly unfamiliar will remember it as sung rather than spoken; and in the second place will remember it in parts and not as a whole. And this establishes two things about it: first, that it is a *lyric* poem, in the strictest pristine sense of 'lyric', and second, that in so far as it has been transmitted to us, the transmission has been oral, not through print. For it is characteristic of orally transmitted poetry that some parts of poems 'drop out', and in fact some of the stanzas I have just read are so habitually 'dropped out' that they may well be said no longer to belong in the poem – in the poem, that is, as it has been smoothed and moulded in the course of oral transmission through one English genera-tion after another. And it is *that* poem – the poem as it has 'come down' to us, not the poem as originally composed and printed – that I am chiefly concerned with. It is wholly to the point to remark that the poem is for most intents and purposes anonymous, in the sense that not one in a hundred of those who partly remember the poem will be able to name its author.

What I am describing is a very ancient kind of poem, perhaps the most ancient kind known to us – from other cultures as well as our own. What we have here, it seems, is a lay, *'le chant de la tribu'*, a kind of poem that pre-dates not just the age of print but the age of script, a kind of poem from before writing was invented.

The existence of this kind of poem has been known for a long time, but it is only quite lately that our knowledge of it has come to be – for many of us – a worry and a reproach. Most of us who study literature have lately come to be uneasy, from time to time, about the extent to which the literature we study is the product not of 'the tribe' but of a self-enclosed *élite* or priestly caste within the tribe. We have become ever more frequently agitated by our awareness that most of what we study and value as 'literature' is just not known, and never has been known, to the mass of the English nation, or English-speakers across the world. Our discomfort about this, in extreme cases our feelings of guilt about it, can be allayed by attending to poems like 'O God, our help in ages past' – a poem that is known to English-speakers far outside the ranks of any highly educated minority as well as outside any Christian church; a poem, indeed, that has attained the ultimate classic status of being known to, and sometimes quoted by, people who know not what it is, nor who it is, that they quote. Poetry like this, which has sunk down so far into the common anonymous stock of our linguistic inheritance, can best allay whatever populist misgivings we have – and most of us have some – about devoting ourselves, so much of the time, to products of 'high' or 'minority' culture. Accordingly we need not be surprised if poems like this one are happily seized upon, and attentively studied, amongst us.

In such a case, I say, we need not be surprised. But what *must* be our surprise when we discover that the case is quite otherwise? That even as we bend our energies more than ever before to the ramifying traditions of the Child ballads, to the recovery and printing of anonymous broadsides and street-ballads, of threshers' songs and weavers' songs and children's songs to the skipping rope (not to speak of barrow-boy poets and Merseyside poets and country-rock poets *à la* Bob Dylan), the attention we pay to a poem like 'O God, our help in ages past' is precisely what it was fifty years ago – which is to say, no attention at all, unless we happen to be either hymnologists or else (less probably) historians of the Nonconformist churches! The reasons we may find for this – mere bad faith, mere sloth, incurious inertia – are true so far as they go; but there are other more specific, historically conditioned, reasons – and these may emerge in due course. For the moment it seems we must say that if 'O God, our help in ages past' represents a very ancient kind of poem, that kind is a great deal too ancient for our self-applaudingly 'modern' criticism to be able to deal with it.

We think of this poem as a hymn. And that sounds right, for 'hymn' is indeed the traditionally appropriate title for one sub-category of the sort of tribal lyric that we seem to have to do with. More precisely, however, our poem is not a hymn but a *psalm*. In fact it is specifically and deliberately a version of one of the Psalms of David, or rather of the first six verses of that psalm, Ps. 90, of which the first six verses in the King James Bible are as follows:

> Lord, thou hast been our dwelling place in all generations.
> Before the mountains were brought forth, or ever thou hadst

formed the earth and the world, even from everlasting to everlasting, thou art God.

Thou turnest man to destruction; and sayest, Return, ye children of men.

For a thousand years in thy sight are but as yesterday when it is past, and as a watch in the night.

Thou carriest them away as with a flood; they are as a sleep: in the morning they are like grass which groweth up.

In the morning it flourisheth, and groweth up; in the evening it is cut down, and withereth.

Need it be said that just such dependence on a sacred or canonical text, and in consequence just such total disregard for 'originality' or 'self-expression', is entirely typical of the poet of the tribal lay? Nevertheless it is clear that our poet has intended more than a metrical translation of the verses of Scripture, such as had been effected for the Psalms by John Calvin himself, by Clément Marot at Calvin's insistence, and in England by Sternhold and Hopkins as well as (memorably) by Philip Sidney and his sister in their collaboration on the Sidney Psalter. Our poet is working in that Calvinist tradition but at the same time transforming it, administering to it a shock which in fact provoked many guardians of that tradition to rise up in arms against him. What he gives us is a psalm, not translated, but paraphrased and modernized, and yet in no sense 'freely adapted', but modernized according to a very strict method. He said himself of these compositions of his that they were 'The Psalms of David Imitated in the Language of the New Testament'. And what this means in effect, schematically, is that every time the ancient Hebrew poet looks back ('Lord, thou hast been our dwelling place in all generations'), our English poet looks back with him, but then immediately looks forward; thus, 'O God, our help in ages past', but then, immediately, 'Our hope for years to come'. Original, he had no wish to be; but independent, a radical innovator, he certainly was. As one of his few modern admirers remarks: 'He worked alone. No pope, bishop, college or committee asked him to undertake his task.' His achievement, she says, is 'a shocking example of Protestant individualism'.

Yet, all this is of no account at all if, when we hear or read or sing 'O God, our help in ages past', it strikes us as merely *dull*. And this may well be the case; for we've already found reasons why current critical precepts, and the reading habits they inculcate, should be ill-adapted to seeing anything responsible or sensitive or distinguished in verses like:

> A thousand ages in thy sight
> Are like an evening gone;
> Short as the watch that ends the night
> Before the rising sun.

or:

> Time like an ever-rolling stream
> Bears all its sons away;
> They fly forgotten as a dream
> Dies at the opening day.

About such matters there can be no argument – at least in this sense, that no one should allow himself to be browbeaten into pretending that what he registers as 'dull' somehow isn't. All that a lecturer can do is to avow quite sincerely that 'dull' isn't how such verses register for him now, though it's true that once they did; to quote from his author to show that dullness was one risk the author foresaw yet decided to take; and finally to offer what he has found for his own part to be an instructive comparison. This I now proceed to …

In the first place Isaac Watts (for he, of course, is the poet we are dealing with), speaking of such compositions as this one, declared:

> In many of these composures, I have just permitted my verse to rise above a flat and indolent style; yet I hope it is everywhere supported above the just contempt of the critics: though I am sensible that I have often subdued it below their esteem; because I would neither indulge any bold metaphors, nor admit of hard words, nor tempt the ignorant worshipper to sing without his understanding.

and in 'A Short Essay toward the Improvement of Psalmody', he made the same point more vehemently: 'It was hard to restrain my verse always within the bounds of my design; it was hard to sink every line to the level of a whole congregation, and yet to keep it above contempt.' This was a poet who, if he practised what Pope and the Scriblerus Club called 'the art of sinking', did so deliberately, after counting the cost, his eyes open to the risk he was running. His endeavour may be thought to be perverse; it was not at all events mere blundering (and if the question be put whether he was capable of any style more elevated, more exuberant and audacious – well yes, there are poems of his that prove that he was).

As for the comparison, it shall be with a poet of genius, Christopher Smart, whose paraphrases of the Psalms, on precisely the same principles, came almost exactly half a century after Watts'. Smart's version of Psalm 90 as a whole should be examined. His stanzas which correspond to the two quatrains lately quoted are these:

> For years thy creatures, as they flee,
> Are all responsible to thee,
>   The present as the past;
> Ev'n thousands in thy perfect sight
> Are as the watch of yester-night
>   When their account is cast.

Thou bidst them off into the deep
Of vast eternity to sleep
   And in their peace remain;
While others like the grass succeed,
For their determin'd goal to speed,
   Nor e'er revolve again.

Does Smart turn to profit the elbow-room that he gets from two extra lines in each stanza? It seems to me quite evident that he does not, that the extra lines, and rhymes, betray him into laxity and vapidity.

Well, but (it may be said) we ask of a poetic style – of a style in any art, and indeed of a style of life – that it possess more than negative virtues. It is a weighty point, and one indeed that takes us at once to the heart of the Calvinist aesthetic.[1] For that is what we are now concerned with. And in the first place a Calvinist aesthetic exists: 'In nothing perhaps has Calvin been more misjudged than in the view that he lacked an aesthetic sense …' It was after all John Calvin who clothed Protestant worship with the sensuous grace, and necessarily the aesthetic ambiguity, of song; and who that has attended worship in a French Calvinist church can deny that – over and above whatever religious experience he may or may not have had – he has had an aesthetic experience, and of a peculiarly intense kind? From the architecture, from church furnishings, from the congregational music, from the Geneva gown of the pastor himself, everything breathes *simplicity*, *sobriety*, and *measure* – which are precisely the qualities that Calvinist aesthetics demands of the art-object. Just here, in fact, is where negative virtues become positive ones. And this is true not just of Calvinist art but of all art, not just of Calvinist ethics but of all ethics. The aesthetic *and* the moral perceptions have, built into them and near to the heart of them, the perception of licence, of abandonment, of superfluity, foreseen, even invited, and yet in the end denied, fended off. Art is measure, *is* exclusion; is therefore simplicity (hard-earned), is sobriety, tense with all the extravagances that it has been tempted by and has denied itself. I appeal to you, and to your experience, whether in making art or in responding to it: Isn't this the way it is? And so, even if we admit for the sake of argument that Calvinism denies sensuous pleasure, we encounter time and again the question, when faced with a Calvinistic occasion: Do we have here a denial of sensuous pleasure, or do we not rather have sensuous pleasure deployed with an unusually frugal, and therefore exquisite, fastidiousness? It is peculiarly of the nature of Puritan art to pose just this question, though that is by no means the account of it that is usually given.

The French critic Brunetière had in mind something different, though related, when he maintained that Calvin's *Institutes* constitute the first book in French of which one might say that it is 'classic': 'It is equally so', he says, 'by reason of the dignity of the plan, and the manner in which the conception of the whole determines the nature and choice of details.' It is important here to take the particular and precise force of the term *classique* in French usage; and Brunetière gives a succinct definition of it in the passage just quoted. In this sense of 'classic' or 'classical' – the subordination of detail to 'the conception of the whole' – Pope is not often classical, and is not so to just the extent that he is, as Dr Leavis showed us, in 'the line of wit'. But classical in this sense is just what, for good or ill, we can call the poet who protested: 'It was hard to restrain my verse always within the bounds of my design ...' 'O God, our help in ages past' is in this sharp, Calvinist, non-English sense, 'classical', as are very few poems by Pope, and also incidentally few hymns by Charles Wesley. In fact I suggest that, just as there is a necessary and compelling and often noted connection between Methodistical Evangelicalism and Romanticism, so between Calvinism and 'classicism' there is a connection no less binding. 'Simplicity, sobriety, and measure' – do the words not speak for themselves?

If this should seem paradoxical, the paradox is not of my making. And I should be very sorry to have it thought that this is special pleading. I suggest in all earnestness that the common cause which the English dissenters felt with the Huguenots gave some of them a more direct access to the culture which produced *Athalie*, than Pope could or did get from reading Boileau or Voiture; for after all the Roman Church produces its own puritans, and Racine's *Athalie*, so far as it is Jansenist, is itself puritan art.[2] Unless we disabuse ourselves of certain stereotyped oppositions in our thinking, we shall lose track of the dissenting thread in our culture, even at this early stage. The first such slack assumption that we need to be rid of looks like a ghost of Matthew Arnold's distinction between the Hellenic and the Hebraic emphases in our inheritance. It is the assumption that the more 'classical' a culture is or aspires to be, the less sympathy it will feel with the Hebrew Scriptures, and vice versa. We need to remember that Racine wrote *Athalie* as well as *Phèdre;* that Dryden wrote *The Hind and the Panther* as well as *Macflecknoe;* and that Isaac Watts is as authentic a voice of Augustan England as is Alexander Pope. A second false assumption is likely to be even more obstructive, if only because it is particularly rife at the present day, and is promoted by the false friends of Dissent rather than by its enemies. It can be symbolized by the latest and now current biography of Cromwell, which has the (as I find it) embarrassing title, *God's Englishman.* There is abroad among us an unformulated assumption that Dissent is in some special ways more 'English' than the Church of England is – and this in contexts where 'English' means, more or less defiantly, 'insular'. However it may be in the twentieth century, or may have been in the seventeenth, English Dissent in the eighteenth century was not insular in the least. The full cultural consequences of the influx of Huguenots into England, after the revocation of the Edict of

Nantes, has I think never been assessed, nor indeed much studied. But in any case a strong and sturdy 'French connection' can be traced among dissenting leaders from before the seventeenth century is out. More surprisingly, the connection is not only with French Protestantism, still less with the lunatic fringe of that Protestantism, the Camisard 'French prophets' who irrupted upon England in 1709–10 and ultimately spawned, by way of the English prophetess Anne Lee, the Shaker communities in America. Watts and Wesley and Cowper, even the Evangelical poet Henry Kirke White, were respectfully and eagerly aware of 'surprising conversions' within French Roman Catholicism. And Isaac Watts drew upon the Counter Reformation more generally, notably upon the Latin poems of 'the Christian Horace', the Polish Jesuit, Matthew Casimire Sarbiewski (1595–1640). In short, English Dissent does not offer an insular alternative to European culture, a way of 'keeping out', but rather a way of 'going in' on special, and specially rewarding, terms.

In any case, the notion of a Calvinist classicism gives us a vantage-point from which there open up, and stretch away, vistas which may be dizzying but are also (to speak for myself) exciting and very tempting. I must resist the temptation to explore any of them except one. Can I be serious when I offer Isaac Watts as a poet of the tribal lay, a true analogue in Augustan England of David, the bard and warrior king of ancient Israel? Calling Watts to mind, undersized and sickly, demure and grave and domesticated in Hanoverian London, the notion seems ludicrous. And yet I do suggest it. The dissenters for whom he wrote conceived themselves to be, very exactly, 'a tribe', a chosen people just as ancient Israelites were chosen, in tension with their neighbours just as ancient Israel was. Watts shared their conviction, and articulated it for them once and for all, magnificently:

> *The Church the Garden of Christ*
>
> We are a Garden wall'd around,
> Chosen and made peculiar Ground;
> A little Spot inclos'd by Grace
> Out of the World's wide Wilderness.
>
> Like Trees of Myrrh and Spice we stand,
> Planted by God the Father's Hand;
> And all his Springs in Sion flow,
> To make the young Plantation grow.
>
> Awake, O heavenly Wind, and come,
> Blow on this garden of Perfume;
> Spirit Divine, descend and breathe
> A gracious Gale on Plants beneath.

Make our best Spices flow abroad
To entertain our Saviour-God:
And faith, and Love, and Joy appear,
And every Grace be active here.

Let my Beloved come, and taste
His pleasant Fruits at his own Feast.
I come, my Spouse, I come, he crys,
With Love and Pleasure in his eyes

Our Lord into his Garden comes,
Well pleas'd to smell our poor Perfumes,
And calls us to a Feast divine,
Sweeter than Honey, Milk, or Wine.

Eat of the Tree of Life, my Friends,
The Blessings that my Father sends;
Your Taste shall all my Dainties prove,
And drink abundance of my Love.

Jesus, we will frequent thy Board,
And sing the Bounties of our Lord:
But the rich Food on which we live
Demands more Praise than Tongues can give.

There are good examples here of what Watts meant by 'sinking' his style.
'The young Plantation' for instance has little to do with afforestation, but
a lot to do with Plymouth Plantation or the Plantation of Ulster – a
pungently topical allusion, historically resonant, which might have been
elaborated into something ingenious and striking, which instead is
subdued to the tenor of the rest. And another example is the way in
which 'spirit' and 'gale' in adjacent lines vivify each other by evoking
their common element, 'breath'. But it is more important to recognize
the strategy and structure of the whole occasion: how the ancient icon
and figure of the *hortus conclusus*, the garden enclosed, is startlingly reno-
vated by being applied to religious Dissent. For the 'We' of the first line
– 'We are a Garden wall'd around' – is not mankind as a whole, not the
whole body of Christians, not even Protestant mankind, but specifically
dissenting mankind. For what sense would it make to describe the Church
of England as 'A little Spot … Out of the World's wide Wilderness'?
How could this be said of a Church whose head is the reigning monarch,
whose bishops sit as Lords Spiritual in Parliament? The Established
Church is the *national* Church; that is what 'establishment' means – it is
by maintaining the strenuous fiction that the Church and the nation are
coterminous that Anglicans claim and attempt to sanctify or spiritualize
the entire secular order. But 'tribe' implies something more intense and

intimate than that, a community much more immediately in tension with its potentially hostile neighbours. And Watts' poem articulates that tribal sentiment, just as the royal psalmist articulated it for Israel. Moreover, hymns like this, and perhaps this very hymn, were composed and sung *from manuscript*, week by week through 1694 and 1695, in the dissenting chapel at Southampton to which the youthful Watts had returned from his dissenting academy in the much more sumptuous though still sober milieu of Stoke Newington. (Hence arises the charming tradition that one of the loveliest of them – 'There is a Land of pure Delight' – was prompted by the view of the Isle of Wight across Southampton Water.) Watts was there in the congregation, hearing his hymns sung at sight by his neighbours, most of whom, no doubt, he knew and could name. Can we conceive of a more tribal situation, or of a relation more immediate and intimate between a poet and his public? And this happened at the very height of what we are taught to call 'the age of print', that sad inter-regnum in the history of poetry from which – we are asked to believe – a Yevtushenko or an Allen Ginsberg or Leonard Cohen has come to save us, by reading his poems through massed microphones and thus (if you please!) reviving poetry as an oral art.

This poem is a hymn, not a psalm. But it is related as closely as the psalm was, to a passage of Scripture – to verses from the Song of Solomon:

> A garden inclosed is my sister, my spouse; a spring shut up, a fountain sealed ...
> Spikenard and saffron; calamus and cinnamon, with all trees of frankincense; myrrh and aloes, with all the chief spices;
> A fountain of gardens, a well of living waters, and streams from Lebanon ...
> I am come into my garden, my sister, my spouse: I have gathered my myrrh with my spice: I have eaten my honeycomb with my honey: I have drunk my wine with my milk: eat, O friends; drink yea, drink abundantly, O beloved.

And the Song of Songs or (more properly, since it is not one song but many) the Book of Canticles is, we all know, the most erotic item in the Scriptures and one of the most intensely and unashamedly erotic pieces of literature that we know of. How comical, we snigger, that our Puritan forebears should not have noticed that! But *of course* they noticed it, and relished it. If they allegorized it into a nuptial mysticism which made Christ the bridegroom and the Church his bride, they knew perfectly well that allegory can work only if the literal sense is coherent and compelling on its own account. Listen to one of them:

> The doctrine of *union* between Christ and his church is of a nature so

copious, that no one metaphor can *properly* represent it; therefore in the scriptures we meet with *various* similitudes, tending to illustrate the important subject. Christ is frequently compared to a *foundation*, on which his people are built; but that conveying only the idea of support, therefore he is compared to a *root*, by which the idea of *influence* is likewise illustrated. But though *branches* are influenced, and rendered fruitful, in consequence of conveyed nourishment, yet Christian *activity* is not thereby properly represented: to supply this defect, Christ and his people are farther illustrated by the union subsisting between *head* and *members*. But though the idea of *activity is* thereby conveyed, there is still a material defect, *for* the relation between these is quite *involuntary*. Had it been otherwise, the *head* might possibly have chosen better feet, or better *hands;* and had *they* been the subject *of* distinct volition, they would probably have chosen to have been in union with a better *head:* therefore to supply the deficiency of the above simile, and to include the idea of *mutual choice* and *social endearments*, Christ and his church are compared to *husband* and *wife*. If then we are in such near and close connection with the blessed Jesus, as the Scriptures assert, and, by so many significant similitudes, illustrate his own people to be, let us frequently think of, and bless God for, that *sovereign* and *inseparable* love which constituted the relation. It is all of God, as is acknowledged by that sweet singer in our British Israel, the late Dr Watts who of the Father's love and choice thus speaks:

> Christ be my first elect, he said,
> Then chose our souls in Christ our Head;
> Nor shall our souls be thence remov'd,
> Till he forgets his first belov'd.

This passage, from Robert Hall the elder's *Help to Zion's Travellers* (1781), is an invaluable example of how carefully, with how much sophistication (literary as well as theological), devout Christians of the eighteenth century read Watts' poetry.

Alas, it couldn't last. Haven't Puritans always had a hang-up about sex? (Vague and vulgar language; but these are vague and vulgar notions.) Well, no, it appears that they haven't. But already by 1736 Watts was printing an apology: 'Solomon's Song was much more in use amongst preachers and writers of divinity when these poems were written than it is now.' His friend and follower Doddridge took the hint, and among Doddridge's 363 scriptural hymns, published in the 1750s, not one is derived from the Song of Songs. The emergence of the hang-up, it seems, can be dated quite precisely; and sure enough, *NED* gives 1746 for the first appearance of both 'pruriency' and 'prurient' in their modern senses. After that everyone gets more and more flustered whenever erotic and devotional experience are found close together. John Wesley in a sermon asked about Watts' hymns: 'Are they not too full of expressions which strongly savour of "knowing Christ after the flesh"? Yea, and in a more gross manner, than anything which was ever before published in the English tongue? What pity is it, that those coarse expressions should appear in many truly spiritual hymns!' And Robert Southey in 1837 is close to panic:

> Pure as was the mind of Dr Watts – and its purity was equal to the lucid clearness of his style – he has in many of these pieces made so bold a use of the sensible imagery proper to amatory verse, that while the unspiritual reader is apt to linger, if not finally to rest, in the mere external sense, there is no small danger, at least in these times, lest the more pious and refined should experience a feeling bordering on disgust.

Whose minds were the more prurient and agitated: Watts' and the Baptist Hall's, or Wesley's and Southey's, both of them High Church Anglicans? 'Puritanical', it seems, may or may not be right for describing repressed sexuality – it rather looks as if it isn't right – but certainly it is something that crops up in Church at least as often as in Chapel.

While we are about it, we may as well look at some things that have been said about Watts up to our own day. Here is Leslie Stephen in 1876:

> The name of Watts, associated with certain hymns still dear to infancy, has contracted a faint flavour of the ludicrous, though other poems of greater pretensions are still preserved in the lower strata of literature. The hymns, indeed, of Watts, Doddridge, and the Wesleys, whatever their literary merit, have been popular enough to show that they are not inadequate expressions of a strong religious sentiment. It is said that for many years 50,000 copies of Watts' 'Psalms and Hymns' were annually printed: and if there be any truth in the commonplace about songs and laws, Watts' influence must have been greater than that of many legislators, and, indeed, many more distinguished writers. But such an influence is too intangible in its nature to be easily measured.

And that is all we hear from Stephen about Watts' hymns, or Watts' poetry generally! In one who, as Noel Annan says, pioneered, if not 'the sociology of literature', at least the consistent relating of literary to social history, that 'influence … too intangible … to be easily measured' is surely a very cavalier way of dismissing the phenomenon of Watts' popularity through nearly two hundred years – with English-speakers, moreover, many of whom knew no other English poetry at all. However, we are in no position to jeer at Stephen; for we, too, a century after him, have no way of dealing with such phenomena, no method by which to translate the quantitative facts of so many copies sold and printed year after year, into the qualitative consideration of how they conditioned the sensibility of the English-speaking peoples. What we can and should do, however, is to confess and insist – as Leslie Stephen does not – just what a vast lacuna this reveals in our pretensions to chart cultural history, and diagnose cultural health, on the evidence of printed literature. There is quite clearly *prima facie* quantitative evidence for supposing that Watts' *Hymns and Psalms* ('Watts Entire', as it came to be called) has been more influential than any of the works of its century that we think of as most popular – more than Johnson's *Dictionary*, more than *Robinson Crusoe* or *Gulliver's Travels*, more even than *The Seasons* or 'Ossian'; and so far are we from taking this into account, that the work in question gets either no notice at all or only marginal notice in histories of our literature!

I am not prepared nor competent to rectify this state of affairs; my concern is to probe a little behind Stephen's lordly or flurried parenthesis: 'Whatever their literary merit.' I am trying to show that their literary merit is very great, and hence that, whatever the extent of their influence, it may well have been an influence for the good, a *civilizing* influence. (And if I had time, incidentally, I would have liked to show this for Philip Doddridge, though Watts was a genius whereas Doddridge was only an exceptionally intelligent and honourable and civilized man.)

What Stephen said of Watts – that his name 'has contracted a faint flavour of the ludicrous' because of its association with 'certain hymns still dear to infancy' – is still true today. At least I can find no other explanation when, as late as 1960, a historian of Dissent declares: 'the greatest imaginative literature of Puritanism is to be found in Watts' hymns', but then goes on – inexcusably, I think – to say that this treasure can be found only 'with perseverance in thrusting through the doggerel and bathos'.[3] This image of Watts is potent among us because Watts' name has become attached to just one of his books: his *Divine and Moral Songs for Children* (1720). And Lewis Carroll's lethal because good-humoured and hilarious parodies have conditioned us so that we cannot read with a straight face such rhymes as 'Let dogs delight to bark and bite', or 'How doth the little busy bee Improve each shining hour', or ''Tis the voice of the Sluggard: I heard him complain, "You have waked me too soon! I must slumber again!"' Not all of these poems by Watts are indefensible. But a defence of them would have to start by placing them in a tradition that runs from Bunyan's *A Book for Boys and Girls: or Country Rhymes for Children* (1686), and takes in the Wesleys' *Hymns and Prayers for Children* (1746), Christopher Smart's *Hymns for the Amusement of Children* (1770), and Mrs Barbauld's *Hymns in Prose for Children* (1782), to culminate in Blake's *Songs of Innocence* (1790). The development is, as Professor Holloway has shown, from songs *to* or *about* innocence to songs *of* innocence. And in this department of poetry Blake so consummately crowns and transcends all his predecessors, that only by a very strenuous exertion of the historical imagination can we get sympathetic access to the climate of feeling about children which Blake's beautiful poems rule out of court. Such an exertion is possible but I do not attempt nor invite it here; and so the case that I want to make for Watts does not rest in any way on the poems he wrote for children. It should be said, however, that William Blake and Lewis Carroll are redoubtable assailants for any poetic reputation to have to contend with; and what should give us pause is that both Blake and Dodgson thought Watts worth spending their ammunition on, as did Emily Dickinson also.

Between the last two authorities that I have cited came A.E. Housman, in *The Name and Nature of Poetry* (1933), quoting four lines of Watts and declaring: 'That simple verse, bad rhyme and all, is poetry beyond Pope.' As I have declared upon another occasion, this is a great deal worse than useless. Pope is one of the greatest poets in our language, and incomparably the greatest poet of England during Watts' lifetime. Because earlier I have suggested that in one crucial and valid sense Watts' poetry is more classical than Pope's – for in how many poems by Pope do we register the whole as greater than the sum of its parts? – I must make it plain that in no way do I contend for Watts' poetry as superior to Pope's (which would be absurd), nor yet as representing an alternative tradition to his. That would be sectarian indeed! (And it's a trap that sectarian commentators have fallen into.) No! Housman is *exactly* wrong: so far from Watts representing an artless tradition rivalling the artfulness of Pope, what we must see in him is a similar artfulness, though less magisterial, in the service of a quite different artistic end.

And who was the man who wrote these poems that I ask you to admire? Was he *all* poet, or all poet-plus-preacher? By no means! But to establish what Watts stood for, what he signifies and represents, over and above whatever one thinks of his poetry – for this we go to another authority, whose testimony redeems the otherwise shabby story of how the memory of Watts has been preserved amongst us. We go – and I think we might have guessed it – to that most magnanimous of Anglicans, Samuel Johnson. Johnson's estimate of Watts is one of the things I shall take up in my next lecture.

Notes

1 On the aesthetic sense of Calvin, and the aesthetics of Calvinism, see Henry. R. Van Til, *The Calvinistic Concept of Culture*, 1959, pp. 107, 109, 111. Brunetière is quoted by Van Til from *The Presbyterian and Reformed Review*, XII, 1901, pp. 392–414.

2 Doddridge's reading of Racine is recorded in a letter of 1723:

> Of all their dramatic poets, I have met with none that I admire so much as Racine. It is impossible not to be charmed with the pomp, elegance, and harmony of his language, as well as the majesty, tenderness, and propriety of his sentiments. The whole is conducted with a wonderful mixture of grandeur and simplicity, which

sufficiently distinguishes him from the dullness of some tragedians, and the bombast of others.

In the same letter Doddridge recommends Fenelon, whom Watts also admired, saying that 'in his *Posthumous Essays* and his *Letters*, there are many admirable thoughts in practical and experimental religion, and very beautiful and divine sentiments in devotion'. On the other hand Watts no more than Bossuet could look with sympathy on Fenelon's enthusiasm for the mystical quietism of Mme Guyon; and we may suppose him to have that side of Fenelon in mind when he goes on to say that 'sometimes in large paragraphs, or in whole chapters together, you find him in the clouds of mystic divinity, and he never descends within the reach of common ideas or common sense'. There speaks the Watts who was a devoted admirer of Locke. (For the whole of this paragraph, see A.G. Matthews and G.F. Nuttall, 'The Literary Interests of Nonconformists in the 18th Century', *Transactions of the Congregational Historical Society*, vol. 12, 1933–6, pp. 337–8.)

As might be expected, the Wesleyans were less chary of Mme Guyon (and the Quakers, incidentally, co-opted her very eagerly). In John Wesley's *Journal* for 1742, we find him reading her *Torrents Spirituels*, and Henry Bett in his *Hymns of Methodism* recognizes imagery from this book in Charles Wesley's *Hymns and Sacred Poems* of 1749. As late as 1776 John Wesley published *An Extract of the Life of Madame Guion*. Cowper translated her extensively, but when his translations were published posthumously in 1801, his editor William Bull remarked with some agitation: 'To infer that the peculiarities of Madame Guion's theological sentiments, were adopted either by Mr C. or by the Editor, would be ... absurd ...'

A more extraordinary case of the French presence in eighteenth-century dissenting and Evangelical concerns is the career in English translation and allusion of a sonnet, 'Grand Dieu, tes jugements ...' by Jacques Vallée, Seigneur des Barreaux (1602–73), a famous libertine whom Pascal described as among those 'who would renounce their reason and become brute beasts', who repented, however, and died in retirement. The full story is extremely complicated, and has been disentangled by the meticulous and indispensable Henry Bett. It encompasses Watts' version, 'The Humble Enquiry', dated 1695 but not published till the second edition of *Lyra Heroica* (1709); Addison quoting the French sonnet in full in *The Spectator;* attacks on John Wesley, by Thomas Church (1745) and Lavington (1749), for having adapted verses from the French: marginalia to Lavington by Mrs Thrale, ascribing the lines to the French source but with a crucial error; numerous reminiscences of the French lines in Charles Wesley's hymns; and a version by the Evangelical Henry Kirke White, 'Thy judgments, Lord, are just ...'

The title of Bishop Lavington's notorious polemic, *The Enthusiasm of Methodists and Papists Compared* (1749–51), hints at how anti-French chauvinism and anti-Papist prejudice could be mustered in some quarters of the Establishment against the often more charitable and cosmopolitan attitudes of dissenters and Wesleyans.

3   Erik Routley, *English Religious Dissent*, 1960, p. 137.

From the Clark Lectures, delivered in Cambridge in 1976; printed as *A Gathered Church: the Literature of the English Dissenting Interest, 1700–1930* (London, 1978).

XVII Dissent and the Wesleyans, 1740–1800

As we have seen, it is hard to find anyone with a good word to say for the dissenters of the early eighteenth century. Even their fellow-sectaries, in the nineteenth and twentieth centuries, customarily appeal over their heads to their seventeenth-century predecessors. A curious instance of this is the blue-stocking historian Lucy Aikin in 1828, writing across the Atlantic to her fellow-Unitarian, William Ellery Channing:

> As for … the Calvinistic dissenters, they had the misfortune of living in one of those middle states between direct persecution and perfect religious liberty, which sours the temper by continual petty vexations, without affording scope for great efforts or great sacrifices – which drives men to find a perverse pleasure in hating and being hated, and to seek indemnification for the contempt of the world in a double portion of spiritual pride and self-importance. 'We can prove ourselves saints', 'being Christ's little flock everywhere spoken against', is the plea put into the mouth of this set by Green, a poet, who was born and bred among them.[1]

Surprisingly, after this contemptuous dismissal of the eighteenth-century dissenters, Lucy Aikin in her very next paragraph pays tribute to the dissenting leader Doddridge, recording how 'my kindred the Jennings, the Belshams, my excellent grandfather Aikin, and his friend and tutor Doddridge, had began to break forth out of the chains and darkness of Calvinism, and their manners softened with their system'. But more immediately to our purpose is her specifying, as the spokesman of 'this set', 'Green, a poet'. This is Mr Matthew Green of the Customs House, whose most sustained performance, *The Spleen*, is one of those delightful but not very consequential poems that are continually being re-discovered, but never by enough readers to save them permanently from obscurity. For my generation the rediscovery was effected by F.R. Leavis in some well-considered and valuable pages of his *Revaluation*. That was in 1936, and over the years since, unless I am mistaken, oblivion has claimed Matthew Green once again. But as Lucy Aikin may remind us, Green *stands for* something; his poem articulates a particular moment in the spiritual and intellectual history of one kind of Englishman – a moment which otherwise in our poetry goes unrecorded. It's on these grounds – which were not Leavis's – that we may pluck him back from oblivion once more, and for as long as anyone is interested.

To say that Green was a dissenter is true, but misleading. He seems to have been in fact a lapsed Quaker – which is a very special kind of dissenter, special at any time but particularly so in 1737, the year of Green's death, when *The Spleen* was published; for George Fox, the farouche and irreconcilable founder of the Society of Friends, had died as recently as 1691, and the process by which, over no more than two generations, the English Quaker transformed himself from that stereotype into becoming the banker and iron-master of the Industrial Revolution, represents an adaptation so extreme and so precipitate that it must give pause even to someone who believes that 'accommodation' (as I have ventured to call it) was the historically necessary and in itself not ignoble duty of Dissent in this period. Accommodation, yes; but at this rate? And on this scale?[2] One thinks the better of those like Matthew Green who could not change so far so fast.

Horace Walpole said of *The Spleen:* 'It has the wit of Butler with the ease of Prior without imitating either.' And the judgement is less facile than it may seem: Butler's *Hudibras*, pillorying once and for all the Old Dissenters and their pretence to 'the inner light', is consistently the presence behind Green's poem, not just as a formal and stylistic mark that Green must steer by, but as an ideological pressure that he must acknowledge and give way before. Hence, for instance, the dissenters of his time, or else of his childhood, unmistakably and excellently pinned down:

> Nor they so pure and so precise,
> Immaculate as their white of eyes,
> Who for the spirit hug the spleen,
> Phylactered throughout their mien;
> Who their ill-tasted home-brewed prayer
> To the state's mellow forms prefer;
> Who doctrines, as infectious, fear,
> Which are not steeped in vinegar,
> And samples of heart-chested grace
> Expose in show-glass of the face ...

The neat, terse gibes strike home; and yet they are predictable, out of common stock. The figure being assailed is after all a stereotype, a cardboard cut-out. Such knowledgeable and spiteful apostasies from Dissent were common in Matthew Green's lifetime; Samuel Wesley the elder is another example out of many. It is permissible to feel that an attempt like Watts', to change Dissent from inside, was a more honourable and forthright endeavour.

Certainly, we may infer, it seemed so to Dr Johnson, who said of

Watts: 'Such he was as every Christian Church would rejoice to have adopted'; who specified Watts' *cultural* achievement by saying:

> He was one of the first authors that taught the dissenters to court atten-
> tion by the graces of language. Whatever they had among them
> before, whether of learning or acuteness, was commonly obscured and
> blunted by coarseness and inelegance of style. He shewed them, that
> zeal and purity might be expressed and enforced by polished diction.

Johnson it was, moreover, who apologized for a long quotation from Gibbons' memoir of Watts, by saying: 'If this quotation has appeared long, let it be considered that it comprises an account of six-and-thirty years, and those the years of Dr Watts.' Johnson it was who concluded his account of Watts by saying: 'happy will be that reader whose mind is disposed by his verses or his prose, to imitate him in all but his non-conformity, to copy his benevolence to man, and his reverence to God.' And it was Johnson who, when the name of Matthew Green was missing from the list of poets whom he was to introduce, made no demur; but who, when Watts' name was missing, insisted that it be included – as he is careful to tell us himself, at the start of his 'Life of Watts'. Johnson's 'Life of Watts' is nearer to hagiography than any other of his *Lives of the English Poets;* and if the significance of thus honouring a dissenter is lost upon us, it impressed and puzzled readers nearer to Johnson's time, as we see for instance from Hazlitt's *Conversations with Northcote*.

As regards poetic style, to compare Green with Watts means ques-tioning whether 'conceited' *wit*, however submerged and subdued – as we can find it in Green but not, except in his apprenticeship, in Watts – can be taken in respect of the eighteenth century, as by and large it can be taken when we deal with the seventeenth, as the measure of imaginative seriousness. *The Spleen* itself supplies evidence that, for good or ill, wit-writing was by 1737 restricted to those parts of a composition that were relatively capricious and irresponsible; for at line 717 Green prepares for his exordium by re-addressing his addressee, Cuthbert Jackson, in the person of 'Memmius'. This signals a shift to a graver tone than the inven-tive banter which has preceded it; and the diction henceforth is nearer to the plain style of Watts than to Marvell:

> In one, no object of our sight,
> Immutable and infinite,
> Who can't be cruel or unjust,
> Calm and resigned, I fix my trust;
> To him my past and present state
> I owe, and must my future fate.
> A stranger into life I'm come,
> Dying may be our going home,

> Transported here by angry Fate,
> The convicts of a prior state;
> Hence I no curious thoughts bestow
> On matters I can never know.

This passage, which some readers will think the most moving and the most seriously intended in the poem, is almost entirely free of wit. On the other hand it is a profession of faith so hedged about with saving clauses – consider only that 'Dying *may be* our going home' – that it can hardly be called 'Christian' at all. Indeed, could it not be subscribed to by any number of nineteenth or twentieth-century agnostics? And isn't this the reason why, when – rarely, as by Leavis – we are directed to *The Spleen*, we are able to respond to it so warmly? In any case it is all very well to say (what is true) that in Green's more vivacious passages we see the urbanity and ease of Andrew Marvell's octosyllabic couplets persisting into the eighteenth century; but we need to count the cost – that in order to reproduce this alert suavity Green permits himself a flippant or weary impudence about the tenets of Christian belief such as Marvell eighty years before neither could nor would have allowed himself.

Nevertheless *The Spleen* is invaluable, indeed irreplaceable, for giving a lively and highly intelligent account of the state of mind and feelings in which a dissenter of the 1730s might either conform to the Establishment or slide out of Christian belief altogether. There is no denying that in the 1720s and 1730s such defections and apostasies were very common. The numbers of the faithful were falling precipitately; and historians for whom as it were the box-office returns are the ultimate test have no difficulty showing that dissenting leaders like Watts and Doddridge quite manifestly in their generation *failed*. This was the reasoning of Elie Halévy when in 1906 he addressed himself to 'The Birth of Methodism in England'. Of the Methodist evangelists Wesley and Whitefield, Halévy says that 'they reanimated, as a side effect of their influence, the other Dissenting sects, which were seemingly dying of old age'. More sweepingly Halévy asserts: 'after fifty years (1688–1738) of professing religious skepticism England had her Puritan revival, and the date can be established firmly; it was in 1739 that the crisis occurred.' One does not lightly disagree with an authority like Halévy, and yet on this point he seems to be quite simply *wrong*.[3] Moreover he backs it up with special pleading. Thus, when Doddridge in his *Free Thoughts* asked that the minister be 'an evangelical, an experimental, a plain & an affectionate preacher', he was not, as Halévy supposes, an exception that proves some quite opposite rule. Nor do the dissenting sermons of the time bear out Halévy when he declares: 'The Dissenting ministers should have been able to assume the leadership of the Protestant opinion; they were its chosen chiefs. But betraying the confidence of their followers, they preached a doctrine more and more like that of Aristotle or Cicero, instead of Christianity according to Saint Paul.' How is it possible to recognize in this description the most famous and influential dissenting minister of the time, the Isaac Watts who wrote that hell-fire sermon in plunging sapphics, 'The Day of Judgment'?

> Hopeless immortals! how they scream and shiver
> While devils push them to the pit wide-yawning
> Hideous and gloomy, to receive them headlong
> Down to the centre!

Is *that* the doctrine of Aristotle or Cicero? We are likely to find it very unaccommodating indeed! And it requires a considerable exertion of the historical imagination to recognize, in the face of such a document, that 'accommodation' (to secular enlightenment and civility) was nevertheless Watts' and Doddridge's steady endeavour – as Johnson realized.

Halévy is not the first to be so dazzled by the massive and heroic figure of John Wesley as not to realize how there could be, and was, resistance to his evangelizing on scrupulous and considered grounds. 'When the Methodists started to preach', he assures us too confidently, 'they were well received by the great majority of Dissenters':

> Was not the religion they preached a revival of Puritanism? But they ran up against the distrust and hatred of the ministers, too enlightened and reasonable to enjoy the doctrine and method of the Awakening. And that is why those ministers were not themselves capable of bringing forth an Awakening; and why the Awakening could not come from the Dissenting Churches.

Even if all this were true, might we not conclude that the congregation failed their ministers, rather than the other way round? That by and large the ministers were too far ahead of their flocks, pursuing a cultural 'accommodation' that their congregations were not ready for? This would avoid having to use 'enlightened' and 'reasonable' as words of opprobrium, when applied to such men as Doddridge or Watts or Edmund Calamy; and it would be in the spirit of Johnson's tribute to Watts.

How some dissenting ministers responded to the Wesleyan challenge may appear from a piece of admirably vigorous mid-century prose:

> I will take this occasion with great freedom to tell you my opinion of those people who are called Methodists. I have carefully inquired after them; was willing to think well of them; loth to censure them or hear others do so. And I think still there are serious people deluded by them. But after a candid attention to them, their proceedings appear not to be wise and good. Their devotion is unseasonable, irregular and injudicious. Their sermons are low and loose and not at all like what

they seem to assume. Their spirits appear to me to be turbulent, unruly and censorious. They practise upon weak men and poor people. They call them up to pray and sing when they should be in their business or their beds. They disturb the peace and order of families. What they pretend above their neighbours, appears to me mere enthusiasm. Their people are rather slothful, mopish and dejected or pragmatical, than sober, considerate, judicious, exemplary and regular Christians. And I have no expectation but that Methodism, like other enthusiasm, will promote infidelity and turn out to the damage of religion and the souls of men. Though I judge not their hearts, views and motives, which are secret things that belong to God, yet I thought it needful very lately to warn my hearers of these people's errors and advise them to avoid them.

This is one of the remonstrances that Philip Doddridge endured in 1743 when he had allowed George Whitefield to preach from his pulpit. Others came from Watts, from John Guyse, and from a trustee of the Coward Trust thinly veiling a threat to withhold Trust funds from Doddridge's Academy; and if this makes it seem that Doddridge was more 'liberal' than his fellow ministers, the point is that on this flank he could afford to be – his distrust of 'enthusiasm' was well established, and it was on his other flank that he was vulnerable, where he joined hands with the more or less Arian circles that we have seen Lucy Aikin connect him with. He represented firm and consistent opposition to Methodism from within Dissent – an attitude that we can find for instance in his friend and editor Job Orton up to the latter's death in 1783. And indeed, though it could be said in 1806 that 'the Independents have gone over in a body to the Methodists', there was, as we shall see, opposition from Old Dissent to the Methodist New Dissent until far into the succeeding century.

To return to Elie Halévy ... His theories about the *birth* of Methodism have been overshadowed by his much more startling and influential argument as to its consequences: an argument advanced in his classic work of 1912, *England in 1815*, though in fact it was already firmly formulated by 1906. The argument is that 'England was spared the revolution toward which the contradictions in her polity and economy might otherwise have led her, through the stabilizing influence of evangelical religion, particularly of Methodism'; in other words, that the potentially revolutionary energies of the unprivileged English were syphoned off by the Wesleys and Whitefield into activities not political at all, but religious. This hypothesis in fact did not originate with Halévy; on the contrary, the bare bones of it are to be found not just in several British and French nineteenth-century historians but in Robert Southey in the first decade of the nineteenth century and indeed in the Methodists themselves as they defended themselves against the punitive measures against them proposed in 1811 by Sidmouth, the Home Secretary. Moreover, 'Halévy, like Weber, was suspicious of all efforts to understand history as the product of a single cause, and he saw religion as capable of altering what appeared to be the otherwise almost "inevitable" tendency of the internal contradictions (as both Ricardo and Marx understood them) of the new industrialism to produce Revolution'. Marxist historians are thus uncomfortable about Halévy's hypothesis, with a discomfort that is compounded by the fact that the hypothesis is rather plainly the product of a speculative and indeed literary intelligence in Halévy, rather than of 'scientific' research. In these circumstances it is remarkable that the hypothesis still stands, and that claims, by Marxists and others, to have overthrown it turn out on examination to be quibbles and qualifications not affecting the central contention, which is that the revolution which ought to have been 'inevitable' was in fact evaded. Accordingly, when a Marxist historian takes over Halévy's thesis, he does so with a specially bitter feeling of mortification.

This is compounded by the historically incontrovertible fact that Wesleyan Methodism springs out of the Moravian movement of Count Zinzendorf, which itself is plainly related to the egalitarian and enthusiastic 'Ranters' of Cromwell's time – a body, or an obscure congeries of bodies, long enshrined in English Marxist mythology as heroic pioneers and precursors. How with equanimity concede that this tradition which should have been, and once was, proto-revolutionary should, in the Wesleys' lifetime and for long after, have produced a movement that was consistently, and at times splenetically, High Tory? Certainly, in the nineteenth century, radicals and trade-union organizers were often Methodists; and in our time some Methodist historians have made much of this. But it is incontestable that radicals like Hazlitt and Leigh Hunt and Cobbett saw Methodism in their day, with reason, as on the contrary a bulwark of the *status quo*.

There is a yet further complication, in the fact that when John Wesley finally broke with the Moravians it was because of the insistent yet devious and grotesque eroticism which characterized their hymns certainly, and perhaps other aspects of their worship also. No one who has looked at the Moravian hymn book of the 1740s will want to deny that Wesley acted with good taste and good judgement in deciding that this would never do. Yet this circumstance is awkward for the Marxist historian when he wants to establish that in Wesleyan hymns 'Love' is private and airless, whereas it ought to be 'social'. Our historian levels the charge none the less:

> the cult of 'Love' was brought to a point of poise between affirmations of a 'social religion' and the pathological aberrations of frustrated social

and sexual impulses. On the one hand, genuine compassion for 'harlots, and publicans, and thieves': on the other hand, morbid preoccupations with sin and with the sinner's confessional. On one hand, real remorse for real wrong-doing: on the other, luxuriating refinements of intro-spective guilt. On one hand, the genuine fellowship of some early Methodist societies: on the other, social energies denied outlet in public life which were released in sanctified emotional onanism ...

... Here was a cult of 'Love' which feared love's effective expres-sion, either as sexual love or in any social form which might irritate relations with Authority. Its authentic language of devotion was that of sexual sublimation streaked through with masochism: the 'bleeding love', the wounded side, the blood of the Lamb ...

We notice how far this twentieth-century authority agrees with the eighteenth-century dissenter, in finding the Methodists 'slothful, mopish and dejected'. But he has in his sights something quite specific, a body of achieved literature, Charles Wesley's hymns. And this being so, the disci-plines of the social historian will serve no longer. All sorts of further considerations now arise – notably the tradition in devotional literature of images of the Lamb and Bleeding Heart, at least from the counter-reformation on; and the traditional use of the erotic analogy over the same period. For instance, is Watts' Calvinism of 1710 to be allotted the same socio-historical significance as the Wesleys' Arminianism of the 1750s, because of Watts' unabashed use of the eroticism of the Song of Songs?

And not only sexual organs like the lips are to be ruled out, but liver and lights also; for we are told:

after the Wesleys broke with the Moravian brethren, the language of their hymns ... had become a public scandal. In the hymns of John and Charles Wesley overt sexual imagery was consciously repressed, and gave way to imagery of the womb and the bowels:

> Come, O my guilty brethren, come,
>   Groaning beneath your load of sin!
> His bleeding heart shall make you room,
>   His open side shall take you in ...

Not all readers will be sure that they find in these indifferent verses either bowels or womb. But if we do find them, what follows? Are all bodily functions and organs too gross to serve as analogies and imagery in poetry, or in devotional poetry? Whoever is being 'puritanical' in this confronta-tion, it seems not to be Charles Wesley.

However, what our historian can't stand the sight of is blood. And there is blood all over the place in the Wesleyan hymns 'as if the underground traditions of Mithraic blood-sacrifice which troubled the early Christian Church suddenly gushed up in the language of 18th century Methodist hymnody'. 'The union with Christ's love', Edward Thompson decides (for he it is that I am quoting), 'unites the feelings of self-mortification, the yearning for the oblivion of the womb, and tormented sexual desire', for 'sacrificial, masochistic, and erotic language all find a common nexus in the same blood-symbolism'. And so to the indignant peroration:

> It is difficult to conceive of a more essential disorganisation of human life, a pollution of the sources of spontaneity bound to reflect itself in every aspect of personality. Since joy was associated with sin and guilt, and pain (Christ's wounds) with goodness and love, so every impulse became twisted into the reverse, and it became natural to suppose that man or child only found grace in God's eyes when performing painful, laborious or self-denying tasks. To labour and to sorrow was to find pleasure, and masochism was 'Love'. It is inconceivable that men could actually *live* like this; but many Methodists did their best.

But this is beyond a joke. A very strenuous protest is surely called for – not on behalf of Methodism, nor on behalf of Christianity (though it is Christianity as such, not just Methodism, that is the target of this sort of rant), but on behalf of poetry; for if poets are to be judged in this way, by scraps of verses torn from their context in poems and their larger contexts in iconographic and literary tradition, with a flurry of words like 'masochistic' that have no place in either literary or social history, which of all our poets will 'scape whipping?

Yet the fault lies with our literary historians, for what I remarked of the hymns and psalms of Watts – that we look in vain through our literary scholarship for any considered assessment of their intrinsic virtues and their historical significance – is hardly less scandalously true of the more than 6,000 hymns composed by Charles Wesley. Where the literary historians have so shamefully failed to do their duty, one can hardly blame the social historian for rushing in. I would not be misunderstood. The text of the Wesley hymns has been reliably established, and this was no light undertaking in respect of such a bulky corpus; there has been valuable examination of Wesley's metres; and a great deal has been done by way of identifying sources and analogues and allusions. The *editorial* challenge has been met. In particular, like every one else who has poked his nose into this field, I must pay tribute to Henry Bett's admirable *The Hymns of Methodism*. But it is precisely the 'field' that must be questioned; Charles Wesley's poetry is thought to be a very special field indeed, something *sui generis* or at most to be compared with a few hymns by other hands. One looks for a long time before finding any attempt to place Charles Wesley, or Isaac Watts either, in relation to the more secular poetry of their times – in relation to Pope, or Thomson, or Gray or Goldsmith. One consequence is that the eighteenth century is thought to have produced little *lyric* poetry, whereas the eighteenth-century lyric is to be found in the hymn books just as surely as seventeenth-century lyric is in George Herbert's *Temple*. The dependence of line after line of Wesley on the precedent of Matthew Prior has been duly noted, but no one has explored the significance, stylistically and historically, of this surprising connection with the suave and frequently improper author of 'Henry and Emma'. Methodism is a sub-culture as Old Dissent is a sub-culture; and the tribal warmth of such a subculture, of what Edmund Burke called 'our own little platoon', is so comforting and agreeable that there is no more incentive from within its ranks to relate the sub-culture to the national culture, than there is on the part of the Establishment to acknowledge what manoeuvres the little platoons have been engaged in.[4]

Yet John Wesley, in striking contrast to his fellow evangelist Whitefield, was at great pains not to let his followers cut themselves off from the culture of the national society as a whole, particularly not from the *literary* culture. He used his *Arminian Magazine* for many purposes; but among them was keeping in currency George Herbert and Prior and other writers he valued. He printed there, to the scandal of some of his readers, Prior's 'Henry and Emma', which Johnson the High Churchman found improper. In his late *Thoughts on the Character and Writings of Mr Prior*, as in such a stray document as a letter of 1764 to the Reverend Mr Furley, Wesley was a master of very acute and unprejudiced practical criticism. Moreover his successful battle through his lifetime to keep Methodism within the Established Church is something that tells the same story: Wesley did not want to found a sect, and he distrusted the tribal, the sectarian temper in culture. On this point his brother the poet was even more determined: Charles jeered and mocked when John began ordaining his own preachers. For the brothers were very different, though they co-operated loyally. It was Charles, the poet, for instance, who governed his sex life better, who made a successful marriage and reared a happy family; and it was Charles's household that rang night and morning with music, some of it highly sophisticated.

One literary scholar has lately broken through the sectarian ring that otherwise still walls off Charles Wesley's poetry from English poetry generally. This is Martha Winburn England, in a volume on which ten years ago she collaborated with John Sparrow for the New York Public Library. To this book, entitled *Hymns Unbidden*, Miss England contributes a series of exceptionally erudite and perceptive papers comparing Wesley with his contemporary William Blake. Blake certainly knew Wesley's work: his autograph, dated 1790, appears in a copy of Wesley's *Hymns for the Nation, in 1782*. Written by Charles Wesley when the defeat of British forces by the American colonists was clearly inevitable, *Hymns for the Nation* sees 'America as Sodom, her leaders as murderers and fanatics, the Continental Congress as like Lucifer in its rage for power and its blind fury of insurrection', and the American Loyalists as 'martyrs, persecuted by usurpers and betrayed by weak leadership'. Blake, of course, saw Washington and his colleagues quite differently, 'not as Albion's enemies but as allies of that visionary spirit of liberated energy as it existed in Britain'. But what matters is not that Wesley and Blake drew opposite conclusions, but that they addressed themselves to the same problem, and in the same spirit; for, as Ms England puts it: 'What *Hymns for the Nation* has in common with Blake is belligerence, exuberance, excess.' And this is, throughout their careers, the common ground between these two poets: 'Wesley and Blake are comparable in their arrogance, vulgarity, and excess. These traits of enthusiasm entered into all their poetic successes and can be seen with greatest clarity in their poetic failures.' But they shared also a common intention: 'Their poetry is prophetic and evangelical, the messages are intensely personal and aimed at reformation of the social order. They meant to bring about an inner change, in the heart, the imagination, and hoped that social changes would come about as a result.'

It is against this background, of the temperamental affinity between the two men and their common dedication to a prophetic role, that the differences between them stand out most sharply. And their political differences are among the least important. In the first place, 'Wesley looked upon himself as transmitting a received dogma', whereas Blake 'claimed no connection with any existing orthodoxy'. If Blake can be called Christian at all (which may well be doubted) 'his Christianity has no institutional aspect at all. All his life, he neglected those "means of grace" to which the Wesleys refer most often'. He seems never to have taken communion nor to have attended any services other than his own christening and wedding. Second, 'the authority of academic standards of excellence had no part in Blake's aesthetic. He thanked God he was never sent to school.' Wesley on the other hand was associated with scholarship all his life. Hence, third, 'Blake professed antagonism to empirical philosophy, experimental science, and the lower and higher criticism of the Bible that were an important product of the Enlightenment', whereas Wesley accepted these ideas early in his life, and wrote his hymns in the light of them. Then again, in Ms England's words:

> An obvious difference is Wesley's acknowledged obligation to clarity. He wrote in three traditions that demanded it. The Augustan aesthetic demanded it, and he added to that demand his own emphasis on the didactic nature of his writings and the nature of the audience he addressed ... None of these pressures operated directly upon Blake. He would not accede to demands for a certain sort of 'clarity', for it involved the writer in those generalizations which seemed to him a blurring of true clarity.

But over and above all these differences, there is one that goes deeper: where Wesley believes in paradox, Blake believes in dialectic. And anyone who attends with proper seriousness to the matters which preoccupied these two nobly dedicated men must, on this crucial issue, side with one of them against the other. R.H. Tawney, who was no worse a theologian and no worse a Christian for being also a historian and a Socialist, remarked:

> There is a distinctively Christian way of life ... This way of life is not, as appears often to be supposed, identical with what is called 'goodness'; for ... Christianity is a religion for sinners. It rests on a peculiar – and superficially, at any rate, a highly improbable – view of the nature of the universe. It implies the acceptance of a scale of spiritual values which no rationalisation can make appear other than extremely paradoxical.

'Extremely paradoxical' – just so:

> What though my shrinking flesh complain,
>   And murmur to contend so long,
> I rise superior to my pain,
>   When I am weak then I am strong,
> And when my all of strength shall fail,
> I shall with the God-Man prevail.
>
> My strength is gone, my nature dies,
>   I sink beneath thy weighty hand,
> Faint to revive, and fall to rise;
>   I fall, and yet by faith I stand,
> I stand, and will not let thee go,
> Till I thy name, thy nature, know.

In these lines, where our social historian would no doubt discover 'masochism', the central paradox of a god who is also man breeds other paradoxes, as that weakness is strength, and falling is rising – as it was for the God-Man who triumphed by being crucified. Such paradoxes are at the heart of Wesley's writing, as of any writing in the centrally Christian tradition; and time and again the laborious clarity of Wesley's verse takes on rhetorical splendour and intensity when paradox is concentrated into its appropriate rhetorical figure, oxymoron. Blake is not so much incapable of this, as profoundly averse to it. This emerges, for instance, when Martha Winburn England compares him with Charles Wesley as regards another of the central Christian paradoxes – that Law is Love: 'Wesley believed law and love were one, paradoxically related in time, but eternally one. Blake ... saw no sweetness in commandment or statute, no love in any discipline imposed from without'. Paradox is what Blake cannot readily live with, though his 'Tyger' is certainly a splendid exception. His famously *dialectical* way of thought solves and evades paradox by separating it out – as it were on a plane surface: love ('Innocence') *leads to* law ('Experience'), as law then *leads to* love (through Revolution). Paradox is multivocal; Blake has to break it down into narrative sequence, into the univocal. Though Blake is commonly thought of – and in part rightly – as an enemy of rationalism, in this defining feature of his thought he is a rationalist all through.

Thus, Blake's relation to English Dissent is tortuous and very far from clear. G.E. Bentley has presented evidence, inconclusive but suggestive, that Blake's father about 1769 joined a Baptist church; and this, if true, would clarify the all but unanimous contention of the early biographers that Blake's parents were dissenters, though no one says of what kind. The question is academic, however, for it has come to seem more and more likely – ever since A.L. Morton's *The Everlasting Gospel* of 1958 – that the Dissent which *effectively* influenced Blake was that of the antinomian and heretical sects, the Ranters and Muggletonians, who (as is now clear) survived in clandestine fashion among the artisans and petty tradesmen of London, from their origins in the Cromwellian Commonwealth until Blake's lifetime and after. These sectaries are now attracting much devoted and admiring attention. But it is not denied by their most fervent admirers that what they express is socio-political resentment and aspiration thinly cloaked in religious terminology; and that, as specifically *religious* insights, their ideas are beneath contempt. Thus none of the research currently being pursued into the Muggletonians and others can seriously qualify the impression that in Blake, as – so I shall suggest – in D.H. Lawrence a century later, we have a case of an imaginative genius born into a stratum of religious experience too shallow to sustain him.

John Holloway has shown invaluably how many of Blake's 'Songs of Innocence and of Experience' are cast in the metrical, the rhetorical and stanzaic forms of Watts' and Doddridge's hymns; and indeed the connection with Watts was noticed as early as 1806. But it must be emphasized that the theological content that is poured into these moulds is such as Watts and Doddridge would have been appalled by, and would have denounced as un-Christian.

One may think William Blake a great poet, and an exceptionally engaging person, and still regard with alarm, as a very ominous symptom, the veneration which nowadays is so freely accorded him; for what we see, I suggest, as the aristocratic Anglicanism of George Herbert modulates into the Old Dissent of Richard Baxter and Watts and Doddridge, and then is overtaken by the evangelizing of the Moravians and Wesleyans – is a test case, historically recorded, of what happens when a body of difficult but momentous truths is taken 'to the people'. To those who draw from this record the sanguine conclusion that in the process nothing, or nothing important, was lost – I have nothing to say. For those who believe that something was lost along the way, it is very difficult to determine just where, in the process, the simplifications and intensifications became 'too much' – so as to damage just those truths that were to be simplified and intensified. To speak for myself, I am much persuaded by those who point to the excesses of the Wesleyan meetings – the fallings about, the paroxysms, the 'speaking with tongues', and the preachers' perfervid and foolish rhetoric that provoked such manifestations – as clear symptoms of religious sentiment perverted, and doctrine coarsened out of recognition. But then I encounter the wonderful figure of John Wesley himself, who regretted these grotesque distortions and diagnosed them (as in his comments on the Flemish prodigy, Antoinette Bourignan), who none the less tolerated them as a price that had to be paid; Wesley, whose level-headedness and fastidious though heartfelt taste is manifest on nearly every page of his that has come down to us. What does seem to me certain is that, by the time and to the extent that the process works itself out in Blake, the game is not worth the candle, the price asked (and paid by Blake) is exorbitant. Blake is lamed by this historical process, not – except in the delusory short run – sustained by it; he is not a hero of the democratizing of Scripture, but a martyr to it.

Notes

1 I quote Lucy Aikin from *Memoirs, Miscellanies and Letters of the Late Lucy Aikin*, edited by Philip Hemery Le Breton, 1864, p. 196. My quotations from and about Halévy's *The Birth of Methodism in England* (originally 1906), together with much of my information about him and his view of Methodism generally, come from the invaluable edition translated and introduced by Bernard Semmel (1971). The letter to Doddridge beginning, 'I will take this occasion...' is reproduced in Duncan Coomer's modest but very useful *English Dissent under the Early Hanoverians* (1946). I have drawn also on Roger Thomas's, 'Philip Doddridge and Liberalism in Religion', in G. Nuttall (ed.), *Philip Doddridge* (1951). The passages about the Wesley hymns quoted from E.P. Thompson's *Making of the English Working Class* (1964) will be found on pp. 40 and 371–2 of the New York edition. All quotations comparing Charles Wesley with William Blake are from Martha Winburn England in *Hymns Unbidden* (1966).

2 It was in 1737 that William Law told his fellow non-juror, John Byrom, 'that the Quakers were a subtle worldly-minded people, that they began with the contempt of learning, riches etc., but now were a politic worldly society, and strange people'. Seven years earlier Byrom had decided for himself: 'It is their life, their love of the world, their wisdom as to this generation, their luxury and neglect of that Spirit which they particularly pretend to, which I blame in a Quaker as well as in myself and others' (see Stephen Hobhouse, *William Law and Eighteenth-Century Quakerism*, 1928, pp. 119, 146). To be sure, 'accommodation' among the Quakers took a special form, since the external marks of it were a newly rigid observance of habits of dress, demeanour and address, which served to mark them off at a glance. On this, and on how nevertheless it masked a profound accommodation with the secular spirit of the age, see A. Neave Brayshaw, *The Quakers: Their Story and Message*, 1927, ch. XII.

   Lucy Aikin, who quotes not from *The Spleen* but from another of Green's poems, 'The Seeker', had good reason to remember Green's poems, and to recognize their significance, for it was her own father, John Aikin, who in 1796 had re-issued them with an introduction that is still the most just and enthusiastic of all tributes to this poet:

> He had not, like a Gray or a Collins, his mind early fraught with all the stores of classic literature; nor could he devote months and years of learned leisure to the exquisite charms of versification or the refined ornaments of diction. He was a man of business, who had only the intervals of his regular employment to improve his mind by reading and reflection; and his poems appear to have been truly no more than hasty effusions for the amusement of himself and his particular friends. Numbers of works thus produced are born and die in the circle of every year; and it is only by the stamp of real genius that these have been preserved from a similar fate. But nature had bestowed on the author a strong and quick conception, and a wonderful power of bringing together remote ideas so as to produce the most novel and striking effects. No man ever thought more copiously or with more originality; no man ever less fell into the beaten track of common-place ideas and expressions. That cant of poetical phraseology which is the only resource of an ordinary writer, and which those of a superior class find it difficult to avoid, is scarcely anywhere to be met with in him. He has no hackneyed combinations of substantives and epithets; none of the tropes and figures of a schoolboy's Gradus. Often negligent, sometimes inaccurate, and not unfrequently prosaic, he redeems his defects by a rapid variety of beauties and brilliancies all his own, and affords more food to the understanding or imagination in a line or a couplet, than common writers in half a page (LUCY AIKIN, *Memoir of John Aikin, M.D.*, 1823, vol. 2, pp. 225–7).

Lucy Aikin declared that 'no one, I believe, of all his critical pieces was composed with greater pleasure in his subject than this'. And it is easy to believe her, for Aikin's own copy of verses in rhyming octosyllabics, 'Horatian Philosophy' – by no means a despicable performance – is quite plainly an exercise in Green's manner, and not just in the manner, but in substance too. As Aikin's daughter says, still speaking of Green's poetry:

> While the profusion of uncommon thoughts and witty allusions with which it is studded amused his fancy, the pervading spirit of the whole had much in it to attract his sympathetic approbation. It is that of a philosophy somewhat on the Horatian model, in which habitual serenity of mind is sought by a renunciation of the common objects of ambition, by temperate enjoyments and modest wishes, by the indulgence of a vein of free speculation, and by a general indifference and neutrality in the disputes which chiefly agitate the world (*op. cit.*, pp. 186–7).

And the natural affinity between the Horatian frame of mind and the Quaker at its best, or indeed the Unitarian at its best, is something that deserves pondering, and perhaps study – for instance, as it bears upon a Quaker poet of our day, like Basil Bunting.

John Aikin is an important witness in any case, as the memorialist of those years, in the 1770s and 1780s, when the success of the Unitarian academy at Warrington shifted the intellectual, if not the imaginative, centre of the kingdom from London to an area bounded by Manchester to the east and Liverpool to the west. In both these cities the influence of the Warrington focus of intellectual endeavour persisted through several decades after the Warrington academy had been disbanded. Aikin's memorials of this 'vortex', and of the several personalities that whirled within it, are invaluable precisely because his own equable and Horatian temperament was not shared by his Warrington colleagues; and so our sense of their injudiciousness is gathered from a testimony that is at pains to minimize it. For example, what an unmanageable coxcomb Gilbert Wakefield was, is conveyed between the lines of Aikin's obituary tribute to him (*op. cit.*, pp. 364–5), and is nowhere so unmistakable as in Wakefield's verses responding to the poem with which Aikin welcomed him from prison (*op. cit.*, pp. 237–8):

> Next to that first of comforts to the soul,
> The plaudit of a conscience self-approv'd,
> AIKIN! I deem the gratulation sweet
> Of sympathising friendship, and a Muse
> Terse, uncorrupt, ingenuous, bold and free.

'The plaudit of a conscience self-approv'd' ('Self in benevolence absorb'd and lost', is what Wakefield modestly claims for himself in a later verse) very clearly characterized the Warrington Unitarian Jacobins as a group, Joseph Priestley not excepted. And such self-righteously self-appointed intellectual *élites*, usually ranging themselves on the revolutionary Left, have been a volatile element in English political life from John Aikin's day to ours. Aikin himself, though he pamphleteered in 1790 against Parliament's refusal to revoke the Test Act, was a more admirable and engaging person than the celebrities he chose to memorialize. And his daughter's memoir of him is, though an unexciting book, a worthy one. Nowhere in it, however, do we find anything to set beside what Lucy Aikin confessed to, in a letter of 1831 to Channing, about what it could mean to be brought up an English Unitarian under George III:

> the atmosphere of a sect and a party, which it was my fate to breathe from childhood, narrowed my affections within strait limits. Under the notion of a generous zeal for freedom, truth, and virtue, I cherished a set of prejudices and antipathies which placed beyond the pale of my charity not the few, but the many, the mass of my compatriots. I shudder now to think how *good a hater* I was in the days of my youth. Time and reflection, a wider range of acquaintance, and a calmer state of the public mind, mitigated by degrees my bigotry; but I really knew not what it was to open my heart to the human race until I had drunk deeply into [*sic*] the spirit of your writings (*Memoirs, Miscellanies and Letters*, pp. 243–4).

3   When Halévy seventy years ago, and E.P. Thompson more recently, saw the Methodist evangelists as doing for the dissenting interest what Hanoverian ministers like Watts and Doddridge should have done but didn't, they were only echoing what historians of Dissent have been saying since the beginning of the nineteenth century. Indeed the unanimity on this point is so remarkable that one would be frightened of questioning it, were it not that there is so plainly no agreed mark by which religious decline and religious revival may be measured. What is a sign of demoralization for one historian – for instance, Doddridge allowing Whitefield to preach from his pulpit – is, for another, a symptom of reawakening vigour.

A clear example of the received opinion – and without doubt an influential one – is the second volume of Henry W. Clark's *History of English Nonconformity* (1913), wherein Book III, concerned with the years 1660 to 1736, is entitled, 'The Fading Ideal', and within that span the years 1714 to 1736 are called 'The Darkness before the Dawn', whereas the Methodist years, from 1736 to 1800, are treated of in Book IV under the title, 'The Partial Return to the Ideal'. If we look in Clark for the proof of these contentions we find that, though indeed he pays lip-service to such immeasurable entities as 'feeling' and 'fervour', his ultimate measure is not religious, certainly not doctrinal, *but political;* he is concerned for Church government, and for the relations between that government and the government of the State. Such matters are certainly important; but to look to them for the measure of religious health or decline is surely inadequate and even pedantic. Thus modern readers can hardly be expected to shake their heads in appalled revulsion, as Clark seems to want them to do, when he reveals (*op. cit.*, p. 166) that Thomas Abney, Watts' patron, as a London alderman took advantage of the Occasional Conformity Act. And Clark is even less compelling, appeals even more pedantically to a pristine Reformation principle which succeeding years had made inapplicable, when he tries to convict Watts himself of back-sliding (pp. 163–4):

> It is worth while in this connection to take a glance at what may be called Congregationalism in a transition stage, as represented in the message sent by Isaac Watts to the Mark Lane Independent Church, when it called him to its pulpit in 1702. Watts had Congregationalism so to say in his blood; for his father was in jail for it when he was born in 1674, and his mother nursed him upon the prison steps; so that the son was from the first too much overshadowed by the Congregational idea to travel as far from it as some were going. Yet, in giving some account of his views to the Mark Lane congregation, although he uses the old language as to every society of saints being a true Church, admits that a Church is not bound to submit itself blindly to its pastor's government, and admits also that in *some* matters a pastor ought to do nothing without the people's consent, he nevertheless declares that in the absence of a pastor a Church is 'incomplete' and without 'power in itself to

administer all ordinances among them': there are various hints that the minister is something more than the *primus inter pares* which true Congregationalism holds him… If one were unaware that such a tendency was at work upon a wider stage, Watts' words and clauses might pass unsuspected by, buried as they are among words and clauses of other tenor; but when one knows, then one discerns, in phrases slipped in here and there, how that tendency was claiming occasional visiting rights where it could not as yet hope to be made perfectly at home. And if Watts, for whom Congregational air had been mingled with the earliest breaths he drew, and for whom there was in heredity's cord so marked a Congregational strand – if Watts could go so far, one may conjecture how much further and how much more easily Congregationalists of less high and strenuous ancestry would be led away.

The strain of special pleading in this account is surely obvious; it provokes the retort that precisely because Watts knew at first hand or at one remove what persecution had meant, he had a better right than any subsequent commentator to decide when, and how far, to take note of the maxim *autres temps, autres moeurs*. One may reflect also that a pastor who has in his flock such black sheep as John Dunton is well advised to preserve some residual authority for himself and his office.

Moreover, with all his enthusiasm for the evangelizing of Wesley and Whitefield, Clark is forced to concede that two important dissenting communions – the Particular Baptists and the Quakers – seem to have gone through the eighteenth century largely unaffected by it. More generally, however, no one should want to deny that Dissent *was* affected, and in many ways profitably, by the Wesleyan and Evangelical Revival. This was not denied by R.W. Dale who, however, stands almost alone among historians of Dissent in maintaining that, if much was gained, much also was lost:

> The Revival … helped to suppress the original type of Independent character. Reserve, a firm self-restraint in habits of expenditure and in amusements, patient, resolute industry, punctuality in the discharge of all obligations, a family life governed by exact method, a keen interest in theology, and a keen interest in politics, a delight in books and in intellectual pursuits of the severer kind, a strict Observance of Sunday – these were the characteristics of the men who had been disciplined by Independent traditions. The great Independents of the Commonwealth who had been formed by other influences were freer and more genial; but in the course of a generation or two the prevailing type of Independent character had taken this austere form. Watts deplored the irregular habits of the Dissenters of his time; but in many Churches the type was still preserved … The authority of the original type of character was still asserted by the public opinion of the Churches. Any serious departure from it was condemned.
>
> But when Congregational Churches began to be thronged with Churchmen who had inherited another ideal of Christian morals and conduct … the whole spirit of the Churches was changed. The moral traditions of Independency were lost. The gravity, severity, and solid strength, to which the habits of an earlier age had formed the members of Congregational Churches, disappeared. The intellectual earnestness also disappeared. Congregationalists ceased to be keen theologians, and they ceased to be keen politicians (R.W. Dale, in A.W.W. Dale (ed.), *History of English Congregationalism*, 1907).

Not everyone will be so attracted as Dale plainly is, by gravity, severity and reserve. However, by his account, what was lost was *culture*, or all those elements of culture which go along with 'intellectual earnestness'.

It was George II who was for the dissenters, and long remained in dissenting tradition, the paragon of princes; and the high-water mark of the dissenters' royalism was when Doddridge and others were active in 1745 in raising levies to oppose the Pretender, despite the civic disabilities which debarred them from serving in arms in any responsible position themselves. George III, though the dissenters had high hopes of him at the start, soon alienated most of them when he identified himself with the policies of Bute; and for the dissenters, conscious of close ties with their fellow sectaries across the Atlantic, the attempt to coerce the American colonies was a bitter pill which many of them (in striking contrast to the Methodists) refused to swallow. The Baptist minister John Collet Ryland scared the schoolboy Robert Hall by the violence with which he declared himself for General Washington; and not many dissenters could be as sorrowfully temperate as John Bowring – a Presbyterian, and grandfather of his celebrated namesake, the Victorian polyglot – when he wrote to his cousin in 1778:

> After the most deliberate consideration of the nature of the quarrel between us, I freely own it appears to me that they are right and we wrong, nor is there anything I more ardently wish for relative to our national concerns than a thorough change both of men and manners in the British Cabinet. Yet, as an Englishman, I by no means wish to see my country vanquished by the arms of France (*Autobiographical Recollections of Sir John Bowring*, 1877, pp. 2–3).

Thenceforward until the end of the century relations between the dissenters and the Crown were strained once again by mutual suspicions. Nevertheless, though the fact is seldom acknowledged, there were in this period dissenters who supported the national policies; and however it may have been earlier in the century, it is not true of this or of later periods that a Tory dissenter is a contradiction in terms:

> Dissenters could always be found who approved of the American War; who petitioned Parliament against the extension of Toleration; who supported Pitt and joined the volunteers during the French Revolution. If we find Richard Price, Joseph Priestley, Robert Hall and Robert Robinson on the one side, there were the Rev. Edward Pickard, the Rev. John Martin, the Rev. John Clayton and the Rev. David Rivers on the other (Anthony Lincoln, *Some Political and Social Ideas of English Dissent, 1763–1800*, 1938, pp. 21–2).

In fact, of the four names cited here as belonging to the less than loyal Opposition in this period, three – Price, Priestley and Robinson – were, or ended up as, heterodox Unitarians quite unrepresentative of Dissent as a whole; and the fourth – Robert Hall, the Baptist – is ranked with them on the score of a couple of youthful polemics which he soon by implication disowned. Of the four 'Tory' names, the most interesting is that of John Clayton (1754–1843).

Clayton was at one time closely associated with the mercurial Sir Harry Trelawney, of the ancient Cornish family, with whom he took Congregationalism into Cornwall, itinerating from the baronet's family seat at Looe. How genteel Dissent could be at this period appears from an account of Sir Harry's being 'publicly set apart to the office of pastor or overseer, in the church of Christ, by the laying on of the hands of the Presbytery':

> This solemnity took place at Southampton, 22 April 1777, with more of pomp and circumstance than usually attend services, when administered according to the simple forms of Protestant Dissenters. A large platform was raised, covered with green cloth, and a velvet cushion provided for the young baronet to kneel upon. Constables were in attendance, to guard against disorder and disturbance. The crowd, anxious to witness the celebration of the rite, under circumstances by no means common, was immense and composed of all classes, fashionable and unfashionable, from the town and neighbourhood …

Alas, Sir Harry later went Socinian.

When the Birmingham mob rioted against Joseph Priestley, Clayton preached a sermon, subsequently published, which – says his Victorian biographer – 'embodied some conservative sentiments, which would not be wholly endorsed by many of his brethren then, and still less now'. To this the 27-year-old Robert Hall replied with a pamphlet, *Christianity Consistent with a Love of Freedom* (1791). But Clayton was not to be deflected –

> When the mind of the public was exasperated by party politics, and the horrors of the French Revolution made every ear tingle, and many hearts bleed, he set his face like a flint against what he termed 'the revolutionary mania'; and while barbarous atrocities were practised in a neighbouring land, and corresponding societies, trea-

sonable plots, seditious libels, and furious demagogues, were in activity at home, he felt it to be his duty to insist much on relative obligations – especially those which refer to the subject and the magistrate ...

... he endeavoured to discriminate between the exploded doctrines of passive obedience and non-resistance, and that rational, just, and religious deference to constituted authorities, so indispensable to the liberty, safety, and prosperity of the empire.

The course he took proved offensive to not a few of his ministerial brethren; and to the whole fraternity of Jacobins and revolutionists, who rose up in arms against him, in squibs, pamphlets, and caricatures ...

... He tasked all his strength to stem the torrent of democratic fury (T.M. Aveling, *Memorials of the Clayton Family*, 1867, pp. 145–6).

It comes as no surprise that Clayton, professing these views (which incidentally were firmly upheld in the next generation from the pulpit of his eldest son), was possessed of private means – which at least takes care of any allegation that he was on the Government payroll. Moreover, by 1800 when he was minister of the Weighhouse Chapel in London (where Mark Rutherford was to admire the preaching of his successor, Thomas Binney), his congregations were affluent and genteel, 'for there might have been counted at the doors of the Weighhouse chapel, from sixteen to twenty equipages, or full-appointed gentlemen's carriages, waiting to convey their owners, after public service, to their respective suburban villages'. What is significant is that his biographer Aveling, sixty years later, conveying this information, seems to speak of it as a phenomenon long vanished from the scene. It looks as if an audience for Dissent recognizably similar in social composition to that of Watts survived as late as 1800, but had vanished from dissenting chapels by 1860. If so, it may be that when it vanished it took with it from dissenting households the secular literary culture represented by what John Clayton read with his children (*op. cit.*, p. 100): 'Watts' *Lyrics*, Cowper's *Poems*, the *Odyssey* of Homer, as versified by that author, Pope's *Iliad*, and the *Dramas* of Hannah More.' Already in 1807 David Bogue and James Bennett in their *History of Dissenters* were very suspicious of Watts' versions of the Psalms, and explicitly lamented that Cowper should have spent any of his time on an author so unserious as Homer. Nineteenth-century Dissent was by and large to follow their lead, not John Clayton's.

4   T.B. Shepherd's *Methodism and the Literature of the Eighteenth Century* (1940), which might seem to address itself to just this topic, fails to live up to the promise of its title. It is particularly barren and perfunctory on the Wesleys' poetry. It has value, however, in directing attention to John Wesley's prose, especially his political and controversial writings like *A Farther Appeal to Men of Reason and Religion*. George Lawton's *John Wesley's English: A Study of his Literary Style* (1962) has more to say on this, but has the opposite defects to Shepherd's book, in that it stays unmanageably close to a card-index concordance to Wesley's works. In both these works may be found hints towards, and material for, a study of Wesleyan prose as carrying forward into the later eighteenth century, for the most part addicted to a more 'Corinthian' and ornamental prose, the easy, trenchant and conversational styles of Swift on the one hand, Robert South on the other – both of them masters whom Wesley appealed to and recommended. Such an investigation would be valuable.

Certainly what might on that showing be claimed for Methodism cannot be claimed for Dissent. By the end of the century dissenters were writing an English that is tumid and glittering; in particular Robert Hall, however estimable on other counts, is nowadays unreadable, though in his own day he was highly praised as an oratorical stylist.

From the Clark Lectures, delivered in Cambridge in 1976; printed as *A Gathered Church: the Literature of the English Dissenting Interest, 1700–1930* (London, 1978).

XVIII Notes on Goldsmith's Politics

There are many things for which we go back to Horace Walpole; but we certainly don't look to him for any just estimate of who among his contemporaries achieved immortality in literature. All the same we must surely be startled when Walpole in his *Memoirs*, writing of the year 1768 and undertaking 'to say a few words on the state of literature during the period I have been describing', remarks: 'Two other poets of great merit arose, who meddled not with politics; Dr Goldsmith, the correct author of *The Traveller;* and Mr Anstey, who produced as original a poem as *Hudibras* itself; the *New Bath-guide.*'[1] In one whose chief correspondent about poetry was the Reverend William Mason, the rating of Goldsmith on a level with Christopher Anstey is not really surprising. (And of Goldsmith Walpole says no more, but of Anstey a great deal: 'the most genuine humour, the most inoffensive satire, the happiest parodies … the most harmonious melody. …') What is startling, surely, is to have it said of the author of *The Traveller* that he 'meddled not with politics'. What did Walpole think that Goldsmith *was* meddling with, when he wrote such lines as these? (ll. 379–92):

> Calm is my soul, nor apt to rise in arms,
> Except when fast approaching danger warms:
> But when contending chiefs blockade the throne,
> Contracting regal power to stretch their own,
> When I behold a factious band agree
> To call it freedom, when themselves are free;
> Each wanton judge new penal statutes draw,
> Laws grind the poor, and rich men rule the law;
> The wealth of climes, where savage nations roam,
> Pillag'd from slaves, to purchase slaves at home;
> Fear, pity, justice, indignation start,
> Tear off reserve, and bare my swelling heart;
> 'Till half a patriot, half a coward grown,
> I fly from petty tyrants to the throne.

---

1   *Horace Walpole: Memoirs and Portraits*, ed. Matthew Hodgart (London, 1963), p. 188. Quotations from Goldsmith are given from the text of the *Collected Works of Oliver Goldsmith*, ed. Arthur Friedman, 5 vols (Oxford, 1966).

What did Walpole think these lines were about, if not about politics? The answer must be that Walpole, that fierce though fluctuating Whig, understood by 'politics' precisely the contentions of the 'contending chiefs', the matter of who was in and who was out of favour and of power, Pelhamites today, Rockingham Whigs tomorrow; just that level of politics which in *Retaliation* Goldsmith was to treat with contempt in his searing lines on Burke (ll. 31–4):

> Who, born for the Universe, narrow'd his mind,
> And to party gave up, what was meant for mankind.
> Tho' fraught with all learning, kept straining his throat,
> To persuade Tommy Townsend to lend him a vote; ...

Which of them do we agree with when we ask ourselves what we mean by 'politics', more particularly when we ask if politics is a proper concern for earnest and impassioned poetry? The answer surely is not far to seek: it is Walpole, we think, who is speaking of *practical* politics, the day-by-day hurlyburly in Westminster; and politics is a practical matter, 'the art of the possible'; accordingly, Goldsmith's loftier view of it is futile. And so we are likely to conclude that politics is what poetry should not stoop to. When it does so stoop, as in *The Traveller*, we tut-tut indulgently and look elsewhere in the poem for whatever it is we admire it for. And is not that indeed how *The Traveller* has been read in every generation, including our own? Because we thus conspire to suppress from our attention and our recollection those passages where the poem is political, and indeed politically *tendentious*, we are more than halfway to agreeing with Walpole that Goldsmith 'meddled not with politics'.

Moreover, if we narrow our sights to the politics of Westminster in Goldsmith's day, and consult those who have made that their special study, we find them in effect vindicating Horace Walpole. For we are nowadays invited by political historians to see the politics of that time as a *system*, and a system that worked. It worked, and *could* work, only because of those elements in it that were denounced, then and later, as 'faction' and as 'corruption'. We must, we are told, tough-mindedly recognize such denunciations for what they were taken to be at the time – a rhetorical ritual expected of politicians out of office; just as we must equally dismiss, as rhetorical smokescreens, all those accounts of Britain in the 1760s which see Liberty, in the person of John Wilkes, threatened by Autocracy, in the person of George III. Accordingly, when we re-read *The Traveller* and find Goldsmith making play with all these notions – 'corruption' and (especially) 'faction', and 'freedom' in relation to 'the throne' – we are presented with a straight choice: either this is an instance of the smoke-screen, and Goldsmith is being disingenuous; or else he has been deluded by the rhetoric, and is being naïve.

And here at last we are on solid ground. For all the contemporary accounts agree: Goldsmith was ingenuous, a naïf. Walpole again is as good a witness as any: time and again, in Walpole's letters, Goldsmith crops up – and always as *a silly*. In several of the anecdotes about him, not just from the poisoned pen of Boswell, we see Goldsmith attempting to 'put on airs' or 'make an impression', and ludicrously failing – when he wanted to be disingenuous, he couldn't, effectively. Thus there can be no question: if indeed Goldsmith in *The Traveller* deceives us about what was at issue in the England of the 1760s, he deceived himself first. He meant what he said; he was not writing in code.

But in that case, what are we to make of the contention that no one at the time was deceived by fulminations about faction, and corruption, and freedoms endangered? Goldsmith may have been naïve, but surely he wasn't uniquely so. And of course the evidence is overwhelming that he was not. However readily the fulminations and protestations may have been discounted by people in the know such as Burke and Walpole, up and down the country patriotic citizens took them at face-value, finding in their own experience much to bear them out. The political system may not in fact have reached a crisis in the 1760s, but plenty of thoughtful people thought it had. And Goldsmith was one of them.

Thus when he says that he will 'tear off reserve, and bare my swelling heart', we may as well believe him. And where does his swelling heart impel him? To 'the throne' (ll. 393–412):

> Yes, brother, curse with me that baleful hour
> When first ambition struck at regal power;
> And thus, polluting honour in its source,
> Gave wealth to sway the mind with double force.
> Have we not seen, round Britain's peopled shore,
> Her useful sons exchang'd for useless ore?
> Seen all her triumphs but destruction haste,
> Like flaring tapers brightening as they waste;
> Seen opulence, her grandeur to maintain,
> Lead stern depopulation in her train,
> And over fields, where scatter'd hamlets rose,
> In barren solitary pomp repose?
> Have we not seen, at pleasure's lordly call,
> The smiling long-frequented village fall?
> Beheld the duteous son, the sire decay'd,
> The modest matron, and the blushing maid,
> Forc'd from their homes, a melancholy train,
> To traverse climes beyond the western main;
> Where wild Oswego spreads her swamps around,
> And Niagara stuns with thund'ring sound?

This is of course a passage that everyone remembers, because it contains in embryo what was to become *The Deserted Village*. But if that later treatment surpasses this one, as of course it does, we ought to recognize a price that is paid: *The Deserted Village* is in crucial ways a great deal less specific. Nothing in *The Deserted Village* is so uncompromising as 'Her useful sons exchang'd for useless ore ...'. Indeed, as is notorious, in the later poem the reason for the expropriation of the villagers is left notably unclear – a vagueness that permits of the time-honoured and still inconclusive debate about whether the village is in Ireland (Lissoy) or in England. The debate to be sure is misconceived, for the poetic imagination surely often transforms disparate experiences by amalgamating and compounding them, and so to the question, 'Ireland or England?' the most plausible answer is no doubt: 'A bit of both.' All the same the pressures on rural Ireland in the 1760s were, surely, significantly different from those that bore in on rural England; and our inability to specify which kingdom is meant shows how far the poem is from specifying the cause of the calamity. In both poems the interests which expropriate the villagers are mercantile, but in reading *The Deserted Village* we have to be attentive, to notice this. If in that poem we identify 'the man of wealth and pride' who throws out the villagers as a *nouveau-riche*, possibly a 'nabob' returned from the East or West Indies, who wants a country-seat without any manorial obligations, this is no more than a plausible conjecture on our part; the poem itself doesn't identify him in that way nor in any other. And we can't help but wonder if it isn't precisely this lack of specificity which (along with other features, to be sure) has always made *The Deserted Village* the more appealing poem. It enunciates sentiments to which, we might say, every bosom returns an echo:

> But a bold peasantry, their country's pride
> When once destroyed, can never be supplied.

Who would not agree? Who would be inconvenienced or put out of countenance, except the perhaps fictitious nabob himself? But in *The Traveller*, where the expropriation is emphatically presented as a direct consequence of commercial imperialism, the sentiment would be embarrassing to any one who practised, or profited by, the import of raw material ('ore') from overseas.

Moreover *The Deserted Village* prescribes no remedy for the state of affairs it deplores, and therefore puts no reader under any obligation to do anything about it. *The Traveller* however *does* prescribe a remedy: enhanced power for George III. How very unappealing that has been, for readers through the generations and still today! It flies in the face of the Whig Interpretation of History – an interpretation which, though we have recognized and diagnosed its partiality, most of us are still bound by more than we realize. It is one thing to exculpate George III from the charges hurled at him by Tom Paine; it is something else to believe, as

Goldsmith wants us to, that in the contention between the King and demagogues like Paine or Wilkes the right (and also the *freedom*) was with the King. For that is certainly what Goldsmith means when he calls on his brother to join him in cursing the inroads made on 'regal power'. *The Traveller* is a fervent apologia for the monarchical form of government, taking the time-honoured ground that, since the unprivileged need a power to appeal to above the power of local privilege, the only such power conceivable is the power of the Monarch, elevated above all sectional interests.

It is astonishing that the British, who live to this day under a monarchical government and have shown their readiness to fight and die for it, still refuse to give a hearing to this most cogent argument in its favour. Among Americans, on the other hand, such reluctance is not astonishing at all. And this reflection is not gratuitous. For 'Auburn' names a city or a settlement in no less than fifteen states of the Union; and whereas Auburn, California, is almost certainly named after Auburn, Massachusetts, or Auburn, Maine, the Auburns in the eastern states must surely have been named by readers of *The Deserted Village*. After all, by 1816 Goldsmith's *Political Works* as well as *The Vicar of Wakefield* had been published in a city as far from the Atlantic sea-board as Pittsburgh.[1] Certainly Auburn University, in Auburn, Alabama, proudly declares its allegiance by calling its campus newspaper, 'The Plainsman'. (And 'Plains' or 'The Plains' crops up as a place-name in Georgia, Kansas, Montana, Ohio and Texas.) 'Sweet Auburn, loveliest village of the plain' would hardly have sired so many communities in republican America, if American readers of *The Deserted Village* had also read *The Traveller*, and had recognized that Goldsmith's Auburn originally looked for its security to powers that would be clawed back by George III from his Parliament. It is a telling instance of how much more palatable and inoffensive *The Deserted Village* is than *The Traveller*.

Nothing has yet been quoted from *The Traveller* which, simply as an exploitation of the resources of English, deserves much more than the tepid commendation of Horace Walpole: 'correct'. But much more can and must be claimed for an earlier passage, where Goldsmith makes a smooth and yet momentous transition from considering the Netherlands to considering Great Britain (ll. 313–34):

> Heavens! how unlike their Belgic sires of old!
> Rough, poor, content, ungovernably bold;
> War in each breast, and freedom on each brow;
> How much unlike the sons of Britain now!
> Fir'd at the sound, my genius spreads her wing,

1   Louis B. Wright, *Culture on the Moving Frontier* (Bloomington, Ill., 1955 and 1961), p. 83. I have ignored 'Auburndale' (Wisconsin, Florida) and 'Auburntown' (Tennessee).

And flies where Britain courts the western spring;
Where lawns extend that scorn Arcadian pride,
And brighter streams than fam'd Hydaspis glide,
There all around the gentlest breezes stray,
There gentle music melts on every spray;
Creation's mildest charms are there combin'd,
Extremes are only in the master's mind;
Stern o'er each bosom reason holds her state.
With daring aims, irregularly great,
Pride in their port, defiance in their eye,
I see the lords of human kind pass by
Intent on high designs, a thoughtful band,
By forms unfashion'd, fresh from Nature's hand;
Fierce in their native hardiness of soul
True to imagin'd right above controul,
While even the peasant boasts these rights to scan,
And learns to venerate himself as man.

Goldsmith never wrote better than this. And there could be no better example of how a stilted convention can, in certain circumstances and in the right hands, achieve effects more suave and economical than are available to more 'natural' idioms. The panegyric is keyed so high, and the diction so fulsome ('courts the western spring' … 'Arcadian pride' … 'fam'd Hydaspis'… 'gentlest/gentle'), precisely so that the sentiment it conveys can be undermined so soon, and so insidiously. The effect is that when this florid oratorical voice begins to drop into its discourse words like 'extremes' and 'irregularly' and 'pride', our first reaction is to ask ourselves: 'Does he understand what he is *saying*?' We begin to think that he does, when we reach 'the lords of human kind', but we are not wholly sure of it until 'True to imagin'd right above controul'. For the claims to be advanced, acceded to, and then denied, all inside twenty lines, is masterly.

And the verses that bite and drive most fiercely are yet to come (ll. 339–48):

That independence Britons prize too high,
Keeps man from man, and breaks the social tie;
The self dependent lordlings stand alone,
All claims that bind and sweeten life unknown;
Here by the bonds of nature feebly held,
Minds combat minds, repelling and repell'd;
Ferments arise, imprison'd factions roar,
Represt ambition struggles round her shore,
Till over-wrought, the general system feels
Its motions stopt, or phrenzy fire the wheels.

The metaphors that blaze in the last two couplets – from chemistry, from medicine, from mechanics – seem 'mixed' only because in a Shakespearean way the imagination is whirling so rapidly from one analogy to the next. And 'factions' here means something more inclusive than power-blocs vying and shouldering at court, in parliament, or in Whitehall offices. It is *minds* that are factious, and more than minds; personalities or sensibilities, human beings, are locked into this prison of unending combat, 'repelling and repell'd'. What we have in fact is what may be the earliest and is certainly to my mind the most caustic indictment of the world of 'free enterprise', unstructured and unrestricted competitiveness, the morality of the market – in ideas, in status, and in feelings, as well as commodities. Why is the passage seldom remembered and extolled? Because for most of us the indictment is launched from the wrong end of what we conceive of as the political spectrum. Such sentiments and insights are thought to be the privileged monopoly of the liberal Left, and we refuse to acknowledge them when they are uttered by a Tory monarchist like Goldsmith or like Johnson.

Already we must suppose it was this prejudice, or something like it, that prevented the Whig Walpole from recognizing in such a passage anything to do with politics. Yet at least once more, before he submerged his analysis in the indulgent haze of *The Deserted Village*, Goldsmith re-stated it. This was in Chapter XIX of *The Vicar of Wakefield* (1766):

'I wish,' cried I, 'that such intruding advisers were fixed in the pillory. It should be the duty of honest men to assist the weaker side of our constitution, that sacred power that has for some years been every day declining, and losing its due share of influence in the state. But these ignorants still continue the cry of liberty, and if they have any weight basely throw it into the subsiding scale.'

Thus Dr Primrose, who subsequently warms to his subject:

Now, Sir, for my own part, as I naturally hate the face of a tyrant, the farther off he is removed from me, the better pleased am I. The generality of mankind also are of my way of thinking, and have unanimously created one king, whose election at once diminishes the number of tyrants, and puts tyranny at the greatest distance from the greatest number of people. Now the great who were tyrants themselves before the election of one tyrant, are naturally averse to a power raised over them, and whose weight must ever lean heaviest on the subordinate orders. It is the interest of the great, therefore, to diminish kingly power as much as possible; because whatever they take from that is naturally restored to themselves; and all they have to do in the state, is to undermine the single tyrant, by which they resume their primaeval authority.

Since wealth is power (thus the argument develops), and since 'an accumulation of wealth … must necessarily be the consequence, when as at present more riches flow in from external commerce, than arise from internal industry', it follows that in proportion as fortunes are made by international trading more and more attempts will be made to abridge the power of the Monarch. The speaker, whom we may as well call Goldsmith as Primrose, accordingly declares his allegiance to 'people without the sphere of the opulent man's influence', a 'middle order of mankind' in whom 'are generally to be found all the arts, wisdom, and virtues of society'. Indeed, he does not scruple to say, 'This order alone is known to be the true preserver of freedom, and may be called the People.' If the historical circumstances are such as he has described, what is in the interest of this middle order? And he replies:

> to preserve the prerogative and privileges of the one principal governor with the most sacred circumspection. For he divides the power of the rich, and calls off the great from falling with tenfold weight on the middle order placed beneath them.

This sustained disquisition in Goldsmith's prose is inferior both in scope and in passion to the passage from *The Traveller*; but it teases out in detail, for those who need the demonstration, the logical coherence of his anti-commercialism and anti-imperialism (why not say, his anti-capitalism?) with his monarchism. And must we not concede that out of the terms of his argument we could contrive an at least plausible explanation of how Whiggism behaved in the next century, how it made way for Liberalism, and how both Whigs and Liberals were able to make accommodations with the Radicals, including some who were overtly or implicitly republican?

There is no doubt in my mind that the arguments and sentiments in Chapter XIX of *The Vicar of Wakefield* are those of Goldsmith himself. And I'm sure Donald Greene was right in *The Politics of Samuel Johnson* (p. 185) to quote from the chapter in that spirit, calling it 'the view of Goldsmith … one of the most vigorous rebuttals of the Whig contention that what was good for Russells and Cavendishes was good for England.' But alas, for those who want to overlook or circumvent the case that Goldsmith makes, there is always available the figure of Dr Primrose. And Dr Primrose is, like his creator, a silly, 'too good for this world', lovable. Thus we are allowed to think that we should not take seriously sentiments put in his mouth. This is unfortunate, and a bad miscalculation on Goldsmith's part. For when Addison had created his lovable old Tory, Sir Roger de Coverley, he had done so as a Whig, adroitly letting the reader's heart go out to Sir Roger even as his head approved the Whig, Sir Andrew Freeport. Goldsmith by contrast was very maladroit indeed, when he put sentiments that mattered to him into the mouth of a speaker who can be discounted so easily.

Cowper told Lady Hesketh in 1785:

> I have read Goldsmith's Traveller and his Deserted Village, and am
> highly pleased with them both, as well for the manner in which they
> are executed, as for their tendency, and the lessons that they inculcate.[1]

Not many readers have, like Cowper, taken seriously the 'tendency' of
Goldsmith's two poems, let alone 'the lessons that they inculcate'. And it
is true that the tendency of *The Deserted Village* can easily be missed unless
that poem is read along with *The Traveller*. No one will deny that in the
later poem Goldsmith tapped new resources, and found new ways to
move us, ways more specifically 'poetic'. But there is more clarity in *The
Traveller*, and more urgency. It is the earlier poem that is challenging.

Andrew Swarbrick (ed.), *The Art of Oliver Goldsmith* (London, 1984).

1   *Letters and Prose Writings of William Cowper*, ed. J. King and C. Ryskamp (Oxford, 1981),
    II, 407.

XIX Goldsmith as Monarchist

In 1771, in his preface to *The History of England, from the Earliest Times to the Death of George II*, Oliver Goldsmith wrote:

> It is not yet decided in politics, whether the diminution of kingly power in England tends to encrease the happiness, or the freedom of the people. For my own part, from seeing the bad effects of the tyranny of the great in those republican states that pretend to be free, I cannot help wishing that our monarchs may still be allowed to enjoy the power of controlling the encroachments of the great at home. A king may easily be restrained from doing wrong, as he is but one man; but if a number of the great are permitted to divide all authority, who can punish them if they abuse it? Upon this principle, therefore, and not from any empty notion of divine or hereditary right, some may think I have leaned towards monarchy.[1]

This had indeed been consistently Goldsmith's principle. But he had not always avowed it so guardedly and suavely as he does here. Eight years before, in *The Traveller*, he had been much more vehement:

> Yes, brother, curse with me that baleful hour
> When first ambition struck at regal power;
> And thus, polluting honour in its source,
> Gave wealth to sway the mind with double force.
> Have we not seen, round Britain's peopled shore,
> Her useful sons exchang'd for useless ore?
> Seen all her triumphs but destruction haste,
> Like flaring tapers brightening as they waste;
> Seen opulence, her grandeur to maintain,
> Lead stern depopulation in her train,
> And over fields, where scatter'd hamlets rose,
> In barren solitary pomp repose?

I have anticipated some of my arguments as 'Notes on Goldsmith's Politics', in *The Art of Oliver Goldsmith*, ed. Andrew Swarbrick (London, 1984).

1 Oliver Goldsmith, *Collected Works*, ed. Arthur Friedman, 5 vols (Oxford, 1966), 5:339–40. Further references to this edition, including volume and page numbers, will be included in the text.

Have we not seen, at pleasure's lordly call,
The smiling long-frequented village fall?
Beheld the duteous son, the sire decay'd,
The modest matron, and the blushing maid,
Forc'd from their homes, a melancholy train,
To traverse climes beyond the western main;
Where wild Oswego spreads her swamps around,
And Niagara stuns with thund'ring sound?

(4:267–8, ll. 393–412)

This passage is generally remembered, because it contains in embryo what
was to become *The Deserted Village*. But if that later treatment surpasses
this one, as is usually but not universally supposed, Goldsmith (and we
also) have to pay a price. For *The Deserted Village* is in important ways
much less specific than *The Traveller*. Nothing in the later poem is so
uncompromising as 'Her useful sons exchang'd for useless ore ...' Indeed
it is notoriously unclear why in *The Deserted Village* the villagers have
been expropriated. And this vagueness permits of the time-honoured
debate whether the village, Auburn, is to be understood as in England or
in Ireland. The debate of course is misconceived, since the poetic imagination surely transforms disparate experiences by amalgamating and
compounding them, often enough. It remains true that agricultural
distress in the 1760s took different forms in England and in Ireland; and
our inability to determine which kingdom is meant shows how far the
poem is from specifying the cause of the calamity. In both poems mercantile interests expropriate the villagers, but in reading *The Deserted Village*
we notice this only if we are very attentive. Indeed, we may go further.
If we identify 'the man of wealth and pride' who drives the villagers out
as a nouveau-riche 'nabob', returned with a fortune from the East or
West Indies, this is only a plausible conjecture; the poem itself does not
identify him in that way, nor in any other. And it is reasonable to wonder
if this lack of specificity is not one of the features that have always made
The Deserted Village more appealing than *The Traveller*. If so, that appeal is
suspect. For instance:

But a bold peasantry, their country's pride,
When once destroyed, can never be supplied.

(4:289, ll. 55–6)

Who would not agree? What bosom does not return an echo? Whom
does the couplet put out of countenance? But in *The Traveller*, where the
expropriation is emphatically and unequivocally laid at the door of
commercial imperialism, the sentiment would embarrass anyone who
practised, or profited from, the import of raw material ('ore') from
overseas.

Moreover *The Deserted Village* prescribes no remedy for the state of affairs that it deplores, and so puts no reader under any obligation to do anything about it. *The Traveller* however does prescribe a remedy: enhanced power for George III. And that prescription is even less palatable for the modern reader than for Goldsmith's contemporaries. For it flies in the face of the Whig Interpretation of History – an interpretation which, though in theory we recognize its partiality, most of us are bound by more than we realize. It is one thing to exculpate George III from the charges thrown at him by Tom Paine and others; it is something else to believe, as Goldsmith would have us do, that in the contention between the king and demagogues like Paine or John Wilkes, the right (and also the *freedom*) was with the king. For that is undoubtedly what Goldsmith means when he calls on his brother to join him in cursing the inroads made on 'regal power'. *The Traveller* is a fervent apologia for the monarchical form of government, taking the time-honoured ground that, since the unprivileged need a power to appeal to above the power of local and financial privilege, the only such power conceivable is the power of the monarch, elevated above all sectional interests. *The Deserted Village* may be the more seductive poem; it is *The Traveller* that is clearer and more challenging.

However, Goldsmith's thinking about the monarchy had gone through an earlier phase before he wrote *The Traveller*. In 1759 in *The Bee* had appeared 'Custom and Laws Compared'. Here Goldsmith (for I follow Arthur Friedman in supposing him the author) finds Tacitus, with his *Corruptissima republica, plurimae leges*, at odds with 'the great Montesquieu, who asserts that every nation is free in proportion to the number of its written laws'. Forced to choose, Goldsmith plumps for Tacitus, and for 'custom' against 'laws', in this anticipating that other Irish political thinker of his day, Edmund Burke. Goldsmith concludes:

> From hence we see how much greater benefit it would be to the state rather to abridge than encrease its laws. We every day find them encreasing; acts and reports, which may be termed the acts of judges, are every day becoming more voluminous, and loading the subject with new penalties. (1:486)

In the next year we find him harping on the same string. This is in a charming paper in *The British Magazine*, 'A Reverie at the Boar's-head-tavern in Eastcheap', where Mr Rigmarole (Goldsmith himself) tells the ghost of Mistress Quickly: 'I rather fancy, madam, that the times then were pretty much like our own; where a multiplicity of laws give a judge as much power as a want of law, since he is ever sure to find among the number some to countenance his partiality' (3:104)

And yet Goldsmith at once sets about reversing this judgement, or rather standing it on its head. According to his new argument, the plethora of legislation in eighteenth-century England, so far from being a sickness in the state, was a sign of its health – but only, he insists, because England was a monarchy. This argument appears first, so far as I can see, already in 1760, in an essay in *The Royal Magazine:*

> Examine every state in Europe, and you will find the people either enjoying a precarious freedom under monarchical government, or what is worse, actually slaves in a republic, to laws of their own contriving. What constitutes the peculiar happiness of Britain, is, that laws may be overlooked without endangering the state. In a mere republic, which pretends to equal freedom, every infringement upon law is a dissolution of government, and must consequently be punished with the most unremitting severity; but in England, laws may be sometimes overlooked without danger. A King who has it in his power to pardon, gives the government at once the strength of the oak, and the flexibility of the yew. (3:68)

However, Goldsmith's fullest exposition of this paradoxical position (which surely again anticipates in its tenor Burke's hostility to written constitutions) had appeared less than two weeks before in the important Letter L of *The Citizen of the World:*

> In all those governments, where laws derive their sanction from the *people alone*, transgressions cannot be overlooked without bringing the constitution into danger. They who transgress the law in such a case, are those who prescribe it, by which means it loses not only its influence but its sanction. In every republic the laws must be strong, because the constitution is feeble: they must resemble an Asiatic husband who is justly jealous, because he knows himself impotent. Thus in Holland, Switzerland, and Genoa, new laws are not frequently enacted, but the old ones are observed with unremitting severity. In such republics therefore the people are slaves to laws of their own making, little less than in unmix'd monarchies where they are slaves to the will of one subject to frailties like themselves.
>
> In England, from a variety of happy accidents, their constitution is just strong enough, or if you will, monarchical enough, to permit a relaxation of the severity of laws, and yet those laws still remain sufficiently strong to govern the people. This is the most perfect state of civil liberty, of which we can form any idea; here we see a greater number of laws than in any other country, while the people at the same time obey only such as are immediately conducive to the interests of society; several are unnoticed, many unknown; some kept to be revived and enforced upon proper occasions, others left to grow obsolete, even without the necessity of abrogation. (2:211)

And Goldsmith expatiates:

Scarce an Englishman who does not almost every day of his life, offend with impunity against some express law, and for which in a certain conjuncture of circumstances he would not receive punishment. Gaming houses, preaching at prohibited places, assembled crowds, nocturnal amusements, public shews, and an hundred other instances are forbid and frequented. These prohibitions are useful; though it be prudent in their magistrates, and happy for their people, that they are not enforced, and none but the venal or mercenary attempt to enforce them.

The law in this case, like an indulgent parent, still keeps the rod, though the child is seldom corrected. Were those pardoned offences to rise into enormity, were they likely to obstruct the happiness of society, or endanger the state, it is then that justice would resume her terrors, and punish those faults she had so often overlooked with indulgence. It is to this ductility of the laws that an Englishman owes the freedom he enjoys superior to others in a more popular government; every step therefore the constitution takes towards a Democratic form, every diminution of the regal authority is, in fact a diminution of the subject's freedom; but every attempt to render the government more popular, not only impairs natural liberty, but even will at last, dissolve the political constitution. (2:211–12)

Thus the Englishman of Goldsmith's time is persuaded that he lives under the rule of law by the assurance that the laws will be enforced only capriciously!

At first sight, this is one of those quixotic, 'Irish' arguments that Goldsmith was famous for in conversation, which made it so difficult for his English friends, even his great champion Johnson, to take him seriously. Yet in fact Goldsmith has here put his finger on an anomaly in eighteenth-century England that recent historians have found exceptionally significant: the anomaly that 'the number of capital statutes grew from about 50 to over 200 between the years 1688 and 1820', and yet 'the available evidence suggests that, compared to some earlier periods, the eighteenth-century criminal law claimed few lives'. What has to be explained is 'the coexistence of bloodier laws and increased convictions with a declining proportion of death sentences that were actually carried out.'[1] I am quoting from an essay of capital importance, Douglas Hay's 'Property, Authority and the Criminal Law'. What Hay shows is that the commuting or pardoning of severe sentences was, at least outside the commercial centres of London and perhaps Bristol, a principal way of

---

1   Douglas Hay, 'Property, Authority and the Criminal Law', in *Albion's Fatal Tree: Crime and Society in Eighteenth-century England*, ed. Hay et al. (London, 1975), pp. 18, 22; further references to this essay, abbreviated 'P', will be included in the text.

knitting English society together, in a way that was hierarchical indeed and inequitable, yet effective and even in a deep sense humane. As in other perspectives, what has been denounced in English eighteenth-century society as 'corrupt' (and was even so denounced at the time) turns out to be the margin of humanity – of humane feelings and human relationships – that that society provided for. Intercession on behalf of inferiors and dependents was taken for granted as an essential part of the mechanism of society, alike by those who needed such help and those who (on conditions, of course) extended it. Without this 'corrupt' play between the majesty of the law and the acknowledgement of special interests, the society would have been less flexible and less stable than it proved to be. And to this extent modern scholarship may be thought to vindicate Goldsmith's speculations, which thus turn out to have been remarkably astute. Moreover, in a curious and devious way Goldsmith may be thought to vindicate his earlier preference for 'custom' over 'laws', since the very multiplicity of laws ensured that their severity would be *customarily* alleviated.

What remains to be justified is Goldsmith's conviction that things could work out this way only under a monarchy. Readers of Hay's essay will be tempted to think that Goldsmith was wrong and starry-eyed about this (if nothing worse). For Hay shows that the system worked so as to put life and death in the hands of those local tyrants, justices of the peace and their cronies, from whom, on Goldsmith's understanding of the matter, the Crown was supposed to liberate the unprivileged. That pardons came from the king was a legal and ideological fiction, masking the fact that they were handed down as a result of interplaying interests in the ruling class. However, this fiction – that all clemency is the king's – has far more power than the more or less squalid or whimsical fact of letters written on behalf of this or that convicted person at this or that level of influence. For it is of the nature of an ideology to be a tissue of fictions, that is to say in the most serious sense a *myth*. Hay abjures this word. And one can hardly blame him. For too often in these contexts 'myth' seems at once facile and pretentious, pretending to explain what in effect it only consigns to the ineffable. Yet where 'monarchy' is in question, though the word itself may be dispensed with, the sense of it hardly can be:

> Where authority is embodied in direct personal relationships, men will often accept power, even enormous, despotic power, when it comes from the 'good King', the father of his people, who tempers justice with mercy. A form of this powerful psychic configuration was one of the most distinctive aspects of the unreformed criminal law. Bentham could not understand it, but it was the law's greatest strength as an ideological system, especially among the poor, and in the countryside. ('P', p. 39)

'Powerful psychic configuration' is certainly a drier expression than 'myth', but it surely means much the same thing. And indeed whenever Hay invokes 'paternalism', as he is compelled to do, he acknowledges the same mythic dimension. For under a monarchical dispensation the fatherliness of a squire to his tenant is thought to mirror in microcosm the fatherliness of the king towards the entire realm.

It is notable moreover that Hay is forced to explain how 'the criminal law, more than any other social institution, made it possible to govern eighteenth-century England without a police force and without a large army' ('P', p. 56), by following through the same logic which, when we first encountered it in Letter L of *The Citizen of the World*, struck us as quixotic:

> An ideology endures not by being wholly enforced and rigidly defined. Its effectiveness lies first in its very elasticity, the fact that men are not required to make it a credo, that it seems to them the product of their own minds and their own experience. And the law did not enforce uniform obedience, did not seek total control; indeed, it sacrificed punishment when necessary to preserve the belief in justice. ('P', p. 55)

This is the same logic that governs the policy of the English monarch even today. The monarch has powers which he or she retains on the tacit understanding that except in barely conceivable circumstances he or she will never exercise them. According to this understanding, the theory of monarchism is analogous to what naval strategists understand by the principle of 'the fleet in being'. So long as the fleet is never hazarded in combat (but only detached units or squadrons), it remains, as a menacing potency, an important pawn in grand strategy and in diplomacy. So too with the unreformed criminal law, as both Hay and Goldsmith understand it.

None of this intricate and perhaps special pleading enters into *The Traveller*. For this poem Goldsmith reverts to the not unconnected but bolder argument of 'The Revolution in Low Life' *(Lloyd's Evening Post*, 1762):

> Wherever we turn we shall find those governments that have pursued foreign commerce with too much assiduity at length becoming Aristocratical; and the immense property, thus necessarily acquired by some, has swallowed up the liberties of all. Venice, Genoa, and Holland, are little better at present than retreats for tyrants and prisons for slaves. The Great, indeed, boast of their liberties there, and they have liberty. The poor boast of liberty too; but, alas, they groan under the most rigorous oppression. (3:197–8)

Goldsmith protested – and coming from Samuel Johnson's very insular

England, the protestation should be attended to – that when he spoke in
this lordly fashion of Venice, Genoa, Holland, he drew on the experience
of one who had travelled, needy and on foot, through their territories.
What poetic capital Goldsmith could make of these experiences appears
in a passage where he makes a smooth and yet momentous transition from
considering the Netherlands to considering Great Britain:

> Heavens! how unlike their Belgic sires of old!
> Rough, poor, content, ungovernably bold;
> War in each breast, and freedom on each brow;
> How much unlike the sons of Britain now!
>
> Fir'd at the sound, my genius spreads her wing,
> And flies where Britain courts the western spring;
> Where laws extend that scorn Arcadian pride,
> And brighter streams than fam'd Hydaspis glide.
> There all around the gentlest breezes stray,
> There gentle music melts on every spray;
> Creation's mildest charms are there combin'd,
> Extremes are only in the master's mind;
> Stern o'er each bosom reason holds her state.
> With daring aims, irregularly great,
> Pride in their port, defiance in their eye,
> I see the lords of human kind pass by
> Intent on high designs, a thoughtful band,
> By forms unfashion'd, fresh from Nature's hand:
> Fierce in their native hardiness of soul,
> True to imagin'd right above controul,
> While even the peasant boasts these rights to scan,
> And learns to venerate himself as man.

(4:262–3, ll. 313–4)

The diction is very stilted. Modern prejudices in favour of the colloquial
will prompt us to say that the language is at no point in touch with spoken
usage. But this is plainly untrue: 'I see the lords of human kind pass by'
could certainly be *said* (sarcastically). And that drop in the level of the
diction has a force that depends on the level in the preceding lines having
been pitched so high. A more 'natural' idiom could not make the point
with such economy. The panegyric is keyed so high, and the diction is so
fulsome ('courts the western spring' ... 'Arcadian pride' ... 'fam'd
Hydaspis'), precisely so that the sentiment conveyed can be undermined
so soon, and so insidiously. The effect is that when this florid oratorical
voice begins to drop into its discourse words like 'extremes' and 'irregularly' and 'pride', our first reaction is to ask ourselves: 'Does he understand what he is *saying*?' We begin to think that he does when we reach
'the lords of human kind', but we are not wholly sure of it until 'True to

imagin'd right above controul'. We see the claims of English complacency advanced, acceded to, and then denied, all inside twenty lines. The
elevated diction is crucial for the achievement of masterly economy.

The verses that bite and drive most fiercely are yet to come:

> That independence Britons prize too high
> Keeps man from man, and breaks the social tie;
> The self dependent lordlings stand alone,
> All claims that bind and sweeten life unknown;
> Here by the bond of nature feebly held,
> Minds combat minds, repelling and repell'd;
> Ferments arise, imprison'd factions roar,
> Represt ambition struggles round her shore,
> Till over-wrought, the general system feels
> Its motions stopt, or phrenzy fire the wheels.

> (4:263–4, ll. 339–48)

The metaphors that flame in the last two couplets – from chemistry, from
the sea, from medicine, from mechanics – seem 'mixed' only because in
a positively Shakespearean way the imagination is whirling so rapidly
from one analogy to the next. And 'factions' here means something more
inclusive than power-blocs vying and shouldering at court, in parliament,
or in Whitehall offices. It is *minds* that are factious, and more than minds;
personalities and sensibilities, human beings, are locked into this prison of
unending combat, 'repelling and repell'd'. We have here in fact what may
be the earliest and also the most caustic indictment of the world of 'free
enterprise', unstructured and unrestricted competitiveness, the morality
of the marketplace – in ideas, in status, and in feelings, as well as
commodities. Nothing can save us from this, or alleviate it, except –
Goldsmith insists – the institution of monarchy. Why is a passage so
memorable seldom remembered or extolled? It is easy to see why. For
most of us the indictment is launched from the wrong end of what we
conceive of as the political spectrum. These sentiments and insights are
thought to be the monopoly of the liberal democratic left, and we refuse
to acknowledge them when they come to us from conservative monar-
chists like Goldsmith and Johnson. The Whig Interpretation is at work
once again.

At least once more, before he submerged his analysis in the indulgent
haze of *The Deserted Village*, Goldsmith restated it. This was in chapter 19
of *The Vicar of Wakefield* (1766):

> 'No, Sir,' replied I, 'I am for liberty, that attribute of Gods! Glorious
> liberty! that theme of modern declamation. I would have all men
> kings. I would be a king myself. We have all naturally an equal right
> to the throne: we are all originally equal. This is my opinion, and was

once the opinion of a set of honest men who were called Levellers. They tried to erect themselves into a community, where all should be equally free. But, alas! it would never answer; for there were some among them stronger, and some more cunning than others, and these became masters of the rest; for as sure as your groom rides your horses, because he is a cunninger animal than they, so surely will the animal that is cunninger or stronger than he, sit upon his shoulders in turn.' (4:99)

The speaker is Dr Primrose, the vicar, who here shows that he knows about primitive communism and anticipates George Orwell's *Animal Farm* in discrediting it by way of a bestial fable. The vicar goes on:

'Since then it is entailed upon humanity to submit, and some are born to command, and others to obey, the question is, as there must be tyrants, whether it is better to have them in the same house with us, or in the same village, or still farther off, in the metropolis. Now, Sir, for my own part, as I naturally hate the face of a tyrant, the farther off he is removed from me, the better pleased am I. The generality of mankind also are of my way of thinking, and have unanimously created one king, whose election at once diminishes the number of tyrants, and puts tyranny at the greatest distance from the greatest number of people. Now the great who were tyrants themselves before the election of one tyrant, are naturally averse to a power raised over them, and whose weight must ever lean heaviest on the subordinate orders. It is the interest of the great, therefore, to diminish kingly power as much as possible; because whatever they take from that is naturally restored to themselves; and all they have to do in the state, is to undermine the single tyrant, by which they resume their primaeval authority.' (4:99–100)

Dr Primrose may here seem to be more tough-minded than Dr Goldsmith, since he asserts that the power of the king is of its nature tyrannical; however, we may suppose that both the learned doctors know, and rely on their hearers to know, that *tyrannos* in ancient Greek is a term morally neutral, as 'tyrant' in English is not.

Since wealth is power (thus the argument develops), and since 'an accumulation of wealth ... must necessarily be the consequence, when as at present more riches flow in from external commerce than arise from internal industry' (4:100), it follows that in proportion as fortunes are made by international trading more and more attempts will be made to abridge the power of the monarch. The speaker, whom we may as well call Goldsmith as Primrose, accordingly declares his allegiance to 'people without the sphere of the opulent man's influence', a 'middle order of mankind' in whom 'are generally to be found all the arts, wisdom, and virtues of society' (4:101, 102). Indeed, he does not scruple to say, 'This order alone is known to be the true preserver of freedom, and may be called the People' (4:102). Here, it might reasonably be proposed, we see the sharp-sightedness of the Irishman, the outsider, detecting what now we take for granted though for observers at the time it was obscured by the conspicuousness of the landed grandees: the truth that eighteenth-century England was essentially a *bourgeois* civilization.

If the historical circumstances are such as he has described, what then, the speaker asks, is in the interest of that 'middle order' with which he has declared himself in sympathy? And he answers, '"to preserve the prerogative and privileges of the one principal governor with the most sacred circumspection. For he divides the power of the rich, and calls off the great from falling with tenfold weight on the middle order placed beneath them"' (4:102). But what began as protestation and proceeded as exposition has by this time become, as the speaker apologetically recognizes, a *harangue*. Accordingly it ends with a peroration:

> 'I am then for, and would die for, monarchy, sacred monarchy; for if there be any thing sacred amongst men, it must be the anointed sovereign of his people, and every diminution of his power in war, or in peace, is an infringement upon the real liberties of the subject. The sounds of liberty, patriotism, and Britons, have already done *much*, it is to be hoped that the true sons of freedom will prevent their ever doing more. I have known many of those pretended champions for liberty in my time, yet do I not remember one that was not in his heart and in his family a tyrant.' (4:102–3)

But it is plain that the alleged sacredness and anointedness of the monarch belong in a quite different dimension of discourse from the hard-nosed calculations of interest that have made the case for monarchy up to this point. That extra dimension can only be called 'mythological'.

Dr Primrose, the vicar, is of course a ninny; an endearingly foolish and unworldly man – as was, so we are assured by numerous but always controvertible witnesses, Oliver Goldsmith himself. But at no point are we invited to make fun of him in his capacity as priest and pastor, spiritual guide to his flock. Nor do we see him as easily deluded by catch-phrases – on the contrary his unworldliness often consists in his taking seriously and literally what other people say only as a matter of form. Accordingly, when he speaks of 'the *anointed* sovereign', we are in duty bound to suppose him in earnest. And indeed to a Christian nation like the eighteenth-century English (not nominally but deeply Christian), the figure of David, shepherd-king and warrior-psalmist of ancient Israel, could not fail to loom behind, and to transfigure, the image of any king whom they knew or knew about. The myth of kingship was for them underpinned by scriptural reading and religious observance. This is surely a main part of that 'powerful psychic configuration' which Hay postulates.

It has been argued that, in creating Dr Primrose, Goldsmith miscalculated. When the Whig Addison had created the lovable but foolish Tory figure of Sir Roger de Coverley, he had taken care not to put in Sir Roger's mouth any arguments that he, Addison, could take seriously; whereas Goldsmith took no such precautions. I now think this is wrong. Addison's Coverley papers are remarkably inventive and insidious political polemic, whereas *The Vicar of Wakefield* is, as Goethe admiringly and astutely recognized, an *idyll*. Within the conventions of the idyll – and the myth of kingship is itself, one might argue, idyllic – Goldsmith could safely expound doctrines that he took in all seriousness. Accordingly Donald Greene was surely right to quote from this chapter 19 and to present it as 'the view of Goldsmith ... one of the most vigorous rebuttals of the Whig contention that what was good for Russells and Cavendishes was good for England.[1] About politics this Irish zany was more levelheaded and penetrating than has ever been acknowledged.

Politics and Poetic Value, ed. R. Von Hallberg (University of Chicago Press, 1987).

1   Donald J. Greene, *The Politics of Samuel Johnson* (New Haven, Conn., 1960), p. 185.

XX Disaffection of the
Dissenters under George III

The last forty years of the eighteenth century have through recent decades attracted disproportionate attention from political historians – disproportionate, yet very natural. For this was the period that saw the political severance of most of the English speakers of North America from Great Britain, and there is every reason why Americans and Britons alike should continue to ask themselves why and how this momentous and drastic surgery came about, to ask even if it could have been avoided. Moreover this period saw some crucial stages in that amorphous but even more momentous development that we call the Industrial Revolution; a social transformation the strain of which, experienced by the British sooner than by any other nation, more than once brought Britain to the brink of a political revolution that nevertheless never quite happened. For these reasons, not to mention others that might be cited, changes in the historical understanding of these decades inevitably and properly continue to inflame passions in the here and now. An American's sense of his own national identity or of the rectitude of his citizenship is in some degree at risk in any retelling of the War of Independence, in any attempt for instance to correct the long-established view of the part played at that time by the king of England. As Edmund S. Morgan remarked more than twenty years ago, 'The righteousness of the Americans is somewhat diminished through the loss of the principal villain of the piece [George III]... no longer the foe of liberty seeking to subvert the British constitution, but an earnest and responsible monarch.'[1] And, on the other hand, a British patriot of today, if he thinks of himself as in some sort a radical, cannot examine without emotion the course of events by which the British Revolution that ought to have happened mysteriously didn't. It cannot be a coincidence that this stretch of British history, this bit of the past that may be dead but clearly won't lie down, should have been chosen by Sir Lewis Namier as the test case on which to push through a revolution in the methods of historical research.

---

1 See Edmund S. Morgan, *William and Mary Quarterly*, 3rd ser., 14 (1957), 3–15. Quoted by Ian R. Christie, *Myth and Reality in Late Eighteenth-Century British Politics* (Berkeley and Los Angeles, 1970), p. 23.

When a period has come in for such intense professional attention, the inevitable consequence is that in the interests of rigour studies are narrowed down to specific problems that reveal their complexity only when considered thus minutely. And there is already a formidable body of scholarship of this kind, much of it very impressive. There remain, however, larger, more general questions, and these tend not to get asked because they call for an altogether looser, more sweeping and foolhardy treatment. One such question concerns the role played in this period by the people called at some times Dissenters, at other times Non-conformists, and nowadays for the most part Free Churchmen. That the Dissenters played a crucial role in politics under George III is what nobody denies; yet who they were, these people called Dissenters, is a question at once too large and too rudimentary to get very much attention from those whose analytical skills have been developed to deal with knottier and more sophisticated problems. This broad and obvious question is the one I am concerned with: who *were* the Dissenters under George III? And are we right to lump them together so confidently as we commonly do?

To begin with, the fluctuating nomenclature is itself significant: it causes difficulties, and it raises questions – of which the most troubling and unwelcome to an English Free Churchman of the present day is whether he is, in any more than a formal sense, the heir to the Nonconformists of yesterday and the Dissenters of two hundred years ago; whether in fact his tradition has not in the past suffered breaches and discontinuities papered over by generous sentiment but become really irreparable, so that today's Free Churchman is a wholly different animal from such as Joseph Priestley and Thomas Hollis. To such as Hollis in the 1750s and 1760s this was already a burning question that presented itself in the form of whether he and those who felt like him were truly, in more than a formal sense, the heirs of Milton and Cromwell; and further, if he was such an heir, what actions and sentiments that inheritance compelled him to, in political situations different from those that Milton and Cromwell had contended with. The answer that such as Hollis found, which made them a significant political force in the 1760s and 1770s, is pointed to in the very title of Caroline Robbins' justly well regarded study *The Eighteenth Century Commonwealthman*.[1] That is to say, they decided that their situation under George III and Lord North was not after all significantly different from the situation of their ancestors under Charles I and Strafford. For making this decision they were applauded by some (mostly) Americans in their own day, and have been applauded ever since by those who think, or else expediently affect to think, that the

---

1 Caroline Robbins, *The Eighteenth-Century Commonwealthman* (New York, 1959).

decision was a correct one because grounded in a correct historical analysis. But this is precisely what twentieth-century historians have challenged and may be thought to have disproved: George III was *not* Charles I, neither in private life nor as a politician, despite what Tom Paine pretended; Lord North was *not* Strafford; and accordingly (it may seem to follow) Cromwellian republicanism was *not* a responsible or apposite political position in the England of the 1770s. Indeed, it may be thought that this was proved by events long before twentieth-century historians addressed themselves to the question; as J.H. Plumb has pointed out,[1] the out-and-out republicanism of an Algernon Sidney, as espoused and promulgated by Hollis's protégés such as the Dissenting minister Richard Baron,[2] merely withered away as soon as the differences with the American colonies became a state of war, and more particularly when the American colonists became the allies of Britain's old enemy, France. And this development casts a shadow backwards so as to raise the question whether the republicanism of Hollis or Baron or the diarist Sylas Neville was ever, even in the 1760s, practical politics.[3] Was it ever more than the irresponsible speculation of persons far from the centres where political decisions were taken? And did the majority of English Dissenters ever regard these republicans as anything more than a lunatic fringe? This question is still debated;[4] but we may certainly suspect that Robbins' 'commonwealthmen' have an interest and an importance in the history of political ideas such as they never had in the history of politics. This is to say that very few English Dissenters at any time under George III harboured sentiments and designs that were positively treasonable; few can be said to have been at any time disloyal, though at certain times many of them can be properly described as 'disaffected'.

And yet even this may be questioned. For who were these people that we are speaking of? James E. Bradley, in an important article,[5] has accused Whig historiographers of 'a preoccupation with the dissenting elite', at the expense of the rank-and-file of English Dissenters up and down the country. And this is surely a true bill; historians of all sorts, and especially those of a literary turn, inevitably pay too much attention to the articulate and self-appointed leaders of opinion, without sufficiently consid-

1   J.H. Plumb, 'British Attitudes to the American Revolution' (1964), in Plumb, *In the Light of History* (Boston, 1973), pp. 70–87.
2   For Baron, see *Memoirs of Thomas Hollis* (1780).
3   *The Diary of Sylas Neville, 1767–1788*, ed. Basil Cozens-Hardy (London, 1950)
4   See Ian R. Christie, *Wilkes, Wyvill and Reform* (London, 1962), p. 15: 'Attacks of a fairly traditional and arid kind came from a little group of *soi-disant* republicans: Thomas Hollis of Lincoln's Inn, his cousin, Timothy, Richard Baron, Thomas Brand, and a few others. Their republicanism, based on a high and dry whiggism drawn directly from later seventeenth-century tradition, had little popular appeal.' But contrast Plumb, pp. 70–87.
5   James E. Bradley, 'Whigs and Nonconformists: "Slumbering Radicalism" in English Politics', *Eighteenth-Century Studies*, 9 (1975), 1–27.

ering that their 'lead' may not have been followed by the relatively inarticulate fellow citizens whom they addressed. Just here indeed we see one of the entering wedges of the Namierite method of political historiography; and Bradley, by applying that method, has no difficulty proving that in one English borough after another Dissenters were no less 'corrupt' than other Englishmen; that the votes of the Dissenting interest were up for sale in a way that was not just time-honoured but essential if the eighteenth-century political machine in England was to function at all. Indeed, while still shirking the laborious Namierite discipline of scrutinizing the electoral returns and division lists on crucial votes, in the municipalities as well as at Westminster, we can cite a case where the 'country' Dissenters quite plainly refused to follow the lead of their metropolitan spokesmen. This was the application to Parliament in 1772 to relieve Church of England clergy from having to subscribe to all the Thirty-Nine Articles and, as regards such subscription, to secure for Dissenters more than the two or three exemptions they enjoyed already. Henry F. May believes that the failure of the initiative 'caused some English dissenters to believe in a new conspiracy against Protestant liberty'. And no doubt he is right; but he fails to remark that the initiative was ultimately defeated, when it was launched again in 1773, by *the country Dissenters*, for these, still mostly Trinitarian Calvinists, rightly saw that those who sought relief were Dissenters of a Socinian or Arian or Unitarian cast.[1] Dissent was not monolithic; and the most taciturn Calvinist Dissenters would on occasion strike down the liberties sought by their more vociferous brethren, Socinians and Arians.

It may be that on other issues besides this one, for instance on the broad issue of loyalty to the Crown, there was at any time a substantial minority of English Dissenters, if not indeed a majority at times, who go unremarked because they were relatively inarticulate. They did indeed sometimes find articulate spokesmen. But these are hard to discern, perhaps because there were disproportionately few of them, more certainly because it has been in nobody's partisan interest, from their day to ours, to have them remembered. One of them, hardly a spokesman at all except in his immediate circle, seems to have been John Merivale of Exeter, described as 'a sturdy conscientious Dissenter of the old school; combining with his dissent an absolute horror of Radicalism and disloyalty.'[2] In 1792, when Timothy Kenrick, avowedly Unitarian minister of the Presbyterian George's Meeting in Exeter, had prayed extempore 'for the success of people struggling for their liberty' (having in mind specifically, as he admitted, the French), Merivale expostulated in a letter: 'It is so utterly repugnant to my Conception of what is right to join in prayers

---

1　Henry F. May, *The Enlightenment in America* (New York, 1976), p. 157.
2　Anna W. Merivale, *Family Memorials* (Exeter, 1884), p. 129.

offer'd up to the God of Mercy for the further success of a wretched Faction which has already involv'd a country in a most deplorable state of Anarchy & Distress, – that I feel myself obliged to seek some other Place of Worship.'[1] And Merivale was as good as his word, signally absenting himself and his family thereafter from Kenrick's ministrations. It is not clear, however, whether he carried out his threat 'to seek some other Place of Worship'. For Kenrick shared the pastorate there with two others, and in his reply to Merivale he explained, 'Mr Tozer, Mr Manning and myself may publickly pray for the spread of Christianity, altho' we each of us affix different ideas to the phrase – the first meaning by it Trinitarianism, the second Arianism, and the last Unitarianism.' This arrangement by which, if he chose, Merivale could still profit by the devotions of Mr Tozer or Mr Manning is of a liberalism so thorough-going that one might suppose it invented only in the present century; but in fact such blithe inclusiveness, like the eager ardour of a Timothy Kenrick who could take pride in it, is as common among nominal Presbyterians in George III's England as among leftward-leaning clerics and confident laymen of our own times. And it had, then as now, the effect of fostering, and absolving in advance, every sort of irresponsible pulpit eloquence, whether in politics or theology.

It may well be asked whether John Merivale belonged, in James E. Bradley's sense of the term, to the dissenting elite. From one point of view, as the son and pupil at the Exeter Dissenting Academy of Samuel Merivale, himself a pupil of the great Doddridge, John Merivale may be thought to belong with the bluest blood of West Country Dissent. And this certainly weighed with Kenrick, may even have dismayed him. But since Merivale published nothing and was a leader of opinion only in his own congregation, I think he does not fall into the category of 'dissenting elite' as Bradley conceives of it. And so the question arises, quite press-ingly: How many John Merivales were there, up and down the country, their very existence perpetuated only in the records, where they survive, of long disbanded and extinct Dissenting churches?

It is not clear how that question can be answered. And that no doubt is one reason why it is never or seldom asked. But there are other more prejudiced reasons why the mere existence of the John Merivales, of loyalist and nonradical yet principled Dissenters, should be passed over in silence. These reasons become clearer if we shift our attention from the 1790s back to the 1770s, from the French Revolution to the American; and if we attend particularly to Free Churchmen of the present day, concerned to celebrate with a proper pride the tradition they inherit.

In 1976 the bicentenary of the Declaration of Independence was

---

1   See Alan Brockett, *Nonconformity in Exeter, 1650–1875* (Manchester, 1962), pp. 142–3.

noticed in Britain by Free Churchmen as by others; and there were obvious and proper reasons why on such occasions radical Dissenters, those who sympathized with the colonists, should be remembered, and loyalist Dissenters like John Merivale should be driven still further into the shadows. An example is the lecture 'Nonconformists and the American Revolution', by the distinguished historian of the English Baptists, Ernest A. Payne.[1] Given the occasion, and deciding sensibly that the Methodists (though not strictly Nonconformists) could hardly be left out of account, Dr Payne had to do something about the vehement and intransigent loyalism of the Wesley brothers. Taking note of Charles Wesley's anguished poem that castigates General Howe for mismanaging the American campaigns, and Lord Shelburne for making peace in 1783 ('That smooth, perfidious perjur'd Shelburne sold / His King his country and his God for gold'), he commented: 'Poor Charles Wesley! This is not the right note to end on, not really fair to the Methodists of that day, certainly not fair to the Colonists and their supporters in this country. The rebels and their friends should not be idealized, but the future was with them.' This is compassionate. And of course that 'the future was with them' is what none of us, two centuries later, can deny. But Charles Wesley's concern in that poem and others was not with which of the opposing bodies of opinion in Britain had the future in its keeping, but with which of them had felt and acted constitutionally; and he was sure that the winning side had been the one that mocked and flouted the British Constitution. The same is true of the other anti-Whig document that Dr Payne takes note of: Johnson's *Taxation No Tyranny*. Johnson was, he says, 'unfortunately prejudiced against Americans', and 'he could not see how people who practised and upheld the slave system could protest against ill-treatment and the denial of rights'. Johnson does indeed gibe at libertarian slaveholders, and who will say that the gibe was unwarranted? But such an argument ad hominem is nowhere near the centre of Johnson's powerful pamphlet, which on the contrary turns upon the strictly constitutional questions of what 'sovereignty' means, and what 'representation' means. And it is not clear that Johnson's argument on these properly dry and philosophical grounds has ever been contro-verted.[2] For Dr Payne, however, it is a case of 'poor Sam Johnson', no less than poor Charles Wesley – to whom we may add poor John Wesley also, who was persuaded by Johnson's pamphlet and thereafter agreed with his brother. Of all three of them it seems we must say that they were left behind by history or, if we agree to think that way, 'proved wrong in the event'. To extend to three such massive and formidable figures the

1   Published in *The Journal of the United Reformed Church History Society*, 1, No. 8 (October 1976), 210–27.
2   See The Yale Edition of the Works of Samuel Johnson, Vol. X, *Political Writings*, ed. Donald Greene (New Haven, 1977), pp. 402–9.

charity of our faintly amused compassion appears somewhat hazardous, but from Payne's point of view it is the best we can do. Certainly among those, Dissenters and others, who took the opposite view, we find no men of comparable stature. And for that matter, if among the Dissenters there were any who made the same mistake as Johnson and the Wesleys did, Dr Payne – understandably enough, considering the occasion – chose not to identify them.

His account in fact is only a little more cautious than that of a Nonconformist spokesman eighty years ago, C. Silvester Horne, in his *Popular History of the Free Churches* (1903):

> If the voice of the Free Churches had been listened to, the American Colonies would have been saved for England. It was natural, doubt-less, that English Nonconformists should sympathize with those who represented their own ideals. Across the thousands of miles of sea they united themselves in sympathy with the brave children of the Puritans who were defying British tyranny and dying in thousands for their independence ... Only John Wesley's political instinct failed him; and his attack on the colonists was unworthy of his shrewd intelligence and generous heart. English Nonconformity was not represented in Parliament, but when Burke and Chatham and Fox pleaded the cause of the Americans, the Free Churchmen at home had no need to be ashamed of the men who defended their opinions in the Legislature.[1]

These ringing tones (Horne in his day was a famous pulpit orator)[2] are not what we are used to. But the substance of what Horne asserts appears still to be the received opinion, and not only among Free Churchmen like Ernest A. Payne. British and American historians alike still assume or assert that the English Dissenters were unanimously on the side of the colonists, though it is sometimes conceded that their enthusiasm cooled rather precipitately soon after the war started. James E. Bradley in some entertaining pages has shown that for Whig historiographers like Lecky and Trevelyan what particularly recommended the Dissenters was precisely that they were, as Horne says, 'not represented in Parliament'. For, once the First Reform Bill had acknowledged how corrupt the parliamentary system had been while it sustained the Whig hegemony, Whig virtue could be saved for the nineteenth century only by vesting it in those Whigs who had been outside the system – which is to say, the Dissenters.[3] Silvester Horne, however, had no such sophisticated ends in view when he roundly declared that under George III 'Nonconformity was winning its soul, and coming to see and to declare the beauty of the

---

1 Horne, p. 323.
2 For Horne, see Clyde Binfield, *So Down to Prayers* (London, 1977), pp. 199–213.
3 Of course they were *not* outside the system (as Bradley points out).

ideal of a Free church in a Free State'. At this point Horne has in mind not so much his Dissenters' opposition to coercion of the colonists as, in domestic policy, their agitation for parliamentary reform. But the two issues can hardly be kept apart, if only because the pro-Americans were almost always active for parliamentary reform also. Horne identifies as heroes of this Dissenting thrust not just Joseph Priestley but also 'the eloquent and impassioned Baptist minister, Robert Robinson'.[1]

Readers of Herbert Butterfield[2] will know Robinson already, as instigator of a notorious meeting for parliamentary reform on 25 March 1780, in Cambridge. This is described by a contemporary as 'a mob of Dissenters of all Hues, Colours & Denominations in every part of the Country, called together ... in order to draw up a Petition of œconomy, Alterations in the Method of Parliament, and other wild and republican Schemes, first engendered at Mr Robinson's conventicle, & then recommended to the notice of the Corporation by a modest Republican, if that is compatible, Alderman Burleigh'. And at the end of a turbulent day, we are told, 'Robinson, the Anabaptist Teacher, who lives at Chesterton, set the Bells a Ringing in that Church as soon as he got Home, and made a great Supper at night for all his Party, where strong Liquors, good Cheer, and Zeal for the Cause, so far got the better of their discretion, that many of the Ebenezers were laid flat on their Back, & had Assistance to convey them to their several Habitations'. There is much other evidence to bear out this image of what Robinson was like. Joseph Ivimey, historian of the Baptists in the next generation, was prepared to think that by the time Robinson died a Socinian and Unitarian, he must have been insane. Is this, we may ask mildly, the sort of figure whom we should find, with the advantage of hindsight, politically more admirable and enlightened than John Wesley or Dr Johnson?

At any rate, Lecky and Payne and Horne notwithstanding, there were in the 1770s English Dissenters who rightly or wrongly found themselves of one mind with Johnson and the Wesleys. One of them was the already venerable Job Orton of Shrewsbury, friend and literary executor of the great Philip Doddridge. On 29 September 1775 we find him already resenting, on behalf of the provincial Dissenters, the politicizing of dissent by the ministers of the metropolis: 'Whatever "the principle of the *Americans*" may be, the spirit they shew is malignant, rebellious, and wicked. My Bible teaches me "not to speak evil of dignities" & − I wish the London ministers would leave Politics to Statesmen, and give themselves wholly to their ministry.'[3] By 1778 his tone has sharpened, and by

13 Horne, p. 326.
14 See Butterfield, *George III, Lord North and the People* (London, 1949), pp. 284–8.
15 Joe Orton, *Letters to Dissenting Ministers*, ed. S. Palmer, 2 vols (1806), I, 167.

a pregnant allusion to Northampton Academy under Doddridge he by implication invokes the authority of that most famous and influential of all Hanoverian Dissenters:

> I have been looking over Sallust's *History of Cataline's Conspiracy;* in which I think you will find some things suitable to your purpose, particularly in his speech to the conspirators; which you will meet with towards the beginning of the history; where he pleads Liberty, as a ground for his undertaking; but mentions honour, power, wealth, &c. as also in their plan, and throws out some bitter reflections against the ministers and placemen of those days ... There is a great deal to the same purpose in *Cataline's* speech, and in other parts of the history; but it is near forty years ago since I last read it, which was with the pupils at *Northampton*, in 1739. I have long thought there are many passages in the account of that conspiracy very parallel to the present case of our nation, between loyal men, and those who are called patriots, and who choose by a figure of speech to call themselves Whigs, just as they call me a Tory. Many are angry with me, because I discountenance their disloyalty; but I despise their anger, as much as I dislike their principles and conduct. I would willingly be doing some good while I am here; and to promote loyalty, subjection, and peace, is doing good. I think I have already softened some sharp spirits amongst us, at least brought them to hold their tongues, or to be less confident.[1]

And in the next year Orton can afford to be contemptuously sarcastic: 'I know nothing of Mr— but by report. It is very well to be "valiant for *liberty*", if the courageous man has a proper idea of it; but I should have rejoiced more to have heard that he had been *valiant for truth*, holiness, and peace, and remarkably alive for the conversion and salvation of souls. We have some ministers who are zealous for liberty, but the souls of their flocks are neglected, and our interest is sinking under them.'[2]

Some may read out of these comments only a pusillanimous quietism. But Orton is addressing ministers of religion; and his contention, which can hardly be denied, is that however ardent a minister's political convictions and however he may interpret his political duties as a perhaps prominent and certainly influential citizen, all such matters must have for him a lower priority than the performing of his pastoral and priestly duties. These comments therefore are of a piece with Orton's sacramentalism: 'I cannot agree with you, that administering the Sacraments is the easiest and least important part of our office. I always considered them as most important, and found it more difficult to administer them, as they should be, than to preach.'[3] To those who when they consider late-

---

1 *Letters to a Young Clergyman from the late Reverend Mr Job Orton* (Shrewsbury, 1791), p. 133.
2 *Letters to Dissenting Ministers*, II, 4.
3 Ibid., I, 131.

Hanoverian dissent think first of Priestley and Richard Price, not to speak of Richard Baron and Robert Robinson, it will come as a surprise that sacramentalism has any part at all in the Dissenting tradition. But the proper administering of the sacraments had a central place in the Dissent of Doddridge, with whom in this emphasis also Orton is keeping faith. Moreover, Orton could, if he chose, appeal behind Doddridge to John Flavel in 1691 declaring, 'When God puts a crown upon the head, and a sceptre into the hand of a man, he engraves upon that man (in a qualified sense) both his name, and the lively characters of his Majesty and authority.' And behind Flavel there is the patriarch Richard Baxter telling the Lord Protector Cromwell that 'we took our ancient monarchy to be a blessing, and not an evil to the land; and humbly craved his patience that I might ask him how England had ever forfeited that blessing, and to whom that forfeiture was made.' In short, Orton's submissive, monarchical, and loyalist Dissent has rather better credentials than the republican Dissent of Hollis and Baron, who can establish their lineage from Milton and Cromwell only by way of the infidel Algernon Sidney.

In 1780 Orton is recommending 'Public and Domestic Devotion, written by one *Martin*, a Baptist minister in London … very sensible, serious, and useful'. This is John Martin (1741–1800) who, far from advancing his loyalist sentiments only in private communications, rushed into print impetuously and often, as he acknowledges in *Some Account of the Life and Writings of the Revd John Martin* (1797). This autobiography is a charming sturdy brief narrative in epistolary form, which could well bear reprinting, both for its intrinsic virtues and for the light it casts on a little-noticed element in the society and ideology of late Hanoverian England. Martin's justification for writing it is explicitly Johnsonian – the famous judgement that 'there has perhaps rarely passed a life, of which a judicious and faithful narrative would not be useful'. The son of a publican and grazier in Lincolnshire, Martin, largely self-educated, abandoned a family tradition of Anglicanism to join the Baptist ministry, and after ministering to various congregations in the East Midlands came to a metropolitan church in Grafton Street only in 1773. His interests and his publications were not in any blatant or invidious sense 'politicized'; yet he published his views on each of the vexing constitutional issues that arose in his lifetime, and always on the loyalist side. Himself aware of this bias in his political sentiments, Martin explains in a very interesting way how he thinks it originated:

> As I was born at Spalding, in the year 1741, at the close of the rebellion in favour of the Pretender I was about five years of age. At that time, and for some years afterwards, the story of him, and of those that countenanced his cause, was often sounded in my ears; and as the inhabitants of Spalding were well affected to Government, this story

made so deep an impression on my mind, that before I was fifteen, I could not see without alarm the shadow of civil disturbance; and Sir, let me add that at fifty-five rebellious positions, on whatever pretence they are brought forward, strongly excite my indignation; above all, when they seem to be sanctioned by religious frenzy.

Accordingly, it comes as no surprise that in 1775, inflamed by talk on behalf of the American colonists, Martin should have published a polemic on the loyalist side, of which he was to say: 'In this paper, called the *Monitor*, I attempted to shew, that rebellion first commenced in heaven; that by the suggestions of a ruined rebel, our adversary, it gained admittance into Paradise; and that since the fall of our first parents, the rebellious of all ages, in all conditions of life, have always had an illicit love for dominion; so that, from the first generation to the present, were they to meet together in one body, they might say to each other, Walked we not in the same spirit? Walked we not in the same steps?' When we consider John Rippon telling John Manning in 1784, 'I believe that all our Baptist ministers in town except two, and most of our brethren in the country, were on the side of the Americans in the late dispute',[1] we cannot doubt that one of the recalcitrant pair was John Martin, who had the year before reasserted his position in *Queries and Remarks on Human Liberty*. (And it is interesting to note that Rippon concedes there were more John Martins in the country than in the town.) Moreover, in 1776 Martin had published *Familiar Dialogues between Americus and Britannicus* in which, he says, he 'attempted to explain ... some things that had given offence in the *Monitor*', but 'daring, in this performance, to censure some things advanced by Dr Price, his partizans were exasperated at my supposed temerity'. From that point to the end of his life Martin was always aware of speaking for an unpopular minority among the articulate Dissenters and, reading between the lines, we recognize in him the sort of personality that relishes such an isolated position, exults in it, and seeks it.

Richard Price can still attract partisans, as do his contemporaries Wilkes and Paine and preeminently Burke. But whereas those men were furiously partisan themselves, and in different ways turbulent and passionate, what distinguishes Price is on the contrary a sort of glacial serenity. And so his pro-American *Observations on the Nature of Civil Liberty ... and the Justice and Policy of the War with America* (1776) should be considered in the light of his later *Discourse on the Love of our Country* (1789) where he asks, of such love, 'What has it been but a love of domination; a desire of conquest, and a thirst for grandeur and glory, by extending territory and enslaving surrounding countries?' When patrio-

1 Cited by Payne, p. 210.

tism is thus dismissed as an unworthy prejudice, the rights and wrongs of
any political situation are wonderfully simplified. But the undoubtedly
irrational yet time-honoured promptings of *pietas* toward kindred and
native land cannot be set aside by most people so serenely; and such
promptings are felt by Dissenters sometimes, even by Dissenters of Price's
own Arian and rationalistic kind. Thus the Presbyterian John Bowring
showed that his rationality fell short of Price's when he wrote to a cousin
in 1778 'After the most deliberate consideration of the nature of the
quarrel between us, I freely own it appears to me that they are right and
we wrong, nor is there anything I more ardently wish for relative to our
national concerns than a thorough change both of men and manners in
the British Cabinet. *Yet, as an Englishman, I by no means wish to see my
country vanquished by the arms of France.*'[1] More remarkably the pioneer
industrialist Josiah Wedgwood, Unitarian and friend of Benjamin
Franklin, is found in 1779 expostulating: 'Methinks I would defend the
land of my nativity, my family and friends against a foreign foe, where
conquest and slavery were inseparable, under any leaders – the best I
could get for the moment, and wait for better times to displace an obnox-
ious minister, and settle domestic affairs, rather than rigidly say, I'll be
saved in my own way and by people of my own choice, or perish and
perish my country with me.'[2] To men like Bowring and Wedgwood,
thus touchingly embroiled in the consequences of their own unargued
patriotism, Richard Price's coolly dispassionate statement of the case
could offer no help at all. As the war went on, *in particular as it went worse
and worse for British arms*, the political conduct and sentiments of a
Bowring or a Wedgwood inevitably became for all practical purposes
indistinguishable from those of a Job Orton or John Martin. For when the
Crown finally admitted defeat it was not under pressure from any body of
persistent pro-American sentiment but, as J.H. Plumb valuably points
out, because 'the country interest, the independent members who sat in
Parliament as Knights of the Shire, who never spoke in debates and
usually voted with the government, finally rebelled'.

Robert E. Schofield's comment on Wedgwood's changing sentiments
seems unimaginative as well as inaccurate: 'How long his "my country,
right or wrong" attitude lasted is hard to say; probably not much longer
than it took to discover that the military alliance between America and
France was not going to result in an invasion of Britain.'[3] The tone and
implication of this remark by a scrupulous American historian are probably inescapable whenever an American observes the sentiments of
Britons during the War of the Revolution. And yet what it overlooks is

1   *Autobiographical Recollections of Sir John Bowring* (London, 1877), pp. 2–3 (my italics).
2   Quoted by J.H. Plumb.
3   Robert E. Schofield, *The Lunar Society of Birmingham* (Oxford, 1963), p. 138.

obvious: once the colonists had declared their independence, Americans constituted for the British 'a foreign foe', just as the French did. A parallel case is when C.H. Guttridge reports on the American correspondence of Richard Champion, no Dissenter but one of Edmund Burke's powerful constituents in Bristol. Guttridge observes that 'Champion remained loyal to the cause of his American friends, even to the extent of conduct which could with some reason be termed unpatriotic.' But, of course, when Champion in December 1775 conveyed to America information about 'where the government intended to concentrate armaments, what the numbers of the reinforced army at Boston would be, and what disposition of troops would be made between New York, Virginia, and South Carolina',[1] the name for such conduct may be thought to be not 'unpatriotic' but 'treasonable'. Burgess and Maclean and Rosenberg, Hiss and Pontecorvo and Philby are names from our own century that suggest how hard it is for intellectuals to acknowledge that treason is a matter not of opinion but of legal fact. Everyone knows that when treason is successful 'none dare call it treason'; but this does not excuse one literary historian after another making delicate comedy out of police agents sent by Pitt's government to eavesdrop on Blake and Coleridge and Wordsworth – without at any point reminding their readers that French agents *were* active in the England of that time, and *did* suborn some Englishmen. This underlining of the obvious seems called for if we are to recognize that when Orton and Martin and Wesley advance submission to the civic power as a religious duty, this is not necessarily a manoeuvre of the ruling class, nor yet an anachronistic survival of feudal sentiments into an enlightened age, but one possible solution to a conflict of loyalties that may entangle us, just as it entangled Josiah Wedgwood in 1779.

What no proponent of the Whig version of events under George III can be brought to admit at all readily is that very few of the zealots for 'civil and religious liberty' had any intention of extending those liberties to Roman Catholics. Thus of Thomas Hollis we are told that he was 'persuaded ... as every sensible and impartial man must be, that the civil and religious liberties of Englishmen will ever be endangered in proportion as popery increases, and is not discouraged'; and that he felt 'the clergy of the established church had been too remiss in their opposition to it'.[2] This we have on the authority of one who was himself a clergyman of the established church, though of a rather peculiar kind. He was Francis Blackburne, archdeacon of Cleveland, author of *Considerations of the present state of the controversy between the protestants and papists of Great*

1 C.H. Guttridge, *The American Correspondence of a Bristol Merchant, 1766–1776* (Berkeley, 1934), pp. 4–5
2 *Memoirs of Thomas Hollis* (London, 1780), p. 251.

Britain and Ireland (1768), of which Hollis, as was his habit with books he approved, bought and distributed 110 copies. Blackburne with much self-congratulation recounts this himself in his *Memoirs of Hollis* (1780). It was Blackburne who issued the invitations to a meeting at the Feathers Tavern in the Strand on 17 July 1771, at which was first mooted a petition to Parliament for the abolition of compulsory subscription to the Thirty-nine Articles, this for the benefit of Anglican ministers who were in fact Unitarians, as Blackburne was. This measure, framed so as to relieve also the Dissenting ministers (mostly Presbyterians) who were Unitarians no less, was as we have seen defeated, largely at the instigation of the Dissenting Calvinists. To regularize their position, some half-dozen Anglican clergy resigned their livings, following Theophilus Lindsey who, like his fellow Cambridge don Jebb, thereby sacrificed also his academic career. Blackburne had no such scruples, or none that he could not swallow; and this sufficiently explains his special interest in applauding libertarian (though of course antipapist) Dissenters such as Hollis. Blackburne is the first of several Anglicans in the period who show unwonted tenderness to the Dissenting interest; their motives for doing so, while not often so impudent as Blackburne's, can in most cases be discerned without too much trouble. The truth is that the rapid growth of Unitarianism in this period, alike among parsons and Dissenting ministers, and in either case mostly masked (however perfunctorily) as something else, blurs the borderline between Establishment and Dissent as perhaps at no other period before or since.

The only Dissenter I have found at this time who was in any way prepared to accept papists as fellow Christians was, to give him his due, Richard Price, who seems to have been ready to contemplate Catholic emancipation, at any rate in Ireland. Perhaps not all Dissenters were quite so ferociously antipapist as some of the Establishment would have wished them to be. Such seems to have been the view of Horace Walpole who was during the war with the colonies an extreme Whig, presumably out of filial piety; who accordingly grumbled into his diary in 1776, 'In all this contest with America, the Presbyterians and other Dissenters, who could not but see the designs of the Court, and its notorious partiality to Roman Catholics, were entirely passive in England, being bribed or sold by their leaders'.[1] It is not clear what Walpole could have pointed to as evidence of 'notorious partiality to Roman Catholics'. It was not until the Catholic Relief Act of 1778 that some of the disabilities imposed on the English papists in 1701 were lifted: officiating Roman Catholic clergy were thereafter no longer liable to life imprisonment; and the requirement was abolished by which land in England and Wales must pass over any papist heir in favour of the next Protestant in line. These reliefs, though

---

1   Quoted by Bradley, p. 23.

conditional on an oath of allegiance being taken before a Court of Record or Quarter Sessions, were protested in a series of petitions which, orchestrated by Lord George Gordon, precipitated the Gordon Riots of 1780; and these, according to Peter Brown, 'combined with the excesses of the French Revolution, delayed parliamentary reform in Britain for forty years'.[1] This casts a sardonic light on Silvester Horne's claim for the Protestant bigots, that they were the pioneering heroes of parliamentary reform. As for Walpole, he can have had in mind only the leave extended to the citizens of vanquished Quebec to practice their Roman Catholicism with impunity. And of this Johnson, who to this day figures in radical and dissenting mythology as a fulminating Blimp if not indeed a court-pensioner, had written nobly in *The Patriot* (1774): 'Persecution is not more virtuous in a Protestant than a Papist; and ... while we blame Lewis the Fourteenth, for his dragoons and his gallies, we ought, when power comes into our hands, to use it with greater equity.' Johnson said also that 'in an age, where every mouth is open for liberty of conscience, it is equitable to shew some regard to the conscience of a Papist, who may be supposed, like other men, to think himself safest in his own religion'; and finally, irrefutably, 'if liberty of conscience be a natural right, we have no power to withhold it; if it be an indulgence it may be allowed to Papists, while it is not denied to other sects'.[2] Alas, far more typical was the platform on which the youthful Lord Mahon stood in 1774 as a candidate for Westminster; a platform in which promises to destroy or diminish bribery in elections, to strive for the repeal of the Septennial Act, and for the expunging of the vote of the Commons which had unseated Wilkes, stood alongside a pledge to seek the repeal of the Quebec Act.[3] So happily, under George III, did measures that we are eager to consider 'liberal' or 'enlightened' or 'democratic' go along with antipapist bigotry! And while it is no doubt too much to hope for that any Dissenter should have declared himself on the issue as fearlessly as Johnson did, it is a pity to have to say so, of people who were 'coming to see and to declare the beauty of the ideal of a Free Church in a free State'.

After Francis Blackburne the next prominent Anglican to take up the cudgels for the Dissenters, or for some of them, was Christopher Wyvill in his *Defence of Dr Price, and the Reformers of England* (1792). Wyvill's motives were more altruistic than Blackburne's, and more responsible. In the 1780s his Yorkshire Association had been the best organized and most level-headed of the movements for parliamentary reform, and the one that came nearest effecting some real change. He had got some support, though it is not clear how much, from the Dissenting interest in

1   Peter Brown, *The Chathamiles* (London, 1967).
2   J.P. Hardy, ed., *The Political Writings of Dr Johnson* (London, 1968), pp. 93, 94.
3   See Butterfield, p. 383.

Yorkshire. And it looks as if, by springing to Price's defence in the wake of Burke's fierce attack on him in the *Reflections on the French Revolution*, Wyvill was trying to defend the Dissenting interest from Burke's accusations of disloyalty, against the day when he, Wyvill, might need to call on the Dissenters once more in the service of what was genuinely a reformist rather than revolutionary objective. Accordingly, Wyvill's pamphlet, though predictably vituperative about Edmund Burke, is on the whole meant to be conciliatory. In particular it marks the disowning, by English liberal reformers, of Tom Paine – and not on religious grounds (Paine's *Age of Reason* was not to appear until 1795), but on the very sensible grounds that 'his avowed purpose is, not to reform or amend the System of our Government, but to overturn and destroy it'. Of the author of *The Rights of Man*, Wyvill writes judiciously and severely:

> He supports the doctrine of Republicanism, with an enthusiastic zeal, with an imposing confidence, and with reasoning often specious, and always daring; some truths are interspersed among many fallacies and misrepresentations, and a vein of coarse, but strongly sarcastic wit runs through and clumsily enlivens the whole. His Counsel, to break up and destroy the noble fabric of our Constitution and rebuild a new political edifice on the plans of America, seems to be conveyed in the most dangerous shape, and far more likely to make an impression on those, to whom it is chiefly addressed, than if it had been delivered in a more classical composition.

It may well be thought that Wyvill should in logic have disowned Price no less than Paine. For Price undoubtedly advocated a unicameral legislature, and to effect that would certainly have been 'to break up and destroy' the Constitution, as that was understood by Montesquieu and John Adams no less than Burke. There are signs in fact that Wyvill was uneasy about some of the positions that Price had taken up, but he was committed to exonerating this alarming and prominent Whig Dissenter if he was to clear Dissenting whiggery in general from any taint of disloyalty. And his protestations to this effect are rather too vehement to carry conviction. Thus he asserts that 'during the miseries of the American war no symptom of dissatisfaction to the Constitution appeared'. But only a few years before that war people in the group around Thomas Hollis were to be heard declaring that 'no person is a true friend of Liberty who is not a Republican'; and during the war many in Britain as well as America were reading with enthusiasm Catherine Macaulay's *History of England from the accession of James I*, that 'imaginative work in praise of republican principles'. It may be that Caroline Robbins and J.H. Plumb have overestimated the influence of Dissenting republicanism, but it can hardly be pooh-poohed so blandly as by Wyvill or his modern biographer Ian Christie. Though it is doubtless true that the views of 'the

Commonwealthmen' had little popular appeal when promulgated by themselves in editions of Algernon Sidney and Marchamont Nedham, they could have such appeal when cautiously and partially enunciated by charismatic or demagogic figures like Chatham and Wilkes (who both had connections with the Hollis group) or by an energetic popularizer like Mrs Macaulay. Thus it seems that there must have been, in the 1790s as in the 1760s and 1770s, Dissenters who were also Jacobins whose reading of their Dissenting heritage pushed them well beyond constitutional reform, however radical. And this means surely that when Burke in his *Reflections* imputed disaffection or disloyalty to the Dissenters generally, his alarm was not so groundless and chimerical as is commonly supposed. Indeed, Wyvill himself in 1792, while seeming to reassure, is really threatening:

> The Proselytes to republican notions are few at present, and inconsiderable: They probably would be increased in number by prosecution; but by impunity a wise forbearance will effectually prevent any eventual danger from their speculations, provided the condition of the People be rendered more easy by the farther diminution of their burthens, and their wishes be gratified by a timely correction of those abuses in the Constitution, which have been so justly complained of. By these means, and by these means alone, the possible growth of a great Republican Party in this Country may be prevented.

There is a clear threat in that last sentence. Was it a real threat? Did not Wyvill, no less than Burke, think that it was?

The Dissenters meanwhile had failed in their agitation for a repeal of parts of the Test and Corporation Acts. John Martin, inflexible as ever, had once again espoused an immovably conservative position, and was so much in a minority that by his own account he was not permitted to speak at the meeting of the London Dissenting ministers in Red Cross Street in December 1789. He therefore published his contribution to the debate as a pamphlet, *A Speech on the Repeal of such parts of the Test and Corporation Acts as affect Conscientious Dissenters* ... (1790). But this is an unhappy and disingenuous performance; and a bitter anonymous rejoinder by 'no Reverend Dissenter' is scurrilous and intemperate, but convincing. There is, however, one passage in Martin's pamphlet that is of interest because it shows that the idea of 'oppressive toleration', brandished as a novelty by radicals of the 1960s, was already part of the dissenters' armoury in 1790:

> We are repeatedly told, 'That the pretended *toleration* of Dissenters is a real *persecution*'. Such language is as impolitic as it is unjust. Toleration and persecution may exist at the same time; but can they be considered as the same thing? All legal persecutions, in this country, have been the

offspring either of *Statute* law or of *Canon* law; nevertheless, that Act which repeals the oppressive power of preceding Acts, and prevents the wasps and hornets in low life from darting out their stings, should ever be mentioned with becoming temper.

What Martin has in mind is the Act of Toleration passed under William III; and he proceeds to a panegyric, in thoroughly Burkean vein, on the wisdom of that monarch and his ministers.

There appeared a new spokesman for loyalist Dissent when the Independent minister John Clayton (1754–1843) took advantage of the Birmingham riots against Joseph Priestley by publishing a sermon in which he argued in effect that Priestley had asked for what he got. This provoked many rejoinders, among them Robert Hall's *Christianity Consistent with a Love of Freedom* (1791). A more curious loyalist document appeared in Adam Callender's *Thoughts on the Peaceable ... Nature of Christ's Kingdom* (1794):

> Let us remember therefore, that it is in heaven where our interest chiefly is. There is our citizenship; and in the view of possessing it shortly will the main of our conversation be directed. We are called upon to set our affections on things above, and not on things on the earth; and our Lord lays it down as a maxim, that if we are laying up treasures above, our hearts will be there also; in the same way as they who heap up treasures here have their hearts on earth. If then heaven be our chief banking house, our conversation will be much taken up about the security of our property there, and we shall find, to our comfort, that if once laid up in the sacred mansions above, they will remain inviolable from thieves and unhurt by the moth.
>
> We are pilgrims in this world, as all our forefathers were, and we, like them, seek a country above. It does not suit well with the idea of a pilgrim, when passing through a strange country, to retard his journey by stopping to dispute and settle the manners of a country, to which he means not to return.

Perhaps not many present-day Christians are sufficiently devout and evangelical to accept this obviously extreme case for political quietism. Yet the argument takes on force when it is seen to rest on the grounds that the church is indeed catholic and universal:

> We ought rather to admire the more excellent way which Jesus has taught us, which leaves no room for doubt, by making it our positive duty to obey every kind of government, without exceptions to the characters of those who rule. Here perplexity is at an end, and we are led to admire the wisdom of Christ in establishing a rule of obedience, so suitable to christians in every age, and in every country where they may dwell on the earth: so that we may conceive of christians in

various nations, all harmoniously sending up their petitions to God for their Kings and governors, and for the good of their respective countries, though the governments ... may be totally different to each other.

One wonders if this evangelical Protestant would follow through the implications of this position so far as to endorse the sentiment in Burke that has infuriated so many from his day to ours – Burke's sympathy with the ejected and persecuted Roman Catholic clergy of France.

This writer must interest us in any case. For in 1795, when his contribution to Adam Callender's volume was reprinted separately under the title *Scriptural Subjection to Civil Government*, the author was revealed as Thomas Sheraton. Yes, the great cabinetmaker – who was also, we discover with surprise, a Baptist minister. Sheraton, though a household name in an unusually literal sense, is a very shadowy figure. If he at any time fulfilled his ministerial function, it seems to have been in his native northeast, not in the London to which he migrated. (And he therefore figures, it is interesting to note, as a *provincial* Dissenter, though domiciled in London.) Moreover, in case it should be thought that Sheraton as purveyor to the luxury trade needed to flatter the prejudices of the nobility and gentry, it should be noted that in his own lifetime his furniture designs seem to have brought him no patronage and no profit; he died unknown, and in penury.

In 1794 Sheraton was not content to keep a lordly and scriptural distance from particular disputed issues in the politics of his time. He goes out of his way, for instance, to emphasize that an English Christian's submission to the civil power involves loyalty to a bicameral legislature: 'But, by honouring the King, according to our present form of government, it implies the two houses of parliament. There are two branches of the legislative authority in this kingdom, without which there is not a supreme power; and therefore we must honour these with our prayers in connection with the King. And if these three are to us the reigning powers, we know then to whom subjection is due.' This passage was shortened and softened in the 1795 reprint, for reasons that we can only guess at, though they may be in the background of what Sheraton says in his Preface to that reissue:

Should the writer's motives for publishing on this subject be inquired into – he has to say, that at a time when the loyalty of Dissenters in general was doubted, he accepted an invitation and opportunity of announcing openly that he was not amongst that class of nonconformists, who scruple not to revile the good constitution under which Divine Providence has happily placed them; *reserving at the same time the important distinction between a good constitution, and those corruptions that may exist in its administration*, to point out which he conceives would be as much beyond his ability as foreign to his duty to attempt it (my italics).

(Sheraton, it will be observed, was not so nimble a craftsman with the English language as he was in rosewood and mahogany.)

Doubtless what is most striking about this Preface is its use of the past tense. As the news came in from France, so the attitudes of observers changed week by week, or month by month; and so it is that in 1795 Sheraton can look back upon public opinion of a year earlier as belonging to a past era. And so it is that by 1797 John Martin, looking back to the 1770s but with sly allusions to the 1790s, can manage a wry urbanity:

> Some of my friends, (for I have had friends of various complexions,) affected to wonder, that I, who had so much trouble and sorrow at Grafton Street, should meddle, as they pleased to call it, with political subjects. This, Sir, is the way of some gentlemen in Town, and I suppose it is so with some in the country. They can meet together, form associations, and corresponding societies, to propagate indecent, and unfounded reports of the powers that are, and aggravate, with pleasure, the inadvertence of our rulers, whatever may be the condition of their own affairs; whereas, if others attempt to make the best of that which is, by pleading for order, and legitimate subordination, these gentlemen are sure to censure their proceedings, and to speak of them in very harsh and disrespectful terms.

In 1799 the tide of opinion had changed so markedly and was so hostile to any who might seem to be pro-French radicals that the alleged though unproven unanimity of the English Dissenters, which before had counted unto them for virtue and has been so taken through many generations since, could be and was turned around so as to validate a comprehensive indictment. This seems to be the significance of *Observations on the Political Conduct of the Protestant Dissenters; ... in Five Letters to a Friend*, by the Reverend David Rivers, who identifies himself on his title page as 'Late Preacher to a Congregation of Dissenters at Highgate'. The line of argument open to a prosecuting counsel like Rivers should be obvious. A few excerpts will give the flavour of it:

> But were not the Dissenters strenuously active in serving the interest of the disaffected Colonies at home? Was not the courage and vigour of the enemy much heightened by the repeated assurances they had of cordial assistance from their brethren on this side of the Atlantic? Did not the Dissenters use their utmost endeavours to blacken the measures of Government, and to weaken and destroy the confidence of the nation in its rulers? and were not their endeavours crowned with too much success? So much so, that I attribute the loss of America to the Protestant Dissenters. Dr Price, that firebrand of sedi-

tion, did the most essential service, by his inflammatory publications, to animate and invigorate the Colonies to persevere in their revolt. His exertions were seconded by the whole phalanx of the Dissenters, headed by the members of the senate in opposition to government; thus, powerfully supported by a rank and discontented party here, they carried on the contest till they gained their independence.

But, I limit not myself to the conduct of Price and Priestley: it may be justly retorted, that the Dissenters as a body, were not to be censured for the imprudent conduct of two of their teachers. I will take a wider range; I will prove to you, Sir, that the Dissenters as a body tacitly approved of the conduct of their leaders ... If they had been that loyal body of men, which they are sometimes arrogant enough to stile themselves, why did they not pass a vote of censure upon Dr Price and Dr Priestley for their political conduct? Why did not they disavow their principles? These queries are easily replied to: because, they secretly *approved of them*. Secretly, did I say, they openly approved of them.

As to calling the *King a fool* and a *blockhead*; refusing to pray for him in their public worship; drinking success to the French; adorning their parlours with portraits of Buonaparte, Tom Paine, Horn Tooke, and others; and, *perhaps,* a *little ivory Guillotine* in some sly corner; I pass over such circumstances as these; what I limit myself to, is their *plotting Treason.*

... Godwin, the author of Political Justice, was a Dissenting Minister at Beaconsfield; Gilbert Wakefield is a Dissenter; Frend, who was expelled the University of Cambridge, now associates with Dissenters ... And among those persons who have been convicted of high treason ... we shall find them altogether Dissenters. Thomas Muir, Fysche Palmer, Gerald, and Skirving, all Presbyterians.

I hope, Sir, that you will acquit me of a want of candour, in what has been stated in these letters; if I have erred, it is in favour of that sect among whom I first drew my breath; but from whom, from motives of the purest integrity, I have now separated.

Rivers' attack has topical point because of the Irish rising of '98 in which, as he does not fail to note, Ulster Presbyterians made common cause with Wexford papists. But his tone is too intemperate, and his polemic falls in too pat with what his public wanted to hear, for us to take him very seriously. Yet he makes a case that needs to be answered. And his judgement – 'I attribute the loss of America to the Protestant Dissenters' – is at least as plausible as Silvester Horne's directly opposite verdict, 'If the voice of the Free Churches had been listened to, the American Colonies could have been saved for England'. No doubt both are equally wide of the truth, which is more nearly caught in the sour retrospect of one of Washington's officers:

> The disappointment of a few smugglers in New England worked upon by the ancient Oliverian spirit, that panted to suffer once more for the 'good old cause', the idle opulence of the Southern provinces, where something was wanted to employ the heavy hours of life, the stupidity of two or three British Governors, & the cruel impolitic behaviour of their government, brought on & kept up the war, which was conducted on both sides, & terminated in a manner that has convinced me, that there are certain extensive operations determined upon by providence, which are not to be foreseen, aided, or obviated by human means.[1]

It is to be hoped, and expected, that scholarship will uncover other loyalist dissenters than those we have taken note of. Those few – Job Orton and John Martin, Clayton and Sheraton, Merivale and Rivers – obviously constitute too small a sample to generalize from. Yet it is worth saying that in surveying them we find nothing to contradict a generalization that has been risked by the distinguished historian of Methodism, Bernard Semmel. Semmel suggests that if we ask what the loyalist Dissenters had in common, one plausible and surprising answer might be: John Calvin. For certainly it seems to be the Calvinists among the Dissenters who are conspicuous by their absence from pro-American and later pro-French demonstrations and writings. And John Martin for one was a fiercely old-style Calvinist, who lived long enough to attack Andrew Fuller of his own church for attempting to moderate the high Calvinism traditional among Particular Baptists. (Martin's account of his own conversion to high Calvinist principles is affecting and impressive.) Thus the church-and-king rhymester in Manchester who wrote a loyalist squib against the Anglican Thomas Walker and his radical friends may have been shrewd and accurate when he accused them of being disloyal to Calvin as well as to the Establishment:

> Next Tommy Tax, that Lad of Wax,
> If Charly Fox said Yea, Sirs,
> Would souse the Church and Calvin lurch,
> And after that, Huzza, Sirs.

In this instance, as time and again, the use of the blanket term *Dissenter*, which darkened counsel at the time, continues to do so today. For the Manchester loyalists wrote of 'Legions of Dissenting Congregations, headed by their respective Pastors' invading a loyalist meeting in 1789;[2]

---

1 Francis Kinloch of South Carolina, in 1785. Quoted by May, p. 146.
2 See Frida Knight, *The Strange Case of Thomas Walker* (London, 1957), pp. 40–2.

but in another of their publications on the same topic, when an inquirer asks, 'What caused so so much turbulence at the Meeting?' the answer he gets is: 'The *Presbyterians'* obtrusion' (my italics). And by 1789, if not indeed ten years earlier, *Presbyterian* nearly always means *Unitarian* – which is to say, the Calvinists' bitterest opponents.

This may explain why, though Presbyterians and many Baptists are to be found at various times in the radical ranks, Congregationalists (the old Independents) are hard to find there. Ernest Payne finds one, Samuel Wilton, of whom we read: 'If in anything he discovered what approached to an enthusiastic zeal, it was for the success of America in her struggle for independence.' Caleb Fleming may have been another. But Fleming, doctrinally liberal like Philip Furneaux of Clapham and Hugh Farmer of Walthamstow, was very far from typical of the Independents' ministry in the 1770s. In the previous decade Independent congregations, like John Hammer's in Plymouth or John Burnett's in Hull, had shown themselves ready to dismiss ministers who did not dispense the pure milk of Calvinism.[1] As Leighton Pullan pointed out long ago in his Bampton Lectures, already in 1761 'Methodism and the general Evangelical movement were not only stemming the whole tide of Arian and Socinian opinions, but were ousting them from the meeting-houses of the Independents', though 'the English Presbyterians showed less power of recovery'.[2] Accordingly, the late Basil Willey seems to have been wrong when he explicitly included the Independents along with Presbyterians and Baptists in his in any case rash judgement that 'Priestley in his development from Calvinism to Unitarianism merely illustrates in epitome what was going on widely amongst the dissenting congregations in the eighteenth century'.[3] In the 1760s and 1770s Calvinism was, on the contrary, regaining lost ground. And by 1780 Calvinists and anti-Calvinists had largely sorted themselves out between the two denominations, the Calvinists deserting Presbyterianism for Independency, in which long-established theological 'liberals' like Furneaux and Farmer were anachronistic survivors. It is thus somewhat disingenuous of Ernest Payne to wonder that historians of Congregationalism like R.W. Dale and Tudur Jones should 'give so little, indeed virtually no attention to the American War and Revolution'; the suspicion is irresistible that Dale and Jones kept silence because otherwise they would have had to concede that most Congregationalists of the 1770s were not, in the matter of America, 'on the side of the future'.

1   See Jeremy Goring, 'The Break-up of the Old Dissent', in C.G. Bolam et al., eds, *English Presbyterians: From Elizabethan Puritanism to Modern Unitarianism* (London, 1968), pp. 209–10.
2   Leighton Pullan, *Religion since the Reformation* (Oxford, 1923), p. 141, and cf. Michael R. Watts, *The Dissenters* (Oxford, 1978), pp. 468–9.
3   Basil Willey, *The Eighteenth Century Background* (London, 1946), pp. 181–2.

The natural affinity between Calvinism and loyalism has been
obscured by John Wesley. For Wesley, even as he wrote his vehemently
loyalist tracts at the time of the war with the Americans, at the same time
persisted in, and stepped up, his polemic against what he called 'antino-
mianism' among his own Methodists; that is to say, against the Calvinistic
Methodism of those who followed George Whitefield. Hence Wesley,
and those who supported him, like John Fletcher of Madeley, identified
the Calvinism of New England with that of old England, and so accused
their opponents, the Calvinistic Baptist Caleb Evans of Bristol and the
Establishment Calvinist Augustus Toplady, of being disloyal revolution-
aries and levellers. But as Bernard Semmel points out, the English
Calvinists were in important ways quite different from their American
fellows, and there is no reason to doubt that both Evans and Toplady
were, though Whigs, entirely loyal. When Evans spoke of the 'superb, I
had almost said, the divine edifice' which was the British Constitution,
there is no reason to think he was insincere or panicked into hypocrisy;
and he made a fair point when he invoked the name of Blackstone, and
asked if Blackstone was 'a *Calvinist*, an *Anabaptist*, an *Antinomian* patriot'
for enunciating the constitutional principles that Evans also held.
Similarly that unamiable character Toplady had a point when he invited
readers to compare 'the loyalty of the Calvinistic archbishop Usher, with
that of the Arminian ranter and fifth monarchy man John Goodwin'.
Wesley had mistaken his enemies; or rather he had rashly confounded his
theological with his political adversaries. As Semmel implies, the truly
disaffected Dissenters were Unitarian or Quaker, not Calvinist.[1] And so it
seems to be high time that, in studies of this period, we stopped taking the
Dissenters as a homogeneous and self-explanatory political entity or pressure group.

But we may fairly go a little further, and take a wider range.
Nonconformist, Dissenter – the old names announce, proudly and exul-
tantly on the part of those who so describe themselves, a condition of
alienation from the consensus, and from (though also within) their societies. This is something with which thinkers about politics have made
great play, ever since the youthful Karl Marx. Gerhart Niemeyer, for
instance, has distinguished three types of alienation: first, that of the
ancient Gnostics; then, that oldest alienation which 'stems from sorrow at
being separated from God, the source of truth, order, and peace'; and
then again, 'modern ideological alienation', that of the man who
'becomes alienated by his own act of accepting an idea structure that
implies a declaration of war by some men on the historical existence of all
men'. Of this last, Niemeyer writes: 'The ideological system bears the

---

1   Bernard Semmel, *The Methodist Revolution* (New York, 1973), pp. 61–71.

stamp of an imperious pretension in rebellion against that which exists.
The symbol of Prometheus, perverted into a modern hero of rebellion, is
present in all modern thinking. Thus modern alienation is based not on
faith but on choice ... The alienation is intentionally entered and its
maintenance deliberately cultivated. Its character is wilful rather than
experiential.'[1] Those who assert that the eighteenth-century English
Dissenter was – or *had to be*, if he thought his position through – a political revolutionary (pro-American in 1780, pro-French in 1790), are
contending that the alienation which the Dissenter by that very title
confessed or proclaimed was alienation of the modern, ideological
variety. But when John Martin contends 'that rebellion first commenced
in heaven; that by the suggestion of a ruined rebel, our adversary, it
gained admittance into Paradise; and that ... the rebellious of all ages ...
have always had an illicit love for dominion', he is asserting that *his* alienation, confessed and embraced, and imposed on him by history, is *not*
alienation of the modern, ideological kind. In particular, by identifying
Prometheus with the other superhuman rebel Lucifer, Martin rejects the
Promethean myth that Niemeyer sees as crucial to the alienation that is
'modern' and 'ideological'. It is in this way, and at this deep mythological
level, that Martin refuses to have 'religious Dissenter' mean 'political
dissident'. It would be rash to suppose that in John Martin's generation,
and in subsequent generations, others have not reached the same position
by the same reasoning.

From *Greene Centennial Studies: essays presented to Donald Greene in the
centennial year of the University of Southern California*, ed. Paul J. Korshin and
Robert R. Allen. (Charlottesville: University Press of Virginia, 1984.)

1   Cerhart Niemeyer, 'Loss of Reality: Gnosticism and Modern Nihilism', *Modern Age*, 22
    (1978), 341.

Index